understanding human
communication

understanding human communication

second edition

Ronald B. Adler
Santa Barbara City College

George Rodman
Brooklyn College,
The City University of New York

Holt, Rinehart and Winston

New York   Chicago   San Francisco   Philadelphia
Montreal   Toronto   London   Sydney
Tokyo   Mexico City   Rio de Janeiro   Madrid

Library of Congress Cataloging in Publication Data

Adler, Ronald B. (Ronald Brian), date.
  Understanding human communication.

  Bibliography: p.
  Includes index.
  1. Communication. 2. Rodman, George R., date.
II. Title.
P90.A32   1985   001.51   84-15658
ISBN 0-03-071626-8

Copyright © 1985, 1982, by CBS College Publishing
Address correspondence to:
383 Madison Avenue
New York, N.Y. 10017
All rights reserved
Printed in the United States of America
Published simultaneously in Canada
5 6 7 8   032   9 8 7 6 5 4

CBS COLLEGE PUBLISHING
Holt, Rinehart and Winston
The Dryden Press
Saunders College Publishing

credits

6 Steinberg drawing. Cartoon reprinted by permission of Julian Bach Literary Agency. Copyright © 1965 by Saul Steinberg. From *The New World,* Harper & Row, Publishers.
27 Chon Day cartoon. © 1970 Saturday Review Magazine Co. Reprinted by permission.
29 Goldstein poem. Reprinted by permission of Lenni Shender Goldstein.
36 Lorenz cartoon. Reprinted from *The Saturday Evening Post* © The Curtis Publishing Co.
37 M.C. Escher print. © BEELDRECHT. Amsterdam/V.A.G.A., New York, Collection Haags Gemeentemusem—The Hague, 1981.

(continued following Index)

preface

Few, if any, academic fields are so obviously important or fascinating as the study of how we understand (and misunderstand) one another. The intrinsic interest and value of the field makes teaching and writing about human communication especially enjoyable. Unlike many other subjects, the challenge is not how to make apparently dull and arcane material appealing, but how to present obviously important information in the most useful, comprehensible way.

The second edition of *Understanding Human Communication* follows the same approach that made its predecessor so well received. Rather than choose sides in the "theory vs. skills" debate, the book shows how the most important theory and research on face-to-face human communication translates into skills that students can use to communicate more effectively in their own lives. The book's approach is just as important as its contents: Along with the readable text itself, the material is illustrated by a wide variety of epigrams, photos, brief readings, sophisticated cartoons, and individual exercises.

Several changes in the new edition add to its usefulness. Most noticeably, a new chapter, "Communicating in Organizations," devotes special attention to the nature of communication in this important context. Prepublication research shows that today's career-oriented students find this material especially useful. In addition, the material on interpersonal relationships has been reorganized in a form that makes it more useful and manageable in the time most instructors have available. Every chapter contains numerous changes that clarify and update the information.

Pedagogical aids also add to the usefulness of this edition. Each chapter now begins with a list of both cognitive and behavioral objectives, giving both students and instructors a clear statement of learning goals. Finally, an expanded, revised Instructor's Manual prepared by Mary Bozik of the University of Northern Iowa provides many ideas of curriculum design and evaluation, as well as an outstanding test bank.

These changes are the result of a team effort. The efforts of the following professionals at Holt, Rinehart and Winston kept us on track and on time: Anne Boynton-Trigg, Jackie Fleischer, Patricia Murphree, Lester Sheinis, Nancy Myers, and Lou Scardino. As always, the talents of Janet Bollow resulted in the book's handsome interior design. We also appreciate the useful suggestions of our reviewers: Barbara Baird, Suffolk Community College; Mary Bozik, University of Northern Iowa; John Bradley, Cleveland State Community College; Dennis E. Brown, El Paso Community College; Susan O. Coffey, Central Virginia Community College; Carol Diekhoff, State Community College of East St. Louis; Claire Jones, Oklahoma City University; Carolyn M. Kuriyama, Chaminade University; E. Joseph Lamp, Anne Arundel Community College; Mary Jane Leary, Kirkwood Community College; James Mancuso, Mesa Community College; Chris Meesey, Tarrant County Junior College; Donald W. Olson, Texas Lutheran College; Rudy Pugliese, Harrisburg Area Community College; Edd H. Sewell, Virginia Polytechnic Institute and State University; James I. Walling, Central Michigan University; John Wanzenreid, University of Nebraska at Omaha; and Alan Zaremba, Northeastern University.

Finally, of course, we would like to thank our wives, Sherri and Linda, for their support, and our kids, Robin, Rebecca, and Jennifer, for making it all worthwhile.

Ronald B. Adler
George Rodman

contents

understanding human
communication

part 1 elements of communication

one

human communication: what and why

After reading this chapter, you should understand:

1. The working definition of communication used in *Understanding Human Communication*.
2. The needs satisfied by communication.
3. The value of a communication model.
4. The elements of the communication model introduced in this chapter.
5. Five common misconceptions about communication.

You should be able to:

1. Give specific examples of the various types of needs you attempt to satisfy by communicating.
2. Identify the elements of the communication model in this chapter as they apply to an incident in your life.
3. Identify the misconceptions about communication you have held and suggest a more accurate belief for each.

3

communication defined

Because this is a book about communication, it makes sense to begin by defining that term. This is not as simple as it might seem, for people use the word in a variety of ways that are only vaguely related:

- Family members, co-workers, and friends make such statements about their relationships as "We just can't communicate" or "We communicate perfectly."

- Business people talk about "office communications systems" consisting of computers, telephones, printers, and so on.

- Scientists study and describe communication among ants, dolphins, and other animals.

- Certain organizations label themselves "communications conglomerates," publishing newspapers, books, and magazines and owning radio and television stations.

There is clearly some relationship among uses such as these, but we need to narrow our focus before going on. A look at the Table of Contents of this book shows that it obviously doesn't deal with animals, computers, or newspapers. Neither is it about Holy Communion, the bestowing of a material thing, or many of the other subjects mentioned in the *Oxford English Dictionary*'s 1,200 word definition.

What, then, *are* we talking about when we use the term "communication"? A survey of the ways in which scholars use the word will show that there is no single, universally accepted usage. Some definitions are long and complex whereas others are brief and simple. This isn't the place to explore the differences between these conceptions or to defend one against the others. What we need is a working definition that will help us in our study. For our purposes we will say that communication refers to *the process of human beings responding to the face-to-face symbolic behavior of other persons.*

A point-by-point examination of this definition reveals some important characteristics of communication as we will be studying it.

communication is human

In this book we'll be discussing communication between human beings. Animals clearly do communicate: Bees instruct their hive-mates about the location of food by a meaning-laden dance. Chimpanzees have been taught to express themselves with the same sign language used by deaf humans, and a few have developed impressive vocabularies. And on a more commonplace level, pet owners can testify to the variety of messages their animals can express. Although this subject of animal communication is a fascinating and an important one, it goes beyond the scope of this book.

communication is a face-to-face activity

Written messages, like books and letters, do not require face-to-face interaction; neither do mass media messages delivered by radio, television, or film. These types of communication are certainly important—so important that they deserve full treatment elsewhere. In this book we will focus on communication between persons who are in each others' presence.

communication is a process

We often talk about communication as if it occurred in discrete, individual acts. In fact, communication is truly a continuous, ongoing process. Consider, for example, a friend's compliment about your appearance. Your interpretation of those words will depend on a long series of experiences stretching far back in time: How have others judged your appearance? How do you feel about your looks? How honest has your friend been in the past? How have you been feeling about one another recently? All this history will help shape your response to the other person's remark. In turn, the words you speak and the way you say them will shape the way your friend behaves toward you and others—both in this situation and in the future.

This simple example shows that it's inaccurate to talk about "acts" of communication as if they occurred in isolation. To put it differently, communication isn't a series of incidents pasted together like photographs in a scrapbook; instead, it is more like a motion picture in which the meaning comes from the unfolding of an interrelated series of images.

communication is symbolic

The next feature of our definition focuses on the symbolic nature of human communication. Chapter 3 discusses the nature of symbols in detail, but this idea is so important that it needs an introduction now. The most significant feature of symbols is their *arbitrary* nature. For example, there's no logical reason why the letters in "book" should stand for the object you're reading now. Speakers of Spanish would call it a *libro*, whereas Germans would label it a *Buch*. Even in English another term would work just as well as long as everyone agreed to use it in the same way. We overcome the arbitrary nature of symbols by linguistic rules and customs. Effective communication depends on agreement among people about these rules. This is easiest to see when we observe people who don't follow linguistic conventions. For example, recall how unusual the speech of children and nonnative speakers of a language often sounds.

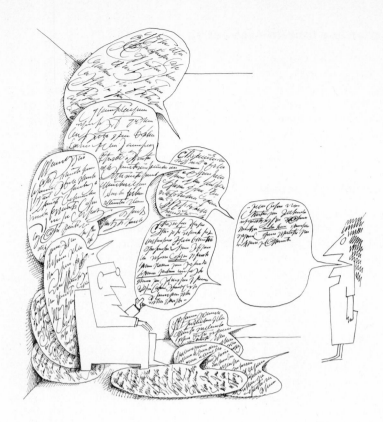

We've already talked about words as one type of symbol. In addition, nonverbal behavior can also have symbolic meaning. As with words, some nonverbal behaviors, though arbitrary, have clearly agreed-upon meanings: For example, to most North Americans, placement of a thumb and first finger together while facing the palm of the hand outward stands for the idea of something being "OK." But even more than words, nonverbal behaviors are ambiguous. Does a frown signify anger or unhappiness? Does a hug stand for a friendly greeting or a symbol of the hugger's romantic interest in you? One can't always be sure. We'll discuss the nature of nonverbal communication in Chapter 5.

communication requires the response of a receiver

Sending by itself isn't sufficient to create an act of communication: There needs to be some response to a message as well. To understand this point, think of a radio station broadcasting late at night without a single listener tuned in. One needn't argue about trees falling in an unpopulated forest to agree that no communication has occurred here. In the same way, a speaker talking at one or more people who aren't listening isn't communicating—at least by our definition.

Ideally we hope that others receive and understand our messages exactly as we intend them; but for our purposes we'll say that this doesn't have to occur for communication to take place. There are many other types of receiver response that qualify as part of the communication process. Sometimes a person who isn't your target receives a message, as when a bystander overhears you muttering about matters that weren't intended for others' ears. In other cases the intended receiver does in fact pick up a message but interprets it incorrectly, as when an overly sensitive friend takes your joking insults seriously. Finally, there are cases where no one seems to have received your message, but where your behavior has created an internal, unobservable response in someone else. We have known students who appeared to be daydreaming through our lecture but who, when questioned, prove to have been listening carefully.

Now that we have a working definition of the term "communication," it is important to discuss why we will spend so much time exploring this subject. Perhaps the strongest argument for studying communication is its central role in our lives. The amount of time we spend communicating is staggering. In one study researchers measured the amount of time a sample group of college students spent on various activities.[1] They found that the subjects spent an average of over 61 percent of their waking hours engaged in some form of communication. Whatever one's occupation, the results of such a study would not be too different. Most of us are surrounded by others, trying to understand them and hoping that they understand us: family, friends, co-workers, teachers, and strangers.

There's a good reason why we speak, listen, read, and write so much: Communication satisfies most of our needs.

physical needs

Communication is so important that it is necessary for physical health. In fact, evidence suggests that an absence of satisfying communication can even jeopardize life itself. Medical researchers have identified a wide range of medical hazards that result from a lack of close relationships. For instance:

1. Socially isolated people are two to three times more likely to die prematurely than are those with strong social ties. The type of relationship doesn't seem to matter: Marriages, friendship, religious and community ties all seem to increase longevity.[2]

2. Divorced men (before age seventy) die from heart disease, cancer, and strokes at double the rate of married men. Three times as many die from hypertension; five times as many commit suicide; seven times as many die from cirrhosis of the liver; and ten times as many die from tuberculosis.[3]

functions of communication

3. The rate of all types of cancer is as much as five times higher for divorced men and women, compared to their single counterparts.[4]

4. Poor communication can contribute to coronary disease. One Swedish study examined thirty-two pairs of identical twins. One sibling in each pair had heart disease whereas the other was healthy. The researchers found that the obesity, smoking habits, and cholesterol levels of the healthy and sick twins did not differ significantly. Among the significant differences, however, were "poor childhood and adult interpersonal relationships": the ability to resolve conflicts and the degree of emotional support given by others.[5]

5. The likelihood of death increases when a close relative dies. In one Welsh village, citizens who had lost a close relative died within one year at a rate more than five times greater than those who had not suffered from a relative's death.[6]

Research like this demonstrates the importance of satisfying personal relationships. Remember: Not everyone needs the same amount of contact, and the quality of communication is almost certainly as important as the quantity. The important point here is that personal communication is essential for our well-being. In other words, "people who need people" aren't "the luckiest people in the world" ... they're the *only* people!

ego needs

Communication does more than enable us to survive. It is the way—indeed, the *only* way we learn who we are. As you'll read in Chapter 2, our sense of identity comes from the way we interact with other people. Are we smart or stupid, attractive or ugly, skillful or inept? The answers to these questions don't come from looking in the mirror. We decide who we are based on how others react to us.

Deprived of communication with others, we would have no sense of identity. In his book *Bridges, Not Walls,* John Stewart dramatically illustrates this fact by citing the case of the famous "Wild Boy of Aveyron," who spent his early childhood without any apparent human contact. The boy was discovered in January 1800 while digging for vegetables in a French village garden. He showed no behaviors one would expect in a social human. The boy could not speak, but uttered only weird cries. More significant than this absence of social skills was his lack of any identity as a human being. As author Roger Shattuck put it, "The boy had no human sense of being in the world. He had no sense of himself as a person related to other persons."[7] Only after the influence of a loving "mother" did the boy begin to behave—and, we can imagine, think of himself as a human.

Like the boy of Aveyron, each of us enters the world with little or no sense of identity. We gain an idea of who we are from the way others

define us. As Chapter 2 explains, the messages we receive in early child-hood are the strongest, but the influence of others continues through-out life.

social needs

Besides helping define who we are, communication is the way we relate socially with others. Psychologist William Schutz describes three types of social needs we strive to fulfill by communicating.[8] The first is *inclusion*, the need to feel a sense of belonging to some personal relationship. Inclusion needs are sometimes satisfied by informal alliances: the friends who study together, a group of runners, or neighbors who help one another with yard work. In other cases, we get a sense of belonging from formal relationships: everything from religious congregations to a job to marriage.

A second type of social need is the desire for *control*—the desire each of us has to influence others, to feel some sense of power over our world. Some types of control are obvious, such as the boss or team captain whose directions make things happen. Much control, however, is more subtle. Experts in child development tell us that preschoolers who insist on staying up past bedtime or having a treat in the supermarket

People don't get along because they fear each other.
People fear each other because they don't know each other.
They don't know each other because they have not properly communicated with each other.

Martin Luther King, Jr.

See that man over there?
Yes.
Well, I hate him.
But you don't know him.
That's why I hate him.

Gordon Allport
The Nature of Prejudice

may be less concerned with the issue at hand than with knowing that they have at least some ability to make things happen.[9] In this case, even driving a parent crazy can satisfy the need for control. This answers the parent's question "Why are you being so stubborn?"

The third social need is *affection*—a desire to care for others and know that they care for us. Affection, of course, is critical for most of us. Being included and having power aren't very satisfying if the important people in our lives don't care for us.

practical needs

We shouldn't overlook the everyday, important functions communication serves. Communication is the tool that lets us tell the hair stylist to take just a little off the sides, the doctor where it hurts, and the plumber that the broken pipe needs attention *now!* Communication is the means of learning important information in school. It is the method you use to convince a prospective employer that you're the best candidate for a job, and it is the way to persuade the boss you deserve a raise. The list of common but critical jobs performed by communicating goes on and on, and it's worth noticing that the inability to express yourself clearly and effectively in every one of the above examples can prevent you from achieving your goal.

Psychologist Abraham Maslow suggested that human needs such as the preceding ones fall into five categories, each of which must be satisfied before we concern ourselves with the following ones.[10] As you read on, think about the ways in which communication is often necessary to satisfy each need. The most basic of these needs are *physical:* sufficient air, water, food, and rest and the ability to reproduce as a species. The second of Maslow's needs involves *safety:* protection from threats to our well-being. Beyond physical and safety concerns are the *social* needs we have mentioned already. Even beyond these, Maslow suggests that each of us has *self-esteem* needs: the desire to believe that we are worthwhile, valuable people. The final category of needs described by Maslow involves *self-actualization:* the desire to develop our potential to the maximum, to become the best person we can be.

modeling communication

So far we have introduced a basic definition of communication and seen the functions communication performs. This information is useful, but it only begins to describe the subject. One way to understand more about communication is to examine a model of that process.

why use models?

A model is a simplified representation of some process. For instance, consider what a model of "digestion" might look like. At one end of a page we could draw a mouth with food going into it, followed by tubes running into a baglike object representing the stomach. To represent the intestines, we could draw a coiled hose connected at the top end to the stomach.

Whereas this representation may begin to tell us something about digestion, it also tells us a great deal about the following characteristics of models:

1. *Models can represent the relevant elements of a process.* Even though our diagram is crude, it does provide a good introduction to the basic parts of the digestive tract.
2. *Models organize the parts of a process and indicate how they are related to each other.* For example, an uninformed viewer would learn from our drawing that the stomach is below the esophagus and above the intestines.
3. *Models simplify a complex event.* This simplification helps promote understanding. It's certainly easier for an uninitiated learner to start exploring the digestion process with a simple model than by looking into the entire process in all its complexity.
4. *Models provide an opportunity to look at a familiar process in a new way.* By doing so, models sometimes make us aware that we've been operating on misconceptions. For instance, adding an explanation of what goes on in each part of our digestion model makes clear how little digestion actually goes on in the stomach, contrary to the belief of many people.

Whereas models clearly offer several advantages, they also suffer from a number of potential drawbacks. First, in an attempt to make a complex event simple, a model may oversimplify and lead viewers into thinking that the event itself is simple. This mistaken assumption has the highest probability of occurring if a learner has little information on what the event is really like. For instance, someone not versed in physics might actually believe that an atom is quite similar to marbles spinning around a grapefruit.

It's also important to remember that a model is an analogy, nothing more. The danger of confusing the map with the territory is illustrated by the story of an elementary school child who, having studied geography by using the classroom map, was surprised to discover that Spain was not a pink country, France green, and so on.

Finally, a model can cause us to stop thinking about the process that it represents and can cause us to conclude that we know everything significant about the subject. This mistake is termed *premature closure* and, of course, should be avoided.

a communication model

Keeping the advantages and dangers of models in mind, we can begin to build a representation of what goes on in the process of communication. Because we need to begin somewhere, let's start with your wanting to express an idea (see Figure 1-1). If you think about it for a

human communication: what and why

11

figure 1–1

moment, you'll realize that most ideas you have don't come to you already put into words. Rather, they are more like mental images, often consisting of unverbalized feelings or ideas.

As people aren't mind readers, you have to translate this mental image into symbols (usually words) that others can understand. No doubt you can recall times when you actually shuffled through a mental list of words to pick exactly the right ones to explain an idea. This process, called *encoding,* goes on every time we speak (see Figure 1–2).

figure 1–2

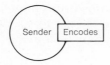

Once the idea is encoded, the next step is to send it. We call this step the *message* phase of our model. There are a number of ways to send a message. For instance, you might consider expressing yourself in a letter, over the telephone, or face-to-face. In this sense, writing, talking on the phone, and speaking in person are three of the *channels* through which we send our messages (see Figure 1–3). All channels aren't equal: The method of communication often influences the type of interaction that occurs between people. For instance, one study revealed that students were more likely to ask questions of professors through computer networks than in person.[11] Another showed that some discussions carried on by computer hookups are more argumentative than face-to-face sessions, but also more equal in terms of shared discussion time and decision making.[12]

figure 1–3

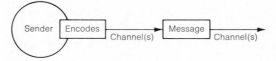

When your message reaches another person, much the same process occurs in reverse. Receivers must make some sense out of the symbols you've sent by *decoding* them back into feelings, intentions, or thoughts that mean something to them (see Figure 1–4).

figure 1–4

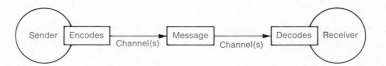

12

Ideally at this point the mental images of the sender and receiver ought to match. If this happens, we can say that an act of successful communication has occurred. However, as you know from your own experience, things often go wrong somewhere between the sender and the receiver. For instance:

Your constructive suggestion is taken as criticism.

Your carefully phrased question is misunderstood.

Your friendly joke is taken as an insult.

Your hinted request is missed entirely.

And so it often goes. Why do such misunderstandings occur? To answer this question, we need to add more detail to our model. We recognize that without several more crucial elements our model would not represent the world accurately.

First, it's important to recognize that communication always takes place in an *environment*. By this term we do not mean simply a physical location, but also the personal history that each person brings to a conversation. The problem here is that each of us represents a different environment because of our differing backgrounds. Although we certainly have some experiences in common, we also see each situation in a unique way. For instance, consider how two individuals' environments would differ if:

A were well rested and *B* were exhausted.

A were rich and *B* were poor.

A were rushed and *B* had nowhere special to go.

A had lived a long, eventful life and *B* were young and inexperienced.

A were passionately concerned with the subject and *B* were indifferent to it.

Obviously this list could go on and on. The problem of differing environments is critical to effective communication. Even now, though, you can see from just these few items that the world is a different place for sender and receiver. We can represent this idea on our model shown in Figure 1–5.

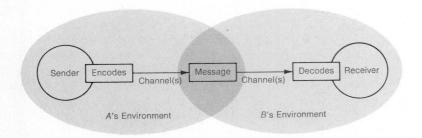

figure 1–5

human communication: what and why

13

Notice that the environments of *A* and *B* overlap. This overlapping represents those things that our communicators have in common. This point is important because it is through our shared knowledge and experiences that we are able to communicate. For example, you can at least partially understand the messages we are writing on these pages because we share the same language, however imprecise it often may be.

Different environments aren't the only cause of ineffective communication. Communicologists use the term *noise* to label other forces that interfere with the process and point out that it can occur in every stage (see Figure 1-6).

figure 1-6

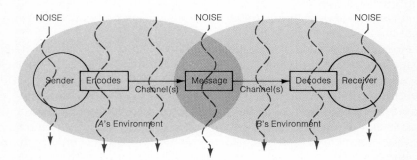

There are primarily two types of noise that can block communication—physical and psychological. Physical noise includes those obvious things that make it difficult to hear as well as many other kinds of distractions. For instance, too much cigarette smoke in a crowded room might make it hard for you to pay attention to another person, and sitting in the rear of an auditorium might make a speaker's remarks unclear. Physical noise can disrupt communication almost anywhere in our model—in the sender, channel, message, or receiver.

Psychological noise refers to forces within the sender or receiver that make these people less able to express or understand the message clearly. For instance, an outdoor person might exaggerate the size and number of fish caught in order to convince himself or herself and others of his or her talents. In the same way, some students might become so upset upon learning that they failed a test that they would be unable (perhaps unwilling is a better word) to understand clearly where they went wrong.

So far we may seem to be talking about one-way communication, consisting of a single sender and receiver who never switch roles. There certainly are situations in which information appears to move in one direction, as in families where parents expect to do all the talking while their children are placed in the position of being merely listeners.

Actually, even in cases like these, communication is *two way,* with each participant both sending and receiving. The most recognizable example of two-way communication is a conversation, in which the participants continually respond to each other's statements. Sometimes the response is verbal and sometimes nonverbal, but in either case each sender can use the other's reaction to see how a message is being received. This discernible response to a message is termed *feedback*.

Nonverbal feedback is almost always present when we communicate, and verbal reactions are usually there as well. This feedback is valuable because it helps us discover how our message has been received. Despite the fact that feedback is generally available and is almost always useful, many communicators fail to take advantage of it. Some teachers, for example, seem to have an uncanny ability to talk for hours without realizing that once-interested listeners have nodded off to sleep, nibbled through their lunches, or slipped quietly out of the room. The feedback was there, but the instructor either ignored it or failed to interpret it correctly.

Feedback isn't always accurate, as we can see by following our classroom example a bit further. Students have learned how to shake their heads in agreement, smile, and look contemplative when faced with boring teachers, thus giving a naive instructor an inaccurate picture of how successful the lesson has been. Failure to check the validity of feedback can lead to misunderstandings.

This completes our representation. Take a moment and look at the detailed model of the communication process that we've built (see Figure 1–7). This picture is probably more complicated than a definition you once might have given. But now you can probably see that every step is important and can't be omitted. Given this model, perhaps you can better understand why effective communication is often so difficult and why spending some time learning the skills that make it possible can be worth your while.

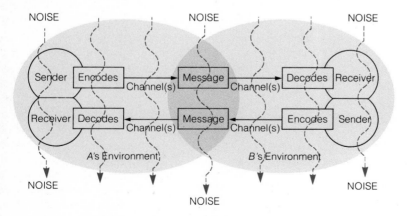

figure 1–7

Although this model provides a good overview of the nature of communication, we need to explain two additional important characteristics of that phenomenon.

human communication: what and why

15

1. **Communication is irreversible.** Though we sometimes wish that we could back up in time, erasing something we've said and replacing it with a better message, such an act is impossible. There certainly are some times when further explanation can clear up another's confusion or when your apology can mollify another's hurt feelings, but there are other cases where no amount of explanation can erase the impression you have created.

2. **Communicators are simultaneously senders and receivers.** At first glance our model implies that at any point a person is either sending or receiving a message. Actually we constantly do both. The two sender-receiver representations in our model should not be one under another, but rather superimposed—hard to do in a two-dimensional drawing. The process does not involve A's sending a message to B, who in turn sends a message back to A. Rather, A and B are both sending and receiving messages *at the same time*. Certainly one may appear to be the predominant sender and the other primarily a receiver, but each party simultaneously does both.

   For example, consider an apparently one-way situation that we mentioned a few pages ago—namely, parents lecturing children. Although the youngsters are certainly receiving information, they are also transmitting messages nonverbally by facial expression, posture, gestures, and so on. The talkative parents are also receivers in this situation, noticing the messages sent by their children. (We know this awareness of a youngster's messages exists because of feedback, such as "You're not paying attention—look at me!")

clarifying misconceptions about communication

Having spent time talking about what communication is, we ought to also identify some things it is not.[13] Recognizing these misconceptions is important, not only because they ought to be avoided by anyone knowledgeable about the subject, but also because following them can get you into personal trouble.

communication is not always a good thing

For most people, belief in the value of communication rates somewhere close to motherhood in their hierarchy of important values. In truth, communication is neither good nor bad in itself. Rather, its value comes from the way it is used. In this sense, communication is similar to fire: Flames in the fireplace on a cold night keep us warm and create a cozy atmosphere, but the same flames can kill if they spread to the surrounding room. Communication can be a tool for expressing warm feelings and useful facts, but under different circumstances the same words and actions can cause both physical and emotional pain.

communication will not solve all problems

"If I could just communicate better . . ." is the sad refrain of many unhappy people who believe that if they could just express themselves better, their relationships would improve. Though this is sometimes true, it's an exaggeration to say that communicating—even communicating clearly—is a guaranteed panacea.

more communication is not always better

Although it's certainly true that not communicating enough is a mistake, there are also situations when *too much* communication is a mistake. Sometimes excessive communication simply is unproductive, as when we "talk a problem to death," going over the same ground again and again without making any headway. And there are times when communicating too much can actually aggravate a problem. We've all had the experience of "talking ourselves into a hole"—making a bad situation worse by pursuing it too far. As McCroskey and Wheeless put it, "More and more negative communication merely leads to more and more negative results."[14]

There are even times when *no* communication is the best course. Any good salesperson will tell you that it's often best to stop talking and let the customer think about the product. And when two people are angry and hurt, they may say things they don't mean and will later regret. At times like these it's probably best to spend a little time cooling off, thinking about what to say and how to say it.

One key to successful communication, then, is to share an *adequate* amount of information in a *skillful* manner. Teaching you how to decide what information is adequate and what constitutes skillful behavior is one major goal of this book.

meanings rest in people, not words

We already hinted that meanings rest in people, not in words, when we said earlier that the symbols we use to communicate are arbitrary. It's a mistake to think that, just because you use a word in one way, others will do so too. Sometimes differing interpretations of symbols are easily caught, as when we might first take the statement "He's gay" to mean the subject has homosexual preferences, only to find out that he is cheerful—and straight. In other cases, however, the ambiguity of words and nonverbal behaviors isn't so apparent ... and thus has more far-reaching consequences. Remember, for instance, a time when someone said to you, "I'll be honest ...," and only later did you learn that those words hid precisely the opposite fact. In Chapter 3 you'll read a great deal more about the problems that come from mistakenly assuming that meanings rest in words.

communication is not simple

Most people assume that communication is an aptitude that people develop without the need for training—rather like breathing. After all, we've been swapping ideas with one another since early childhood, and there are lots of people who communicate pretty well without ever having had a class on the subject. Though this picture of communication as a natural ability seems accurate, it's actually a gross oversimplification.

Throughout history there have been cases of infants raised without human contact. In all these instances the children were initially unable to communicate with others when brought into society. Only after extensive teaching (and not even then in some cases) were they able to speak and understand language in ways we take for granted. But what about the more common cases of effective communicators who have had no formal training, yet are skillful at creating and understanding messages? The answer to this question lies in the fact that not all education occurs in a classroom: Many people learn to communicate skillfully because they have been exposed to models of such behavior by those around them. This principle of modeling explains why children who grow up in homes with stable relationships between family members have a greater chance of developing such relationships themselves. They know how to do so because they've seen effective communication in action.

Does the existence of these good communicators mean that certain people don't need courses like the one you're taking? Hardly. Even the best communicators aren't perfect: They often suffer the frustration of being unable to get a message across effectively, and they frequently misunderstand others. Furthermore, even the most successful people you know can probably identify ways in which their relationships could profit by better communication. These facts show that communication skills are rather like athletic ability: Even the most inept of us can learn to be more effective with training and practice, and those who are talented can always become better.

summary

This chapter introduced some key concepts that provide a foundation for the material that follows in the rest of the book. It explained the nature of communication as it will be studied here: a face-to-face symbolic process between human beings, in which the receiver is involved. The chapter described several types of needs communication satisfies: physical, ego, social, and practical.

The chapter explained the value of models as a way of understanding any process and introduced a model of human communication. It also introduced several misconceptions about communication.

activities

1. List the needs you have attempted to satisfy by communicating during a recent twenty-four-hour period. Since describing every need-satisfying act would call for writing a small book, choose a sample of incidents representing each of the categories described in the text.

2. Describe three incidents in which you communicated to satisfy each of the following social needs:
   a. inclusion
   b. control
   c. affection

3. Identify an important message that you would like to communicate within the next week. Describe:
   a. The idea you want to send and the various ways you could encode it.
   b. The channels by which you could send it.
   c. The ways in which your receiver might decode it.

d. Possible differences between your environment and that of the receiver that might make it difficult for your message to be accurately understood.

e. Likely sources of physical and psychological noise that might interfere with the communication transaction.

f. Types of feedback you can utilize to see whether or not you have succeeded in having your message understood.

Based on your answers to these questions, describe the steps you can take to construct and deliver your message in a way that it has the greatest chance of being accurately received.

4. To recognize that communication can be either good or bad, recall three incidents in which communication improved a situation and three in which acts of communication made matters worse.

5. What evidence can you provide to show that effective communication is not a natural ability? Include in your answer instances when people communicated poorly owing to

a. lack of training

b. exposure to ineffective models

c. reinforcement of poor behavior

d. punishment for effective behavior

Although the last two categories might seem unlikely, a bit of reflection will show you that many people do get social or material payoffs for communicating in ways that would generally be defined as unacceptable whereas others are punished for acting in a manner that would be regarded positively by most people.

notes

1. Rudolph Verderber, Ann Elder, and Ernest Weiler, "A Study of Communication Time Usage Among College Students," unpublished study, University of Cincinnati, 1976.

2. R. Narem, "Try a Little TLC," research reported in *Science* 80: 1 (1980):15.

3. J. Lynch, *The Broken Heart: The Medical Consequences of Loneliness* (New York: Basic Books, 1977), pp. 239–242.

4. Ibid.

5. E. A. Liljefors and R. H. Rahe, "Psychosocial Characteristics of Subjects with Myocardial Infarction in Stockholm," in E. K. Gunderson and R. H. Rahe (eds.), *Life Stress Illness* (Springfield, Ill.: Charles C. Thomas, 1974), pp. 90–104.

6. W. D. Rees and S. G. Lutkins, "Mortality of Bereavement," *British Medical Journal* 4 (1967):13.

7. R. Shattuck, *The Forbidden Experiment: The Story of the Wild Boy of Aveyron* (New York: Farrar, Straus & Giroux, 1980), p. 37.

8. W. Schutz, *The Interpersonal Underworld* (Palo Alto, Calif.: Science and Behavior Books, 1966).

9. E. H. Erikson, *Childhood and Society* (New York: Norton, 1963).

10. A. H. Maslow, *Toward a Psychology of Being* (New York: Van Nostrand Reinhold, 1968).

11. D. Goleman, "The Electronic Rorschach," *Psychology Today* 17:2 (February 1983):42.

12. Ibid., p. 41.

13. Adapted from J. C. McCroskey and L. R. Wheeless, *Introduction to Human Communication* (Boston: Allyn and Bacon, 1976), pp. 3–10.

14. Ibid., p. 5.

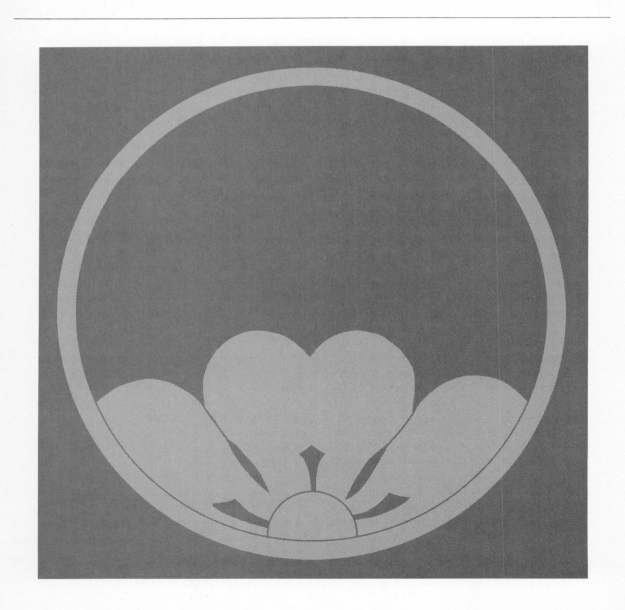

two

perception and the self

After reading this chapter, you should understand:

1. The communicative influences that shape the self-concept.
2. The three elements of the perception process.
3. The perceptual errors that distort perception of others.
4. How self-fulfilling prophecies can influence behavior.
5. The requirements for changing one's self-concept.

You should be able to:

1. Identify the ways you influence the self-concept of others and the way significant others influence your self-concept.
2. Describe the different ways that you and at least one other person perceive an event, showing how selection, organization, and interpretation lead to the differing perceptions.
3. Identify the errors listed in this chapter that have led you to develop distorted perceptions of others.
4. Identify communication-related self-fulfilling prophecies that you have imposed on yourself, that others have imposed on you, and that you have imposed on others.
5. List the steps you could take to change an important part of your self-concept that affects your communication.

A student is practicing his first assigned speech with several friends.

"This is a stupid topic," he laments. The other students sincerely assure him that the topic is an interesting one and that the speech sounds good.

Despite these reassurances, the student remains unconvinced. Later in class he becomes flustered because he believes that his speech is no good. As a result of his unenthusiastic delivery, the student receives a low grade on the assignment.

Despite her nervousness, a job candidate does her best in a job interview. She leaves the session convinced that she botched her big chance. A few days later she is surprised to receive a job offer.

At a party several guests have been emptying a keg of beer with great gusto. They are now engaged in conversation that they think is witty, but that a sober observer would find foolish. However, as there are no sober observers present, the reality of the situation is lost on the participants.

Stories like these are probably familiar to you. Yet behind this familiarity lie principles that are perhaps the most important ones in this book:

1. Two or more people often perceive an event in radically different ways.
2. The beliefs each of us holds about ourselves—our self-concept—has a powerful effect on our behavior, even when these beliefs are inaccurate.

These simple truths play a role in virtually all the important messages we send and receive. The goal of this chapter is to demonstrate the significance of these principles by describing the nature of perception and showing how it influences the way we view ourselves and how we relate to others.

understanding the self-concept

We will begin our study by examining the nature of the self-concept. We will first define that term and next go on to explore how the self-concept develops. Then after looking at the role of perception in human interaction, we will discuss how the self-concept affects communication.

self-concept defined

The *self-concept* is an internalized set of relatively stable perceptions each of us holds about ourselves. The self-concept includes our conception about what is unique about us and what makes us both similar to and different from others.[1] To put it differently, the self-concept is

rather like a mental mirror that reflects how we view ourselves: not only physical features, but also emotional states, talents, likes and dislikes, values, and roles.

We will have more to say about the nature of the self-concept shortly, but first you will find it valuable to gain a personal understanding of how this theoretical construct applies to you. You can do so by answering a simple question: "Who are you?"

How do you define yourself? As a student? A man or woman? By your age? Your religion? Occupation?

There are many ways of identifying yourself. Take a few more moments, and list as many ways as you can to identify who you are. You'll need this list later in this chapter, so be sure to complete it now. Try to include all the characteristics that describe you:

your moods or feelings

your appearance and physical condition

your social traits

talents you possess or lack

your intellectual capacity

your strong beliefs

your social roles

Even a list of twenty or thirty terms would be only a partial description. To make this written self-portrait complete, your list would have to be hundreds—or even thousands—of words long.

perception and the self

25

Retrospectively, one can ask "Who am I?" But in practice, the answer has come before the question.

J. M. Yinger

Of course, not every item on such a list would be equally important. For example, the most significant part of one person's self-concept might consist of social roles whereas for another it could consist of physical appearance, health, friendships, accomplishments, or skills.

You can begin to see how important these elements are by continuing this personal experiment. Pick the ten items from your list that describe the most fundamental aspects of who you are. Rank these ten items so that the most fundamental one is in first place, with the others following in order of declining importance. Now, beginning with the tenth item, imagine what would happen if each characteristic in turn disappeared from your makeup. How would you be different? How would you feel?

For most people, this exercise dramatically illustrates just how fundamental the concept of self is. Even when the item being abandoned is an unpleasant one, it's often hard to give it up. And when they are asked to let go of their most central feelings or thoughts, most people balk. "I wouldn't be *me* without that," they insist. Of course this proves our point: The concept of self is perhaps our most fundamental possession. Knowing who we are is essential, for without a self-concept it would be impossible to relate to the world.

communication and development of the self

So far we've talked about what the self-concept is; but at this point you may be asking what it has to do with the study of human communication. We can begin to answer this question by looking at how you came to possess your own self-concept.

Newborn babies come into the world with very little sense of self.[2] In the first months of life infants have no awareness of their bodies as being separate from the rest of the environment. At eight months of age, for example, a child will be surprised when a toy grabbed from the grip of another child "resists." Not until somewhere between their first and second birthday are children able to recognize their reflections in a mirror.[3]

How does this rudimentary sense of identity grow into the rich, multi-dimensional self-concept you identified in the preceding section? It develops almost exclusively from communication with others. As psychologists Arthur Combs and Donald Snygg put it:

> The self is essentially a social product arising out of experience with people. ... We learn the most significant and fundamental facts about ourselves from ... "reflected appraisals," inferences about ourselves made as a consequence of the ways we perceive others behaving toward us.[4]

The term "reflected appraisal," coined by Harry Stack Sullivan,[5] is a good one, for it metaphorically describes the fact that we develop an image of ourselves from the way we think others view us. This notion of the "looking-glass self" was first introduced in 1902 by Charles H. Cooley, who suggested that we put ourselves in the position of other

"Guess who Miss Price picked to play poison ivy in the class play."

people and then in our mind's eye view ourselves as we imagine they see us.[6] In other words, we interpret (or "decode," to use the terminology of our communication model) the behavior of others, assuming that this interpretation is an accurate representation of how they view us.

The stream of messages about who we are begins early in life, long before we have developed sufficiently to think about them in any systematic way. During this prelinguistic stage the messages are nonverbal. The amount of time parents allow their infant to cry before responding can, over time, communicate how important the child is to them. Their method of handling the baby also speaks volumes: Do they affectionately play with it, joggling it gently and holding it close, or do they treat it like so much baggage, changing diapers and feeding and bathing it in a brusque, impersonal manner? Does the tone of voice they use express love and enjoyment or disappointment and irritation?

As the youngster learns to speak and understand language, verbal messages—both positive and negative—also contribute to the developing self-concept. These messages continue later in life, especially when they come from what social scientists term *significant others*— people whose opinions we especially value. A teacher from long ago, a special friend or relative, or perhaps a barely known acquaintance whom you respected can all leave an imprint on how you view yourself. To see the importance of significant others, ask yourself how you arrived at your opinion of you as a student ... as a person attractive to the

perception and the self
27

We are not only our brother's keeper; in countless large and small ways, we are our brother's maker.

Bonaro Overstreet

opposite sex . . . as a competent worker . . . and you will see that these self-evaluations were probably influenced by the way others regarded you.

Research supports the importance of reflected appraisals. One study identified the relationship between adult attitudes toward children and the children's self-concepts.[7] The researcher first established that parents and teachers expect children from higher socioeconomic backgrounds to do better academically than socioeconomically disadvantaged youngsters. In other words, parents and teachers have higher expectations for socioeconomically advantaged students. Interestingly, when children from a higher socioeconomic class performed poorly in school their self-esteem dropped; but children from less advantaged backgrounds did not lose self-esteem. Why was there this difference? Because the parents and teachers sent messages about their disappointment to the higher status children whereas no such messages went to their less-advantaged counterparts. The relationship between others' evaluations of an individual and his or her self-concept persists

into adulthood. Researchers conducted a study using several groups—fraternities, sororities, and sociology classes.[8] Each student rated himself or herself on a five-point scale for intelligence, self-confidence, physical attractiveness, and likableness. Next the subjects rated the other members of their group in terms of the same characteristics. The researchers found that the students whom others regarded highly also viewed themselves positively, whereas those with lower peer ratings had less self-esteem.

You might argue that not every part of one's self-concept is shaped by others, insisting there are certain objective facts that are recognizable by self-observation. After all, nobody needs to tell you that you are taller than others, speak with an accent, can run quickly, and so on. These facts are obvious.

Though it's true that some features of the self are immediately apparent, the *significance* we attach to them—the rank we assign them in the hierarchy of our list and the interpretation we give them—depends greatly on the opinions of others. After all, there are many of your features that are readily observable, yet you don't find them important at all because nobody has regarded them as significant.

Recently we heard a woman in her eighties describing her youth. "When I was a girl," she declared, "we didn't worry about weight. Some people were skinny and others were plump, and we pretty much accepted the bodies God gave us." Compare this attitude with what you find today: It's seldom that you pick up a popular magazine or visit a bookstore without reading about the latest diet fads, and television ads are filled with scenes of slender, happy people. As a result you'll find many people who complain about their need to "lose a few pounds." The reason for such concern has more to do with the attention paid to slimness these days than with any increase in the number of people in the population who are overweight. Furthermore, the interpretation of characteristics such as weight depends on the way people important to us regard them. We generally see fat as undesirable because others tell us it is. In a society where obesity is the ideal (and there are such societies), a heavy person would feel beautiful. In the same way, the fact that one is single or married, solitary or sociable, aggressive or passive takes on meaning depending on the interpretation society attaches to those traits. Thus, the importance of a given characteristic in your self-concept has as much to do with the significance you and others attach to it as with the existence of the characteristic.

By now it should be clear that the self-concept is not an objective characteristic, like height or hair color. Sometimes an individual's self-evaluation is unrealistically high. You might, for instance, see yourself as a witty joke teller when others can barely tolerate your attempts at humor; or you might consider yourself an excellent worker, in contrast to the employer who is thinking about firing you. In other cases, people

---

premier artiste

Watch me perform!
I walk a tightrope of unique
   design.
I teeter, falter, recover
  And bow.
     You applaud.
I run forward, backward,
   hesitate
  And bow.
     You applaud.
If you don't applaud
  I'll fall.
Cheer me! Hurray me!
Or you push me
Down.

Lenni Shender Goldstein

I am not what I think I am.
I am not what you think I am.
I am what I think you think I
  am.

Aaron Bleiberg and Harry
Leubling

---

perception and communication

29

For the most part we do not see first and then define; we define first and then see.

Walter Lippmann

view themselves more harshly than objective facts suggest. You may have known people, for instance, who insist they are unattractive or incompetent in spite of your honest insistence to the contrary.

Because we react to ourselves and others according to the perceptions we hold rather than objective events themselves, it is important to take a look at the process of perception and see how it influences communication.

the perception process

We need to begin our discussion of perception by talking about the gap between "what is" and what we know. Our idea of reality is only a partial one: The world contains far more than we are able to experience with our limited senses. Infrared photos, electron microscopes, and other technological tools reveal a world our ancestors never imagined. Certain animals can hear sounds and detect scents not apparent to humans.

Even within the realm of our senses we are only aware of a small part of what is going on around us. For instance, most people who live in large cities find that the noises of traffic, people, and construction soon fade out of awareness. Others can take a walk through the forest without distinguishing one bird's call from another or noticing the differences between various types of vegetation. On a personal level we have all had the experience of failing to notice something unusual about a friend—perhaps a new hair style or a sad expression—until it's called to our attention.

Sometimes our failure to recognize some events while noticing others comes from not paying attention to important information. But in other cases it simply isn't possible to be aware of everything, no matter how attentive we might be: There is just too much going on.

William James said that "to the infant the world is just a big blooming, buzzing confusion." One reason for this is the fact that infants are not yet able to sort out the myriad impressions with which we're all bombarded. As we grow, we learn to manage all this data, and as we do so, we begin to make sense out of the world.

Because this ability to organize our perceptions in a useful way is such a critical factor in our ability to function, we need to begin our study of perception by taking a closer look at this process. We can do so by examining the three steps by which we attach meaning to our experiences.[9]

Selection   As we are exposed to more input than we can possibly manage, the first step in perceiving is to select what data we will attend to. There are several factors that cause us to notice some messages and ignore others.

Stimuli that are *intense* often attract our attention. Something that is louder, larger, or brighter stands out. This explains why—other things being equal—we're more likely to remember extremely tall or short people and why someone who laughs or talks loudly at a party attracts more attention (not always favorable) than do more quiet guests.

Repetitious stimuli, repetitious stimuli, repetitious stimuli, repetitious stimuli, repetitious stimuli, repetitious stimuli also attract attention.* Just as a quiet but steadily dripping faucet can come to dominate our awareness, people to whom we're frequently exposed become noticeable.

ATTENTION IS ALSO FREQUENTLY RELATED TO contrast OR change IN STIMULATION. Put differently, unchanging people or things become less noticeable. This principle gives an explanation (excuse?) for why we come to take wonderful people for granted when we interact with them frequently. It's only when they stop being so wonderful or go away that we appreciate them.

Motives also determine what information we select from our environment. If you're anxious about being late for a date, you'll notice whatever clocks may be around you, and if you're hungry, you'll become aware of any restaurants, markets, and billboards advertising food in your path. Motives also determine how we perceive people. For example, someone on the lookout for a romantic adventure will be especially aware of attractive potential partners whereas the same person at a different time might be oblivious to anyone but police or medical personnel in an emergency.

Organization Along with selecting information from the environment, we must arrange that data in some meaningful way. Many messages are ambiguous and can be organized in more than one manner. For example, consider Figure 2–1. How many ways can you view the boxes? Most people have a hard time finding more than one perspective. (There are four.) If you can't find all of them, turn to Figure 2–2 for some help.

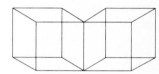

figure 2–1

We can see the principle of alternative organizing patterns in human interaction. Young children usually don't classify people according to their skin color. They are just as likely to identify a black person, for example, as being tall, wearing glasses, or being a certain age. As they become more socialized, however, they learn that one common organizing principle in today's society is race, and then their perceptions of others change. Figure 2–3 shows how different linguistic categories alter perception.[10] In the same way it's possible to classify people or behaviors according to many schemes, each of which will result in different consequences. Do you organize according to age, education, occupation, physical attractiveness, astrological sign, or some other scheme? Imagine how different your relationships would be if you used different criteria for organizing.

---

* We borrowed the graphic demonstrations in this and the following paragraph from Dennis Coon's *Introduction to Psychology,* 2d ed. (St. Paul: West Publishing, 1981).

figure 2–2

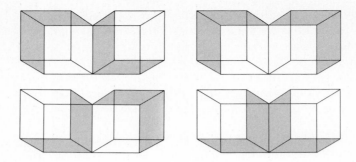

Interpretation There are many ways to interpret a single event. Is the person who smiles at you across a crowded room interested in romance or simply being polite? Is a friend's kidding a sign of affection or an indication of irritation? Should you take an invitation to "Drop by any time" literally or not?

There are several factors that cause us to interpret an event in one way or another:

1. **Past experience.** What meanings have similar events held? If, for example, you've been gouged by landlords in the past, you might be skeptical about an apartment manager's assurances that careful housekeeping will assure the refund of your cleaning deposit.
2. **Assumptions about human behavior.** "People generally do as little work as possible to get by." "In spite of their mistakes, people are doing the best they can." Beliefs like these will shape the way we interpret another's actions.
3. **Expectations.** Anticipation shapes interpretations. If you imagine that your boss is unhappy with your work, you'll probably feel threatened by a request to "see me in my office first thing Monday morning." On the other hand, if you imagine that your work will be rewarded, your weekend will probably be a pleasant one as you anticipate a reward from the boss.
4. **Knowledge.** If you know that a friend has just been jilted by a lover or been fired from a job, you'll interpret her aloof behavior differently than if you were unaware of what had happened. If you know that an instructor speaks sarcastically to all students, then you won't be as likely to take any such remarks personally.
5. **Personal moods.** When you're feeling insecure, the world is a very different place from what it is when you're confident. The same goes for happiness and sadness or any other opposing emotions. The way we feel determines how we interpret events.

accuracy and inaccuracy in person perception

Not all interpretations are accurate. Research has uncovered several common perceptual errors we need to guard against if we are to gain a clear understanding of ourselves and others.[11]

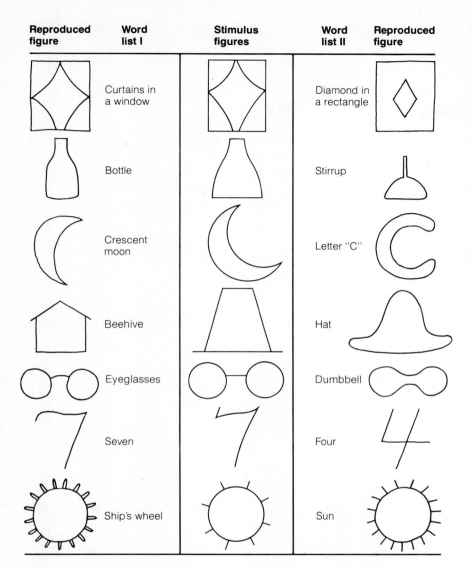

Reproduced figure	Word list I	Stimulus figures	Word list II	Reproduced figure
	Curtains in a window		Diamond in a rectangle	
	Bottle		Stirrup	
	Crescent moon		Letter "C"	
	Beehive		Hat	
	Eyeglasses		Dumbbell	
	Seven		Four	
	Ship's wheel		Sun	

figure 2–3

An illustration of the way in which labels shape organization and interpretation of events. Subjects were presented with stimulus figures along with the descriptions in either Word list I or Word list II. Notice how the subjects' belief about what the stimulus figure represented shaped their perception and subsequent drawings. Think of several everyday examples in which the label given to people, objects, or events shapes the way in which they are perceived. (Carmichael, Hogan, and Walter, 1932)

We are influenced by what is most obvious The error of being influenced by what is most obvious is understandable. As you read earlier, we select stimuli from our environment that are noticeable: intense, repetitious, unusual, or otherwise attention-grabbing. The problem is that the most obvious factor is not necessarily the only cause—or the most significant one for an event. For example:

- When two children (or adults, for that matter) fight, it may be a mistake to blame the one who lashes out first. Perhaps the other one was at least equally responsible, teasing or refusing to cooperate.
- You might complain about an acquaintance whose malicious gossiping or arguing has become a bother, forgetting that by putting up

with that kind of behavior you have been at least partially responsible.

■ You might blame an unhappy working situation on the boss, overlooking other factors beyond her control such as a change in the economy, the policy of higher management, or demands of customers or other workers.

We cling to first impressions, even if wrong   Labeling people according to our first impressions is an inevitable part of the perception process. These labels are a way of making interpretations. "She seems cheerful." "He seems sincere." "They sound awfully conceited."

If they're accurate, impressions like these can be useful ways of deciding how to respond best to people in the future. Problems arise, however, when the labels we attach are inaccurate; for once we form an opinion of someone, we tend to hang onto it and make any conflicting information fit our image.

Suppose, for instance, you mention the name of your new neighbor to a friend. "Oh, I know him," your friend replies. "He seems nice at first, but it's all an act." Perhaps this appraisal is off-base. The neighbor may have changed since your friend knew him, or perhaps your friend's

judgment is simply unfair. Whether the judgment is accurate or not, once you accept your friend's evaluation, it will probably influence the way you respond to the neighbor. You'll look for examples of the insincerity you've heard about . . . and you'll probably find them. Even if the neighbor were a saint, you would be likely to interpret his behavior in ways that fit your expectations. "Sure he *seems* nice," you might think, "but it's probably just a front." Of course, this sort of suspicion can create a self-fulfilling prophecy, transforming a genuinely nice person into someone who truly becomes an undesirable neighbor.

Given the almost unavoidable tendency to form first impressions, the best advice we can give is to keep an open mind and be willing to change your opinion as events prove that the first impressions were mistaken.

We tend to assume others are similar to us People commonly imagine others possess the same attitudes and motives that they do. For example, research shows that people with low self-esteem imagine that others view them unfavorably whereas people who like themselves imagine that others like them too.[12] The frequently mistaken assumption that others' views are similar to our own applies in a wide range of situations. For example:

- You've heard a slightly raunchy joke that you found funny. You might assume that it won't offend a somewhat straight friend. It does.
- You've been bothered by an instructor's tendency to get off the subject during lectures. If you were a professor, you'd want to know if anything you were doing was creating problems for your students, so you decide that your instructor will probably be grateful for some constructive criticism. Unfortunately, you're wrong.
- You lost your temper with a friend a week ago and said some things you regret. In fact, if someone said those things to you, you would consider the relationship was finished. Imagining that your friend feels the same way, you avoid making contact. In fact, your friend feels that he was partly responsible and has avoided you because he thinks you're the one who wants to end things.

Examples like these show that others don't always think or feel the way we do and that assuming similarities exist can lead to problems. How can you find out the other person's real position? Sometimes by asking directly, sometimes by checking with others, and sometimes by making an educated guess after you've thought the matter out. All these alternatives are better than simply assuming everyone would react the way you do.

We tend to favor negative impressions over positive ones What do you think about Harvey? He's handsome, hardworking, intelligent, and honest. He's also very conceited.

Did the last quality make a difference in your evaluation? If it did, you're not alone. Research shows that when people are aware of both

THE SATURDAY EVENING POST

"The truth is, Cauldwell, we never
see ourselves as others see us."

the positive and negative characteristics of another, they tend to be more influenced by the undesirable traits. In one study, for example, researchers found that job interviewers were likely to reject candidates who revealed negative information even when the total amount of information was highly positive.[13]

Sometimes this attitude makes sense. If the negative quality clearly outweighs any positive ones, you'd be foolish to ignore it. A surgeon with shaky hands and a teacher who hates children, for example, would be unsuitable for their jobs, whatever their other virtues. But much of the time it's a bad idea to pay excessive attention to negative qualities and overlook good ones. This is the mistake some people make when screening potential friends or dates. They find some who are too outgoing or too reserved, others who aren't intelligent enough, and still others who have the wrong sense of humor. Of course, it's important to find people you truly enjoy, but expecting perfection can lead to much unnecessary loneliness.

We blame innocent victims for their misfortunes The blame we assign for misfortune depends on who the victim is. When others suffer, we often blame the problem on their personal qualities. On the other hand, when we're the victims, we find explanations outside ourselves. Consider a few examples:

- When *they* botch a job, we might think they weren't listening well or trying hard enough; when *we* make the mistake, the problem was unclear directions or not enough time.
- When *he* lashes out angrily, we say he's being moody or too sensitive; when *we* blow off steam, it's because of the pressure we've been under.
- When *she* gets caught speeding, we say she should have been more careful; when *we* get the ticket, we deny we were driving too fast or say, "Everybody does it."

There are at least two explanations for this kind of behavior. As most of us want other people to approve of us, we defend ourselves by finding explanations for our own problems that make us look good. Basically what we're doing here is saying, "It's not *my* fault." And because

looking good is so often a personal goal, putting others down can be a cheap way to boost our own self-esteem, stating in effect, "I'm better than he is."

Don't misunderstand: We don't always commit the kind of perceptual errors described in this section. Sometimes, for instance, people *are* responsible for their misfortunes, and our problems are not our fault. Likewise, the most obvious interpretation of a situation may be the correct one. Nonetheless, a large amount of research has proved again and again that our perceptions of others are often distorted in the ways listed here. The moral, then, is clear: Don't assume that your first judgment of a person is accurate.

perception, self-concept, and communication

So far in this chapter we've talked about two important factors that influence communication: the self-concept and the perception process. Now we are ready to look at how these two factors influence each other.

how the self-concept influences perception

You have already seen that we learn about ourselves through the reflected appraisal of others. But *what* others? And *what* appraisals? Every day we are bombarded with information about ourselves that is often contradictory. A letter from your family says, "We're proud of your work at school" whereas an instructor's comments suggest you're doing poorly. An old friend's phone call implies that you're important and valued, but a potential date's rejection of your invitation suggests the opposite.

Although it would be theoretically possible to incorporate contradictory messages like these into a single self-concept, in reality this usually doesn't happen. Rather than juggle conflicting messages, we strive for *simplicity* and *consistency* in our self-perception.[14]

You can verify the drive for consistency in your own life by looking at the self-concept list you developed on page 25. You will almost certainly find that it describes you in relatively simple, consistent terms: either intelligent or unintelligent, attractive or ugly, industrious or lazy, and so on.

Because messages about ourselves aren't consistent, we build and maintain a self-concept by creating perceptual filters that allow us to view the world in a way that fits our beliefs. We said earlier that perception is selective; now we see that our selection is guided by this desire for consistency.

Our perceptual filters maintain a consistent self-concept in two ways: by selecting and by distorting information. To see how the process of *selection* operates, imagine that the person with whom you live accuses you of being a slob and not doing your share of the housework. Unless your self-concept fits this description, you might defend yourself by pointing out all the neat, helpful things you've done while forgetting to

It has become something of a cliché to observe that if we do not love ourselves, we cannot love anyone else. This is true enough, but it is only part of the picture. If we do not love ourselves, it is almost impossible to believe fully that we <u>are loved</u> by someone else. It is almost impossible to <u>accept</u> love. It is almost impossible to <u>receive</u> love. No matter what our partner does to show that he or she cares, we do not experience the devotion as convincing because we do not feel loveable to ourselves.

Nathaniel Branden
The Psychology of Romantic Love

remember the chores you've left unfinished. It's important to realize that in cases like this you probably wouldn't be lying, but rather remembering selectively.

Because your housemate's perceptions aren't limited by the need to maintain an image of you as conscientious and tidy, your selective memory would probably be met with a reminder of all the unfinished and sloppy housekeeping you forgot to mention. At this point the second perceptual filter, namely *distortion,* might come into play. You could protest that it really wasn't your fault that you failed to do your share of the work; that illness, schoolwork ... anything but your unwanted habits were responsible for the undone chores. Although distortions like these probably wouldn't impress your housemate, they would serve the purpose of maintaining your self-image as a responsible, reasonably neat person. Distortions like these often take the form of defense mechanisms; as you can imagine, they can lead to troublesome conflicts.

the self-fulfilling prophecy

The self-concept is such a powerful force on the personality that it not only determines how we communicate in the present, but it can actually influence our future behavior and that of others. Such occurrences come about through a phenomenon called the self-fulfilling prophecy.

A *self-fulfilling prophecy* occurs when a person's expectation of an event makes the outcome more likely to occur than would otherwise have been true. Self-fulfilling prophecies occur all the time, although you might never have given them that label. For example, think of some instances you may have known:

You expected to become nervous and botch a job interview and later did so.

You anticipated having a good (or terrible) time at a social affair and found your expectations being met.

A teacher or boss explained a new task to you, saying that you probably wouldn't do well at first. You did not do well.

A friend described someone you were about to meet, saying that you wouldn't like the person. The prediction turned out to be correct—you didn't like the new acquaintance.

In each of these cases there is a good chance that the event happened because it was predicted to occur. You needn't have botched the interview, the party might have been boring only because you helped make it so, you might have done better on the job if your boss hadn't spoken up, and you might have liked the new acquaintance if your friend hadn't given you preconceptions. In other words, what helped make each event occur was the expectation that it would happen.

There are two types of self-fulfilling prophecies. The first occurs when your own expectations influence your behavior. Like the job interview and the party described earlier, there are many times when an event that needn't have occurred does happen because you expect it to. In sports you have probably psyched yourself into playing either better or worse than usual, so that the only explanation for your unusual performance was your attitude that you would behave differently. Similarly, you have probably faced an audience at one time or another with a fearful attitude and forgotten your remarks, not because you were unprepared, but because you said to yourself, "I know I'll blow it." (We'll offer advice on overcoming this kind of stage fright in Chapter 13.)

A second type of self-fulfilling prophecy occurs when the expectations of one person govern another's actions. The classic example was demonstrated by Robert Rosenthal and Lenore Jacobson:

> 20 percent of the children in a certain elementary school were reported to their teachers as showing unusual potential for intellectual growth. The names of these 20 percent were drawn by means of a table of random numbers, which is to say that the names were drawn out of a hat. Eight months later these unusual or "magic" children showed significantly greater gains in IQ than did the remaining children who had not been singled out for the teachers' attention. The change in the teachers' expectations regarding the intellectual performance of these allegedly "special" children had led to an actual change in the intellectual performance of these randomly selected children.[15]

In other words, some children may do better in school, not because they are any more intelligent than their classmates, but because they learn that their teacher, a significant other, believes they can achieve.

To put this phenomenon in context with the self-concept, we can say that when a teacher communicates to students the message, "I think you're bright," they accept that evaluation and change their self-concepts to include that evaluation. Unfortunately, we can assume that the same principle holds for those students whose teachers send the message, "I think you're stupid."

This type of self-fulfilling prophecy has been shown to be a powerful force for shaping the self-concept and thus the behavior of people in a wide range of settings outside the schools. In medicine, patients who

There is an old joke about a man who was asked if he could play a violin and answered, "I don't know. I've never tried." This is psychologically a very wise reply. Those who have never tried to play a violin really do not know whether they can or not. Those who say too early in life and too firmly, "No, I'm not at all musical," shut themselves off prematurely from whole areas of life that might have proved rewarding. In each of us there are unknown possibilities, undiscovered potentialities—and one big advantage of having an open self-concept rather than a rigid one is that we shall continue to expose ourselves to new experiences and therefore we shall continue to discover more and more about ourselves as we grow older.

S. I. Hayakawa

unknowingly use placebos—substances such as injections of sterile water or doses of sugar pills that have no curative value—often respond just as favorably to treatment as people who actually received a drug. The patients believe they have taken a substance that will help them feel better, and this belief actually brings about a "cure." In psychotherapy, Rosenthal and Jacobson describe several studies that suggest that patients who believe they will benefit from treatment do so, regardless of the type of treatment they receive. In the same vein, when a doctor believes a patient will improve, the patient may do so precisely because of this expectation whereas another person for whom the physician has little hope often fails to recover. Apparently the patient's self-concept as sick or well—as shaped by the doctor—plays an important role in determining the actual state of health.

The self-fulfilling prophecy operates in families as well. If parents tell their children long enough that they can't do anything right, the children's self-concepts will soon incorporate this idea, and they will fail at many or most of the tasks they attempt. On the other hand, if children are told they are capable or lovable or kind persons, there is a much greater chance of their behaving accordingly.

The self-fulfilling prophecy is an important force in communication, but it doesn't explain all behavior. There are certainly times when the expectation of an event's outcome won't bring about that occurrence. Your hope of drawing an ace in a card game won't in any way affect the chance of that card's turning up in an already shuffled deck, and your belief that good weather is coming won't stop the rain from falling. In the same way, believing you'll do well in a job interview when you're clearly not qualified for the position is unrealistic. Similarly, there will probably be people you don't like and occasions you won't enjoy, no matter what your attitude. To connect the self-fulfilling prophecy with the "power of positive thinking" is an oversimplification.

In other cases, your expectations will be borne out because you are a good predictor and not because of the self-fulfilling prophecy. For example, children are not equally well equipped to do well in school, and in such cases it would be wrong to say that a child's performance was shaped by a parent or teacher, even though the behavior did match that which was expected. In the same way, some workers excel and others fail, some patients recover and others don't—all according to our predictions but not because of them.

Keeping these qualifications in mind, it's important to recognize the tremendous influence that self-fulfilling prophecies play in our lives. To a great extent we are what we believe we are. In this sense we and those around us constantly create our self-concepts and thus ourselves.

changing the self-concept

Having read this far, you know more clearly just what the self-concept is, how it is formed, and how it affects communication. But we still haven't focused on what may be the most important question of all: How can you change the parts of your self-concept with which you aren't happy? Sometimes the answer involves changing your *self* (for example, getting a responsible job or losing weight), and sometimes it means changing your *beliefs* (recognizing your strengths or decreasing self-criticism). Neither of these processes are simple, for there's usually no quick method for becoming the person you'd like to be: Personal growth and self-improvement are lifelong activities. But there are several suggestions that can help you move closer to your goals.

have realistic expectations

It's extremely important to realize that some of your dissatisfaction might come from expecting too much of yourself. If you demand that you handle every act of communication perfectly, you're bound to be disappointed. Nobody is able to handle every conflict productively, to be totally relaxed and skillful in conversations, to ask consistently perceptive questions, or to be 100 percent helpful when others have problems. Expecting yourself to reach such unrealistic goals is to doom yourself to unhappiness at the start.

Sometimes it's easy to be hard on yourself because everyone around you seems to be handling themselves so much better than you. It's important to realize that much of what seems like confidence and skill in others is a front to hide uncertainty. They may be suffering from the same self-imposed demands of perfection that you place on yourself.

Even in cases where others definitely seem more competent than you, it's important to judge yourself in terms of your own growth, not against the behavior of others. Rather than feeling miserable because you're not as talented as an expert, realize that you probably are a better, wiser, or more skillful person than you used to be and that this is a legitimate source of satisfaction. Perfection is fine as an ideal, but you're being unfair to yourself if you expect actually to reach that state.

have a realistic perception of yourself

One source of a poor self-concept is an inaccurate self-perception. As you've already read, such unrealistic pictures sometimes come from being overly harsh on yourself, believing that you're worse than the facts indicate. By sharing the self-concept list you recorded on page 25, you will be able to see whether you have been selling yourself short. Of course, it would be foolish to deny that you could be a better person than you are, but it's also important to recognize your strengths.

An unrealistically poor self-concept can also come from the inaccurate feedback of others. Perhaps you are in an environment where you receive an excessive number of "downer" messages, many of which are undeserved, and a minimum of upper messages. We have known many housewives, for example, who have returned to college after many years spent in homemaking where they received virtually no recognition for their intellectual strengths. It's amazing that these women have the courage to come to college at all, so low is their self-esteem; but come they do, and most are thrilled to find that they are much brighter and more competent intellectually than they suspected. In the same way workers with overly critical supervisors, children with cruel

"friends," and students with unsupportive teachers all are prone to suffering from low self-concepts owing to excessively negative feedback.

If you fall into this category, it's important to put the unrealistic evaluations you receive into perspective and then to seek out more supportive people who will acknowledge your assets as well as point out your shortcomings. Doing so is often a quick and sure boost to self-esteem.

have the will to change

Often we claim we want to change but we aren't willing to do the necessary work. You might, for instance, decide that you'd like to become a better conversationalist. Taking the advice offered in the next section of this book, you ask your instructor or some other communication adviser how to reach this goal. Suppose you receive two suggestions: first, to spend the next three weeks observing people who handle themselves well in conversations and to record exactly what they do that makes them so skillful; second, to read several books on the subject of conversational skills. You begin these tasks with the best intentions, but after a few days the task of recording conversations becomes a burden—it would be so much easier just to listen to others talk. And your diligent reading program becomes bogged down as the press of other work fills up your time. In other words, you find you just "can't" fit the self-improvement plan into your busy schedule.

Let's be realistic. Becoming a better communicator is probably one of many goals in your life. It's possible that you'll find other needs more pressing, which is completely reasonable. However, you should realize that changing your self-concept often requires a good deal of effort, and without that effort your good intentions alone probably won't get you much closer to this goal. In communication, as in most other aspects of life, "there's no such thing as a free lunch."

have the skill needed to change

Often trying isn't enough. There are some cases where you would change if you knew of a way to do so. To see if this is the case for you, check the list of "can'ts" and "won'ts" from the exercise on page 46, and see if any items there are more appropriately "don't know how." If so, then the way to change is to learn how. You can do so in two ways.

First, you can seek advice—from books such as this one, the references listed at the end of each chapter, and other printed sources. You can also get suggestions from instructors, counselors and other experts, as well as friends. Of course, not all the advice you receive will be useful, but if you read widely and talk to enough people, you have a good chance of learning the things you want to know.

A second method of learning how to change is to observe models—people who handle themselves in the ways you would like to master. It's often been said that people learn more from models than in any other way, and by taking advantage of this principle you will find that the world is full of teachers who can show you how to communicate more successfully. Become a careful observer. Watch what people you admire do and say, not so that you can copy them, but so that you can adapt their behavior to fit your own personal style.

At this point you might be overwhelmed at the difficulty of changing the way you think about yourself and the way you act. Remember, we never said that this would be easy (although it sometimes is). But even when change is difficult, you know that it's possible if you are serious. You don't need to be perfect, but you can improve your self-concept if you choose to.

summary

The chapter began by introducing the role of the self in communication. It defined the self-concept and showed the forces contributing to its development.

The chapter next examined the nature of perception, both of oneself and others. It began by introducing the steps in the perception process: selection, organization, and interpretation. It next listed several common errors in person perception and suggested ways of overcoming them.

The final section of the chapter showed how the self-concept influences perception. It discussed the desire for consistency and explained how it leads people to interpret events in ways that fit with their existing beliefs and attitudes. It showed how self-fulfilling prophecies can influence both one's own communication and the behavior of others. Finally, the chapter suggested ways of changing the self-concept.

activities

1. This exercise will help you identify the importance of significant others in shaping a self-concept.

   a. Think of several people who have played a role in shaping your self-concept. Recall one person who was influential in your earliest years and two or three who have had a more recent impact. For each name you list, remember one or two incidents that show how the person's behavior influenced the way you view yourself. Do you think that these people were intentionally shaping your self-perception in these incidents? Were there any cases in which the people you named weren't even aware of how their actions affected you?

   b. Now describe at least three people whose self-concepts you have influenced in some way. As earlier, describe exactly what you've done in each case to have this effect; then reflect upon whether you were aware of what was happening at the time. You can make this part of the exercise even more interesting by actually asking other people about your effect on them. There's a good chance that you'll be surprised at how some things you do without being aware have a strong impact on others.

perception and the self

45

2. Choose a controversial event: a personal dispute, a questionable decision by a boss or instructor, a disagreement among members of a group, or a hotly debated public issue. Describe the issue from two separate points of view, showing how each one selects, organizes, and interprets the same information differently.

3. Identify two cases in which you committed the perceptual errors listed on pages 33–38.

4. What communication-related self-fulfilling prophecies do you impose on yourself? What prophecies have others imposed on you? What prophecies have you imposed on others?

5. How committed are you to changing your self-concept? You can find out by responding to the steps that follow.

a. Choose a partner and for five minutes or so take turns making and listing statements that begin with ''I can't . . .'' Try to focus your statements on your relationships with family, friends, co-workers and students, and even strangers: whomever you have a hard time communicating with.

Sample statements:

''I can't be myself with strangers I'd like to get to know at parties.''

''I can't tell a friend how much I care about her.''

''I can't bring myself to ask my supervisor for the raise I think I deserve.''

''I can't ask questions in class.''

b. Notice the feelings you experience as you make each statement: self-pity, regret, concern, frustration, and so on, and share these with your partner.

c. Now go back and repeat aloud each statement you've just made, except this time change each ''can't'' to a ''won't.'' After each sentence, share with your partner whatever thoughts you have about what you've just said.

d. After you've finished, decide whether ''can't'' or ''won't'' is more appropriate for each item, and explain your choice to your partner.

e. Are there any instances of the self-fulfilling prophecy in your list— times when your decision that you ''couldn't'' do something was the only force keeping you from doing it?

notes

1. Anthony G. Athos and John J. Gabarro, *Interpersonal Behavior: Communication and Understanding in Relationships* (Englewood Cliffs, N.J.: Prentice-Hall, 1978), p. 140.
2. Kathleen S. Berger, *The Developing Person* (New York: Worth, 1980), pp. 243–244.
3. Michael Lewis and Jeanne Brooks, "Self-Knowledge and Emotional Development" in Michael Lewis and Leonard A. Rosenblum (eds.), *The Development of Affect* (New York: Plenum, 1978), pp. 205–226.
4. Arthur W. Combs and Donald Snygg, *Individual Behavior,* rev. ed. (New York: Harper & Row, 1959), p. 134.
5. Harry S. Sullivan, *The Interpersonal Theory of Psychiatry* (New York: Norton, 1953).
6. Charles H. Cooley, *Human Nature and the Social Order* (New York: Scribner's, 1902).
7. Monte D. Smith, S. A. Zingalc, and J. M. Coleman, "The Influence of Adult Expectations/Child Performance Discrepancies upon Children's Self-Concepts," *American Educational Research Journal* 15 (1978): 259–265.
8. S. Frank Miyamoto and Sanford M. Dornbusch, "A Text of Interactionist Hypotheses of Self-Conception," *American Journal of Sociology* 61 (1956): 399–403.
9. Dennis Coon, *Introduction to Psychology,* 2d ed. (St. Paul: West Publishing, 1981).
10. L. Carmichael, H. P. Hogan, and A. A. Walter, "An Experimental Study of the Effect of Language on the Reproduction of Visually Perceived Form," *Journal of Experimental Psychology* 15 (1932): 73–86.
11. Summarized in Don E. Hamachek, *Encounters with Others* (New York: Holt, Rinehart and Winston, 1982), pp. 23–30.
12. See, for example, Penny Baron, "Self-Esteem, Ingratiation, and Evaluation of Unknown Others," *Journal of Personality and Social Psychology* 30 (1974): 104–109; and Elaine Walster, "The Effect of Self-Esteem on Romantic Liking," *Journal of Experimental and Social Psychology* 1 (1965): 184–197.
13. See, for example, D. E. Kanouse and L. R. Hanson, "Negativity in Evaluations," in E. E. Jones, D. E. Kanouse, H. H. Kelley, R. E. Nisbett, S. Valins, and B. Weiner (eds.), *Attribution: Perceiving the Causes of Behavior* (Morristown, N.J.: General Learning Press, 1972).
14. See F. Heider, *The Psychology of Interpersonal Relations* (New York: Wiley, 1968); C. Osgood and P. Tannenbaum, "The Principle of Congruity in the Prediction of Attitude Change," *Psychological Review* 62 (1955): 42–55; and L. Festinger, *A Theory of Cognitive Dissonance* (Stanford, Calif.: Stanford University Press, 1957).
15. Robert Rosenthal and Lenore Jacobson, *Pygmalion in the Classroom* (New York: Holt, Rinehart and Winston, 1968).

three

language

After reading this chapter, you should understand:

1. The symbolic, person-centered nature of language.
2. The syntactic and semantic characteristics of language.
3. The ways in which language shapes the perceptions of users.
4. How language reflects the attitudes of users.
5. The types of linguistic misunderstandings listed in this chapter.

You should be able to:

1. Identify at least two ways in which language has shaped your perceptions of a person, object, or event.
2. Identify at least two ways in which your language reflects your attitudes about a person, object, or event.
3. Identify and correct the linguistic misunderstandings listed in this chapter in a conversation or written text.
4. Translate overly abstract problems, goals, appreciations, complaints, and requests into more specific, behavioral terms.

And the whole earth was of one language, and of one speech.

2 And it came to pass, as they journeyed from the east, that they found a plain in the land of Shinar; and they dwelt there.

3 And they said to one another, Go to, let us make brick, and burn them thoroughly. And they had brick for stone, and slime had they for mortar.

4 And they said, Go to, let us build us a city and a tower, whose top may reach unto heaven; and let us make us a name, lest we be scattered abroad upon the face of the whole earth.

5 And the Lord came down to see the city and the tower, which the children of men builded.

6 And the Lord said, Behold, the people is one, and they have all one language; and this they begin to do: and now nothing will be restrained from them, which they have imagined to do.

7 Go to, let us go down, and there confound their language, that they may not understand one another's speech.

8 So the Lord scattered them abroad from thence upon the face of all the earth: and they left off to build the city.

9 Therefore is the name of it called Babel; because the Lord did there confound the language of all the earth: and from thence did the Lord scatter them abroad upon the face of all the earth.

Genesis 11:1–9

It is no accident that the story of the Tower of Babel is the opening passage for this chapter. Sometimes it seems as if none of us speaks the same language. Others hear, but don't understand us; and we often fail to grasp the full meaning of what others say or write.

In this chapter we will explore the nature of linguistic communication. After reading the following pages, you should have a better understanding of both how we use—and misuse—language to express our thoughts and how the language we use shapes our perception of people and events.

the nature of language

Because we use language almost constantly, we often assume that carefully chosen words can paint an accurate picture of any idea. Actually, the matter isn't this simple.

language is symbolic

As we said in Chapter 1, words are symbols that represent things—ideas, events, objects, and so on. Words are not the things themselves. For instance, it's obvious that the word *coat* is not the same as the piece of clothing it describes. You would be a fool to expect the letters *c-o-a-t* to keep you warm in a snowstorm. This point seems so obvious as to be hardly worth mentioning, yet people often forget the nature of language and confuse symbols with their referents. For example, some students will cram facts into their heads just long enough to regurgitate them into a blue book in order to earn a high grade, forgetting that letters like A or B are only symbols and that a few lines of ink on paper don't necessarily represent true learning. In the same way, simply saying the words "I care about you" isn't necessarily a reflection of the truth, although many disappointed lovers have learned this lesson the hard way.

So far we have been using the terms *language* and *symbol* interchangeably, which isn't quite correct. *Languages* consist of collections of symbols, which possess certain properties.[1] First, a language must contain certain *elements*. In English these elements consist of the letters of our alphabet along with punctuation marks such as commas, periods, and so on. In the language of mathematics the elements are the integers zero through nine plus other symbols such as plus and minus signs. Morse code has only two elements—dots and dashes.

The elements of any language have no meaning by themselves. And in many combinations they are also meaningless. For example, the letters "flme oo usi oysk" are pure gibberish. But when rearranged into a more recognizable pattern, they become more understandable: "Kiss me, you fool!" This example illustrates the second characteristic of language, which is the existence of a body of *rules* that dictate the way in which symbols can be used.

Languages contain two types of rules. *Syntactic* rules govern the ways in which symbols can be arranged. For example, in English syntactic

language

51

figure 3-1
Ogden and Richards' triangle
of meaning

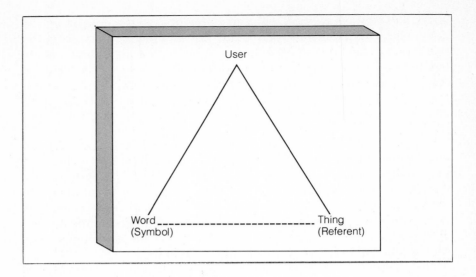

rules require that every word contain at least one vowel, and prohibit sentences such as "Have you the cookies brought?" which is a perfectly acceptable word order in a language such as German. Although most of us aren't able to describe the rules that govern our language, it's easy to recognize the existence of such rules by noting how odd a statement that violates them appears.

Semantic rules also govern our use of the language. But where syntax deals with structure, semantics governs meaning. Semantic rules reflect the ways in which speakers of a language respond to a particular symbol. Semantic rules are what make it possible for us to agree that "bikes" are for riding and "books" are for reading; they also help us to know who we will and won't encounter when we use rooms marked "Men" or "Women." Without semantic rules, communication would be impossible, for each of us would use symbols in unique ways, unintelligible to one another.

After reading the last sentence, you might object, thinking about the many cases in which people don't follow the same semantic rules. Of course, you would be correct, for there are many times when a single word has different meanings for different people. This is possible because words, being symbols, have no meaning in themselves. Ogden and Richards have illustrated this point graphically in their well-known "triangle of meaning" (Figure 3-1).[2] This triangle shows that there is only an indirect relationship—indicated by a broken line—between a word and the thing it claims to represent.* Problems arise when people mistakenly believe that words automatically represent things or when we

---

* Some of these "things" or referents do not exist in the physical world. For instance, some referents are mythical (such as unicorns), some are no longer tangible (such as the deceased Mr. Smith), and others are abstract ideas (such as "love").

assume that our meaning for a word is the same as someone else's. We will spend most of this chapter discussing how to avoid such linguistic problems.

meanings are in people, not words

Show a dozen people the same symbol and ask them what it means, and you are likely to get twelve different answers. Does an American flag bring up associations of soldiers giving their lives for their country? Fourth of July parades? Mom's apple pie? How about a cross: What does it represent? The gentleness and wisdom of Jesus Christ? Fire-lit rallies of Ku Klux Klansmen? Your childhood Sunday school? The necklace your sister always wears?

Like these symbols, words can be interpreted in many different ways. And, of course, this is the basis for many misunderstandings. It's possible to have an argument about *feminism* without ever realizing that you and the other person are using the word to represent entirely different things. The same goes for *communism, Republicans, rock music,* and thousands upon thousands of other symbols. Words don't mean, people do—and often in widely different ways.

It might seem as if one remedy to misunderstandings like these would be to have more respect for the dictionary meanings of words. After all, you might think, if people would just consult a dictionary whenever they send or receive a potentially confusing message, there would be little problem.

This approach has three shortcomings. First, dictionaries show that many words have multiple definitions, and it isn't always clear which one applies in a given situation. The 500 words most commonly used in

COON!!

HONKIE!!

Reproduced by special permission of *Playboy* Magazine; copyright © 1972 by *Playboy*

"I don't know what you mean by 'glory,' " Alice said.

Humpty Dumpty smiled contemptuously. "Of course you don't—till I tell you. I meant 'there's a nice knock-down argument for you!' "

"But 'glory' doesn't mean 'a nice knock-down argument,' " Alice objected.

"When *I* use a word," Humpty Dumpty said, in a rather scornful tone, "it means just what I choose it to mean—neither more nor less."

"The question is," said Alice, "whether you *can* make words mean so many different things."

"The question is," said Humpty Dumpty, "which is to be master—that's all."

Lewis Carroll
Through the Looking Glass

everyday communication have over 14,000 dictionary definitions, which should give you an idea of the limitations of this approach.

A second problem is that people often use words in ways you would never be able to look up. Sometimes the misuse of words is due to a lack of knowledge, as when you might ask your auto parts dealer for a new generator when you really need an alternator.

The third shortcoming of dictionaries is that they define most words in terms of *other* words, and this process often won't tell you any more about a term than you already know. In fact, it's possible to talk endlessly about a subject and sound very knowledgeable without ever having the slightest idea of what your words refer to. Jessica Davidson's quiz is an example of this. Read the paragraph; then see if you can answer the questions:

Because public opinion is sometimes marsiflate, empetricious insoculences are frequently zophilimized. Nevertheless, it cannot be overemphasized that carpoflansibles are highly traculate.

1. In the author's opinion, carpoflansibles are
   a. Empetricious
   b. Traculate
   c. Zophilimized
2. Public opinion is sometimes
   a. Insoculent
   b. Variable
   c. Marsiflate
3. According to the text insoculences are zophilimized
   a. Often
   b. Never
   c. Sometimes[3]

You can see that the correct answers are 1(b), 2(c), and 3(a). But even if you scored perfectly on the quiz, do you know the meaning of the paragraph? Of course not, for the words are gibberish. But if you look closely, you'll find that many people use their own language in the same way, talking in terms they can define only by other terms.

language shapes perception

Earlier in this chapter we said that meanings rest in people, not words. This statement doesn't mean language is unimportant. In fact, just the opposite is true: In many cases, the labels we use shape the way we look at an event. And on a more fundamental level, the structure of language shapes the very way we view the world.

The power of language is so great that it even extends to personal names. Research shows that these names are more than just a simple means of identification; that, in fact, they shape the way others think of us, the way we view ourselves, and the way we act.[4]

Different names have different connotations. In one study psychologists asked college students to rate over a thousand names according to their likability, how active or passive they seemed, and their masculinity or femininity. In spite of the large number of subjects, the responses were quite similar. Michael, John, and Wendy were likable and active and were rated as possessing the masculine or feminine traits of their sex. Percival, Isadore, and Alfreda were less likable, and their sexuality was more suspect. Other research also suggests that names have strong connotative meanings. More common names are generally viewed as being more active, stronger, and better than unusual ones.

The preconceptions we hold about people because of their names influence our behavior toward them. In another well-known study, researchers asked a number of teachers to read several essays supposedly written by fifth-grade students. The researchers found that certain names—generally the most popular ones such as Lisa, Michael, and Karen—received higher grades regardless of which essay they were attached to whereas other less popular names—Elmer, Bertha, Hubert— were consistently graded as inferior. There was one exception to the link between popular names and high grades: Unpopular Adelle received the highest evaluation of all. The researchers speculated that the teachers saw her as more "scholarly."

It's not surprising to find that the attitudes others hold toward a person because of his or her name have an effect on that person's self-concept. Over 40 years ago, researchers found that students at Harvard who had unusual names were more likely to be neurotic and to flunk out of school. The negative effect of unusual names seems to be more damaging to men than women, perhaps owing to our social convention that makes such labels acceptable for females. At any rate, research such as this makes it clear that the question "What shall we name the baby?" is an important one for more than aesthetic reasons.

Personal names are just one way that language shapes perception. Another is through metaphors—terms that describe one object or idea in terms of another. Most of us think of metaphors as poetic or rhetorical devices: The ocean roars, the brook babbles, a sign shouts, and so on. Viewed in this narrow sense, metaphors are ingredients of extraordinary, not ordinary language. In fact, scholars like George Lakoff and Mark

language

55

Johnson have demonstrated that metaphors operate in everyday life, shaping the way we think and act.[5]

Consider, for example, the metaphors based on the linguistic implication that "up" is good ("Things are looking up." "She has high ideals.") and "down" is bad ("You sound depressed." "That was a low thing to do."):

- *Having control or force is up; being subject to control or force is down.*
  She is *under* my control. He is *low man* on the totem pole. She's *moved up* to *top management.*
- *Rational is up; emotional is down.*
  The discussion *fell* to the emotional level, but I *raised* it to a rational plane. He can't *rise above* his emotions.

Still another metaphor implies that size is desirable:

- *Big is significant; small is unimportant.*
  He's a *big man* in the garment industry. It's a *small-time* operation. It was only a *little* white lie.

These metaphors create attitudes every time we hear them used. They subtly tell us that being in control is good and being in a subordinate position is undesirable, that emotions should be discarded in favor of deliberate thought, and that more is better. Although this isn't the place to debate the value of propositions like these, we should recognize that they aren't the only way to view life. Nonetheless, familiar metaphors subtly brainwash us into thinking they are accurate descriptions of reality. In other words, the metaphors we hear often do more than simply describe perceptions: They often *shape* them.

Many social scientists believe that the structure of a culture's language shapes the world view of its members. This idea has been most widely circulated in the writings of Benjamin Lee Whorf and Edward Sapir.[6] Although their writings focused on cultures unfamiliar to most of

The problems crop up when we start talking about other types of deviant behavior. We say of a person who drinks too much that he "is" an alcoholic, and we say of people who think bizarre thoughts that they "are" schizophrenic. This person is a drug addict and that person is a homosexual. Others are sadomasochists, pedophiliacs, juvenile delinquents. The English language is constructed in such a way that we speak of people *being* (certain things) when all we know is that they do certain things. . . .

That kind of identity is a myth. Admittedly, if a person believes the myth, the chances rise that he will assume the appropriate, narrowly defined role. Believing that one is an addict, an alcoholic, a schizophrenic, or a homosexual can result in relinquishing the search for change and becoming imprisoned in the role.

Edward Sagarian

---

us, Neil Postman illustrates the principle with an example closer to home. He describes a culture where physicians identify patients they treat as "doing" arthritis and other diseases instead of "having" them and where criminals are diagnosed as "having" cases of criminality instead of "being" criminals.[7]

The implications of such a linguistic difference are profound. We believe that characteristics people "have"—what they "are"—is beyond their control whereas they are responsible for what they "do." If we changed our view of what people "have" and what they "do," our attitudes would most likely change as well. Postman illustrates the consequences of this linguistic difference as applied to education:

In schools, for instance, we find that tests are given to determine how smart someone is or, more precisely, how much smartness someone "has." If one child scores a 138, and another a 106, the first is thought to "have" more smartness than the other. But this seems to me a strange conception—every bit as strange as "doing" arthritis or "having" criminality. I do not know anyone who *has* smartness. The people I know sometimes *do* smart things (as far as I can judge) and sometimes *do* stupid things—depending on what circumstances they are in, and how much they know about a situation, and how interested they are. "Smartness," so it seems to me, is a specific performance, done in a particular set of circumstances. It is not something you *are* or have in measurable quantities. In fact, the assumption that smartness is something you *have* has led to such nonsensical ideas as "over-" and "underachievers." As I understand it, an overachiever is someone who doesn't *have* much smartness but does a lot of smart things. An underachiever is someone who *has* a lot of smartness but does a lot of stupid things.

In any case, I am not prepared here to argue the matter through. Although I have not heard of them, there may be good reasons to imagine that smartness or honesty or sensitivity are "qualities" that people *have* in measurable proportions and that exist independently of what people actually do. What I am driving at is this: All language is metaphorical, and often in the subtlest ways. In the simplest sentence, sometimes in the simplest word, we do more than merely express ourselves. We construct reality along certain lines. We make the world according to our own imagery.[8]

language
57

The Sapir-Whorf hypothesis has never been conclusively proved or disproved. In spite of its intellectual appeal, some critics point out that it is possible to conceive of flux even in static languages like English. They suggest that Sapir and Whorf overstated the importance of their idea. Supporters of the hypothesis respond that though it is *possible* to conceptualize an idea in different languages, some make it much easier to recognize a term than do others.

language reflects attitudes

Besides shaping perceptions, language often reflects the speaker's attitudes. Consider love as an example: As the quote on page 57 suggests, this is a word with many meanings. Lakoff and Johnson show how the metaphors people choose can reflect their attitudes toward a relationship:[9]

- *Love is a physical force (beyond the power of the people involved).*
  I was *attracted* to him. His life *revolves* around her. I could feel the *electricity* between us.
- *Love is war.*
  She *fought* for him; the other woman *won out.* He is slowly *gaining ground* with her. He *enlisted the aid* of her friends.

the semantics of "i love you"

"I love you" [is] a statement that can be expressed in so many varied ways. It may be a stage song, repeated daily without any meaning, or a barely audible murmur, full of surrender. Sometimes it means: I desire you or I want you sexually. It may mean: I hope you love me or I hope that I will be able to love you. Often it means: It may be that a love relationship can develop between us or even I hate you. Often it is a wish for emotional exchange: I want your admiration in exchange for mine or I give my love in exchange for some passion or I want to feel cozy and at home with you or I admire some of your qualities: A declaration of love is mostly a request: I desire you or I want you to gratify me, or I want your protection or I want to be intimate with you or I want to exploit your loveliness.

Sometimes it is the need for security and tenderness, for parental treatment. It may mean: My self-love goes out to you. But it may also express submissiveness: Please take me as I am, or I feel guilty about you, I want, through you, to correct the mistakes I have made in human relations. It may be self-sacrifice and a masochistic wish for dependency. However, it may also be a full affirmation of the other, taking the responsibility for mutual exchange of feelings. It may be a weak feeling of friendliness, it may be the scarcely even whispered expression of ecstasy. "I love you,"—wish, desire, submission, conquest; it is never the word itself that tells the real meaning here.

J. A. M. Meerloo
Conversation and Communication

Philosopher Robert Solomon points out other metaphorical attitudes about love:[10]

- *Love is a game.*
  I'm *playing the field.* She's *playing* hard to get. Did you *score?*
- *Love is an exchange.*
  Our relationship is a *good arrangement.* We're both *getting a lot* out of it. It isn't *worth it* any more.
- *Love is work.*
  We're *working* on our marriage. We've *made it work.* We've had problems in the past, but we *worked them out.*
- *Love is a flame.*
  We need to *spice up* our relationship. Things have *cooled down* between us.

Language reflects attitudes in many other ways. Morton Wiener and Albert Mehrabian describe several ways in which word choice and grammatical construction suggest the speaker's degree of liking:[11]

- *Demonstrative pronoun choice.*
  These people want our help (positive) vs. *Those* people want our help (less positive).
- *Negation.*
  It's *good* (positive) vs. It's *not bad* (less positive).

how to tell a businessman from a businesswoman

A businessman is aggressive; a businesswoman is pushy.

He is careful about details; she's picky.

He loses his temper because he's so involved in his job; she's bitchy.

He's depressed (or hung over), so everyone tiptoes past his office; she's moody, so it must be her time of the month.

He follows through; she doesn't know when to quit.

He's firm; she's stubborn.

He makes wise judgments; she reveals her prejudices.

He is a man of the world; she's been around.

He isn't afraid to say what he thinks; she's opinionated.

He exercises authority; she's tyrannical.

He's discreet; she's secretive.

He's a stern taskmaster; she's difficult to work for.

- *Sequential placement.*
  Dick and Jane (Dick is more important) vs. Jane and Dick (Jane is more important).*

In addition to suggesting liking and importance, language can also reveal the speaker's willingness to accept responsibility for a message.

- *"It" vs. "I" statements.*
  It's not fair (less responsible) vs. *I* don't think it's fair (more responsible).
- *"You" vs. "I" statements.*
  Sometimes *you* wonder if he's honest (less responsible) vs. Sometimes *I* wonder if he's honest (more responsible).
- *"But" statements.*
  It's a good idea, *but* it won't work. You're really terrific, *but* I think we ought to spend less time together. ("But" cancels everything that went before the word.)
- *Questions vs. statements.*
  Do you think we ought to do that? (less responsible) vs. I don't think we ought to do that (more responsible).

the language of misunderstandings

After reading this far, you should understand that language isn't the simple tool for expressing ideas that it first seems to be. Some terms have especially high potential for being misunderstood. By becoming more aware of them, your chances for communicating accurately will grow.

* Sequential placement isn't always significant. You may put "toilet bowl cleaner" at the top of your shopping list simply because it's closer to the market door than champagne.

60

equivocal language

Equivocal terms have more than one correct dictionary definition. Some equivocal misunderstandings are simple and humorous. Not long ago we were ordering dinner in a Mexican restaurant and noticed that the menu described each item as coming with rice or beans. We asked the waitress for "a tostada with beans," but when the order arrived, we were surprised to find that instead of a beef tostada with beans on the side as we expected, the waitress had brought a tostada *filled* with beans. Looking back on the incident, it's obvious that the order was an equivocal one.

Other equivocal misunderstandings are more serious. A nurse once told her patient that he "wouldn't be needing" the materials he requested from home. He interpreted the statement to mean he was near death, when the nurse meant he would be going home soon. A colleague of ours mistakenly sent some confidential materials to the wrong person after his boss told him to "send them to Richard," without specifying *which* Richard.

As we mentioned earlier, most of the words people use can be interpreted in a number of ways. A good rule to remember if you want to keep misunderstandings to a minimum is "If a word can be interpreted in more than one way, it probably will be." The paraphrasing and questioning skills you will learn in Chapter 4 can help overcome equivocal misunderstandings.

relative terms

Relative words gain their meaning by comparison. For example, is the school you attend large or small? This depends on what you compare it to: Alongside a campus like UCLA, with its almost 30,000 students, it probably looks small; but compared with a smaller institution it might seem quite large. In the same way relative words like *fast* and *slow, smart* and *stupid, short* and *long* depend for their meaning upon what they're compared to. (The "large" size can of olives is the smallest you can buy; the larger ones are "giant," "colossal," and "supercolossal.")

Using relative terms without explaining them can lead to communication problems. Have you ever responded to someone's question about the weather by saying it was warm, only to find out that what was warm to you was cold to the other person? Or have you followed a friend's advice and gone to a "cheap" restaurant, only to find that it was twice as expensive as you expected? Have you been disappointed to learn that classes you've heard were "easy" turned out to be hard, that journeys you were told would be "short" were long, that "unusual" ideas were really quite ordinary? The problem in each case came from failing to anchor the relative term used to a more precisely measurable term.

emotive language

To understand how emotive language works we need to distinguish between *denotative* and *connotative* meanings. A denotative definition describes an event in purely objective terms whereas connotative interpretations contain an emotional element. Consider, for example, the term *pregnant*. The denotative meaning of this word involves a condition in which a female is carrying her offspring during a gestation period. When used in this purely biological sense, most people could hear the term without a strong emotional reaction. But imagine the additional turmoil this word would create when an unmarried teenage couple find it stamped on the young woman's lab report. Certainly the meaning to these people would go far beyond the dictionary definition.

Some words have little or no connotative meaning: *the, it, as,* and so on. Others are likely to evoke both denotative and connotative reactions: *cancer, income tax,* and *final examination,* for example. There are also terms that are almost exclusively connotative, such as the *damn!* (or other oath) you would probably utter if you hammered your thumb instead of a nail.

Connotative meanings are a necessary and important part of human communication. Being creatures with emotions, it's a fact of life that people will use some words that will evoke strong reactions. Without connotative meanings, we'd be unable to describe our feelings fully.

Problems occur, however, when people claim to use words in a purely denotative way when they are really expressing their attitudes. *Emotive language,* then, contains words that sound as if they're describing something when they are really announcing the speaker's attitude toward something. Do you like that old picture frame? If so, you would probably call it "an antique," but if you think it's ugly, you would likely describe it as "a piece of junk." Now whether the picture frame belongs on the mantel or in the garbage can is a matter of opinion, not fact, but it's easy to forget this when emotive words are used. Emotive words may sound like statements of fact, but are always opinions. The humorous guide "How to Tell a Businessman from a Businesswoman" illustrates how emotive language indirectly expresses the speaker's attitude.

As this list suggests, problems occur when people use emotive terms without labeling them as such. You might, for instance, have a long and bitter argument with a friend about whether a third person was "assertive" or "obnoxious," when a more accurate and peaceable way to handle the issue would be to acknowledge that one of you approves of the behavior and the other doesn't.

cathy   by **Cathy Guisewite**

63

A group of synonyms does not define an object. A careful description may help bring it into focus for the listener, but is not conclusive. Final identification is achieved only by pointing to the apple, touching it with the hand, seeing it with the eyes, tasting it with the mouth, and so recognizing it as nonverbal. Here is the base from which all our proud words rise—every last one of them—and to it they must constantly return and be refreshed. Failing this, they wander into regions where there are no apples, no objects, no acts, and so they become symbols for airy chunks of nothing at all.

Stuart Chase
The Tyranny of Words

overly abstract language

Most objects, events, and ideas can be described with varying degrees of specificity. Consider the material you are reading. You could call it:

A book

A textbook

A communication textbook

Understanding Human Communication

Chapter 3 of *Understanding Human Communication*

Page 64 of Chapter 3 of *Understanding Human Communication*

In each case your description would be more and more specific. Semanticist S. I. Hayakawa created an "abstraction ladder" to describe this process.[12] This ladder consists of a number of descriptions of the same person, object, or event. Lower items focus specifically on the thing under discussion, and higher terms are generalizations that include the subject as a member of a larger class. These higher-level generalizations are absolutely necessary, for without them language would be too cumbersome to be useful. But though higher level abstractions allow us to focus on similarities, they also cause us to ignore differences between the objects being discussed in the category. Thus, overly abstract language can lead to several problems.

1. Stereotyping. Imagine someone who has had a bad experience while traveling abroad and as a result blames an entire country. "Yeah, those damn Hottentots are a bunch of thieves. If you're not careful, they'll steal you blind. I know, because one of 'em stole my camera last year." You can see here how lumping people into highly abstract categories ignores the fact that for every thieving Hottentot there are probably 100 honest ones. It's this kind of thinking that leads to mistaken assumptions that keep people apart: "None of those kids are any damn good!" "You can't trust anybody in busi-

instant blap

Anyone who is familiar with the academic, business, or government worlds knows that there often seems to be a rule which says "When choosing between a simple and a more abstract term, always pick the more confusing one."

In the past this has been a great setback for clear-headed writers and speakers. But now modern technology has found a solution: the Systematic Buzz Phrase Projector.

The projector is simple to use. Whenever you want to say nothing in an authoritative way, simply pick any three-digit number, and then find the matching word from each column. For example, 424 produces "functional monitored programing," which should impress anyone untrained in detecting high-level abstractions.

column 1	column 2	column 3
0 integrated	0 management	0 options
1 total	1 organizational	1 flexibility
2 systematized	2 monitored	2 capability
3 parallel	3 reciprocal	3 mobility
4 functional	4 digital	4 programing
5 responsive	5 logistical	5 concept
6 optional	6 transitional	6 time-phase
7 synchronized	7 incremental	7 projection
8 compatible	8 third-generation	8 hardware
9 balanced	9 policy	9 contingency

---

ness." "Those cops are all a bunch of goons." Each of these statements ignores the very important fact that sometimes our descriptions are too general; that they say more than we really mean.

When you think about examples like these, you begin to see how thinking in abstract terms can lead to ignoring individual differences, which can be as important as similarities. In this sense, semantics isn't "just" a matter of words. People in the habit of using highly abstract language begin to *think* in generalities, ignoring uniqueness. And as we discussed in Chapter 2, expecting people to be a certain way can become a self-fulfilling prophecy. If I think all police officers are brutal, I'm more likely to react in a defensive, hostile way toward them, which in turn increases the chance that they'll react to me as a threat. If I think that no teachers care about their classes, then my defensive indifference is likely to make a potentially helpful instructor into someone who truly doesn't care.

2. Confusing others. Imagine the lack of understanding that results from imprecise language in situations like this:

A: "We never do anything that's fun anymore."
B: "What do you mean?"
A: "We used to do lots of unusual things, but now it's the same old stuff, over and over."
B: "But last week we went on that camping trip, and tomorrow we're going to that party where we'll meet all sorts of new people. Those are new things."
A: "That's not what I mean. I'm talking about *really* unusual stuff."
B: (*becoming confused and a little impatient*) "Like what? Taking hard drugs or going over Niagara Falls in a barrel?"

A: "Don't be stupid. All I'm saying is that we're in a rut. We should be living more exciting lives."

B: "Well, I don't know what you want."

Overly abstract language also leads to confusing directions:

Professor "I hope you'll do a thorough job on this paper."
Student "When you say thorough, how long should it be?"
P: "Long enough to cover the topic thoroughly."
S: "How many sources should I look at when I'm researching it?"
P: "You should use several—enough to show me that you've really explored the subject."

S: "And what style should I use to write it?"
P: "One that's scholarly but not too formal."
S: "Arrgh!!!"

Along with unclear complaints and vague instructions, even appreciations can suffer from being expressed in overly abstract terms. Psychologists have established that behaviors that are reinforced will recur with increased frequency. This means that your statements of appreciation will encourage others to keep acting in ways you like. But if they don't know just what it is that you appreciate, the chances of that behavior being repeated are lessened. There's a big difference between "I appreciate your being so nice" and "I appreciate the way you spent that time talking to me when I was upset."

The best way to avoid this sort of overly abstract language is to use *behavioral descriptions* instead. Behavioral descriptions clarify the speaker's meaning whether the message describes a problem, goal, appreciation, complaint, or request. They do so by moving down the abstraction ladder to identify the specific, observable phenomenon being discussed. A thorough behavioral description should contain three elements:

1. **Who is involved?** Are you speaking for just yourself or for others as well? Are you talking about a group of people ("the neighbors," "women") or specific individuals ("the people next door with the barking dog," "Lola and Lizzie")?

2. **In what circumstances does the behavior occur?** Where does it occur?: Everywhere or in specific places (at parties, at work, in public)? When does it occur?: When you're tired? When a certain subject comes up?

   The behavior you are describing probably doesn't occur all the time. In order to be understood, you need to pin down what circumstances set this situation apart from other ones.

3. **What behaviors are involved?** Though terms such as "more cooperative" and "helpful" might sound like concrete descriptions of behavior, they are usually too vague to do a clear job of explaining what's on your mind. Behaviors must be *observable,* ideally both to

---

table 3–1   abstract and behavioral descriptions

	abstract description		behavioral description		remarks
		Who is involved	In what circumstances	Specific behaviors	
Problem	I'm no good at meeting strangers.	People I'd like to date	When I meet them at parties or at school	Think to myself, ''They'd never want to date me.'' Also, I don't originate conversations.	Behavioral description more clearly identifies thoughts and behaviors to change.
Goal	I'd like to be more assertive.	Telephone and door-to-door solicitors	When I don't want the product or can't afford it	Instead of apologizing or explaining, say, ''I'm not interested'' and keep repeating this until they go away.	Behavioral description clearly outlines how to act; abstract description doesn't.
Appreciation	''You've been a great boss.''	(no clarification necessary)	When I've needed to change my schedule because of school exams or assignments	''You've rearranged my hours cheerfully.''	Give both abstract and behavioral descriptions for best results.
Complaint	''I don't like some of the instructors around here.''	Professors A and B	In class when students ask questions the professors think are stupid	Either answer in a sarcastic voice (you might demonstrate) or accuse us of not studying hard enough.	If talking to A or B, use only behavioral description. With others, use both abstract and behavioral descriptions.
Request	''Quit bothering me!''	You and your friends X and Y	When I'm studying for exams	Instead of asking me over and over to party with you, I wish you'd accept my comment that I need to study and leave me to do it.	Behavioral description will reduce defensiveness and make it clear that you don't *always* want to be left alone.

you and to others. For instance, moving down the abstraction ladder from the relatively vague term "helpful," you might come to behaviors such as "does the dishes every other day," "volunteers to help me with my studies," or "fixes dinner once or twice a week without being asked." It's easy to see that terms like these are easier for both you and others to understand than are more vague abstractions.

There is one exception to the rule that behaviors should be observable, and that involves the internal processes of thoughts and emotions. For instance, in describing what happens to you when a friend has kept you waiting for a long time, you might say, "My stomach felt as if it were in knots—I was really worried. I kept thinking that you had forgotten and that I wasn't important enough to you for you to remember our date." What you're doing when offering such a description is to make unobservable events clear.

You can get a clearer idea of the value of behavioral descriptions by looking at the examples in Table 3–1. Notice how much more clearly they explain the speaker's thought than do the vague terms.

summary

To the uninitiated, using language effectively means little more than having an adequate vocabulary and following grammatical rules. This chapter shows that the business of understanding one another through the spoken and written word is much more complex.

The chapter discussed the symbolic nature of language, showing that words are arbitrary symbols that represent reality. But as meanings are in people and not in words, the mistake of assuming that others use language as we do is a dangerous one. The chapter showed that language not only describes events but also shapes our perception of them. This point is true for individual labels, which create favorable or unfavorable images for the receiver and, perhaps more significantly, for entire languages, the structure of which shapes the very way its users perceive reality.

Within the English language we saw that there are many types of words that have great potential to create misunderstandings or to distort meanings. Equivocal language, relative words, emotive descriptions, and fiction terms all need to be recognized and then either qualified or avoided.

Finally, the chapter examined the abstract nature of language, showing the problems that can arise from being overly abstract and then providing suggestions about how to begin expressing ideas in more specific, understandable ways.

1. Recall an instance when you or another person mistakenly assumed that a set of symbols was an accurate reflection of reality.

Next, describe a time when two people interpreted the same symbol in different ways.

2. Check your skill at using labels to shape perceptions by describing the following incident twice: First use language that makes the parent's behavior sound justified. Then rewrite the account to favor the child's position.

The time is 3:30 A.M. A teenager who was due home from a party at 1:00 enters the house quietly, hoping to avoid waking his parents. This attempt fails, however, because they have been awake worrying for two hours.

The parents ask their child why he wasn't home on time, and he explains that the family car struck a police cruiser after he failed to stop at a traffic signal.

Both parents and teenager are upset. The parents believe that the teenager behaved irresponsibly, and the teenager claims that the accident, though unfortunate, could have happened to anyone.

3. Here's a way to see how emotive words work. According to S. I. Hayakawa the idea of "conjugating irregular verbs" this way originated with Bertrand Russell.

a. The technique is simple: Just take an action or personality trait and show how it can be viewed either favorably or unfavorably, according to the label we give it. For example:

I'm casual.
You're a little careless.
He's a slob.

Or try this one:

I read love stories.
You read erotic literature.
She reads pornography.

Or:

I'm thrifty.
You're money-conscious.
He's a tightwad.

b. Now try a few conjugations yourself using the following statements:
(1) I'm tactful.
(2) I'm conservative.
(3) I'm quiet.

(4) I'm relaxed.

(5) My child is high-spirited.

(6) I have a lot of self-pride.

c. Now recall at least two situations in which you used an emotive word as if it were a description of fact and not an opinion. A good way to remember these situations is to think of a recent argument you had and imagine how the other people involved might have described it. How would their words differ from yours?

4. Explore your everyday use of abstract language by following these steps:

a. Complete each of these sentences:

(1) Women are . . .

(2) Men are . . .

(3) In my opinion, conservatives . . .

(4) Blacks in America . . .

(5) This college is . . .

b. Share your results with another person who has also completed each of these sentences. Notice any differences in the way each of you used the same terms.

c. Now go back over your list, reducing the subject of each sentence to whatever lower level abstractions better describe the original idea.

d. Reflect on the unnecessarily abstract terms you use in your everyday communication. In what ways are those terms inaccurate? What misunderstandings do they cause?

notes

1. Erwin P. Bettingshaus and Mark Milkovich, "Codes and Code Systems," in Cassandra Book (ed.), 1980, *Human Communication: Principles, Contexts, and Skills* (New York: St. Martin's), pp. 42–45.

2. C. K. Ogden and I. A. Richards, *The Meaning of Meaning* (New York: Harcourt, Brace, 1923), p. 11.

3. Jessica Davidson, "How to Translate English," in Joseph Fletcher Littell (ed.), *The Language of Man*, vol. 4 (Evanston, Ill.: McDougal Littell, 1971).

4. Research on the following pages is cited in Mary G. Marcus, "The Power of a Name," *Psychology Today* (October 1976): 75–77, 108.

5. George Lakoff and Mark Johnson, *Metaphors We Live By* (Chicago: University of Chicago Press, 1980), pp. 3, 15–17, 22.

6. Benjamin Lee Whorf, in John B. Carroll (ed.), *Language, Thought, and Reality: Selected Writings of Benjamin Lee Whorf* (Cambridge, Mass.: MIT Press, 1966).

7. Neil Postman, *Crazy Talk, Stupid Talk* (New York: Delta, 1976), p. 122.

8. Ibid., pp. 123–124.

9. Lakoff and Johnson, op. cit., p. 49.
10. Robert C. Solomon, "The Love List in Clichés," *Psychology Today* (October 1981): 83–94.
11. Morton Wiener and Albert Mehrabian, *A Language Within Language* (New York: Appleton-Century-Crofts, 1968).
12. S. I. Hayakawa, *Language in Thought and Action* (New York: Harcourt, Brace, 1964).

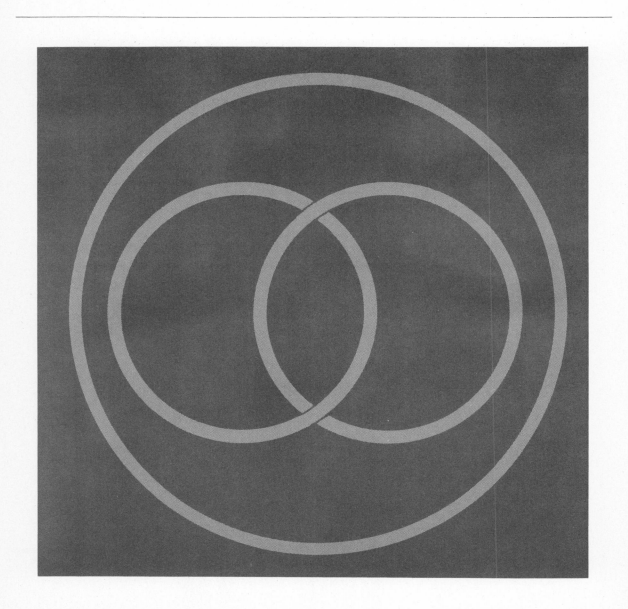

four   **listening**

After reading this chapter, you should understand:

1. The common misconceptions about listening.
2. The four components of the listening process.
3. The nine common types of listening failure.
4. The reasons why people fail to listen effectively.
5. The characteristics of one-way and two-way listening.

You should be able to:

1. Appreciate the effort required to listen effectively.
2. Identify the situations in which you listen poorly and explain the reasons for your lack of effectiveness.
3. Identify and practice the appropriate listening spyle (passive, questioning, or paraphrasing) in a variety of settings you frequently encounter.
4. Follow the guidelines for effective listening contained in this chapter.

In a world where almost everyone acknowledges the importance of better communication, the experience of not being listened to is all too common. The problem is especially bad when you realize that listening is the most frequent type of communication behavior. This fact was established as early as 1926, when Paul Rankin surveyed a group of businesspeople, asking them to record the percentage of time they spent speaking, reading, writing, and listening.[1] Rankin found that his subjects spent more time listening than in any other communication activity, devoting 42 percent of their time to it. Research over the past sixty years continues to show the importance of listening. Businesspeople, homemakers, and students all spend more time engaged in listening than in any other communication activity.[2]

Listening, then, is one of the most frequent activities in which we engage. Despite this fact, our experience shows that much of the listening we and others do is not at all effective. We misunderstand others and are misunderstood in return. We become bored and feign attention while our minds wander. We engage in a battle of interruptions where each person fights to speak without hearing the other's ideas.

As you'll soon read, some of this poor listening is inevitable. But in other cases we can be better receivers by learning a few basic listening skills. The purpose of this chapter is to help you become a better listener by giving you some important information about the subject. We'll talk about some common misconceptions concerning listening and show you what really happens when listening takes place. We'll discuss some poor listening habits and explain why they occur.

In spite of its importance, listening is misunderstood by most people. Because these misunderstandings so greatly affect our communication, let's take a look at three common misconceptions that many communicators hold.

misconceptions about listening

listening and hearing are not the same thing

Hearing is the process wherein sound waves strike the eardrum and cause vibrations that are transmitted to the brain. *Listening* occurs when the brain reconstructs these electrochemical impulses into a representation of the original sound and then gives them meaning. Barring illness, injury, or earplugs, hearing cannot be stopped. Your ears will pick up sound waves and transmit them to your brain whether you want them to or not.

Listening, however, is not so automatic. Many times we hear but do not listen. Sometimes we deliberately do not listen. Instead of paying attention to words or other sounds, we avoid them. This most often occurs when we block irritating sounds, such as a neighbor's power lawn mower or the roar of nearby traffic. We also stop listening when we find a subject unimportant or uninteresting. Boring stories, TV commercials, and nagging complaints are common examples of messages we avoid.

There are also cases when we honestly believe we're listening, even though we're merely hearing. For example, recall times when you think you've "heard it all before." It's likely that in these situations you might claim you were listening when, in fact, you had closed your mental doors to new information.

People who confuse listening with hearing often fool themselves into thinking that they're really understanding others when in fact they're simply receiving sounds. As you'll see by reading this chapter, true listening involves much more than the passive act of hearing.

listening is not a natural process

Another common myth is that listening is like breathing: a natural activity that people do well. "After all," this common belief goes, "I've been listening since I was a child. Why should I have to study the subject in school?"

This attitude is understandable considering the lack of attention most schools devote to listening in comparison with other communication skills. From kindergarten to college, most students receive almost constant training in reading and writing. Every year the exposure to literature continues, from Dick and Jane through Dostoevski. Likewise, the emphasis on writing continues without break. You could probably retire if you had a dollar for every composition, essay, research paper, and bluebook you have written since the first grade. Even spoken commu-

nication gets some attention in the curriculum. It's likely that you had a chance to take a public speaking class in high school and another one in college.

Compare all this training in reading, writing, and speaking with the almost total lack of instruction in listening. Even in college there are few courses devoted exclusively to the subject. This state of affairs is especially ironic when you consider the fact that, as mentioned, over 60 percent of our communication involves listening.

The truth is that listening is a skill much like speaking: Virtually everyone listens, though few people do it well. Your own experience should prove that communication often suffers owing to poor listening. How many times have others misunderstood directions or explanations because they didn't seem to be receiving your ideas clearly? And how often have you failed to understand others accurately because you weren't receiving their thoughts accurately? The answers to these questions demonstrate the need for effective training in listening.

all listeners do not receive the same message

When two or more people are listening to a speaker, we tend to assume that they are each hearing and understanding the same message. In fact, such uniform comprehension isn't the case. Communication is *proactive:* Each person involved in a transaction of ideas or feelings responds uniquely. Recall our discussion of perception in Chapter 2, where we pointed out the many factors that cause each of us to perceive an event differently. Physiological factors, social roles, cultural background, personal interests, and needs all shape and distort the raw data we hear into uniquely different messages.

components of listening

In his book *Listening Behavior,* Larry Barker describes the process of listening as having four components: hearing, attending, understanding, and remembering.[3]

hearing

As we have already discussed, *hearing* is the physiological aspect of listening. It is the nonselective process of sound waves impinging on the ear and the ear responding to those waves that fall within a certain frequency range and are sufficiently loud. Hearing is also influenced by background noise. If such noise is the same frequency as the speech sound, then the speech sound is said to be masked; however, if the background noise is of a different frequency from speech, it is called "white noise" and may or may not detract greatly from our ability to hear. Hearing is also affected by auditory fatigue, a temporary loss of hearing caused by continuous exposure to the same tone or loudness. People who spend an evening dancing to a loud band may experience auditory fatigue, and if they are exposed often enough, permanent hearing loss may result.[4]

attending

After the sounds are converted into electrochemical impulses and transmitted to the brain, a decision—often unconscious—is made whether to focus on what was heard. Though the listening process started as a physiological one, it quickly became a psychological one. An individual's needs, wants, desires, and interests determine what is *attended to.* If you're hungry, you are more likely to attend to the message about restaurants in the neighborhood from the person next to you than the competing message on the importance of communication from the speaker in front of the room.

understanding

The component of understanding is composed of several elements. First, understanding a message involves some recognition of the grammatical rules used to create that message. We find the children's books by Dr. Seuss amusing because he breaks the rules of grammar and spelling in interesting ways, and we are familiar enough with the rules to recognize this. Second, understanding depends upon our knowledge about the source of the message—whether the person is sincere, prone to lie, friendly, an adversary, and so on. Third, there is the *social context.* The time and place, for example, helps us decide whether to take a friend's insults seriously or as a joke. Understanding depends, generally, upon sharing common assumptions about the world. Consider the following two sentences.[5]

1. I bought alligator shoes.
2. I bought horseshoes.

Both sentences can be interpreted the same way because they have the same grammatical structure and may be uttered by the same person (the first two components of understanding). Both could indicate that a person bought two pairs of shoes, one made from alligator, the other from horse, or that two pairs of shoes were purchased, one for an alligator, the other for a horse. However, because of the common assumptions we share about the world, we understand that the first sentence refers to shoes made *from* alligator hides and that the second refers either to shoes *for* horses (or for playing a game).

Finally, understanding often depends on the ability to organize the information we hear into recognizable form. As early as 1948, Ralph Nichols related successful understanding to a large number of factors, most prominent among which were verbal ability, intelligence, and motivation.[6]

remembering

The complaint "You didn't listen to me" often means "You didn't remember what I said."[7] The ability to recall information is a function of several factors: the number of times the information is heard or re-

---

at a lecture—only 12% listen

Bright-eyed college students in lecture halls aren't necessarily listening to the professor, the American Psychological Association was told yesterday.

If you shot off a gun at sporadic intervals and asked the students to encode their thoughts and moods at that moment, you would discover that:
• About 20 percent of the students, men and women, are pursuing erotic thoughts.
• Another 20 percent are reminiscing about something.
• Only 20 percent are actually paying attention to the lecture; 12 percent are actively listening.
• the others are worrying, daydreaming, thinking about lunch or—surprise—religion (8 percent).

This confirmation of the lecturer's worst fears was reported by Paul Cameron, 28, an assistant professor at Wayne State University in Detroit. The annual convention, which ends Tuesday, includes about 2,000 such reports to 10,000 psychologists in a variety of meetings.

Cameron's results were based on a nine-week course in introductory psychology for 85 college sophomores. A gun was fired 21 times at random intervals, usually when Cameron was in the middle of a sentence.

San Francisco Sunday Examiner and Chronicle

77

peated, how much information there is to store in the brain, and whether the information may be "rehearsed" or not.

Research has revealed that people remember only about half of what they hear *immediately after* hearing it.[8] This is true even if people work hard at listening. This situation would probably not be too bad if the half remembered right after were retained, but it isn't. Within two months half of the half is forgotten, bringing what we remember down to about 25 percent of the original message. This loss, however, doesn't take two months: People start forgetting immediately (within eight hours the 50 percent remembered drops to about 35 percent). Given the amount of information we process every day—from instructors, friends, the radio, TV, and other sources—the *residual message* (what we remember) is a small fraction of what we hear.

faulty listening behaviors

Although it may not be necessary or desirable to listen effectively all the time, most people possess one or more bad habits that keep them from understanding truly important messages.

1. **Pseudolistening.** Pseudolistening is an imitation of the real thing. "Good" pseudolisteners give the appearance of being attentive: They look you in the eye, nod and smile at the right times, and even may answer you occasionally. Behind that appearance of interest, however, something entirely different is going on, for pseudolisteners use a polite facade to mask thoughts that have nothing to do with what the speaker is saying. Often pseudolisteners ignore you because of something on their mind that's more important to them than your remarks. Other times they may simply be bored or think that they've heard what you have to say before, and so they tune out your remarks. Whatever the reasons, the significant fact is that pseudolistening is really counterfeit communication.

2. **Stage hogging.** Stage hogs are only interested in expressing their ideas and don't care about what anyone else has to say. These

B. C.   by Johnny hart

people will allow you to speak from time to time, but only so they can catch their breath, use your remarks as a basis for their own babbling, or keep you from running away. Stage hogs really aren't conversing when they dominate others—they are making a speech . . . and at the same time probably making an enemy.

3. **Selective listening.** Selective listeners respond only to the parts of a speaker's remarks that interest them, rejecting everything else. All of us are selective listeners from time to time, as for instance when we screen out media commercials and music as we keep an ear cocked for a weather report or an announcement of time. In other cases selective listening occurs in conversations with people who expect a thorough hearing but only get their partner's attention when the subject turns to the partner's favorite topic—perhaps money, sex, a hobby, or some particular person. Unless and until you bring up one of these pet subjects, you might as well talk to a tree.

4. **Filling in gaps.** People who fill in the gaps like to think that what they remember makes a whole story. Because we remember half or less of what we hear, these people manufacture information so that when they retell what they listened to, they can give the impression they "got it all." Of course, filling in the gaps is as dangerous as selective listening: The message that's left is only a distorted (not merely incomplete) version of the message that could have been received.

5. **Assimilation to prior messages.** We all have a tendency to interpret current messages in terms of similar messages remembered from the past. This phenomenon is called *assimilation to prior input.* A problem arises for those who go overboard with this and push, pull, chop, squeeze, and in other ways mutilate messages they receive to *make sure* they are consistent with what they heard in the past. This unfortunate situation occurs when the current message is in some way uniquely different from past messages.

6. **Insulated listening.** Insulated listeners are almost the opposite of their selective-listening cousins. Instead of looking for something, these people avoid it. Whenever a topic arises they'd rather not deal with, insulated listeners simply fail to hear it or, rather, to acknowledge it. If you remind them about a problem—perhaps an unfinished job, poor grades, or the like—they'll nod or answer you and then promptly forget what you've just said.

7. **Defensive listening.** Defensive listeners take innocent comments as personal attacks. Teenagers who perceive parental questions about friends and activities as distrustful snooping are defensive listeners, as are insecure breadwinners who explode anytime their mates mention money or touchy parents who view any questioning by their children as a threat to their authority and parental wisdom. It's fair to assume that many defensive listeners are suffering from shaky public images and avoid admitting this by projecting their own insecurities onto others.

i have just
wandered back
into our conversation
and find
that you
are still
rattling on
about something
or other
i think i must
have been gone
at least
twenty minutes
and you
never missed me

now this might say
something
about my
acting ability
or it might say
something about
your sensitivity

one thing
troubles me tho
when it
is my turn
to rattle on
for twenty minutes
which i
have been known to do
have you
been missing too

Ric Masten

listening
79

Bore, *n.* A person who talks when you wish him to listen.

Conversation, *n.* A fair for the display of the minor mental commodities, each exhibitor being too intent upon arrangement of his own wares to observe those of his neighbor.

Egotist, *n.* A person of low taste more interested in himself than me.

Heaven, *n.* A place where the wicked cease from troubling you with talk of their personal affairs, and the good listen with attention while you expound your own.

Ambrose Bierce
The Devil's Dictionary

reasons for poor listening

8. **Ambushing.** Ambushers listen carefully, but only because they are collecting information to attack what you have to say. The cross-examining prosecution attorney is a good example of an ambusher. Needless to say, using his kind of strategy will justifiably initiate defensiveness on the other's behalf.

9. **Insensitive listening.** Insensitive listeners offer the final example of people who don't receive another person's messages clearly. People often don't express their thoughts or feelings openly but instead communicate them through subtle and unconscious choice of words and/or nonverbal clues. Insensitive listeners aren't able to look beyond the words and behavior to understand their hidden meanings. Instead, they take a speaker's remarks at face value.

It's important not to go overboard in labeling listeners as insensitive. Often a seemingly mechanical comment is perfectly appropriate. This most often occurs in situations involving *phatic* communication, in which a remark derives its meaning totally from context. For instance, the question "How are you?" doesn't call for an answer when you pass an acquaintance on the street. In this context the statement means no more than "I acknowledge your existence, and I want to let you know that I feel friendly toward you." It is not an inquiry about the state of your health. Although insensitive listening is depressing, you would be equally discouraged to hear a litany of aches and pains everytime you asked, "How's it going?"

Listening well is obviously important, yet often we do just the opposite. Why? Sad as it may be, it's impossible to listen *all* the time, for several reasons.

message overload

The amount of speech most of us encounter everyday makes careful listening to everything we hear impossible. As we've already seen, many of us spend as much as one-third of the time we're awake listening to verbal messages—from teachers, co-workers, friends, family, salespeople, and total strangers. This means we often spend five hours or more a day listening to people talk. If you add this to the amount of time we tune in radio and television, you can see that it's impossible for us to keep our attention totally focused for this amount of time. Therefore we have to let our attention wander at times.

preoccupation

Another reason we don't always listen carefully is that we're often wrapped up in personal concerns that are of more immediate importance to us than the messages others are sending. It's hard to pay attention to someone else when you're anticipating an upcoming test or thinking about the wonderful time you had last night with good friends. Yet we still feel we have to "listen" politely to others, and so we continue with our charade.

rapid thought

Listening carefully is also difficult for a physiological reason. Although we are capable of understanding speech at rates up to 300 words per minute,[9] the average person speaks between 100 and 140 words per minute.[10] Thus we have a great deal of mental "spare time" to spend while someone is talking. And the temptation is to use this time in ways that don't relate to the speaker's ideas, such as thinking about personal interests, daydreaming, planning a rebuttal, and so on. The trick is to use this spare time to understand the speaker's ideas better rather than letting your attention wander.

physical "noise"

The physical world in which we live often presents distractions that make it hard to pay attention to others. The sound of traffic, music, others' speech, and the like interfere with our ability to hear well. Also, fatigue or other forms of discomfort can distract us from paying attention to a speaker's remarks. Consider, for example, how the efficiency of your listening decreases when you are seated in a crowded, hot, stuffy room that is surrounded by traffic and other noises. In such circumstances even the best intentions aren't enough to ensure clear understanding.

hearing problems

Sometimes a person's listening ability suffers from a physiological hearing problem. Once a hearing problem has been diagnosed, it's often possible to treat it. The real tragedy occurs when a hearing loss goes undetected. In such cases both the person with the defect and others can become frustrated and annoyed at the ineffective communication that results. If you suspect that you or someone you know suffers from a hearing loss, it's wise to have a physician or audiologist perform an examination.

faulty assumptions

We often make incorrect assumptions that lead us to believe that we're listening attentively when quite the opposite is true. When the subject is a familiar one, it's easy to think that you've "heard it all before" when in fact the speaker is offering new information. A related problem arises if you assume that a speaker's thoughts are too simple or obvious to deserve careful attention when the truth is that you ought to be listening

duet

When we speak we do not
   listen, my son and I.
I complain of slights, hurts
   inflicted on me.
He sings a counterpoint, but
   not in harmony.
Asking a question, he doesn't
   wait to hear.
Trying to answer, I interrupt
   his refrain.
This comic opera excels in
   disharmony only.

Lenni Shender Goldstein

"What? I'm sorry. I wasn't listening."

carefully. At other times just the opposite occurs: You think that another's comments are too complex to possibly understand (as in some lectures), and so give up trying to make sense of them. A final mistake people often make is to assume that a subject is unimportant and to stop paying attention when they ought to be listening carefully.

talking has more apparent advantages

It often appears that we have more to gain by speaking than by listening. One big advantage of speaking is that it gives you a chance to control others' thoughts and actions. Whatever your goal—to have a prospective boss hire you, to convince others to vote for the candidate of your choice, or to describe the way you want your hair cut—the key to success seems to be the ability to speak well.

Another apparent advantage of speaking is the chance it provides to gain the admiration, respect, or liking of others. Tell jokes, and everyone will think you're a real wit. Offer advice, and they'll be grateful for your help. Tell them all you know, and they'll be impressed by your wisdom. But keep quiet . . . and it seems as if you'll look like a worthless nobody.

Finally, talking gives you the chance to release energy in a way that listening can't. When you're frustrated, the chance to talk about your problems can often help you feel better. In the same way, you can often lessen your anger by letting it out verbally. It is also helpful to share your excitement with others by talking about it, for keeping it inside often leaves you feeling as if you might burst.

Although it's true that talking does have many advantages, it's important to realize that listening can pay dividends, too. As you'll soon read, being a good listener is one way to help others with their problems; and what better way is there to have others appreciate you? As for controlling others, it may be true that it's hard to be persuasive while you're listening, but your willingness to hear others out will often leave them open to thinking about your ideas in return. Like defensiveness, listening is often reciprocal: You get what you give.

lack of training

Even if we want to listen well, we're often hampered by a lack of skill. As we've already said, listening is a skill much like speaking: Virtually everybody does it, though few people do it well. As you read through this chapter, you'll see that one reason so much poor listening exists is because most people fail to follow the important steps that lead to real understanding.

Before going any further, we want to make it clear that it isn't always desirable to listen intently, even when the circumstances permit. Given the number of messages to which we're exposed, it's impractical to expect yourself to listen well 100 percent of the time. This fact becomes even more evident when you consider how many of the messages sent at us aren't especially worthwhile: boring stories, deceitful commercials, remarks we've heard many times before, and so on. Given this deluge of relatively worthless information, it's important for you to realize that behaviors such as insulated listening, pseudolistening, and selective listening are often reasonable. But there are times when you do want very much to understand others. At times like these you may try hard to get the other person's meaning and yet *still* seem to wind up with misunderstandings.

What can you do in such cases? It takes more than good intentions to listen well—there are skills that you can learn to use. To begin understanding these skills we need to look at two styles of listening.

one-way listening

One-way communication occurs when a listener tries to make sense out of a speaker's remarks without actively taking part in the exchange of a message. Another term that describes this style of communication is *passive listening*. Probably the most familiar examples of passive listening occur when students hear a professor lecture or when viewers watch television. One-way communication also takes place in interpersonal settings, as when one person dominates a conversation while

styles of listening

listening
83

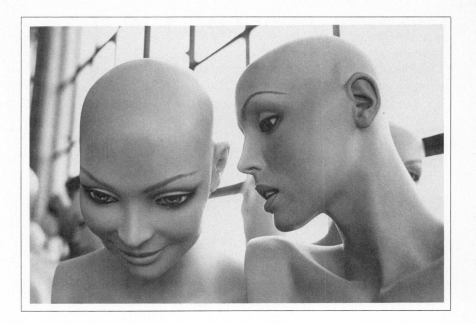

the others fall into the role of audience members or when some parents lecture their children without allowing them to respond.

The most important feature of one-way communication is that it contains little or no feedback. The receiver may deliberately or unintentionally send nonverbal messages that show how the speaker's ideas are being received—nods and smiles, stifled yawns, more or less eye contact—but there's no verbal response to indicate how—or even whether—the message has been received.

Because the speaker isn't interrupted in this type of lecture-conversation, one-way communication has the advantage of being relatively quick. We've all felt like telling someone, "I'm in a hurry. Just listen carefully and don't interrupt." What we're asking for here is one-way communication.

Sometimes one-way communication is an appropriate way of listening. As you'll soon read, sometimes the best way to help people with problems is to hear them out. In many cases they're not looking for, nor do they need, a verbal response. At times like these, when there's no input by the receiver, *anybody* who will serve as a sounding board will do as a "listener." This explains why some people find relief talking to a pet or a photograph.

One-way communication also works well when the listener wants to ease back mentally and be entertained. It would be a mistake to interrupt a good joke or story or to stand up in the middle of a play and shout out a question to the performers.

But outside of these cases one-way listening isn't very effective for the simple reason that it almost guarantees that the listener will misunderstand at least some of the speaker's ideas. There are at least three types of misunderstandings. As you read about each of them, think about how often they occur for you.

The first kind of misunderstanding happens when a speaker sends a clear, accurate message that the receiver simply gets wrong. Somehow a quarter-cup of sugar is transformed into four cups, or "I'll see you at twelve" is translated into "I'll see you at two."

In other cases the receiver is listening carefully enough, but the speaker sends an incorrect message. These instances are the reverse of the ones just mentioned, and their results can be just as disastrous.

The third mix-up that comes from one-way communication is probably the most common. The speaker sends a message that may not be incorrect but is overly vague, and the receiver interprets the words in a manner that doesn't match the speaker's ideas. In Chapter 3 we talked about the problems that come from failing to check out interpretations. In this statement, "I'm a little confused," does "little" mean "slightly" or is it an understatement that could be translated into "very"? When a lover says, "You're my best friend," is this synonymous with the message, "Besides being such a romantic devil, I also feel comfortable with you," or does it mean, "I want to become less of a lover and more of a pal"? You could make your own personal list of confusing messages and in doing so prove the point: Assuming you understand another's words isn't always a sure thing. Fortunately, there's another, usually better way of listening.

two-way listening

The element that distinguishes two-way from one-way communication is verbal feedback. You'll recall from our communication model in Chapter 1 that feedback occurs whenever a listener sends some sort of message to the sender indicating how the original idea was received. There are at least two types of verbal feedback you can use as a listener.

Questioning This type of response involves asking for additional information to clarify your idea of the sender's message. If you ask directions to a friend's house, typical questions might be "Is your place an apartment?" or "How long does it take to get there from here?" In more serious situations, questions could include "What's bothering you?" or "Why are you so angry?" or "Why is that so important?" Notice that one key element of these questions is that they request the speaker to elaborate on information already given.

Questioning is often a valuable tool for increasing understanding. Sometimes, however, it won't help you receive a speaker's ideas any more clearly, and it can even lead to further communication breakdown. To see how this can be so, consider our example of asking directions to a friend's home. Suppose the instructions you've received are to "drive about a mile and then turn left at the traffic signal." Now imagine that a few common problems exist in this simple message. First, sup-

"I have a pet at home"

"Oh, what kind of a pet?"

"It is a dog."

"What kind of a dog?"

"It is a St. Bernard."

"Grown up or a puppy?"

"It is full grown."

"What color is it?"

"It is brown and white."

"Why didn't you say you had a full-grown, brown and white St. Bernard as a pet in the first place?"

pose that your friend's idea of a mile is different from yours: Your mental picture of the distance is actually closer to two miles whereas hers is closer to 300 yards. Next, consider the very likely occurrence that though your friend said "traffic signal," she meant "stop sign"; after all, it's common for us to think one thing and say another. Keeping these problems in mind, suppose you tried to verify your understanding of the directions by asking, "After I turn at the light, how far should I go?" to which your friend replied that her house is the third from the corner. Clearly, if you parted after this exchange, you would encounter a lot of frustration before finding the elusive residence.

What was the problem here? It's easy to see that questioning didn't help, for your original idea of how far to drive and where to turn were mistaken. And contained in such mistakes is the biggest problem with questioning, for such inquiries don't tell you whether you have accurately received the information that has *already* been sent.

Active listening Now consider another kind of feedback—one that would tell you whether you understood what had already been said before you asked additional questions. This sort of feedback involves restating in your own words the message you thought the speaker had just sent, without adding anything new. In the example of seeking directions that we've been using, such rephrasing might sound like this: "So you're telling me to drive down to the traffic light by the high school and turn toward the mountains, is that it?" Immediately sensing the problem, your friend could then reply, "Oh no, that's way too far. I

So the first simple feeling I want to share with you is my enjoyment when I can really hear someone. I think perhaps this has been a long-standing characteristic of mine. I can remember this in my early grammar school days. A child would ask the teacher a question and the teacher would give a perfectly good answer to a completely different question. A feeling of pain and distress would always strike me. My reaction was, "But you didn't hear him!" I felt a sort of childish despair at the lack of communication which was (and is) so common.

Carl R. Rogers

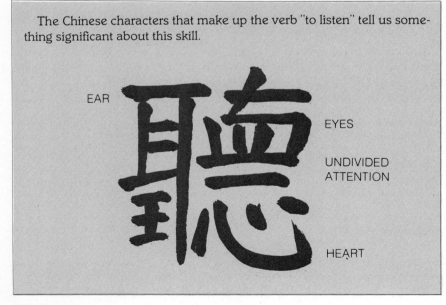

The Chinese characters that make up the verb "to listen" tell us something significant about this skill.

EAR

EYES

UNDIVIDED ATTENTION

HEART

Caligraphy by Angie Au.

meant that you should drive to the four-way stop by the park and turn there. Did I say stop light? I always do that when I mean stop sign!"

This simple step of restating what you think the speaker has said before going on is commonly termed *active listening*[11] and it is a very important tool for effective listening. The thing to remember in active listening is to *paraphrase* the sender's words, not to parrot them. In other words, restate what you think the speaker has said in your own terms as a way of cross-checking the information. If you simply repeat the speaker's comments verbatim, you'll sound as if you're foolish or hard of hearing, and, just as important, you still might be misunderstanding what's been said.

At first, active listening might seem to have little to recommend it. After all, it's an unfamiliar tool, which means that you'll have to go through a stage of awkwardness while learning it. And until you become skillful at responding in this new way, you run the risk of getting odd reactions from the people to whom you're responding. In spite of these very real problems, learning to listen actively is worth the effort, for it offers some very real advantages.

First, it boosts the odds that you'll accurately and fully understand what others are saying. We've already seen that one-way listening or even asking questions may lead you to think that you've understood a speaker when, in fact, you haven't. Active listening, on the other hand, serves as a way of double-checking your interpretation for accuracy. A second advantage of active listening is that it guides you toward sincerely trying to understand another person instead of using non-listening styles such as stage hogging, selective listening, and so on. If you force yourself to reflect the other person's ideas in your own words, you'll spend your mental energy trying to understand that speaker instead of spending it elsewhere: planning retorts, daydreaming, or defending yourself.

guidelines for listening effectively

After reading this far, you probably recognize the need for better listening in many contexts. What steps can you take to become a better receiver? Read on and see.

1. **Choose the proper environment.** In Chapter 1 we introduced the concept of "noise"—psychological and physical distractions that interfere with communication. Whenever listening (or speaking), do your best to pick a time and place that will have a minimal amount of noise. Whenever possible, be sure that you and your partner won't be bothered by any interruptions and will be free of pressing thoughts or feelings. In addition, choose a setting that is physically comfortable.

2. **Stop talking.** Zeno of Citium put it most succinctly: "We have been given two ears and but a single mouth, in order that we may hear more and talk less." It is difficult to listen and talk at the same time. This includes the silent debating, rehearsing, and retorting that often

goes on in our minds. The first step to better listening, then, is to keep quiet when another person speaks.

3. **Concentrate on the speaker's ideas.** Focus your attention on the words, ideas, and the feelings of the speaker. Use the "extra" time you have listening to put the speaker's ideas into your own words, relate them to your experience, and think about any questions you might have.

4. **Don't be overly critical.** Give the speaker a fair hearing; control your anger. If you argue mentally, you lose the opportunity to concentrate on what the speaker is saying. Also, it is often the case that when we mentally argue, we tend to place the other person in a fixed category, and thus cease responding to a unique person, albeit a unique person with whom we disagree.

5. **Listen for main points and supporting evidence.** Careful listening will show that a speaker almost always advances one or more main points and backs them up with examples, stories, analogies, and other types of supporting material. One key to successful listening is to search for these main points and then see if the speaker's support bears them out. A far less productive method is to dwell on an interesting story or comment while forgetting the speaker's main idea.

6. **Share responsibility for the communication.** Remember that communication is a transaction, that we are simultaneously senders and receivers. Just as a good marriage requires both partners to give 100 percent of their effort, so a successful conversation demands the energy and skill of both parties.

7. **Ask questions.** Thus far, we have been discussing listening methods basically passive in nature, that is, those we can carry out silently. It's also possible to verify or increase your understanding in a more active way by asking questions to be sure you are receiving the speaker's thoughts and feelings accurately.

Although the suggestion to ask questions may seem so obvious as to be trivial, honestly ask yourself whether you take full advantage of this simple but effective method. It's often tempting to remain silent instead of being a questioner. Sometimes you may be reluctant to show your ignorance by asking for further explanation of what seems to be an obvious point. This reluctance is especially strong when the speaker's respect or liking is important to you. At such times it's a good idea to remember a quotation attributed to Confucius: "He who asks a question is a fool for five minutes. He who does not ask is a fool for life."

A second reason people are often disinclined to ask questions is that they think they already understand a speaker. But do we in fact understand others as often or as well as we think? You can best answer by thinking about how often people understand *you* while feeling certain that they know what you've meant. If you are aware that others should ask questions of you more often, then it's logical to assume that the same principle holds true in reverse.

8. Use active listening. Questioning is certainly an important tool in the listener's repertoire. But as we saw a few pages ago with our example of jumbled street directions, it won't always clarify a speaker's meaning. Remember that questioning can give you *new* information, but it doesn't necessarily clarify any misunderstandings about messages you've already received. Another problem involves the difficulty of knowing exactly *what* questions to ask in order to get a clear picture of a speaker's ideas.

Because active listening is an unfamiliar way of responding, it may feel awkward at first. But by paraphrasing occasionally in the beginning and then gradually increasing the frequency of such responses, you can begin to gain the benefits of this method without feeling foolish or sounding odd to others.

summary

Even the best message imaginable is useless if it goes unreceived or if it is misunderstood. For this reason, listening—the process of giving meaning to an oral message—is a vitally important part of the communication process. We began our look at the subject by identifying and refuting several myths about listening. Our conclusion here was that effective listening is a skill that needs to be developed in order for us to be truly effective in understanding others.

We next took a close look at four steps in the process of listening: hearing, attending, understanding, and remembering. We examined nine types of faulty listening behavior that block understanding, showing the many ways in which we screen out or distort the messages of others.

Next we identified several reasons—physical, psychological, and environmental—that prevent us from listening effectively even when we want to do so.

We identified two distinctly different styles of listening, one-way and two-way. We took a closer look at two-way listening, describing questioning and paraphrasing as separate types of responses within this category.

We concluded by listing eight guidelines for listening effectively. Each of these suggestions makes it clear that the process of understanding is not only the responsibility of the sender, but rests just as much on the intentions and skills of the receiver.

activities

1. Although failing to listen is a crime we both commit and suffer from, it often goes unnoticed. Trying this activity with a partner will demonstrate its seriousness.
   a. Each person in turn should take two minutes to discuss with the other his or her ideas about a current issue (abortion, capital punishment, or some other idea that is personally important). But,

as the talker shares his or her ideas, the other person should think about the unfinished business in his or her life—incomplete assignments, on-the-job work, things to discuss with the family. The partner shouldn't be rude but should respond politely every so often to the speaker, putting on a good appearance of paying close attention. Nonetheless, the idea is to think about personal concerns, not the speaker's remarks.

b. After each partner completes step **a,** spend some time sharing the feelings you experienced when you were talking and being listened to by the other. Also discuss how you felt as you thought about your problems instead of listening to the speaker.

c. Next conduct a five-minute discussion with a partner in which each of you shares one personal communication problem you hope to solve. Try to be as sincere and open with your feelings as you can. But as both partners talk, each should try to keep the discussion focused on his or her own problem. Every time the other shares an idea or experience, try to turn it around to relate to your situation. Don't get sidetracked by his or her comments. Your task is to tell the other about your communication problem.

d. After your discussion, take a few minutes to talk about how you felt during the conversation—when the other person ignored your message and when you ignored his or hers.

2. Use the categories on pages 78–80 to describe the faulty listening behaviors you use in your everyday interactions. In what circumstances do you use these behaviors: Around whom? With what subjects? In what settings? At what times? What are the main reasons for your failure to listen in these circumstances? How satisfied are you with your findings? How could you change your behavior in the unsatisfying areas?

3. You can see for yourself what a difference active listening can make by trying this exercise, either in class or with a companion on your own.

a. Find a partner; then move to a place where you can talk comfortably. Designate one person as A and the other as B.

b. Find a subject on which you and your partner apparently disagree—a personal dispute, a philosophical or moral issue, or perhaps a matter of personal taste.

c. A begins by making a statement on the subject. B's job is then to paraphrase the idea back, beginning by saying something like "What I hear you saying is . . ." It is very important that in this step B feeds back only what he or she heard A say without adding any judgment or interpretation. B's job is simply to *understand* here, and doing so in no way should signify agreement or disagreement with A's remarks.

listening
91

d. A then responds by telling B whether or not the response was accurate. If there was some misunderstanding, A should make the correction, and B should feed back a new understanding of the statement. Continue this process until you're both sure that B understands A's statement.

e. Now it's B's turn to respond to A's statement and for A to help the process of understanding by correcting B.

f. Continue this process until both partners are satisfied that they have explained themselves fully and that they have been understood by the other person.

g. Now discuss the following questions:

  (1) As a listener, how accurate was your first understanding of the speaker's statements?

  (2) How did your understanding of the speaker's position change after you used active listening?

  (3) Did you find that the gap between your position and that of your partner narrowed as a result of your both using active listening?

  (4) How did you feel at the end of your conversation? How does this feeling compare to your usual emotional state after discussing controversial issues with others?

  (5) How might your life change if you used active listening at home? At work? With friends?

notes

1. Paul T. Rankin, "The Measurement of the Ability to Understand Spoken Language," *Dissertation Abstracts* 12 (1926): 847.

2. See, for example, J. D. Weinrauch and J. R. Swanda, Jr., "Examining the Significance of Listening: An Exploratory Study of Contemporary Management," *The Journal of Business Communication* 13 (February 1975): 25–32; and Larry L. Barker, *Listening Behavior* (Englewood Cliffs, N.J.: Prentice-Hall, 1971), p. 4.

3. Ibid., p. 17.

4. For a complete discussion of the physiology of hearing, see Hayes A. Newby, *Audiology* (New York: Appleton-Century-Crofts, 1972).

5. Jerrold J. Katz and Jerry A. Foder, "The Structure of a Semantic Theory," in Jay F. Rosenberg and Charles Travis (eds.) *Readings in the Philosophy of Language* (Englewood Cliffs, N.J.: Prentice-Hall, 1971).

6. Ralph G. Nichols, "Factors in Listening Comprehension," *Speech Monographs* 15 (1948): 154–163.

7. For a more complete discussion of memory and listening, see Robert N. Bostrom and Carol L. Bryant, "Factors in the Retention of Information Presented Orally: The Role of Short-Term Listening," *Western Journal of Speech Communication* 44 (Spring 1980): 137–145.

8. Nichols, op. cit.

9. David B. Orr, "Time Compressed Speech—A Perspective," *Journal of Communication* 17 (1967): 223.
10. Bert E. Bradley, *Fundamentals of Speech Communication,* 3d ed. (Dubuque, Iowa: W. C. Brown, 1981), pp. 205–206.
11. Thomas Gordon, *Parent Effectiveness Training* (New York: Wyden, 1970).

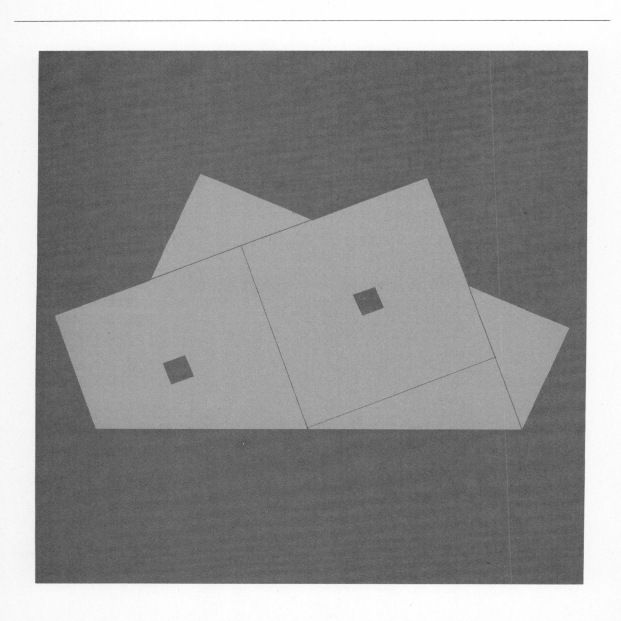

five

nonverbal communication

After reading this chapter, you should understand:

1. The four characteristics of nonverbal communication listed in this chapter.
2. The six functions nonverbal communication can serve.
3. How the types of nonverbal communication described in this chapter function.

You should be able to:

1. Identify and describe the nonverbal behaviors of yourself or another person in a given situation.
2. Identify nonverbal behaviors that repeat, substitute for, complement, accent, regulate, and contradict verbal messages.
3. Recognize the emotional and relational dimensions of your own nonverbal behavior.
4. Share your interpretation of another person's nonverbal behavior in a tentative manner when such sharing is appropriate.

There is often a big gap between what people say and what they feel. An acquaintance says, "I'd like to get together again" in a way that leaves you suspecting the opposite. (But how do you know?) A speaker tried to appear confident but acts in a way that almost screams out, "I'm nervous!" (What tells you this?) You ask a friend what's wrong, and the "nothing" you get in response rings hollow. (Why does it sound untrue?)

Then, of course, there are times when another's message comes through even though there are no words at all. A look of irritation, a smile, a sigh . . . signs like these can say more than a torrent of words.

Sometimes unspoken messages are so obvious that anyone could read them. In other cases they are subtle, leaving you with a hunch about what's going on but unable to figure out the source of your feeling. And then there are times when you miss an unstated message so completely that the truth comes later as a complete surprise.

All situations like these have one point in common—that the message was sent nonverbally. The goal of this chapter is to introduce you to this world of nonverbal communication. Although you have certainly recognized nonverbal messages before, the following pages should introduce you to a richness of information you have never noticed. And though your experience won't transform you into a mind reader, it will make you a far more accurate observer of others . . . and yourself.

nonverbal communication defined

We need to begin our study of nonverbal communication by defining this term. At first this might seem like a simple task. If *non* means "not" and *verbal* means "words," then *nonverbal communication* appears to mean "communication without words." This is a good starting point once we distinguish between *vocal* communication (by mouth) and *verbal* communication (with words). Once this distinction is made, it becomes clear that some nonverbal messages are vocal, and some are not. Likewise, although many verbal messages are vocal, some aren't. Table 5–1 illustrates these differences.

table 5–1   types of communication

	vocal communication	nonvocal communication
verbal communication	Spoken words	Written words
nonverbal communication	Tone of voice, sighs, screams, vocal qualities (loudness, pitch, and so on)	Gestures, movement, appearance, facial expression, and so on

Adapted from John Stewart and Gary D'Angelo, *Together: Communicating Interpersonally*, 2d ed. (Reading, Mass.: Addison-Wesley, 1980), p. 22.

What about languages that don't involve words? Does American Sign Language, for example, qualify as nonverbal communication? Most scholars would say not.[1] Keeping this fact in mind, we arrive at a working definition of nonverbal communication: "oral and nonoral messages expressed by other than linguistic means." This rules out not only sign languages but written words as well, but it includes messages transmitted by vocal means that don't involve language—sighs, laughs, and other utterances we will discuss soon.

Our brief definition only hints at the richness of nonverbal messages. You can begin to understand their prevalence by trying a simple experiment. Spend an hour or so around a group of people who are speaking a language you don't understand. (You might find such a group in the foreign students' lounge on campus, in an advanced language class, or in an ethnic neighborhood.) Your goal is to see how much information you can learn about the people you're observing from means other than the verbal messages they transmit. This experiment will reveal several characteristics of nonverbal communication.

characteristics of nonverbal communication

nonverbal communication exists

Your observations in the earlier experiment demonstrated that even without understanding speech it is possible to get an idea about how others are feeling. You probably noticed that some people were in a hurry whereas others seemed happy, confused, withdrawn, or deep in thought. The point is that without any formal experience you were able to recognize and to some degree interpret messages that other people sent nonverbally. In this chapter we want to sharpen the skills you already have and to give you a better grasp of the vocabulary of nonverbal language.

one can't not communicate

The pervasiveness of nonverbal communication brings us to its second characteristic. Suppose you were instructed to avoid communicating any messages at all. What would you do? Close your eyes? Withdraw into a ball? Leave the room? You can probably see that even these behaviors communicate messages, suggesting that you are avoiding contact. A moment's thought will show that there is no way to avoid communicating nonverbally.

This impossibility of not communicating is extremely important to understand, for it means that each of us is a kind of transmitter that cannot be shut off. No matter what we do, we give off information about ourselves.

Stop for a moment and examine yourself as you read this. If someone were observing you now, what nonverbal clues would they get about how you are feeling? Are you sitting forward or reclining back? Is your

Writer (to movie producer Sam Goldwyn): Mr. Goldwyn, I'm telling you a sensational story. I'm only asking for your opinion, and you fall asleep.

Goldwyn: Isn't sleeping an opinion?

posture tense or relaxed? Are your eyes wide open, or do they keep closing? What does your facial expression communicate? Can you make your face expressionless? Don't people with expressionless faces communicate something?

Of course, we don't always intend to send nonverbal messages. Consider, for instance, behaviors like blushing, frowning, sweating, or stammering. We rarely try to act in these ways, and often we are unaware of doing so. Nonetheless, others recognize signs like these and make interpretations about us based on their observations.

The fact that you and everyone around you is constantly sending nonverbal clues is important because it means that you have a constant source of information available about yourself and others. If you can tune into these signals, you will be more aware of how those around you are feeling and thinking, and you will be better able to respond to their behavior.

nonverbal communication transmits feelings

Although feelings are communicated quite well nonverbally, thoughts don't lend themselves to nonverbal channels.

You can test this principle for yourself. Following is a list that contains both thoughts and feelings. Try to express each item nonverbally, and see which ones come most easily:

You're tired.

You're in favor of capital punishment.

You're attracted to another person in the group.

You think marijuana should be legalized.

You're angry at someone in the group.

nonverbal communication is ambiguous

Before you get the idea that this chapter will turn you into some sort of mind reader, we want to caution you and in so doing introduce a fifth feature of nonverbal communication: A great deal of ambiguity surrounds nonverbal behavior. To understand what we mean, examine the photo on this page. What emotions do you imagine the couple are feeling: grief? anguish? agony? In fact, none of these is even close. The couple have just learned that they won $1 million in the New Jersey state lottery.

Nonverbal behavior is just as ambiguous in everyday life. For example, think of at least two meanings of a partner's silence at the end of an evening together. (Table 5–2 lists some possibilities.) Or suppose a much admired person you have worked with suddenly begins paying more attention to you than ever before. What might this mean?

Although nonverbal behavior can be quite revealing, it can have so many possible meanings that it is a serious mistake to assume your interpretations will always be accurate.

How does this couple feel? See the preceding text for the answer. (Photo courtesy of *The Record,* Hackensack, N.J.)

nonverbal communication

99

table 5–2 some meanings of silence

Agreement	Disagreement ("Silent Treatment.")
Thoughtfulness	Ignorance
Revelation (We often say much about the people we are describing by what we choose to omit.)	Secrecy ("If he didn't have something to hide, he'd speak up.")
Warmth (Bind the participants.)	Coldness (Separate the participants.)
Submission	Attack (Not answering a letter—or worse, not answering a comment directed at you.)
Gaining attention	Boredom
Consideration	Inconsideration

Reprinted with permission from Mark L. Knapp, *Interpersonal Communication and Human Relationships* (Boston: Allyn & Bacon, 1984).

When you do try to make sense out of ambiguous nonverbal behavior, you need to consider several factors: The *context* in which they occur (e.g., smiling at a joke suggests a different feeling from what is suggested by smiling at another's misfortune); the *history of your relationship* with the sender (friendly, hostile, etc.); *the other's mood* at the time; and *your feelings* (when you're feeling insecure, almost anything can seem like a threat). The important idea is that when you become aware of nonverbal messages, you should think of them not as facts, but as *clues* that need to be checked out.

much nonverbal communication is culture-bound

Besides nonverbal communication being ambiguous, it also varies from one culture to another. Depending on your background, you may interpret a particular nonverbal behavior differently from someone who was raised in other circumstances. Also, the meaning you attribute to a particular nonverbal behavior may be the same meaning attributed to some *other* nonverbal behavior by a member of a culture different from yours. Finally, although a particular nonverbal behavior may have meaning for you, in another culture it may be perceived as little more than idiosyncratic or random behavior.

A quick look at many cultures shows the diversity of nonverbal behaviors.[2] Consider the expression of affection, for example. As members of contemporary Western civilization, we are used to embracing and kissing as signs of deepest caring. But to Mongols, the same feelings would be expressed by smelling heads; to Burmese, by pressing mouths and noses upon the other's cheek and inhaling strongly; and to Samoans, by juxtaposing noses and smelling heartily. Salutation behavior is just as varied: Polynesians stroke their own faces with the other person's hands, Lapps and Malays smell each others' cheeks, and the Dahomeans snap fingers.

Before you jump to the conclusion that examples like these are only important to anthropologists, consider the importance of understanding cross-cultural communication in this time of frequent international communication. Take, for instance, the differences between the cultural conventions of North Americans and Arabs.[3] To the former, one unstated rule about nonverbal communication is that a speaker maintains occasional eye contact with a listener, looking away from time to time during a conversation. To most Arabs, however, a greater degree of eye contact is considered normal and acceptable. Another difference between the two cultures involves body orientation. Whereas Americans are comfortable speaking to others without facing them directly, Arabs consider anything less than total confrontation impolite. Given these differences, it's easy to see how uncomfortable an American and an Arab might be, each being unaware of the other's cultural norms, and how suspiciously they could regard one another. Whereas the American might view the Arab as pushy and aggressive, the Arab would think his North American counterpart aloof and unfriendly. Imagine these feelings present during an important political or economic meeting, and you will realize the importance of learning the nonverbal as well as the verbal languages of others with whom we deal.

Nonverbal communication operates in a number of ways. Although nonverbal cues often do operate independently of verbal messages, they more commonly relate to spoken words in one of several ways.

functions of nonverbal communication

1. **Repeating.** If someone asked you for directions to the nearest drugstore, you could say, "North of here about two blocks" and then repeat your instructions nonverbally by pointing north.
2. **Substituting.** When you see a familiar friend wearing a certain facial expression, you don't need to ask, "How's it going?" In the same way, experience has probably shown you that other kinds of looks, gestures, and other clues say, "I'm angry at you" or "I feel great" far better than words.
3. **Complementing.** If you saw a student talking to a teacher and his head was bowed slightly, his voice was low and hesitating, and he shuffled slowly from foot to foot, you might conclude that he felt inferior to the teacher, possibly embarrassed about something he did. The nonverbal behaviors you observed provided the context for the verbal behaviors—they conveyed the relationship between the teacher and student. Complementing nonverbal behaviors signal the attitudes the interactants have for one another.
4. **Accenting.** Just as we can use *italics* in print to underline an idea, we can emphasize some part of a face-to-face message in various ways. Pointing an accusing finger adds emphasis to criticism (as well as

probably creating defensiveness in the receiver). Shrugging shoulders accent confusion, and hugs can highlight excitement or affection. As you'll see later in this chapter, the voice plays a big role in accenting verbal messages.

5. **Regulating** By lowering your voice at the end of a sentence, "trailing off," you. indicate that the other person may speak. You can also convey this information through the use of eye contact and by the way you position your body.

6. **Contradicting.** People often simultaneously express different and even contradictory messages in their verbal and nonverbal behaviors. A common example of this sort of "double message" is the experience we've all had of hearing someone with a red face and bulging veins yelling, "Angry? No, *I'm not angry!*"

   Usually, however, the contradiction between words and nonverbal clues isn't this obvious. At times we all try to seem different from what we are. There are many reasons for this contradictory behavior: to cover nervousness when giving a speech or in a job interview, to keep someone from worrying about us, or to appear more attractive than we believe we really are.

Even though some of the ways in which people contradict themselves are subtle, double messages have a strong impact. Research suggests that when a receiver perceives an inconsistency between verbal and nonverbal messages, the unspoken one carries more weight.[4] Table 5-3 lists situations in which double messages are most likely to be obvious.

table 5-3   leakage of nonverbal cues to deception

deception cues are most likely when the deceiver	deception cues are least likely when the deceiver
Wants to hide emotions being experienced at the moment.	Wants to hide information unrelated to his or her emotions.
Feels strongly about the information being hidden.	Has no strong feelings about the information being hidden.
Feels apprehensive about the deception.	Feels confident about the deception.
Feels guilty about being deceptive.	Experiences little guilt about the deception.
Gets little enjoyment from being deceptive.	Enjoys the deception.
Needs to construct the message carefully while delivering it.	Knows the deceptive message well and has rehearsed it.

Based on material from "Mistakes When Deceiving" by Paul Ekman, in Thomas A. Sebeok and Robert Rosenthal (eds.), *The Clever Hans Phenomenon: Communication with Horses, Whales, Apes, and People* (New York: New York Academy of Sciences, 1981), pp. 269–278.

Keeping these characteristics in mind, we can examine some of the specific types of nonverbal communication.

The first area of nonverbal communication we will survey is the broad field of *kinesics,* or body motion. In this section we will explore the role that posture, gestures, body orientation, facial expressions, and eye behaviors play in our relationships with each other.

posture

Posture is one type of kinesic communication. See for yourself: Stop reading for a moment, and notice how you are sitting. What does your position say nonverbally about how you feel? Are there any other people near you now? What messages do you get from their present posture?

The main reason we miss most posture messages is that they aren't very obvious. It's seldom that people who feel weighted down by a problem hunch over so much that they stand out in a crowd, and when we're bored, we usually don't lean back and slump enough to embarrass another person. In reading posture, then, look for small changes that might be shadows of the way people feel inside.

For example, a teacher who has a reputation for interesting classes told us how he uses his understanding of micropostures to do a better job. "Because of my large classes, I have to lecture a lot," he said, "and that's an easy way to turn students off. I work hard to make my talks entertaining, but you know that nobody's perfect, and I do have my off days. I can tell when I'm not doing a good job of communicating by picking out three or four students before I start my talk and watching how they sit throughout the class period. As long as they're leaning forward in their seats, I know I'm doing OK, but if I look up and see them starting to slump back, I know I'd better change my approach."

Psychologist Albert Mehrabian has found that other postural keys to feelings are tension and relaxation.[5] He says that we take relaxed postures in nonthreatening situations and tighten up when threatened. Based on this observation he says we can tell a good deal about how others feel simply by watching how tense or loose they seem to be. For example, he suggests that watching tenseness is a way of detecting status differences: The lower-status person is generally the more rigid, tense-appearing one whereas the one with higher status is more relaxed. This is the kind of situation that often happens when we picture a "chat" with the boss (or other authority figures), when we sit ramrod straight while the authority figure leans back, relaxed. The same principle applies to social situations, where it is often possible to tell who is uncomfortable by looking at postures. You may see people laughing and talking as if they were perfectly at home, but whose posture almost shouts nervousness. Some people never relax, and their posture shows it.

categories of nonverbal communication

Fie, fie upon her!
There's language in her
    eyes, her cheek, her lip.
Nay, her foot speaks; her
    wanton spirits look out at
    every joint and motive in
    her body.

William Shakespeare
Troilus and Cressida

Who's there? . . .
Stand, and
    unfold yourself.

William Shakespeare
Hamlet

nonverbal communication
103

Copr. © 1943 James Thurber. Copr. © 1971 Helen W. Thurber and Rosemary T. Sauers. From *The War Between Men and Women* in *My World and Welcome to It*, published by Harcourt Brace Jovanovich. Originally printed in *The New Yorker*.

gesture

Gestures are another source of nonverbal messages. In an article titled "Nonverbal Leakage and Clues to Deception" Paul Ekman and Wallace Friesen observed how gestures transmit emotions.[6] They explain that because most of us know, at least unconsciously, that the face is the most obvious channel of expressing emotions, we are especially careful to control our facial expressions when trying to hide our feelings. But most of us are less aware of the ways we move our hands, legs, and feet, and because of this these movements are better indicators of how we truly feel.

Probably the clearest example of those whose feelings are expressed through unconscious gestures is fidgeters. They are the kind of people who assure us that "everything is fine" while almost ceaselessly biting their fingernails, flicking their cigarette, bending paperclips, and so on. Even when fidgeters are aware of these gestures and try to control them, their nervousness usually finds another way of leaking out, as with toe tapping, leg crossing and uncrossing, or other restless movements.

Besides nervousness, you can often detect other emotions from a person's gestures. It's possible to observe anger by looking beyond a smile and noticing the whitened knuckles and clenched fists. When people would like to express their friendship or attraction toward us, but for some reason feel they can't, we can sometimes notice them slightly reaching out or maybe even opening their hands. Albert Scheflen describes how a person's sexual feelings can be signaled through gestures.[7] He describes "preening behaviors" that draw attention to the sender's body and advertise a "come-on" message. Movements such as stroking or combing their hair, glancing in a mirror, and rearranging the clothing are sometimes signals of sexual interest in another person. (It's important not to overemphasize the sexual angle: Such gestures also are more general signals of interest in the topic of conversation or one's partner.)

Ekman and Friesen describe another kind of double message—the "lie of omission." These deceivers nonverbally show their true feelings by failing to accompany their words with the appropriate gestures. This is the kind of behavior we see from a person who talks about being excited or happy while sitting almost motionless with hands, arms, legs, and posture signaling boredom, discomfort, or fatigue. In addition to sending double messages, gestures play other roles—repeating, substituting, complementing, accenting, and regulating in conversations.

face and eyes

The face and eyes are probably the most noticed parts of the body, but this doesn't mean that their nonverbal messages are the easiest to read. The face is a tremendously complicated channel of expression for several reasons.

First, it is hard even to describe the number and kinds of expressions we commonly produce with our face and eyes. For example, researchers have found that there are at least eight distinguishable positions of the eyebrows and forehead, eight more of the eyes and lids, and ten for the lower face. When you multiply this complexity by the number of emotions we experience, you can see why it would be almost impossible to compile a dictionary of facial expressions and their corresponding emotions.

Another reason for the difficulty in understanding facial expressions is the speed with which they can change. For example, slow-motion films have been taken that show expressions fleeting across a subject's face in as short a time as a fifth of a second. Also, it seems that different emotions show most clearly in different parts of the face: happiness and surprise in the eyes and lower face, anger in the lower face and brows and forehead, fear and sadness in the eyes, and disgust in the lower face.

Ekman and Friesen have identified six basic emotions that facial expressions reflect—surprise, fear, anger, disgust, happiness, and sadness.[8] Expressions reflecting these feelings seem to be recognizable in and between members of all cultures. Of course, affect blends—the combination of two or more expressions in different parts of the face—are possible. For instance, it's easy to imagine how someone would look who is fearful and surprised or disgusted and angry.

Research also indicates that people are quite accurate at judging facial expressions of these emotions.[9] Accuracy increases when judges know the "target" or have knowledge of the context in which the expression occurs or when they have seen several samples of the target's expressions.

Pleads he in earnest?—Look
upon his face,
His eyes do drop no tears; his
prayers are jest;
His words come from his
mouth; ours, from our
breast;
He prays but faintly, and
would be denied;
We pray with heart and soul.

Shakespeare
Richard II

"An enormous face, more than a meter wide: the face of a man of about forty-five, with a heavy black mustache and ruggedly handsome features . . . gazed down from every commanding corner." The caption: "BIG BROTHER IS WATCHING YOU."

"It was terribly dangerous to let your thoughts wander when you were in any public place or within range of a telescreen. The smallest thing could give you away. A nervous tic, an unconscious look of anxiety, a habit of muttering to yourself—anything that carried with it the suggestion of abnormality, of having something to hide. In any case, to wear an improper expression on your face (to look incredulous when a victory was announced, for example) was itself a punishable offense. There was even a word for it in Newspeak: *facecrime*, it was called."

George Orwell
1984

In spite of the complex way in which the face shows emotions, you can still pick up messages by watching it. One of the easiest ways is to look for expressions that seem to be overdone. Often when people are trying to fool themselves or someone else they will emphasize this mask to a point where it seems too exaggerated to be true. Another way to detect people's feelings is by watching their expression at moments when they aren't likely to be thinking about appearances. Everyone has had the experience of glancing into another car while stopped in a traffic jam or looking around at a sporting event and seeing expressions that the wearer would probably never show in more guarded moments. At other times it's possible to watch a microexpression as it flashes across a person's face. For just a moment we see a flash of emotion quite different from the one a speaker is trying to convey. Finally, you may be able to spot contradictory expressions on different parts of someone's face: The eyes say one thing, but the expression of the mouth or eyebrows might be sending quite a different message.

The eyes themselves can send several kinds of messages. In our culture meeting someone's glance with your eyes is usually a sign of involvement whereas looking away signals a desire to avoid contact. This is why solicitors on the street—panhandlers, salespeople, petitioners—try to catch our eye. Once they've managed to establish contact with a glance, it becomes harder for the approached person to draw away. A friend explained how to apply this principle to hitchhiking. "When I'm hitching a ride, I'm always careful to look each driver in the eye as he or she comes toward me. Most of them will try to look somewhere else as they pass, but if I can catch somebody's eye, that person will almost always stop." Most of us remember trying to avoid a question we didn't understand by glancing away from the teacher. At times like these we usually became very interested in our textbooks, fingernails, the clock—anything but the teacher's stare. Of course, the teacher always seemed to know the meaning of this nonverbal behavior and ended up picking on those of us who signaled uncertainty.

voice

The voice itself is another channel of nonverbal communication. Social scientists use the term *paralanguage* to describe nonverbal, vocal messages. If you think about it for a moment, you'll realize that a certain way of speaking can give the same word or words many meanings. For example, look at the possible meanings from a single sentence just by changing the word emphasis:

This is a fantastic communication book.
(Not just any book, but *this* one in particular.)

This is a *fantastic* communication book.
(This book is superior, exciting.)

This is a fantastic *communication* book.
(The book is good as far as communication goes; it may not be so great as literature or drama.)

This is a fantastic communication *book*.
(It's not a play or record, it's a book.)

There are many other ways our voice communicates—through its tone, speed, pitch, volume, number and length of pauses, and disfluencies (such as stammering, use of "uh," "um," "er," and so on). All these factors can do a great deal to reinforce or contradict the message our words convey.

Sarcasm is one instance in which both emphasis and tone of voice help change a statement's meaning to the opposite of its verbal message. Experience this yourself with the following three statements. The first time through, say them literally, and then say them sarcastically.

Darling, what a beautiful little gown!

I really had a wonderful time on my blind date.

There's nothing I like better than calves' brains on toast.

touch

Besides being the earliest means we have of making contact with others, touching is essential to our healthy development. During the nineteenth and early twentieth centuries many babies died from a disease then called *marasmus,* which, translated from Greek, means "wasting away." In some orphanages the mortality rate was quite high, but even children in "progressive" homes, hospitals, and other institutions died regularly from the ailment. When researchers finally tracked down the causes of this disease, they found that many infants suffered from lack of physical contact with parents or nurses rather than poor nutrition, medical care, or other factors. They hadn't been touched enough, and as a result they died. From this knowledge came the practice of "mothering" children in institutions—picking the baby up, carrying it

The derivation of the word "personality" proves that there was originally a profound understanding of the close connection between voice and personality. The word comes from the Latin *persona,* which originally meant the mouthpiece of a mask used by actors (persona: the sound of the voice passes through). From phe mask the term shifted to the actor, the "person" in drama. The word eventually came to mean any person and finally "personality," but over the centuries it lost its symbolic connection with the voice.

Paul Moses, M.D.
The Voice of Neurosis

The unconscious parental feelings communicated through touch or lack of touch can lead to feelings of confusion and conflict in a child. Sometimes a ''modern'' parent will say all the right things but not want to touch his child very much. The child's confusion comes from the inconsistency of levels: if they really approve of me so much like they say they do, why won't they touch me?

William Schutz
Here Comes Everybody

around, and handling it several times each day. At one hospital that began this practice the death rate for infants fell from between 30 and 35 percent to below 10 percent.[10]

As a child develops, the need for being touched continues. In his book *Touching: The Human Significance of the Skin,* Ashley Montagu describes research that suggests that allergies, eczema, and other health problems are in part caused by a person's lack of contact as an infant with his or her mother.[11] Although Montagu says that these problems develop early in life, he also cites cases where adults suffering from conditions as diverse as asthma and schizophrenia have been successfully treated by psychiatric therapy that uses extensive physical contact.

Touch seems to increase a child's mental functioning as well as physical health. L. J. Yarrow has conducted surveys that show that babies who have been given plenty of physical stimulation by their mothers have significantly higher IQs than those receiving less contact.[12]

Touch can communicate many messages. In addition to the nurturing/caring function we just discussed, it can signify many relationships:[13]

functional/professional (dental exam, haircut)

social/polite (handshake)

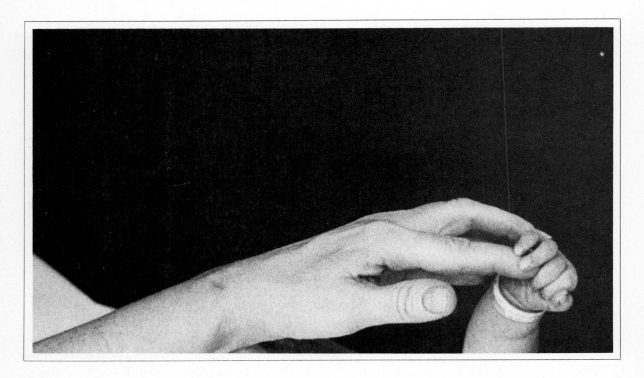

108

In our now more than slightly cockeyed world, there seems to be little provision for someone to get touched without having to go to bed with whomever does the touching. And that's something to think about. We have mixed up simple, healing, warm touching with sexual advances. So much so, that it often seems as if there is no middle way between "Don't you dare touch me!" and "Okay, you touched me, so now we should make love!"

A nation which is able to distinguish the fine points between offensive and defensive pass interference, bogies, birdies, and par, a schuss and a slalom, a technical, a personal, and a player-control foul should certainly be able to make some far more obvious distinctions between various sorts of body contact.

Sidney Simon
Caring, Feeling, Touching

friendship/warmth (clap on back, Spanish *abrazo*)

love/intimacy (some caresses, hugs)

sexual arousal (some kisses, strokes)*

You might object to the examples following each of these categories, saying that some nonverbal behaviors occur in several types of relationship. A kiss, for example, can mean anything from a polite but superficial greeting to the most intense arousal. What makes a given touch more or less intense? Researchers have suggested a number of factors:

what part of the body does the touching

what part of the body is touched

how long the touch lasts

how much pressure is used

whether there is movement after contact is made

whether anyone else is present

the situation in which the touch occurs

the relationship between the persons involved

From this list you can see that there is, indeed, a complex language of touch. As nonverbal messages are inherently ambiguous, it's no surprise that this language can often be misunderstood. Is a hug playful or suggestive of stronger feelings? Is a touch on the shoulder a friendly gesture or an attempt at domination? Research suggests the interpretation can depend on a variety of factors, including the sex of the people involved, ethnic background, and marital status, among others.

* Other types of touch can indicate varying degrees of aggression.

clothing

Besides protecting us from catching colds, clothes can be decorative, a means of identification with groups, devices for sexual attraction, indicators of status, markers of certain roles, and even means of concealment. Clothes communicate some of these functions far more clearly than others. For instance, there's little doubt that someone dressed in a uniform, wearing a badge, and carrying handcuffs and a gun is a police officer. On the other hand, though wrinkled, ill-fitting, dirty old clothes might be a sign that the wearer is a destitute drifter, they might also be the outfit of a worker on vacation, a normally stylish person who is on the way to clean a fireplace, of an emotionally upset person, or even of an eccentric millionaire.

In spite of the ambiguity of clothing as a means of communication, people do intentionally send messages about themselves by what they

"A general! Goodness gracious, you don't look like a general!"
Drawing by Richter; © 1968 The New Yorker Magazine, Inc.

wear, and we make interpretations about others on this basis. Think about the people you know. See if you can tell anything about their personal attitudes or social philosophies by the way they dress.

proxemics

Proxemics is the study of the way people and animals use space.

Anthropologist Edward T. Hall has defined four distances that we use in our everyday lives.[14] He says that we choose a particular distance depending on how we feel toward the other person at a given time, the context of the conversation, and our personal goals. (These distance zones describe the behavior of North Americans and don't necessarily apply to members of other cultures.)

Intimate distance The first of Hall's zones begins with skin contact and ranges out to about eighteen inches. The most obvious context for intimate distance involves interaction with people to whom we're emotionally close—and then mostly in private situations—making love, roughhousing playfully, comforting, and protecting. Intimate distance between individuals also occurs in less intimate circumstances: visiting the doctor or dentist, at the hairdresser's, and during some athletic contests. Allowing someone to move into the intimate zone usually is a sign of trust, an indication that we've willingly lowered our defenses. On the other hand, when someone invades this most personal area without our consent, we usually feel threatened. This explains the discomfort that sometimes comes with being forced into crowded places such as buses or elevators with strangers. At times like these the standard behavior in our society is to draw away or tense the muscles and avoid contact. This is a nonverbal way of signaling "I don't like this invasion of personal territory, but the situation has forced it."

In courtship situations a critical moment usually occurs when one member of a couple first moves into the other's intimate zone. If the partner being approached does not retreat, this usually signals that the relationship is moving into a new stage. On the other hand, if the reaction to the advance is withdrawal to a greater distance, the initiator should get the message that it isn't yet time to get more intimate. We remember from our dating experiences the significance of where on the car seat our companions chose to sit. If they moved close to us, it meant one thing; if they stayed jammed against the opposite door, quite a different message was communicated.

Personal distance The second spatial zone, personal distance, ranges from eighteen inches at its closest point to four feet at its farthest. Its closer phase is the distance at which most couples stand in public. But if someone of the opposite sex stands this near one partner at a party, the other partner is likely to feel uncomfortable. This "moving in" often is taken to mean that something more than casual conversation is tak-

Once I heard a hospital nurse describing doctors. She said there were beside-the-bed doctors, who were interested in the patient, and foot-of-the-bed doctors, who were interested in the patient's condition. They unconsciously expressed their emotional involvement—or lack of it—by where they stood.

Edward Hall

Some thirty inches from my
 nose
The frontier of my Person
 goes,
And all the untilled air
 between
Is private pagus or demesne.
Stranger, unless with
 bedroom eyes
I beckon you to fraternize,
Beware of rudely crossing it:
I have no gun, but I can spit.

W. H. Auden

111

The interrogator should sit fairly close to the subject, and between the two there should be no table, desk, or other piece of furniture. Distance or the presence of an obstruction of any sort constitutes a serious psychological barrier and also affords the subject a certain degree of relief and confidence not otherwise attainable. . . .

As to the psychological validity of the above suggested seating arrangement, reference may be made to the commonplace but yet meaningful expressions such as "getting next" to a person, or the "buttonholing" of a customer by a salesman. These expressions signify that when a person is close to another one physically, he is closer to him psychologically. Anything such as a desk or a table between the interrogator and the subject defeats the purpose and should be avoided.

Inbau and Reid
Criminal Interrogation and Confessions

ing place. The far range of personal distance runs from about two and a half to four feet. It's the zone just beyond the other person's reach. As Hall puts it, at this distance we can keep someone "at arm's length." This choice of words suggests the type of communication that goes on at this range: The contacts are still reasonably close, but they're much less personal than the ones that occur a foot or so closer.

Test this for yourself. Start a conversation with someone at a distance of about three feet, then slowly move a foot or so closer. Do you notice a difference? Does the distance affect your conversation?

Social distance The third zone is social distance. It ranges from four to about twelve feet out. Within it are the kinds of communication that usually occur in business situations. Its closer phase, from four to seven feet, is the distance at which conversations usually occur between salespeople and customers and between people who work together. Most people feel uncomfortable when a salesclerk comes as close as three feet whereas four or five feet nonverbally signals, "I'm here to help you, but I don't mean to be too personal or pushy."

We use the far range of social distance—seven to twelve feet—for more formal and impersonal situations. This is the range at which we generally sit from our boss. Sitting at this distance signals a far different and less relaxed type of conversation than if we were to pull a chair around to the boss's side of the desk and sit only three or so feet away.

Public distance *Public distance* is Hall's term for the farthest zone, running outward from twelve feet. The closer range of public distance is the one most teachers use in the classroom. In the farther reaches of public space—twenty-five feet and beyond—two-way communication becomes difficult. In some cases it's necessary for speakers to use public distance owing to the size of their audience, but we can assume that anyone who voluntarily chooses to use it when he or she could be closer is not interested in having a dialog.

Physical invasion isn't the only way people penetrate our spatial bubble; we're just as uncomfortable when someone intrudes on our visual territory. If you've had the unpleasant experience of being stared at, you know this can be just as threatening as having someone get too close. In most situations, however, people respect each other's visual privacy. You can test this the next time you're walking in public. As you approach other people, notice how they shift their glance away from you at a distance of a few paces, almost like a visual dimming of headlights. Generally, strangers maintain eye contact at a close distance only when they want something—information, assistance, signatures on a petition, recognition, a handout.

territoriality

Whereas personal space is the invisible bubble we carry around as an extension of our physical being, "territory" is fixed space. Any geographical area such as a room, house, neighborhood, or country to which we assume some kind of "rights" is our territory. What's interesting about territoriality is that there is no real basis for the assumption of proprietary rights of "owning" some area, but the feeling of "owning" exists nonetheless. Your room in the house is *your room* whether you're there or not (unlike personal space, which is carried around with you), and it's your room because you say it is. Although you could probably make a case for your room's *really being* your room (and not the family's or the mortgage holder's), what about the desk you sit at in each class? You feel the same way about the desk, that it's yours, even though it's certain that the desk is owned by the school and is in no way really yours.

The way people use space can communicate a good deal about power and status relationships. Generally we grant people with higher status more personal territory and greater privacy.[15] We knock before entering our boss's office whereas a supervisor can usually walk into our work area without hesitating. In traditional schools, professors have offices, dining rooms, and even toilets that are private whereas the students, who are presumably less important, have no such sanctuaries. In the military, greater space and privacy usually come with rank: Privates sleep forty to a barracks, sergeants have their own private rooms, and generals have government-provided houses.

environment

A large amount of research that shows how the design of an environment can shape the kind of communication that takes place in it. In one experiment at Brandeis University, researchers found that the attractiveness of a room influenced the happiness and energy of people working in it.[16] The experimenters set up three rooms: an "ugly" one, which resembled a janitor's closet in the basement of a campus building; an "av-

A good house is planned from the inside out. First, you decide what it has to do for its occupants. Then, you let the functions determine the form. The more numerous and various those functions, the more responsive and interesting the house should be. And it may not look at all like you expect.

Dan MacMasters
Los Angeles Times

erage" room, which was a professor's office; and a "beautiful" room, which was furnished with carpeting, drapes, and comfortable furniture. The subjects in the experiment were asked to rate a series of pictures as a way of measuring their energy and feelings of well-being while at work. Results of the experiment showed that while in the ugly room the subjects became tired and bored more quickly and took longer to complete their task. When they moved to the beautiful room, however, they rated the faces they were judging higher, showed a greater desire to work, and expressed feelings of importance, comfort, and enjoyment. The results teach a lesson that isn't surprising: Workers generally feel better and do a better job when they're in an attractive environment.

Many business people show an understanding of how environment can influence communication. Robert Sommer, a leading environmental psychologist, described several such cases in his book *Personal Space: The Behavioral Basis for Design*. He pointed out that dim lighting, subdued noise levels, and comfortable seats encourage people to spend more time in a restaurant or bar.[17] Knowing this, the management can control the amount of customer turnover. If the goal is to run a

Copr. © 1943 James Thurber. Copr. © 1971 Helen W. Thurber and Rosemary T. Sauers. From *The War Between Men and Women* in *My World and Welcome to It*, published by Harcourt Brace Jovanovich. Originally printed in *The New Yorker*.

Campuses are full of conscious and unconscious architectural symbolism. While the colleges at Santa Cruz evoke images of Italian hill towns as they might have been if the peasants had concrete, the administration building is another story. It appears to anticipate the confrontations between students and administration that marked the sixties. At Santa Cruz, administrative offices are located in a two-story building whose rough sloped concrete base with narrow slit windows gives it the look of a feudal shogun's palace. The effect is heightened by the bridge and landscaped moat that one crosses to enter the building. "Four administrators in there could hold off the entire campus," joked one student.

Sym Van Der Ryn
Chief Architect, State of California

high-volume business that tries to move people in and out quickly, it's necessary to keep the lights shining brightly and not worry too much about soundproofing. On the other hand, if the goal is to keep customers in the bar or restaurant for a long time, the proper technique is to lower the lighting and use absorbent building materials that will keep down the noise level.

Furniture design can control the amount of time a person spends in an environment too. From this knowledge came the Larsen chair, which was designed for Copenhagen restaurant owners who felt their customers were occupying their seats too long without spending enough money. The chair is constructed to put an uncomfortable pressure on the sitter's back if occupied for more than a few minutes. (We suspect that many people who are careless in buying furniture for their homes get much the same result without trying. One environmental psychologist we know refuses to buy a chair or couch without sitting in it for at least half an hour to test its comfort.)

In a more therapeutic and less commercial way, physicians have also shaped environments to improve communication. Sommer found that redesigning the convalescent ward of a hospital greatly increased the interaction among patients. In the old design, seats were placed shoulder to shoulder around the edges of the ward. When the chairs were grouped around small tables so that patients faced each other at a comfortable distance, the amount of conversations doubled.[18]

The design of an entire building can shape communication among its users. Architects have learned that the way housing projects are designed controls to a great extent the contact neighbors have with each other. People who live in apartments near stairways and mailboxes have many more neighbor contacts than do those living in less heavily traveled parts of the building, and tenants generally have more contacts with immediate neighbors than with people even a few doors away.[19] Architects now use this information to design buildings that either encourage communication or increase privacy, and house hunters can use the same knowledge to choose a home that gives them the neighborhood relationships they want.

So far we have talked about how designing an environment can shape communication, but there is another side to consider. Watching how people use an already existing environment can be a way of telling what kind of relationships they want. For example, Sommer watched students in a college library and found that there's a definite pattern for people who want to study alone. While the library was uncrowded, students almost always chose corner seats at one of the empty rectangular tables.[20] Finally each table was occupied by one reader. New readers would then choose a seat on the opposite side and far end of an occupied table, thus keeping the maximum distance between themselves and the other readers. One of Sommer's associates tried violating these "rules" by sitting next to and across from other female readers when more distant seats were available. She found that the approached women reacted defensively, either by signaling their discomfort through shifts in posture or gesturing or by eventually moving away.

summary

Nonverbal communication consists of messages expressed by nonlinguistic means. Thus, it is inaccurate to say that all wordless expressions are nonverbal or that all spoken statements are totally verbal.

There are several important characteristics of nonverbal communication. First is the simple fact that it exists—that communication occurs even in the absence of language. This leads to the second principle, namely, that it is impossible not to communicate nonverbally; humans constantly send messages about themselves that are available for others to receive. The third principle is that nonverbal communication is ambiguous; that there are many possible interpretations for any behavior. This ambiguity makes it important for the receiver to verify any interpretation before jumping to conclusions about the meaning of a nonverbal message. The fourth principle states that much nonverbal communication is culture-bound. In other words, behaviors that have special meanings in one culture may express different messages in another. Finally, we stated that nonverbal communication serves many functions: repeating, substituting, complementing, accenting, regulating, and contradicting verbal behavior.

The remainder of this chapter introduced the many ways humans communicate nonverbally: through posture, gesture, use of the face and eyes, voice, touch, clothing, distance, territoriality, and physical environment.

activities

1. This exercise will both increase your skill in observing nonverbal behavior and show you the dangers of being too sure that you're a perfect reader of body language. You can try the exercise either in or out of class, and the period of time over which you do it is flexible, from a single-class period to several days. In any case, begin by choosing a partner, and then follow these directions:

   a. For the first period of time (however long you decide to make it), observe the way your partner behaves. Notice how he or she moves, his or her mannerisms, postures, way of speaking, how he or she dresses, and so on. To remember your observations, jot them down. If you're doing this exercise out of class over an extended period of time, there's no need to let your observations interfere with whatever you'd normally be doing: Your only job here is to compile a list of your partner's behaviors. In this step you should be careful <u>not</u> to interpret your partner's actions; just record what you <u>see</u>.

   b. At the end of the time period, share what you've seen with your partner. He or she will do the same with you.

   c. For the next period of time, your job is not only to observe your partner's behavior but also to <u>interpret</u> it. This time in your conference you should tell your partner what you thought his or her actions revealed. For example, if your partner dressed carelessly, did you think this meant he or she overslept, that he or she is losing interest in his or her appearance, or that he or she was trying to be more comfortable? If you noticed him or her yawning frequently, did you think this meant he or she was bored, tired from a late night, or sleepy after a big meal? Don't feel bad if your guesses weren't all correct. Remember, nonverbal clues tend to be ambiguous. You may be surprised how checking out the nonverbal clues you observe can help build a relationship with another person.

2. Use your own nonverbal behavior and that of others to provide examples of each function:

   a. Repeating
   b. Substituting
   c. Complimenting
   d. Accenting
   e. Regulating
   f. Contradicting

3. Explore the significance of nonverbal behavior by violating some cultural rules that govern appropriate communication. *Note:* Be sure your violations aren't so extreme that they generate a harmful reaction.

Commit one violation in each of the following areas:

a. Eye contact
b. Vocal cues
c. Touch
d. Clothing
e. Distance
f. Territoriality

Report the results of your experiments in class.

notes

1. For a survey of the issues surrounding the definition of nonverbal communication, see Mark Knapp, *Nonverbal Communication in Human Interaction,* 2d ed. (Englewood Cliffs, N.J.: Prentice-Hall, 1978), pp. 2–12.
2. Maurice M. Krout, "Symbolism," in Haig A. Bosmajian (ed.), *The Rhetoric of Nonverbal Communication* (Glenview, Ill.: Scott, Foresman, 1971), pp. 19–22.
3. Edward T. Hall, *The Hidden Dimension* (Garden City, N.Y.: Anchor, 1969), pp. 160–161.
4. Knapp, op. cit., p. 22.
5. Albert Mehrabian, *Silent Messages,* 2d ed. (Belmont, Calif.: Wadsworth, 1981), pp. 47–48.
6. Paul Ekman and Wallace V. Friesen, "Nonverbal Leakage and Clues to Deception," *Psychiatry* 32 (1969): 88–106.
7. Albert E. Scheflen, "Quasi-Courtship Behavior in Psychotherapy," *Psychiatry* 28 (1965): 245–257.
8. Paul Ekman and Wallace V. Friesen, *Unmasking the Face* (Englewood Cliffs, N.J.: Prentice-Hall, 1975).
9. Paul Ekman, Wallace V. Friesen, and P. Ellsworth, *Emotion in the Human Face: Guidelines for Research and an Integration of Findings* (Elmsford, N.Y.: Pergamon, 1972).
10. Ashley Montagu, *Touching: The Human Significance of the Skin* (New York: Harper & Row, 1972), p. 93.
11. Ibid., pp. 244–249.
12. Ibid., pp. 216–217.
13. Richard Heslin and Tari Alper, "Touch: A Bonding Gesture," in John M. Wiemann and Randall Harrison (eds.), *Nonverbal Interaction* (Beverly Hills, Calif.: Sage, 1983).
14. Hall, op. cit., pp. 113–130.
15. Mehrabian, op. cit., p. 69.
16. A. H. Maslow and N. L. Mintz, "Effects of Esthetic Surroundings," *Journal of Psychology* 41 (1956): 247–254.
17. Robert Sommer, *Personal Space: The Behavioral Basis of Design* (Englewood Cliffs, N.J.: Spectrum), pp. 122–123.
18. Leon Festinger, S. Schachter, and K. Back, *Social Pressures in Informal Groups: A Study of Human Factors in Housing* (New York: Harper & Row, 1950).
19. Sommer, op. cit., p. 78.
20. Ibid., p. 35.

part 2 interpersonal communication

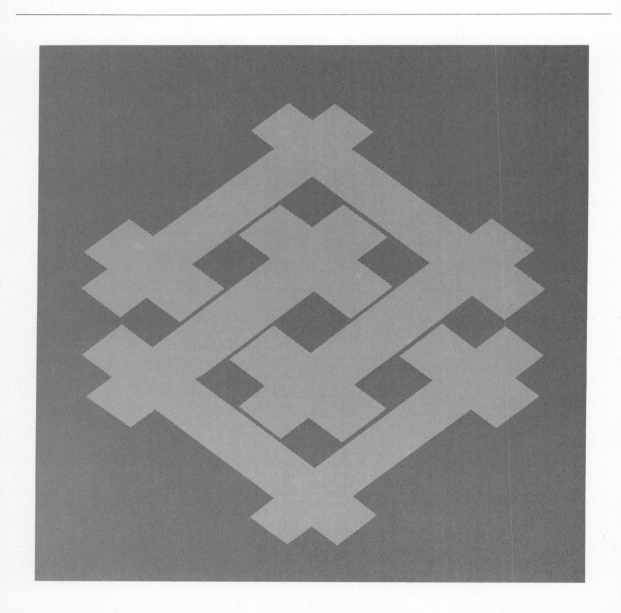

six

understanding interpersonal relationships

After reading this chapter, you should understand:

1. How interpersonal relationships can be defined in terms of breadth and depth.
2. The content and relational dimensions of interpersonal messages.
3. The seven reasons for forming relationships discussed in this chapter.
4. The stages of relational development and dissolution outlined in this chapter.
5. How the Johari Window describes self-disclosure and self-knowledge.
6. The four levels of self-disclosure outlined in this chapter.
7. The characteristics of interpersonal conflict.
8. The characteristics of nonassertion, direct aggression, indirect aggression, and assertion.
9. The characteristics of win-lose, lose-lose, and win-win conflict resolution.

You should be able to:

1. Identify the breadth and depth of your interpersonal relationships.
2. Identify the content and relational dimensions of an interpersonal message.
3. Analyze the reasons you have formed significant interpersonal relationships.
4. Describe your self-disclosure with another person by using the Johari Window model.
5. Develop messages to a significant other on the levels of clichés, facts, opinions, and feelings.
6. Describe nonassertive, directly aggressive, indirectly aggressive, and assertive communication in a conflict situation.
7. Use the win-win problem-solving method whenever appropriate.

"Relationship" is one of those words people use a great deal, yet have a hard time defining. See if you can explain the term before reading on: It isn't as easy as it might seem.

The dictionary defines a relationship as "the mode in which two or more things stand to one another." This is true enough: You are tall in relation to some people and short in relation to others, and we are more or less wealthy only in comparison to others. But physical and economic relationships don't tell us much that is useful about interpersonal communication.

Interpersonal relationships involve the way people deal with one another *socially.* But what is it about their social interaction that defines a relationship? What makes some relationships "good" and others "bad"? We can answer this question by recalling the three kinds of social needs introduced in Chapter 1: inclusion, control, and affection. When we judge the quality of personal relationships, we are usually describing how well those social needs are being met. Having come this far, we can define the term *interpersonal relationship* as an association in which the parties meet each other's social needs to a greater or lesser degree.

In this chapter we will take a close look at the nature of interpersonal relationships. You will see that almost every exchange of messages between two people has a social dimension. You will read a number of explanations for why we form positive relationships with some people and not with others. You'll learn and practice some messages that can build the strength and quality of relationships, and you will read about other ways of communicating that can weaken the bonds between people. Finally, we will examine the subject of self-disclosure, looking at its effects on interpersonal relationships and offering guidelines about when it is and is not appropriate.

characteristics of relational communication

Because we define, maintain, and change relationships by communicating with one another, a good place to begin is by looking at the types of messages that affect relationships.

breadth and depth

One way to look at relationships is in terms of their scope or magnitude. Some relationships are rich and intense, and others are superficial and almost meaningless.

Social psychologists Irwin Altman and Dalmas Taylor developed a model that shows two ways in which a relationship can be more or less intimate.[1] These authors suggest that relationships develop in increments, moving from superficial to more personal levels. As two people learn more about each other, primarily through the process of self-disclosure, the relationship gains importance. Depending on the *breadth* of the information shared (for example, the number of topics

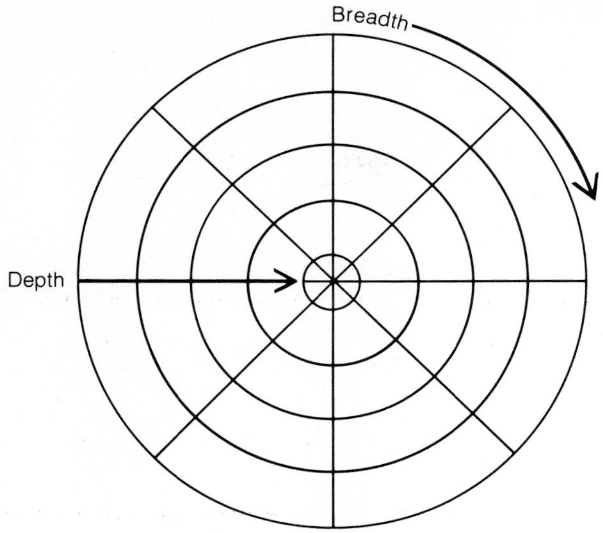

figure 6-1
Social penetration model

you discuss) and the *depth* of that information, a relationship can be defined as casual or intimate. In the case of a casual relationship, the breadth may be high, but not the depth. A more intimate relationship is likely to have high breadth and high depth. Altman and Taylor visualize these two factors as an image of concentric circles (see Figure 6-1). Depth increases as you disclose information that is central to the relationship, information not available unless you provide it, for example, your personal goals, fears, and self-images. Altman and Taylor see relationship development as a progression from the periphery to the center of the circle, a process that typically occurs over time.

Based on this model of *social penetration,* you can visualize a diagram in which a husband's relationship with his wife has high breadth and high depth, his relationship with his friend has low breadth and high depth, and his relationship with his boss is one of low breadth-low depth. Imagine what your own relationship with various people would look like. Figure 6-2 provides one example.

The social penetration model is useful in two ways. First, it can help you identify why certain relationships are strong or weak. If your communication with another person lacks sufficient breadth or depth, for example, it should not be surprising that there is little to hold you together; and if you want to increase those bonds, the Altman-Taylor model shows you the kinds of communication that are necessary.

Another benefit of the theory is its emphasis on the fact that breadth and depth usually occur in small stages over time. According to the theory, relationships that proceed rapidly to central areas can be quite fragile. For example, experiences such as a "one-night stand" of sexual intimacy often lack the personal knowledge in other areas that builds understanding and trust. Without a buildup of communication in other

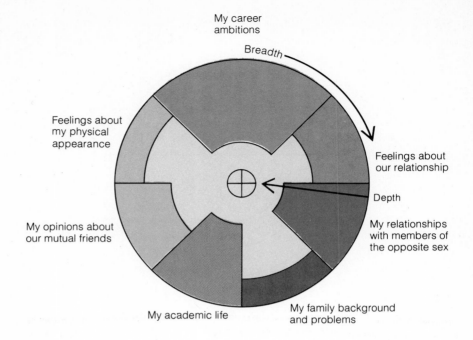

figure 6-2

Sample model of social penetration illustrating a college student's relationship with a friend

My career ambitions

Breadth

Feelings about my physical appearance

Feelings about our relationship

Depth

My opinions about our mutual friends

My relationships with members of the opposite sex

My academic life

My family background and problems

areas, the relationship is likely to crumble at the first strain. We'll have more to say about the importance of self-disclosure later in this chapter.

content and relational messages

The most obvious component of most messages is their *content*—the subject being discussed. The content of messages such as "It's your turn to do the dishes" or "Let's get together Saturday night" is obvious.

Content messages aren't the only information being exchanged when two people communicate. In addition, almost every message—both verbal and nonverbal—also has a second, *relational* dimension, which makes statements about how the parties feel toward one another.[2] These relational messages deal with one or more of the social needs we have been discussing. Consider the two examples we just mentioned:

- Imagine two ways of saying, "It's your turn to do the dishes": One that is demanding and another that is matter-of-fact. Notice how the different nonverbal messages make statements about how the sender views control in this part of the relationship. The demanding tone says, in effect, "I have a right to tell you what to do around the house," whereas the matter-of-fact one suggests, "I'm just reminding you of something you might have overlooked."

- You can easily visualize two ways to deliver the statement "I'm busy Saturday night": one with little affection and the other with much liking.

Most conversations seem to be carried out on two levels, the verbal level and the emotional level. The verbal level contains those things which are socially acceptable to say, but it is used as a means of satisfying emotional needs. Yesterday a friend related something that someone had done to her. I told her why I thought the person had acted the way he had and she became very upset and started arguing with me. Now, the reason is clear. I had been listening to her words and had paid no attention to her feelings. Her words had described how terribly this other person had treated her, but her emotions had been saying, "Please understand how I felt. Please accept my feeling the way I did." The last thing she wanted to hear from me was an explanation of the other person's behavior.

Hugh Prather

Notice that in each of these examples the relational dimension of the message was never discussed. In fact, most of the time we aren't conscious of the many relational messages that bombard us every day. Sometimes we are unaware of relational messages because they match our belief about the amount of respect, inclusion, control, and affection that is appropriate. For example, you probably won't be offended if your boss tells you to do a certain job because you agree that supervisors have the right to direct employees. There are other cases, however, when conflicts arise over relational messages even though content is not disputed. We can see this by returning to a previous example. At home you might object to the reminder "It's your turn to do the dishes," not because of the content (it may be your turn, after all), but because to you the comment sounds too much like an order or reprimand. "Lay off," you might think. "You're not my boss."

The abundance of relational messages means that we have a constant source of clues about how others regard us. It's important to realize, however, that our hunches about relational messages are interpretations, not facts, and that these perceptions might be mistaken. Your friend's yawn at the conclusion of your story might be a sign of boredom (low inclusion)—or it might be the result of a late night. Before you jump to conclusions about relational clues, it's a good idea to share your interpretation to see if it is accurate. For instance: "When you tell me it's my turn to do the dishes, I get the idea you think I ought to do them now and not later tonight—that you think I'm a slob, and that you want me to clean up my act. Is that right?" If your interpretation was indeed correct, you can talk about the control issues. On the other hand, if you were overreacting, the perception check can prevent a needless fight.

Why do we start to develop relationships with some people and prefer not to develop relationships with others? Social scientists have explored several possible reasons, each of which represents a theory of relationship formation and maintenance.[3]

reasons for forming relationships

"It would work with us, Francine. We share the same narrow personal interests and concerns."

Drawing by Dana Freden, © 1979 by *The New Yorker Magazine*, Inc.

we like people who are similar to us—usually

That we like people who are like us should come as no surprise. One of the first steps in getting acquainted with a stranger is the search for common ground—interests, experiences, or other factors you share. When you find similarities, you usually feel some kind of attraction toward the person who is like you.

This doesn't mean that the key to popularity is to agree with everyone about everything. Research shows that attraction is greatest when we are similar to others in a high percentage of important areas. For example, a couple who support each other's career goals, like the same friends, and have similar beliefs about human rights can tolerate trivial disagreements about the merits of sushi or Miles Davis. With enough similarity in key areas, they can even survive disputes about more important subjects, such as how much time to spend with their families or whether separate vacations are acceptable. But if the number and content of disagreements becomes too great, the relationship may be threatened.

Similarity turns from attraction to repulsion when we encounter people who are like us in many ways but who behave in a strange or socially offensive manner. For instance, you have probably disliked people others have said were "just like you" but who talked too much, were complainers, or had some other unappealing characteristic. In fact, there is a tendency to have stronger dislike for similar but offensive people than for those who are offensive but different. One likely reason is that such people threaten our self-esteem, causing us to fear that we may be as unappealing as they are. In such circumstances, the reaction is often to put as much distance as possible between ourselves and this threat to our ideal self-image.

we like people who are different from us—in certain ways

The fact that "opposites attract" seems to contradict the principle of similarity we just described. In truth, though, both are valid. Differences strengthen a relationship when they are *complementary*—when each partner's characteristics satisfy the other's needs. Couples, for instance, are more likely to be attracted to each other when one partner is dominant and the other passive. Relationships also work well when the partners agree that one will exercise control in certain areas ("You make the final decisions about money") and the other will take the lead in different ones ("I'll decide how we ought to decorate the place"). Strains occur when control issues are disputed.

Studies that have examined successful and unsuccessful couples over a twenty-year period show the interaction between similarities and differences. The research demonstrates that partners in successful mar-

129

riages were similar enough to satisfy each other physically and mentally, but were different enough to meet each other's needs and keep the relationship interesting. The successful couples found ways to keep a balance between their similarities and differences, adjusting to the changes that occurred over the years.

we like people who like us—usually

Being liked by others is a strong source of attraction, especially in the early stages of a relationship. At that time we are attracted to people who we believe are attracted to us. Conversely, we will probably not feel good about people who either attack or seem indifferent to us. After we get to know others, their liking becomes less of a factor. By then we form our preferences more from the other reasons listed in this section.

It's no mystery why reciprocal liking builds attractiveness. People who approve of us bolster our feelings of self-esteem. This approval is rewarding in its own right, and it can also confirm a self-concept that says, "I'm a likable person."

You can probably think of cases where you haven't liked people who seemed to like you. These experiences usually fall into two categories. Sometimes we think the other person's supposed liking is counterfeit— an insincere device to get something from us. The acquaintance who becomes friendly whenever he or she needs to borrow your car or the employee whose flattery of the boss seems to be a device to get a raise are examples. This sort of behavior really isn't "liking" at all. The second category of unappealing liking occurs when the other person's approval doesn't fit with our own self-concept. We cling to an existing self-concept even when it is unrealistically unfavorable. When someone says you're good-looking, intelligent, and kind, but you believe you are ugly, stupid, and mean, you may choose to disregard the flattering information and remain in your familiar state of unhappiness. Groucho Marx summarized this attitude when he said he would never join any club that would have him as a member.

we are attracted to people who can help us

Some relationships are based on a semieconomic model called *exchange theory*. It suggests that we often seek out people who can give us rewards—either physical or emotional—that are greater than or equal to the costs we encounter in dealing with them. When we operate on the basis of exchange, we decide (often unconsciously) whether dealing with another person is "a good deal" or "not worth the effort."

At its most blatant level, an exchange approach seems cold and calculating, but in some dimensions of a relationship it can be reasonable. A healthy business relationship is based on how well the parties help one another out, and some friendships are based on an informal kind of barter: "I don't mind listening to the ups and downs of your love life because you rescue me when the house needs repairs." Even close relationships have an element of exchange. Husbands and wives tolerate each other's quirks because the comfort and enjoyment they get make the unhappy times worth accepting. Most deeply satisfying relationships, however, are built on more than just the benefits that make them a good deal.

we like competent people—particularly when they are "human"

We like to be around talented people, probably because we hope their skills and abilities will rub off on us. On the other hand, we are uncomfortable around those who are *too* competent—probably because we look bad by comparison.

Given these contrasting attitudes, it's no surprise that people are generally attracted to others who are talented, but who have visible flaws that show they are human, just like us. There are some qualifications to this principle. People with especially high or low self-esteem find "perfect" people more attractive than those who are competent but flawed, and some studies suggest that women tend to be more impressed by uniformly superior people of both sexes whereas men find desirable but "human" subjects especially attractive. On the whole, though, the principle stands: The best way to gain the liking of others is to be good at what you do, but to admit your mistakes.

we are attracted to people who disclose themselves to us—appropriately

Telling others important information about yourself can help build liking. Sometimes the basis of this attraction comes from learning about ways we are similar, either in experiences ("I broke off an engagement myself") or in attitudes ("I feel nervous with strangers too"). Another reason why self-disclosure increases liking is because it is a sign of regard. When people share private information with you, it suggests they respect and trust you—a kind of liking that we've already seen increases attractiveness.

Not all disclosure leads to liking. People whose sharing is poorly timed often meet with bad results. It's probably unwise, for example, to talk about your sexual insecurities with a new acquaintance or to express your pet peeves to a friend at her birthday party. In addition to bad timing, opening up too much can also be a mistake. Research shows that people are judged as attractive when they match the amount and content of what they share with that of the other person in a relationship. See pages 142–144 for more guidelines about when and how to self-disclose.

understanding interpersonal relationships

131

we feel strongly about people we encounter often

As common sense suggests, we are likely to develop relationships with people we interact with frequently. In many cases, proximity leads to liking. We're more likely to develop friendships with close neighbors than with distant ones, for instance; and several studies show that the chances are good that we'll choose a mate whom we cross paths with often. Facts like these are understandable when we consider that proximity allows us to get more information about the other people and benefit from a relationship with them.

Familiarity, on the other hand, can also breed contempt. Evidence to support this fact comes from police blotters as well as university laboratories. Thieves frequently prey on nearby victims even though the risk of being recognized is greater. Most aggravated assaults occur within the family or among close neighbors. Within the law, the same principle holds: You are likely to develop strong personal feelings of either like or dislike regarding others you encounter frequently.

stages of relational development

Although relationships come in many types and "sizes," social scientists have found that they all grow and dissolve by passing through similar phases. These phases can be broken into as few as three parts (initiation, maintenance, and dissolution) or as many as ten, which we'll now examine. These ten stages are outlined by Mark Knapp.[4] (See Table 6-1.)

1. **Initiation.** This stage involves the initial making of contact with another person. Knapp restricts this stage to conversation openers, both in initial contacts and with previous acquaintances: "Nice to meet you," "How's it going?" and so on.

   Although an initial encounter *is* necessary to the succeeding interaction, its importance is overemphasized in books advising how to pick up men and women. These books suggest fail-proof openers ranging from "Excuse me, I'm from out of town, and I was wondering what people do around here at night?" to "How long do you cook a leg of lamb?" Whatever your preference for opening remarks, this stage is important because you are formulating your first impressions and presenting yourself as interested in the other person.

2. **Experimenting.** In this stage the conversation develops as the people get acquainted by making "small talk." We ask: "Where are you from?" or "What do you do?" or "Do you know Josephine Mandoza? She lives in San Francisco, too."

   Though small talk might seem meaningless, Knapp points out that it serves four purposes:
   a. It is a useful process for uncovering integrating topics and openings for more penetrating conversation.
   b. It can be an audition for a future friendship or a way of increasing the scope of a current relationship.

table 6–1 an overview of interaction stages

process	stage	representative dialog
Coming together	Initiating	"Hi, how ya doin'?" "Fine. You?"
	Experimenting	"Oh, so you like to ski . . . so do I." "You do?! Great. Where do you go?"
	Intensifying	"I . . . I think I love you." "I love you too."
	Integrating	"I feel so much a part of you." "Yeah, we are like one person. What happens to you happens to me."
	Bonding	"I want to be with you always." "Let's get married."
Coming apart	Differentiating	"I just don't like big social gatherings." "Sometimes I don't understand you. This is one area where I'm certainly not like you at all."
	Circumscribing	"Did you have a good time on your trip?" "What time will dinner be ready?"
	Stagnating	"What's there to talk about?" "Right. I know what you're going to say and you know what I'm going to say."
	Avoiding	"I'm so busy, I just don't know when I'll be able to see you." "If I'm not around when you try, you'll understand."
	Terminating	"I'm leaving you . . . and don't bother trying to contact me." "Don't worry."

Reprinted with permission from Mark L. Knapp, *Interpersonal Communication and Human Relationships* (Boston: Allyn & Bacon, 1984).

c. It provides a safe procedure for indicating who we are and how another can come to know us better (reduction of uncertainty).

d. It allows us to maintain a sense of community with our fellow human beings.

The relationship during this stage is generally pleasant and uncritical, and the commitments are minimal. Experimenting may last ten minutes or ten years. (Knapp thinks most relationships never go beyond the experimentation stage.)

3. Intensifying. When a relationship does go beyond experimenting, the intensification phase is one in which it develops a character of its own indicated by a commonality identity: "We like to dance."

You come to know the other person and develop accuracy in predicting the other's wants and whims. You are more accessible to that person and may use less formal terms, including nicknames and special terms of endearment. A truly *interpersonal relationship* begins on this level.

4. **Integrating.** At this point the sense of union of the two people is heightened further—the interpersonal synchrony is high. You become identified by others as "a pair," "an item." This oneness may be accented by similar clothing styles, increased similarities in what you talk about, phrasing of terms, and the designation of common property—for example, *our* song, *our* meeting time, or *our* project.

5. **Bonding.** When the relationship reaches this stage, it achieves some formal social recognition. This can take the form of a contract to be business partners or a license to be married. During this stage more regulations for the interaction are established, and the participants may experience some disorientation and uneasiness until they adjust to the social formality and institutionalization of their relationship. Newlyweds, for example, may feel a need to rebel once the ceremony sanctions their relationship—the husband might take up car maintenance and spend all his free time in the garage, and the wife might work late.

6. **Differentiating.** Now that the two people have formed this commonality, they need to reestablish individual identities. How are we different? How am I unique? Former identifications as "we" now emphasize "I." Differentiation often first occurs when a relationship begins to experience the first, inevitable stress. Whereas a happy employee might refer to "our company," the description might change to "their company" when a raise or some other request isn't forthcoming. We see this kind of differentiation when parents argue over the misbehavior of a child: "Did you see what *your* son just did?"

Differentiation can be positive, too, for people need to be individuals as well as parts of a relationship. The key to successful differentiation is the need to maintain commitment to a relationship while creating the space for members to be individuals as well.

7. **Circumscribing.** So far we have been looking at the growth of relationships. Although some reach a plateau of development, going on successfully for as long as a lifetime, others pass through several stages of decline and dissolution. In the circumscribing stage communication between members decreases in quantity and quality. Restrictions and restraints characterize this stage, and dynamic communication becomes static. Rather than discuss a disagreement (which requires some degree of energy on both parts), members opt for withdrawal: either mental (silence or daydreaming and fantasizing) or physical (where people spend less time together). Circumscribing doesn't involve total avoidance, which comes later. Rather, it entails a certain shrinking of interest and commitment.

8. **Stagnation.** If circumscribing continues, the relationship begins to stagnate. Members behave toward each other in old, familiar ways without much feeling. No growth occurs. The relationship is a hollow shell of its former self. We see stagnation in many workers who have lost enthusiasm for their job, yet who continue to go through the motions for years. The same sad event occurs for some couples who unenthusiastically have the same conversations, see the same people, and follow the same routines without any sense of joy or novelty.

9. **Avoiding.** When stagnation becomes too unpleasant, parties in a relationship begin to create distance between each other. Sometimes this is done under the guise of excuses ("I've been sick lately and can't see you") and sometimes it is done directly ("Please don't call me; I don't want to see you now"). In either case by this point the handwriting about the relationship's future is clearly on the wall.

10. **Termination.** Characteristics of this final stage include summary dialogs of where the relationship has gone and the desire to dissociate. The relationship may end with a cordial dinner, a note left on the kitchen table, a phone call, or a legal document stating the dissolution. Depending on each person's feelings, this stage can be

quite short, or it may be drawn out over time, with bitter jabs at one another. In either case, termination doesn't have to be totally negative. Understanding one another's investments in the relationship and needs for personal growth may dilute the hard feelings.

After outlining these ten steps, Knapp discusses several assumptions about his model. First, movement through the stages is generally sequential and systematic. We proceed at a steady pace and don't usually skip steps in the development. Second, movement can be forward or backward, and there is movement within stages. A relationship, for example, may experience a setback—a lessening of intimacy, a redefining of the relationship. Two people may repeat certain stages, and although the stages are the same, each cycle is a new experience. It may also be the case that certain relationships will stabilize at a particular stage. Many relationships stabilize at the experimenting stage (friend and work relationships), some stabilize at the intensifying stage, and others stabilize at the bonding stage. With these assumptions in mind we can use Knapp's model as a set of developmental guidelines for movement within and between the stages of initiation and dissolution.

self-disclosure in relationships

We have already seen that one way to judge the strength of a relationship is by the breadth and depth of information about themselves that the parties share with one another. Furthermore, we've cited research on attraction showing that appropriate self-disclosure can increase a person's attractiveness. Given these facts, we need to take a closer look at the subject of self-disclosure. Just what is it? When is it desirable? How is it best done?

The best place to begin is with a definition. *Self-disclosure is the process of deliberately revealing information about one's self that is significant and that would not normally be known by others.* Let's take a closer look at some parts of this definition. Self-disclosure must be *deliberate*. If you accidentally mentioned to a friend that you were thinking about quitting a job or proposing marriage, that information would not fit into the category we are examining here. On the other hand, if you intentionally shared information that wasn't *significant*—the fact that you like fudge, for example—it's obvious that no important disclosure occurred. Our third requirement is that the information being disclosed would *not be known by others*. There's nothing noteworthy about telling others that you are depressed or elated if they already know how you're feeling.

Though it's hard to deny the importance of self-disclosure in building and maintaining relationships, the process of opening up is a threatening one for all of us at one time or another. Why are we so often afraid of letting others know who we really are? In a thoughtful book on this subject, John T. Wood suggests an answer:

The personality of man is not an apple that has to be polished, but a banana that has to be peeled. And the reason we remain so far from one another, the reason we neither communicate nor interact in any real way, is that most of us spend our lives in polishing rather than peeling.

Man's lifelong task is simply one, but it is not simple: To remove the discrepancy between his outer self and his inner self, to get rid of the "persona" that divides his authentic self from the world.

This persona is like the peeling on a banana: It is something built up to protect from bruises and injury. It is not the real person, but sometimes (if the fear of injury remains too great) it becomes a lifelong substitute for the person.

The "authentic personality" knows that he is like a banana, and knows that only as he peels himself down to his individuated self can he reach out and make contact with his fellows by what Father Goldbrunner calls "the sheer maturity of his humanity." Only when he himself is detached from his defensive armorings can he then awaken a true response in his dialogue with others.

Most of us, however, think in terms of the apple, not the banana. We spend our lives in shining the surface, in making it rosy and gleaming, in perfecting the "image." But the image is not the apple, which may be wormy and rotten to the taste.

Almost everything in modern life is devoted to the polishing process, and little to the peeling process. It is the surface personality that we work on—the appearance, the clothes, the manners, the geniality. In short, the salesmanship: We are selling the package, not the product.

Sydney J. Harris

I am afraid to be who I am with you . . . I am afraid to be judged by you, I am afraid you will reject me. I am afraid you will say bad things about me. I am afraid you will hurt me. I am afraid, if I really am myself, you won't love me— and I need your love so badly that I will play the roles you expect me to play and be the person that pleases you, even though I lose myself in the process.[5]

There probably isn't a person over the age of six who wouldn't understand these words. At one time or another, all of us are afraid to be real with others. As Wood suggests, the biggest reason for hiding our true selves is usually fear of rejection. As we'll soon see, there are other reasons as well. Because the issue of self-disclosure is such a crucial one in interpersonal communication, we want to look at it in detail.

a model of self-disclosure

One way to illustrate how self-disclosure operates in communication is to look at a device called the *Johari Window,* developed by Joseph Luft and Harry Ingham.[6]

Imagine a frame that contains everything there is to know about you: your likes and dislikes, your goals, your secrets, your needs—everything (see Figure 6-3).

Everything
about
you

figure 6-3

137

figure 6-4

Known to self | Not known to self

figure 6-5

Known to others

Not known to others

	Known to self	Not known to self
Known to others	1 OPEN	2 BLIND
Not known to others	3 HIDDEN	4 UNKNOWN

figure 6-6

Of course you aren't aware of everything about yourself. Like most people, you're probably discovering new things about yourself all the time. To represent this aspect, we can divide the frame containing everything about you into two parts: the part you know about, and the part of which you're not aware (see Figure 6-4).

We can also divide the frame containing everything about you in another way. In this division one part represents the things about you that others know, and the second part contains the things about you that you keep to yourself. Figure 6-5 represents this view.

When we impose these two divided frames one atop the other, we have a Johari Window. By looking at Figure 6-6, you can see that the window divides everything about you into four parts.

Part 1 represents the person of which both you and others are aware. This area is labeled your *open* area. Part 2 represents the part of you that you yourself are not aware of, but others are. This is called your *blind* area. Part 3 represents your *hidden* area; you're aware of this part of yourself, but you don't allow others to know it. Part 4 represents the part of you that is known neither to you nor to others and is therefore referred to as the *unknown* area.

Interpersonal communication of any significance is virtually impossible if·the individuals involved have little open area. Taking this a step further, you can see that a relationship is limited by the individual who is less open, that is, who possesses the smaller open area. Figure 6-7 illustrates this situation with two Johari Windows.

We've set up *A*'s window in reverse so that the Part 1 areas of both *A*'s and *B*'s Joharis appear next to each other. Note that the amount of successful communication (represented by the arrows connecting the two open areas) is dictated by the size of the smaller open area of *A*. The arrows originating from *B*'s open area and being turned aside by *A*'s hidden and blind areas represent unsuccessful attempts to communicate.

Can you put yourself into one of the windows in Figure 6-7? Have you had the experience of not being able to "really get to know" some-

figure 6-7

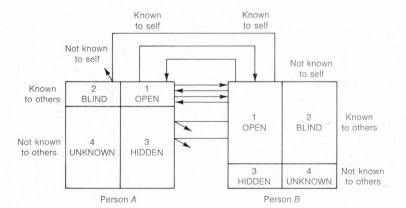

one because he or she was too reserved or closed? Or perhaps you've frustrated another person's attempts to build a relationship with you in the same way. Whether you picture yourself as more like Person A or Person B in Figure 6-7, the fact is that self-disclosure is necessary for the success of any interpersonal relationship.

levels of self-disclosure

The term "self-disclosure" actually describes several very different types of interaction. Identifying them will help you understand the process better and also give you some idea of how to go about increasing the depth of your relationships.[7]

You can begin to understand the types of self-disclosure by picturing a series of four concentric circles surrounding a core. (See Figure 6-8.) Imagine that this core represents the essential you—your beliefs, moods, strengths, weaknesses, likes, and dislikes—every important fact and trait that makes you who you are, all rolled into one. If it were possible to share yourself to the fullest all at once, the other person would know everything contained in that core. Because, in most cases, this kind of intense, immediate sharing comes only with the passage of time and growth of trust, the way we come to let others know about ourselves is by offering information from the various levels that surround our core.

Clichés The layer farthest from the core consists of clichés: "How are you doing?" "Fine!" "We'll have to get together some time."

Remarks such as these usually aren't meant to be taken literally; in

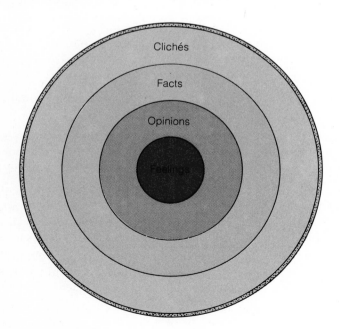

figure 6-8
Levels of self-disclosure

understanding interpersonal relationships

139

fact, the other person would be surprised if you responded to a casual "How are you?" with a lengthy speech on your health, state of mind, love life, and finances. Yet it's a mistake to consider clichés as meaningless, for they serve several useful functions. For instance, they can give two speakers time to size each other up and decide whether it's desirable to carry their conversation any further. Our first impressions are generally based more on the nonverbal characteristics of the other person than on the words we hear spoken. Things like eye contact, vocal tone, facial expression, posture, and so on can often tell us more about another person than can the initial sentences in a conversation. Given the value of these nonverbal cues and the awkwardness of actually saying, "I want to take a few minutes to look you over before I commit myself to getting acquainted," the exchange of a few stock phrases can be just the thing to get you through this initial period comfortably.

Clichés can also serve as codes for other messages we don't usually express directly, such as "I want to acknowledge your presence" (for instance when two acquaintances walk past each other). Additional unstated messages often contained in clichés are "I'm interested in talking if you feel like it" or "Let's keep the conversation light and impersonal; I don't feel like sharing much about myself right now." Accompanied by a different set of nonverbal cues, a cliché can say, "I don't want to be impolite, but you'd better stay away from me for now." In all these cases, clichés serve as a valuable kind of shorthand that makes it easy to keep the social wheels greased and indicates the potential for further, possibly more profound conversation.

Facts Moving inward from clichés to the next circle on the communication model brings us to the level of exchanging *facts,* such as

"You probably can get your car fixed at a garage in town. It looks as if you need a rebuilt generator."

"I'm a professor at a small college in California."

"If you go camping in the mountains this weekend, you'll probably get rain."

Whereas facts may at first seem impersonal, they can tell you a great deal about the other person and in so doing form the basis for a future conversation. For instance, consider the three preceding pieces of information:

You've learned that the speaker is familiar with the town and knows at least a little about how cars work. If you're interested in either of these subjects, you've found a starting point for a conversation.

The speaker is involved in higher education. Are you? Would you like to share more about colleges or to find out what subject the person teaches or to learn something about California? Here's your chance.

How does the speaker know that it might rain in the mountains? Perhaps the information came from a weather forecast, which doesn't give you much to talk about. On the other hand your partner here might be familiar with the area you've headed for, in which case you have something in common.

Facts can be interesting in themselves, and they can be a good clue as to whether a relationship with your conversational partner is worth pursuing.

Opinions Still closer to the core of a speaker's personality is the level of *opinions.*

"I used to be a political volunteer for some cause in every election, but I think politics is so corrupt now that I don't even bother to vote."

"If you like Mexican food, you've got to try Lupita's. It's great!"

"I think Jack is a phony."

It's clear that opinions like these tell you a great deal about the other person—much more than do facts and clichés. If you know where the speaker stands on a subject, you can get a clearer picture of whether your conversation has any potential. In the same way, every time you offer a personal opinion, you're giving people valuable information about yourself, as well as providing some material that they can respond to in order to keep the conversation flowing.

Feelings The fourth level of communication—and the one closest to one's personal core—is the realm of *feelings.* At first glance, feelings might appear to be the same as opinions, but there is a big difference. As we saw earlier, "I think Jack is a phony" is an opinion. Now notice how much more we learn about the speaker by looking at three different feelings upon which this judgment could be based:

"I think Jack is a phony, and *I'm sad that he won't act naturally around me.*"

"I think Jack is a phony, and *I get angry when he doesn't say what's on his mind.*"

"I think Jack is a phony, and *I'm uncomfortable when I see him put on a front when everybody knows what he's doing.*"

Once you can recognize the difference between these four levels of communication, it's easy to see several reasons why it's hard to keep a conversation going. Sometimes the speakers might remain exclusively on the level of facts. This might be suitable for a business relationship but wouldn't be very likely in most other circumstances. Even worse, other communicators never get off the level of clichés. And just as a diet of rich foods can become unappealing if carried to excess, the overuse of feelings and opinions can also become disagreeable. In most cases, the successful conversation is one in which the participants move from one level to another, depending on the circumstances.

Another common problem occurs when two communicators want to relate to each other on different levels. If one is willing to deal only with facts and perhaps an occasional opinion while the other insists on revealing personal feelings, the results are likely to be uncomfortable for both. Consider the following meeting between Jack and Roger at a party.

J Hi. My name's Jack. I don't think we've met before. (*cliché*)

R I'm Roger. Nice to meet you. (*cliché*)

J Do you know anybody here? I've just moved in next door and don't know a soul except for the host. What's his name . . . Lou? (*fact*)

R Lou's right. Well, I'm here with my wife—that's her over there—and we know a few other people. (*fact; both speakers are comfortable so far*)

J Well, I used to have a wife, but she split. She really did me in. (*fact and opinion*)

R Oh? (*cliché; he doesn't know how to reply to this comment*)

J Yeah. Everything was going along great—I thought. Then one day she told me she was in love with her gynecologist and that she wanted a divorce. I still haven't gotten over it. (*feeling and fact*)

R Well, uh, that's too bad. (*cliché; Roger is now very uncomfortable*)

J I don't think I'll ever trust another woman. I'm still in love with my wife, and it's killing me. She really broke my heart. (*feeling and fact*)

R I'm sorry. Listen, I've got to go. (*cliché*)

Clearly, Jack moved to the level of sharing feelings long before Roger was prepared to accept this kind of communication. Though this kind of discussion might have helped a friendship if it had come at a later time, Jack only succeeded in driving Roger away by coming on too fast. Remember the hazards of moving too quickly to a level your partner is likely to find uncomfortable.

This model needs a few words of qualification. Some facts are certainly more revealing than opinions or feelings. Telling a lover you are dating someone else, for example, is more disclosing than giving your opinion about his or her new haircut. Nevertheless, the principle of depth is still valid: Giving your lover an opinion of *why* you are seeing someone else (you think he or she doesn't appreciate you) reveals more than the facts alone, and sharing your feelings (guilt or hurt) is even more disclosing.

guidelines for appropriate self-disclosure

One fear we've had while writing this chapter is that a few over-enthusiastic readers may throw down their books after reading half of what we've written and rush away to begin sharing every personal detail of their lives with whomever they can find. As you can imagine, this kind of behavior isn't an example of effective interpersonal communication.

No single style of self-disclosure is appropriate for every situation. Let's take a look at some guidelines that can help you recognize how to express yourself in a way that's rewarding for you and the others involved.

1. **Is the other person important to you?** There are several ways in which someone might be important. Perhaps you have an ongoing relationship deep enough so that sharing significant parts of yourself justifies keeping your present level of togetherness intact. Or perhaps the person to whom you're considering disclosing is someone with whom you've previously related on a less personal level. But now you see a chance to grow closer, and disclosure may be the path toward developing that personal relationship.

2. **Is the risk of disclosing reasonable?** Take a realistic look at the potential risks of self-disclosure. Even if the probable benefits are great, opening yourself up to almost certain rejection may be asking for trouble. For instance, it might be foolhardy to share your important feelings with someone you know is likely to betray your confidences or ridicule them. On the other hand, knowing that your partner is trustworthy and supportive makes the prospect of speaking out more reasonable. In anticipating risks be sure that you are realistic. It's sometimes easy to indulge in catastrophic expectations in which you begin to imagine all sorts of disastrous consequences of your opening up, when in fact such horrors are quite unlikely to occur.

3. **Is the amount and type of disclosure appropriate?** A third point to realize is that there are degrees of self-disclosure, so that telling others about yourself isn't an all-or-nothing decision you must make. It's possible to share some facts, opinions, or feelings with one person while reserving riskier ones for others. In the same vein, before sharing very important information with someone who does matter to you, you might consider testing reactions by disclosing less personal data.

4. **Is the disclosure relevant to the situation at hand?** Self-disclosure doesn't require long confessions about your past life or current

Before I built a wall I'd ask to know
What I was walling in or walling out.
And to whom I was like to give offense,
Something there is that doesn't love a wall,
That wants it down.

Robert Frost

143

thoughts unrelated to the now. On the contrary, it ought to be directly pertinent to your present conversation. It's ludicrous to picture the self-disclosing person as someone who blurts out intimate details of every past experience. Instead, our model is someone who, when the time is appropriate, trusts us enough to share the hidden parts of self that affect our relationship.

Usually, then, the subject of appropriate self-disclosure involves the present, the "here and now" as opposed to "there and then." "How am I feeling now?" "How are we doing now?" These are appropriate topics for sharing personal thoughts and feelings. There are certainly times when it's relevant to bring up the past, but only as it relates to what's going on in the present.

5. Is the disclosure reciprocated? There's nothing quite as disconcerting as talking your heart out to someone only to discover that the other person has yet to say anything to you that is half as revealing as what you've been saying. And you think to yourself, "What am I doing?!" Unequal self-disclosure creates an imbalanced relationship, one doomed to fall apart.

There are few times when one-way disclosure is acceptable. Most of them involve formal, therapeutic relationships in which a client approaches a trained professional with the goal of resolving a problem. For instance, you wouldn't necessarily expect to hear about a physician's personal ailments during a visit to a medical office. Nonetheless, it's interesting to note that one frequently noted characteristic of effective psychotherapists, counselors, and teachers is a willingness to share their feelings about a relationship with their clients.

6. Will the effect be constructive? Self-disclosure can be a vicious tool if it's not used carefully. Psychologist George Bach suggests that every person has a psychological "belt line." Below that belt line are areas about which the person is extremely sensitive. Bach says that jabbing at a "below-the-belt" area is a surefire way to disable another person, though usually at great cost to the relationship. It's important to consider the effects of your candor before opening up to others. Comments such as "I've always thought you were pretty unintelligent" or "Last year I made love to your best friend" *may* sometimes resolve old business and thus be constructive, but they also can be devastating—to the listener, to the relationship, and to your self-esteem.

7. Is the self-disclosure clear and understandable? When expressing yourself to others, it's important that you share yourself in a way that's intelligible. This means describing the *sources* of your message clearly. For instance, it's far better to describe another's behavior by saying, "When you don't answer my phone calls or drop by to visit anymore . . ." than to vaguely complain, "When you avoid me . . ."

It's also vital to express your *thoughts* and *feelings* explicitly. "I feel worried because I'm afraid you don't care about me" is more understandable than "I don't like the way things have been going."

Self-disclosure doesn't guarantee harmony. Regardless of what we may wish for or dream about, a conflict-free world just doesn't exist. Even the best communicators, the luckiest people, are bound to wind up in situations when their needs don't match the needs of others. Money, time, power, sex, humor, aesthetic taste, as well as a thousand other issues arise and keep us from living in a state of perpetual agreement.

For many people the inevitability of conflict is a depressing fact. They think that the existence of ongoing conflict means that there's little chance for happy relationships with others. Effective communicators know differently, however. They realize that although it's impossible to *eliminate* conflict, there are ways to *manage* it effectively. And those effective communicators know the subject of this chapter—that managing conflict skillfully can open the door to healthier, stronger, and more satisfying relationships.

resolving interpersonal conflict

the nature of conflict

Whatever forms they may take, all interpersonal conflicts share certain similarities. Joyce Frost and William Wilmot provide a thorough definition of conflict. They state that conflict is an expressed struggle between at least two interdependent parties who perceive incompatible goals, scarce rewards, and interference from the other parties in achieving their goals.[8] Let's look at the various parts of this definition so as to develop a clearer idea of conflicts in people's lives.

Expressed struggle   Another way to describe this idea is to say that both parties in a conflict know that some disagreement exists. For instance, you may be upset for months because a neighbor's loud stereo keeps you from getting to sleep at night, but no conflict exists between the two of you until the neighbor learns about your problem. Of course, the expressed struggle doesn't have to be verbal. You can show your displeasure with somebody without saying a word. A dirty look, the silent treatment, or avoiding the other person are all ways of expressing yourself. But one way or another both parties must know that a problem exists before they're in conflict.

Perceived incompatible goals   All conflicts look as if one party's gain will be another's loss. For instance, consider the neighbor whose stereo keeps you awake at night. Does somebody have to lose? A neighbor who turns down the noise loses the enjoyment of hearing the music at full volume; but if the neighbor keeps the volume up, then you're still awake and unhappy.

But the goals in this situation really aren't completely incompatible—solutions do exist that allow both parties to get what they want. For instance, you could achieve peace and quiet by closing your windows and getting the neighbor to do the same. You might use a pair of earplugs. Or perhaps the neighbor could get a set of earphones and listen to the music at full volume without bothering anyone. If any of these solutions prove workable, then the conflict disappears.

Unfortunately, people often fail to see mutually satisfying answers to their problems. And as long as they *perceive* their goals to be mutually exclusive, then, although the conflict is unnecessary, it is still very real.

Perceived scarce rewards Conflicts also exist when people believe there isn't enough of something to go around. The most obvious example of a scarce resource is money—a cause of many conflicts. If a person asks for a raise in pay and the boss would rather keep the money or use it to expand the business, then the two parties are in conflict.

Time is another scarce commodity. As authors and family men, both of us are constantly in the middle of struggles about how to use the limited time we have to spend. Should we work on this book? Visit with our wives? Play with our kids? Enjoy the luxury of being alone? With only twenty-four hours in a day we're bound to wind up in conflicts with our families, editors, students, and friends—all of whom want more of our time than we have available to give.

Interdependence However antagonistic they might feel toward each other, the parties in a conflict are usually dependent on each other. The welfare and satisfaction of one depends on the actions of another. If this weren't true, then even in the face of scarce resources and incompatible goals there would be no need for conflict. Interdependence exists between conflicting nations, social groups, organizations, friends, and lovers. In each case, if the two parties didn't need each other to solve the problem, each would go separate ways. In fact many conflicts go unresolved because the parties fail to understand their interdependence. One of the first steps toward resolving a conflict is to take the attitude that "we're all in this together."

styles of conflict

There are four ways in which people can act when their needs are not met. Each one has very different characteristics.

Nonassertive behavior Nonassertive communicators handle conflict in one of two ways. Sometimes they ignore their needs, keeping quiet when things don't go their way. A second nonassertive course of action is to acknowledge that a problem exists and then simply to accept the situation, hoping that it will clear up by itself.

Unfortunately, most problems don't solve themselves. In addition, a nonassertive person often grows more and more angry at the other party, poisoning the relationship. Furthermore, failing to act often leads to a loss of self-respect. Clearly, nonassertion is usually not a very satisfying course of action.

Direct aggression Where the nonassertive person underreacts, a directly aggressive person overreacts. The usual consequences of aggressive behaviors are anger and defensiveness or hurt and humiliation on the part of the receiver. In either case, aggressive communicators build themselves up at the expense of others.

Indirect aggression In several of his works, psychologist George Bach describes behavior that he terms "crazymaking."[9] Crazymaking occurs when people have feelings of resentment, anger, or rage that they are unable or unwilling to express directly. Instead of keeping these feelings to themselves, the crazymakers send these aggressive messages in subtle, indirect ways, thus maintaining the front of kindness: hinting, joking, gossiping, and so on. This amiable facade eventually crumbles, however, leaving the crazymaker's victim confused and angry at having been fooled. The targets of the crazymaker can either react with aggressive behavior of their own or retreat to nurse their hurt feelings. In either case, indirect aggression seldom has anything but harmful effects on a relationship.

Assertion Assertive people handle conflicts skillfully by expressing their needs, thoughts, and feelings clearly and directly, but without judging others or dictating to them. They have the attitude that most of the time it is possible to resolve problems to everyone's satisfaction. Possessing this attitude and the skills to bring it about doesn't guarantee that assertive communicators will always get what they want, but it does give them the best chance of doing so. An additional benefit of such an approach is that whether or not it satisfies a particular need, it maintains the self-respect of both the assertors and those with whom they interact. As a result, people who manage their conflicts assertively may experience feelings of discomfort while they are working through the problem. They usually feel better about themselves and each other afterward—quite a change from the outcomes of no assertiveness or aggression.

approaches to conflict resolution

So far, we've looked at individual styles of communication. Whereas assertive problem solving may be the most satisfying and productive of these, it's obvious that not everyone uses it. Even when one person behaves assertively, there's no guarantee that others will do so. There are three quite different outcomes of the various interactions among nonassertive, indirectly aggressive, directly aggressive, and assertive com-

table 6–2   styles of conflict

	nonassertive	directly aggressive	indirectly aggressive	assertive
Approach to others	I'm not OK, you're OK.	I'm OK, you're not OK.	I'm OK, you're not OK. (But I'll let you think you are.)	I'm OK, you're OK
Decision making	Let others choose	Chooses for others. They know it.	Chooses for others. They don't know it.	Chooses for self
Self-sufficiency	Low	High or low	Looks high but usually low	Usually high
Behavior in problem situations	Flees, gives in	Outright attack	Concealed attack	Direct confrontation
Response of others	Disrespect, guilt, anger, frustration	Hurt, defensiveness, humiliation	Confusion, frustration, feelings of manipulation	Mutual respect
Success pattern	Succeeds by luck or charity of others	Beats out others	Wins by manipulation	Attempts ''no lose'' solutions

Adapted with permission from Stanlee Phelps and Nancy Austin, *The Assertive Woman* (San Luis Obispo, Calif.: Impact, 1975), p. 11; and Gerald Piaget, American Orthopsychiatric Association, 1975. Further reproduction prohibited.

municators. By looking at each of them, you can decide which ones you'll seek when you find yourself facing an interpersonal conflict.

Win-lose Win-lose conflicts are ones in which one party gets what he or she wants while the other comes up short. People resort to this method of resolving disputes when they perceive a situation as being an "either-or" one: Either I get what I want or you get your way. The most clear-cut examples of win-lose situations are certain games such as baseball or poker in which the rules require a winner and a loser. Some interpersonal issues seem to fit into this win-lose framework: two co-workers seeking a promotion to the same job, for instance, or a couple who disagree on how to spend their limited money.

Power is the distinguishing characteristic in win-lose problem solving, for it is necessary to defeat an opponent to get what you want. The most obvious kind of power is physical. Some parents threaten their children with warnings such as "Stop misbehaving, or I'll send you to your room." Adults who use physical power to deal with each other usually aren't so blunt, but the legal system is the implied threat: "Follow the rules, or we'll lock you up."

Real or implied force isn't the only kind of power used in conflicts. People who rely on authority of many types engage in win-lose methods without ever threatening physical coercion. In most jobs supervisors have the potential to use authority in the assignment of working hours, job promotions, and desirable or undesirable tasks and, of course, in the power to fire an unsatisfactory employee. Teachers can use the power of grades to coerce students to act in desired ways.

Even the usually admired democratic principle of majority rule is a win-lose method of resolving conflicts. However fair it may be, this system results in one group getting its way and another being unsatisfied.

There are some circumstances when the win-lose method may be necessary, as when there are truly scarce resources and where only one party can achieve satisfaction. For instance, if two suitors want to marry the same person, only one can succeed. And to return to an earlier example, it's often true that only one applicant can be hired for a job. But don't be too willing to assume that your conflicts are necessarily win-lose: As you'll soon read, many situations that seem to require a loser can be resolved to everyone's satisfaction.

There is a second kind of situation when win-lose is the best method. Even when cooperation is possible, if the other person insists on trying to defeat you, then the most logical response might be to defend yourself by fighting back. "It takes two to tango," the old cliché goes, and it also often takes two to cooperate.

A final and much less frequent justification for trying to defeat another person occurs when the other party is clearly behaving in a wrong manner and where defeating that person is the only way to stop the wrongful behavior. Few people would deny the importance of restraining a person who is deliberately harming others, even if the aggressor's freedom is sacrificed in the process. The danger of forcing wrongdoers to behave themselves is the wide difference in opinion between people about who is wrong and who is right. Given this difference, it would only seem justifiable to coerce others into behaving as we think they should in the most extreme circumstances.

Lose-lose In lose-lose methods of problem solving neither side is satisfied with the outcome. Although the name of this approach is so discouraging that it's hard to imagine how anyone could willingly use the method, in truth lose-lose is a fairly common approach to handling conflicts.

Compromise is the most respectable form of lose-lose conflict resolution. In it all the parties are willing to settle for less than they want because they believe that partial satisfaction is the best result they can hope for.

In his valuable book on conflict resolution, Albert Filley offers an interesting observation about our attitudes toward this method.[10] Why is it, he asks, that if someone says, "I will compromise my values," we view the action unfavorably, yet we talk admiringly about parties in a conflict who compromise to reach a solution? Though compromises may be the best obtainable result in some conflicts, it's important to realize that both people in a dispute can often work together to find much better solutions. In such cases *compromise* is a negative word.

Most of us are surrounded by the results of bad compromises. Consider a common example: the conflict between one person's desire to smoke cigarettes and another's need for clean air. The win-lose outcomes on this issue are obvious: Either the smoker abstains or the nonsmoker gets polluted lungs—neither very satisfying. But a compromise in which the smoker only gets to enjoy a rare cigarette or must retreat outdoors and in which the nonsmoker still must inhale some fumes or feel like an ogre is hardly better. Both sides have lost a considerable amount of both comfort and goodwill. Of course, the costs involved in other compromises are even greater. For example, if divorced parents compromise on child care by haggling over custody and then finally grudgingly agree to split the time with their youngsters, it's hard to say that anybody has won.

Compromises aren't the only lose-lose solutions or even the worst ones. There are many instances in which the parties will both strive to be winners, but as a result of the struggle both wind up losers. On the international scene many wars illustrate this sad point. A nation that gains military victory at the cost of thousands of lives, large amounts of resources, and a damaged national consciousness hasn't truly won much. On an interpersonal level the same principle holds true. Most of us have seen battles of pride in which both parties strike out and both suffer. It seems as if there should be a better alternative, and fortunately there often is.

Win-win In this type of problem solving, the goal is to find a solution that satisfies the needs of everyone involved. Not only do the partners avoid trying to win at the other's expense, but there's also a belief that by working together it is possible to find a solution in which all parties reach their goals without needing to compromise.

One way to understand how win-win problem solving works is to look at a few examples.

A boss and a group of employees get into a conflict over scheduling. The employees often want to shift the hours they're scheduled to work in order to accommodate personal needs, while the boss needs to be sure that the operation is fully staffed at all times. After some discussion they arrive at a solution that satisfies everyone: The boss works up a monthly master schedule indicating the hours during which each employee is responsible for being on the job. Employees are free to trade hours among themselves as long as the operation is fully staffed at all times.

A conflict about testing arises in a college class. Owing to sickness or other reasons, certain students need to take exams on a makeup basis. The instructor doesn't want to give these students any advantage over their peers and doesn't want to go through the task of making up a brand-new test for just a few people. After working on the problem together, instructor and students arrive at a win-win solution. The instructor will hand out a list of twenty possible exam questions in advance of the test day. At examination time five of these questions are randomly drawn for the class to answer. Students who take makeups will draw from the same pool of questions at the time of their test. In this way, makeup students are taking a fresh test without the instructor's having to create a new exam.

A newly married husband and wife found themselves arguing frequently over their budget. The wife enjoyed buying impractical but enjoyable items for herself and the house whereas the husband feared that such purchases would ruin their carefully constructed budget. Their solution was to set aside a small amount of money each month for such purchases. The amount was small enough to be affordable, yet gave the wife a chance to escape from their Spartan life-style. Additionally, the husband was satisfied with the arrangement because the luxury money was now a budget category by itself, which got rid of the "out-of-control" feeling that came when his wife made unexpected purchases. The plan worked so well that the couple continued to use it even after their income rose, by increasing the amount devoted to luxuries.

The point here isn't that these solutions are the correct ones for everybody with similar problems: The win-win approach doesn't work that way. Different people might have found other solutions that suited them better. What the win-win method does is give you an approach—a way of creatively finding just the right answer for your unique problem. By using it, you can tailor-make a way of resolving your conflicts that everyone can live with comfortably.

You should understand that the win-win approach doesn't call for compromises in which the participants give up something they really want or need. Sometimes a compromise is the only alternative, but in the method we're talking about you find a solution that satisfies everyone—one in which nobody has to lose.

win-win problem solving

Of these three styles the win-win approach is clearly the most desirable one in most cases. It is also the hardest one to achieve—for two reasons. First, it requires a noncompetitive attitude and a number of skills that we'll soon discuss. Second, it requires a certain amount of cooperation from the other person, for it's difficult to arrive at a win-win solution with somebody who insists on trying to defeat you.

In spite of these challenges, it is definitely possible to become better at resolving conflicts. In the following pages we will outline a method to increase your chances of being able to handle your conflicts in a win-win manner, so that both you and others have your needs met. As you learn to use this approach, you should find that more and more of your conflicts wind up with win-win solutions. And even when total satisfaction isn't possible, this method can help by showing you how to solve problems in the most satisfying way possible and also by preventing individual conflict from spoiling your future interactions with the person involved.

The method is patterned after techniques developed by George Bach[11] and Thomas Gordon,[12] and it has proved successful with many people, both young and old, in a variety of settings.

Before we introduce you to this method, there are a few ideas you should keep in mind. This technique is a highly structured activity. While you're learning how to use it, it's important that you follow all the stages carefully. Each step is essential to the success of your encounter, and skipping one or more can lead to misunderstandings that might threaten your meeting and even cause a "dirty fight." After you've practiced the method a number of times and are familiar with it, this style of conflict will become almost second nature to you. You'll then be able to approach your conflicts without the need to follow the step-by-step approach. But for the time being try to be patient, and trust the value of the following pattern.

As you read the following steps, try to imagine yourself applying them to a problem that's bothering you now.

Step 1—Identify your problem and unmet needs Before you speak out, it's important to realize that the problem that is causing conflict is yours. Whether you want to return an unsatisfactory piece of merchandise, complain to a noisy neighbor because your sleep is being disturbed, or request a change in working conditions from your employer, the problem is yours. Why? Because in each case *you* are the person who is dissatisfied. You are the one who has paid for the defective article; the merchant who sold it to you has the use of your good money. You are the one who is losing sleep as a result of your neighbors' activities; they are content to go on as before. You are the one who is unhappy with your working conditions, not your boss.

Realizing that the problem is yours will make a big difference when the time comes to approach your partner. Instead of feeling and acting in an evaluative way, you'll be more likely to share your problem in a descriptive way, which will not only be more accurate but will also reduce the chance of a defensive reaction.

Once you realize that the problem is yours, the next step is to identify the unmet needs that leave you feeling dissatisfied. For instance, in the barking dog incident your need may be to get some sleep or to study without interruptions. In the case of a friend who teases you in public, your need would probably be to avoid embarrassment.

Sometimes the task of identifying your needs isn't as simple as it first seems. Consider these cases:

A friend hasn't returned some money you loaned long ago. Your apparent need in this situation might be to get the cash back. But a little thought will probably show that this isn't the only, or even the main, thing you want. Even if you were rolling in money, you'd probably want the loan repaid because of your most important need: *to avoid feeling victimized by your friend's taking advantage of you.*

Someone you care about who lives in a distant city has failed to respond to several letters. Your apparent need may be to get answers to the questions you've written about, but it's likely that there's another, more fundamental need: *the reassurance that you're still important enough to deserve a response.*

As you'll soon see, the ability to identify your real needs plays a key role in solving interpersonal problems. For now, the point to remember is that before you voice your problem to your partner, you ought to be clear about which of your needs aren't being met.

Step 2—Make a date Unconstructive fights often start because the initiator confronts a partner who isn't ready. There are many times when a person isn't in the right frame of mind to face a conflict: perhaps owing to fatigue, being in too much of a hurry to take the necessary time, upset over another problem, or not feeling well. At times like these it's unfair to "jump" a person without notice and expect to get full attention for your problem. If you do persist, you'll probably have an ugly fight on your hands.

After you have a clear idea of the problem, approach your partner with a request to try to solve it. For example: "Something's been bothering me. Can we talk about it?" If the answer is yes, then you're ready to go further. If it isn't the right time to confront your partner, find a time that's agreeable to both of you.

understanding interpersonal
relationships
153

Our marriage used to suffer from arguments that were too short. Now we argue long enough to find out what the argument is about.

Hugh Prather
Notes to Myself

Step 3—Describe your problem and needs Your partner can't possibly meet your needs without knowing why you're upset and what you want. Therefore it's up to you to describe your problem as specifically as possible. When doing so, it's important to use terms that aren't overly vague or abstract. Recall our discussion of behavioral descriptions in Chapter 3 when clarifying your problem and needs.

Step 4—Partner checks back After you've shared your problem and described what you need, it's important to make sure that your partner has understood what you've said. As you can remember from our discussion of listening in Chapter 4, there's a good chance—especially in a stressful conflict situation—of your words being misinterpreted.

It's usually unrealistic to insist that your partner paraphrase your problem statement, and fortunately there are more tactful and subtle ways to make sure you've been understood. For instance, you might try saying, "I'm not sure I expressed myself very well just now—maybe you should tell me what you heard me say so I can be sure I got it right." In any case be absolutely sure that your partner understands your whole message before going any further. Legitimate agreements are tough enough, but there's no point in getting upset about a conflict that doesn't even exist.

George Bach suggests a very good idea at this point. Because being really understood is so rare and gratifying, once you're sure your partner understands you, why not express your appreciation with a "thank-you"? Besides reinforcing the importance of good listening, such a gesture can show caring at what is probably a tense time.

Step 5—Solicit partner's needs Now that you've made your position clear, it's time to find out what your partner needs in order to feel satisfied about this issue. There are two reasons why it's important to discover your partner's needs. First, it's fair. After all, the other person has just as much right as you to feel satisfied, and if you expect help in meeting your needs, then it's reasonable that you behave in the same way. But in addition to decency there's another, practical reason for concerning yourself with what the other person wants. Just as an unhappy partner will make it hard for you to become satisfied, a happy one will be more likely to cooperate in letting you reach your goals. Thus, it is in your own self-interest to discover and meet your partner's needs.

You can learn about your partner's needs simply by asking about them: "Now I've told you what I want and why. Tell me what you need to feel okay about this." Once your partner begins to talk, your job is to use the listening skills discussed earlier in this book to make sure you understand.

Not having studied interpersonal communication, your partner might state intentions in terms of means rather than ends, for instance, saying things like "I want you to be around when I call" instead of "I need to know where you are when I need you." In such cases, it's a good idea to

We struggled together, knowing. We prattled, pretended, fought bitterly, laughed, wept over sad books or old movies, nagged, supported, gave, took, demanded, forgave, resented—hating the ugliness in each other, yet cherishing that which we were. . . . Will I ever find someone to battle with as we battled, love as we loved, share with as we shared, challenge as we challenged, forgive as we forgave? You used to say that I saved up all of my feelings so that I could spew forth when I got home. The anger I experienced in school I could not vent there. How many times have I heard you chuckle as you remembered the day I would come home from school and share with you all of the feelings I had kept in. "If anyone had been listening they would have thought you were punishing me, striking out at me. I always survived and you always knew that I would still be with you when you were through." There was an honesty about our relationship that may never exist again.

Vian Catrell

rephrase the statements in terms of ends, thus making it clear to you both what your partner really needs to feel satisfied.

Step 6—Check your understanding of partner's needs Reverse the procedure in Step 4 by paraphrasing your partner's needs until you're certain you understand them. The surest way to accomplish this is to use the active listening skills you learned in Chapter 4.

Step 7—Negotiate a solution Now that you and your partner understand each other's needs, the goal becomes finding a way to meet them. This is done by trying to develop as many potential solutions as possible and then evaluating them to decide which one best meets everyone's needs.

Probably the best description of the win-win approach has been written by Thomas Gordon in his book *Parent Effectiveness Training*. The following steps are a modification of his approach.

A. **Identify and define the conflict.** We've discussed this process in the preceding pages. It consists of discovering each person's problem and needs, setting the stage for meeting all of them.

B. **Generate a number of possible solutions.** In this step the partners work together to think of as many means as possible to reach their stated ends. The key word here is *quantity:* It's important to generate as many ideas as you can think of without worrying about which ones are good or bad. Write down every thought that comes up, no matter how unworkable; sometimes a farfetched idea will lead to a more workable one.

C. **Evaluate the alternative solutions.** This is the time to talk about which solutions will work and which ones won't. It's important for all concerned to be honest about their willingness to accept an idea. If a solution is going to work, everyone involved has to support it.

D. **Decide on the best solution.** Now that you've looked at all the alternatives, pick the one that looks best to everyone. It's important to be sure everybody understands the solution and is willing to try it out. Remember, your decision doesn't have to be final, but it should look potentially successful.

Step 8—Follow up the solution You can't be sure the solution will work until you try it out. After you've tested it for a while, it's a good idea to set aside some time to talk over how things are going. You may find that you need to make some changes or even rethink the whole problem. The idea is to keep on top of the problem, to keep using creativity to solve it.

Win-win solutions aren't always possible. There will be times when even the best-intentioned people simply won't be able to find a way of meeting all their needs. In cases like this, the process of negotiation has to include some compromising. But even then the preceding steps haven't been wasted. The genuine desire to learn what the other person wants and to try to satisfy those desires will build a climate of goodwill that can help you find the best solution to the present problem and also improve your relationship in the future.

letting go

One typical comment people have after trying the preceding method of handling conflicts is "This is a helpful thing sometimes, but it's so rational! Sometimes I'm so uptight I don't care about defensiveness or listening or anything . . . I just want to yell and get it off my chest!"

When you feel like this, it's almost impossible to be rational. At times like these, probably the most therapeutic thing to do is to get your feelings off your chest in what Bach calls a "Vesuvius"—an uncontrolled, spontaneous explosion. A Vesuvius can be a terrific way of blowing off steam, and after you do so, it's often much easier to figure out a rational solution to your problem.

So we encourage you to have a Vesuvius with the following qualifications: Be sure your partner understands what you're doing and realizes that whatever you say doesn't call for a response. He or she should let you rant and rave for as long as you want without getting defensive or "tying in." Then, when your eruption subsides, you can take steps to work through whatever still troubles you.

summary

An interpersonal relationship is an association in which two or more people meet one another's social needs to a greater or lesser degree. Relationships can be described in terms of their breadth and depth and by examining both content and relational dimensions of the messages exchanged.

People are attracted to one another for a number of reasons: similarity, complementary traits, mutual liking, net gain, competency, self-disclosure, and frequency of interaction. Each of these factors has its limits, however. Whatever their basis, relationships can be divided into stages of development. These stages are sequential, though not all relationships reach the final stages.

Self-disclosure is the process of deliberately revealing significant information about one's self that would not normally be known. Self-disclosure can be characterized using a Johari Window, which reveals an individual's open, blind, hidden, and unknown areas. Self-disclosure can exist on several levels of depth. The most superficial level is that of clichés, followed by facts, opinions, and feelings. Self-disclosure is not always desirable: The chapter listed several guidelines to help determine when it is and is not appropriate.

The chapter concluded by describing the nature of interpersonal conflict, which is inevitable in any ongoing relationship. There are four individual conflict styles: nonassertive, directly aggressive, indirectly aggressive, and assertive. Two or more people can approach a conflict with either a win-lose or a win-win attitude. The text outlined the steps to follow when seeking a win-win outcome.

activities

1. List the names of five people with whom you have strong positive personal relationships. Use the list that follows to identify the basis of your attraction.
   a. Are their interests, attitudes, values, beliefs, or backgrounds similar to yours?
   b. Do they fill a complementary need for you?
   c. Are they attracted to you?

157

d. Is your relationship a fair exchange of rewards?

e. Are they competent but human?

f. Have they shared personal information with you?

g. Do you encounter them frequently?

Now consider five people with whom you would like to build a stronger relationship. Use the same list to decide whether you are the kind of person they would be attracted to.

2. You can use the Johari Window model to examine the level of self-disclosure in your own relationships.

a. Use the format described in Figure 6–7 to draw two Johari Windows, representing the relationship between you and one other person. Remember to reverse one of the windows so that your open areas and those of the other person face each other.

b. Describe which parts of yourself you keep in the hidden area. Explain your reasons for doing so. Describe the costs and / or benefits of not disclosing these parts of yourself.

c. Look at the blind area of your model. Is this area large or small because of the amount of feedback (much or little) that you get from your partner or because of your willingness to receive the feedback that is offered?

d. Explain whether or not you are satisfied with the results illustrated by your answers. If you are not satisfied, explain what you can do to remedy the problem.

3. Think of a person you would like to know better. Using the levels of self-disclosure in this section, identify the kind of sharing that goes on between you now. Think of two factual statements, two opinions, and two expressions of feeling that you could share as a way of increasing the level of disclosure. Before actually delivering these messages, be sure to read the guidelines on pages 142–144.

4. What is your conflict style? You can find out by answering the following questions.

a. Recall five conflicts you've been involved in. The more recent they are, the better, and they should be involvements with people who are relatively important to you.

b. Turn an 8½-by-11-inch sheet of paper horizontally, and divide it into three columns. In the first one describe the nature of each conflict: who it involved and what it was about. In the second column describe how you handled the conflict: what you said and how you acted. Use the third column to describe the results of each conflict: how you felt, how the others involved felt, and your satisfaction with the outcome.

c. Based on your findings here, answer the following questions:

(1) Are you happy with the way you've handled your conflicts? Do you come away from them feeling better or worse than before?

(2) Have your conflicts left your relationships stronger or weaker?

(3) Do you recognize any patterns in your conflict style? For example, do you hold your angry feelings inside, are you sarcastic, do you lose your temper easily?

(4) If you could, would you like to change the way you deal with your conflicts?

5. This exercise will help you develop a win-win solution for a problem in your own life.

  a. Make a list of the situations in your life where there's a conflict of needs that's creating tension between you and someone else.

  b. Analyze what you're doing at present to resolve such conflicts, and describe whether your behavior is meeting with any success.

  c. Pick at least one of the problems you just listed and, together with the other people involved, try to develop a win-win solution by following the steps listed earlier.

  d. After working through Steps 1 to 7, listed on pages 152–156, share the results of your conference with the class. After you've had time to test your solution, report the progress you've made, and discuss the follow-up conference described in Step 8.

notes

1. I. Altman and D. A. Taylor, *Social Penetration: The Development of Interpersonal Relationships* (New York: Holt, Rinehart and Winston, 1973).

2. P. Watzlawick, J. Beavin, and D. D. Jackson, *Pragmatics of Human Communication* (New York: W. W. Norton, 1967), pp. 80–83.

3. These theories are summarized in D. E. Hamachek, *Encounters with Others: Interpersonal Relationships and You* (New York: Holt, Rinehart and Winston, 1982), pp. 52–69; and E. Berscheid and E. H. Walster, *Interpersonal Attraction,* 2d ed. (Reading, Mass.: Addison-Wesley, 1978).

4. Mark L. Knapp, *Interpersonal Communication and Human Relationships* (Boston: Allyn & Bacon, 1984), Chapter 2. See also J. G. Delia, "Some Tentative Thoughts Concerning the Study of Interpersonal Relationships and Their Development," *Western Journal of Speech Communication* 44 (1980): 97–103; and R. Lacoursiere, *The Life Cycle of Groups* (New York: Human Sciences Press, 1980).

5. John T. Wood, *What Are You Afraid Of?: A Guide to Dealing with Your Fears* (Englewood Cliffs, N.J.: Spectrum, 1976).

6. Joseph Luft, *Of Human Interaction* (Palo Alto, Calif.: National Press, 1969).

7. Adapted from John Powell, *Why Am I Afraid to Tell You Who I Am?* (Niles, Ill.: Argus, 1969).

8. Joyce H. Frost and William W. Wilmot, *Interpersonal Conflict* (Dubuque, Iowa: W. C. Brown, 1978), pp. 9–14.

9. George R. Bach and Herb Goldberg, *Creative Aggression* (Garden City, N.Y.: Doubleday, 1974).

10. Albert C. Filley, *Interpersonal Conflict Resolution* (Glenview, Ill.: Scott, Foresman, 1975), p. 23.

11. George Bach and Yetta Bernhard, *Aggression Lab: The Fair Fight Training Manual* (Dubuque, Iowa: Kendall-Hunt, 1971).

12. Thomas Gordon, *Parent Effectiveness Training* (New York: New American Library, 1975), pp. 263–264.

seven

interviewing

After reading this chapter, you should understand:

1. The most common types of interviews.
2. The characteristics that define interviewing and distinguish it from other types of communication.
3. The types and uses of interview questions.
4. The roles of interviewer and interviewee, both before and during an interview.
5. The functions of each stage in an interview.

You should be able to:

1. Identify the types of interviews you will most commonly encounter.
2. Define the purpose of an interview in which you might participate.
3. Develop a list of questions to accomplish the goal of an interview.
4. Participate effectively in an interview, both as interviewer and interviewee.

A potential employer greets a job applicant: "Let's begin by talking about exactly why you're interested in this opening."

A professor calls a student aside after class: "Neither of us was very happy with your grade on the last exam. I'd like to see where the problem is so you'll do better on the final."

A customer replies to the salesperson's offer of help: "I've been thinking about buying a tape deck, and I'd like to see what you have."

One guest approaches another at a party: "I want to do some backpacking next summer, and I've heard that you've spent a lot of time in the mountains. I was hoping you could suggest some trails and tell me what to expect."

Mention the word *interview*, and most people will think of a news correspondent questioning some public figure or a job applicant facing a potential employer. Though these images are accurate, they only tell part of the story. We all take part in interviews. Some are work-related, determining whether you will get the job you want and how you will do once you have landed the position. Others center around important personal relationships, focusing on everything from finding the perfect birthday gift to solving personal problems. Interviewing also comes into play when you want to learn important information from people with whom you aren't personally involved, perhaps about school, vacationing, how to fix a car, where to find a good restaurant, or what it was like to meet a famous person. Some interviews are formal, and others are casual. Sometimes you are the one who asks the questions; sometimes you are the person who responds. But in all these cases, the ability to get and give information is an important one.

the nature of interviewing

What is interviewing, and how does it differ from other kinds of communication? These are the questions the next few pages will answer.

interviewing defined

Most communication experts would agree with a definition of interviewing as *a form of oral communication involving two parties, at least one of whom has a preconceived and serious purpose, and both of whom speak and listen from time to time.*[1] This description tells us several important characteristics of interviewing.

The phrase *oral communication* emphasizes the critical role of the spoken word. A verbal interview is far superior to a written one in several ways. First, a spoken exchange gives the interviewer a chance to follow up on ideas that emerge as important. Another advantage of face-to-face interviewing comes from the nonverbal messages that accompany a spoken exchange. Tone of voice, emphasis on certain words, disfluencies such as stammers and stutters, and the other paralinguistic clues we discussed in Chapter 5 add a new dimension to any inter-

action. For the same reason, in-person interviewing with its accompanying postures, gestures, facial expressions, and so on offers more information than does a written exchange or even one over the telephone.

The phrase *two parties* needs some explanation. There are certainly cases when one person is questioned by a panel of interviewers and other times when two or more respondents face a single interviewer. But no matter how many participants are involved, in every case interviews are *bipolar:* One person or group is exploring issues with another person or group.

When we say that at least one party *has a preconceived and serious purpose,* we distinguish interviews from casual interactions in which the only goal is to pass the time. The fact that an interview has a serious purpose doesn't mean that enjoyment is against the rules—simply that the goal goes beyond sociability.

The words *both of whom speak and listen from time to time* make it clear that interviews are exchanges of messages. In most cases this exchange involves questions and answers. If either the speaker or the listener dominates the situation, then the interaction becomes a public-speaking situation, even though there may be only one person in the audience.

how interviewing differs from conversation

One way to understand the nature of interviewing is to see what it is not. There are several ways in which interviews differ from conversations. We have already seen that conversations can occur without the

interviewing
163

No talking reporter ever held a decent interview.

John Hohenberg

participants having any serious preconceived purpose: Two people chat between floors in an elevator, friends swap jokes at a party, boss and employees take a break around the coffee machine. An interview, on the other hand, always has a goal.

A second difference involves the amount of structure present. Conversations can be aimless affairs in which neither person knows (or cares) when the exchange will end or exactly what topics will be covered. Any good interview, in contrast, has several distinct parts, which we'll discuss in a few pages.

A third difference involves control. Whereas conversations don't require any guidance from one of the parties, an interviewer should always be acting in ways that keep the exchange moving toward the preset purpose.

A final difference between conversations and interviews involves the amount of speaking done by both parties. Though most conversations involve roughly the same amount of input from each person, authorities on interviewing suggest that participation ought to be in the 70 to 30 percent ratio, with the interviewee doing most of the talking.[2]

planning the interview

A good interview begins long before you sit down to face the other person. There are several planning steps you can take to boost your chances for success.

the interviewer's role

Using Tables 7–1 and 7–2 as guides, choose the most important situation in which you will be an interviewer. Think about yourself in this situation as you read the following section.

table 7–1   types of interviews

Information-gathering	Problem and evaluation
Investigating products and services	Appraisal/performance (employment and academic)
Research	
Career exploration	Counseling (personal and professional)
On-the-job (caseworker, medical, and so on)	Complaint/grievance
Personal interest	
Survey (market, political, and so on)	**Persuasive**
Journalistic	Selling products
	Selling services
Selection	Quasi-commercial selling (charitable, political, religious, and so on)
Hiring	
Promotion	
Placement	

table 7–2   subjects of interviews

Job-related	**Financial**
Investigating career	Advice
Employment selection	Assistance (loans, and so on)
Job performance	Investigation (tax audit, and so on)
Employee grievance	Other _____
Counseling	
Sales	**Other**
Other _____	Personal problems
	Information
School	Family
Investigating courses, major, and so on	Recreation
Understanding coursework	Other_____
Expressing dissatisfaction with course, program, and sk on	Other _____
Other _____	
Consumer	
Investigating products	
Investigating services	
Complaining about products or services	
Other _____	

Clarify the purpose   What do you want to accomplish in the interview? The answer to this question will often seem obvious. For example, in an information-gathering interview you might want to find the best places to go on an upcoming vacation or to find out more about "the old days" from an older relative. But often a purpose that seems clear will prove too vague to get you what you want. For example, your questions about a vacation could result in a list of places too expensive for you or unrelated to your interests. In the same way, your request for information about the old days could bring on a string of stories about long-dead (and uninteresting) relatives when you are really interested in events rather than personalities.

The more clearly you can define the goal of your interview, the greater your chances for success will be. One way to set clear goals is to think about specific content areas you'll need to explore to achieve your general purpose. See how this process of focusing on a goal works in the following situations:

general goal	**specific content objectives**
Learn best place to go.	Discover affordable, beautiful place that is different from home.

Learn about old days.	Learn how daily routines differed from now, how area looked before it was built up, what social relationships were like, what people did for recreation.
Choose best roommate to fit with present occupants of apartment.	Find person with similar or compatible study habits, dating life, ideas about neatness; also, person must be financially responsible.
Get mechanic's opinion about whether I should fix up present car or get a newer one.	Explore cost of repairing old one vs. expense of fixing up newer one, determine life expectancy, performance, mileage of old vs. new.

Develop tentative questions More than any other factor the quality of the interviewer's questions and the way they are asked will determine the success or failure of an interview. Truly good questions rarely come spontaneously, even to the best of interviewers. After you define your goals and content objectives, the next step is to develop a list of questions. You need to think about several factors in planning questions:

1. **Relationship to purpose.** Your questions should cover all the content objectives you developed in the previous step. Furthermore, it's important to cover each area in the amount of depth that suits your needs. For example, in interviewing an instructor about how best to prepare for an exam, you should briefly cover the areas you feel confident about while spending enough time on tougher subjects to be sure you're prepared. This suggestion may seem obvious, but many inexperienced interviewers find to their dismay that they have wasted most of their time discussing trivial areas and have failed to get their most important questions answered.

2. **Factual vs. opinion questions.** Some questions involve matters of fact: "What's the difference between an integrated amplifier and a preamplifier?" or "How many points will I need to earn an *A* for the course?" Questions like these can be called *factual.* In other cases, you'll want to ask questions that seek the subject's *opinion:* "What occupations do you think will offer the best chance for advancement in the next few years?" or "How do you think I should go about apologizing?" When planning an interview, you should ask yourself whether you're more interested in facts or opinions and plan your questions accordingly.

   In some cases, you can approach a question either factually or subjectively, often with quite different results. For example, imagine that you're interviewing two close friends, trying to resolve a conflict between them. Notice the difference between asking, "Where do you think the problem lies?" (a broad, subjective question that invites disagreement between the disputants) and "What are some of the things bothering each of you?" (a factual question that doesn't call for the parties to read each other's minds). Again, you need to think clearly about whether you're seeking facts or opinions.

3. **Open vs. closed questions.** You have almost certainly had the frustrating experience of trying to draw out an uncommunicative partner:

You	"How've you been?"
Other	"Fine."
You	"Up to anything new lately?"
Other	"Nope. Same old stuff."
You	"You look good. Have you been getting a lot of exercise?"
Other	"Not really."

   Although the respondent here could have certainly done better at holding up the other end of the conversation, much of the problem grew out of the type of questions being asked. All of them were *closed:* questions that could be answered in a word or two. Though some talkative subjects will freely amplify on a closed question, less outgoing ones will give you the briefest response possible. The best way to encourage interviewees to talk up is by asking *open questions,* which require the subject to answer in detail:

interviewing

167

Judge a man, not by his answers, but by his questions.

Voltaire

"If you had the chance to start your career over again, what things would you do differently?"

"What were some of the things you liked best about New York?"

"Start at the beginning and tell me just what happened."

It will take time and thought to develop a list of open questions to cover all your content areas, but your effort will be rewarded in several ways. First, you will almost certainly have enough lengthy responses to fill the allotted time, soothing a common fear of inexperienced interviewers. Your open questions, inviting comment as they do, will also make your subject feel more comfortable. Furthermore, the way in which your subject chooses to answer your open questions will tell you more about him or her than you could probably learn by only asking more restrictive closed questions.

Closed questions aren't all bad: For one thing they're easy for many subjects to answer, and you can ask many of them in a short period of time. Also, closed questions are appropriate for some subjects. For example, you wouldn't want long-winded replies to questions such as "What's the cost of part #1234?" or "What is your social security number?" As an interviewer, you should decide what type of information you need, then choose the combination of open and closed questions that will get it for you.

4. Direct vs. indirect questions. Most of the time the best way to get information is to ask for it clearly and directly:

"Have you had any experience in this kind of work?"

"How much were you planning to spend for a new coat?"

"What kinds of things are you looking for in an apartment and new roommates?"

There are times, however, when a subject won't be able to answer a direct question. At one time or another, most of us have been so confused that we've answered the question "What don't you understand?" by replying in exasperation, "Everything!" In other cases, you've heard yourself or someone else sincerely answer the question "Do you understand?" in the affirmative, only to find out later that this wasn't true.

There are also times when a subject might be *able* to answer a question sincerely but isn't *willing* to do so. This sort of situation usually occurs when a candid answer would be embarrassing or risky. For instance, when interviewing a prospective roommate, you'd be naive to ask, "Do you always pay your share of the rent on time?" because a truly shifty person would probably answer yes.

At times like these it's wise to seek information by using indirect questions. You could ask potential roommates whether their share of the rent money would be coming from current work (then check to see if they're employed) or from savings. In the same way, instead of asking, "Are you creative?," a prospective employer might present a job applicant with a typical or hypothetical situation, looking for an innovative solution.

5. **Primary vs. secondary questions.** Sometimes you will only need to ask one question—called *primary*—to get the fact or opinion you need in a given content area. But more often you will need to follow up your first question with others to give you all the information you need. These follow-up probes are called *secondary* questions.

Primary question: "In your opinion who are the best people for me to ask about careers in the computer field?"

Secondary questions: "How could I meet them?" "Do you think they'd be willing to help?" "How could each one help me?"

It's a good idea to develop a list of secondary questions in each content area so you can be sure to get all the information you need. Why fumble on the spot for a way to follow up an incomplete answer when you can plan in advance?

Arrange the setting Even the best questions won't help an interview that takes place in a bad setting. To avoid such problems, keep these two considerations in mind as you arrange a meeting with your subject.

The first is *time*. Just as you should pick a time that is convenient for you, it's equally important for you to do the same for the interviewee. When arranging an appointment with your subject, be sure you've avoided predictably busy days or hours when the press of unfinished business may distract your interviewee. If you can, tactfully discover whether the subject is a morning or evening person—some people function especially well or poorly at certain times of the day. You should also make sure that the interviewee doesn't have appointments or other obligations that will overlap with your scheduled time.

The right *place* for an interview is also important. The most important consideration is to have a spot that is free of distractions. A constantly ringing telephone or other people dropping by to ask questions or chat can throw you and your subject off the track. If any of your questions call for confidential answers, the setting should be private. It's also important for the location to be convenient for both parties. Neither you nor the interviewee will do best if you've had to struggle for a parking place or gotten lost trying to find the right spot. Finally, your setting should be comfortable and attractive enough to put your subject at ease. Don't go overboard and choose too relaxed a setting: Too many beers or the pleasures of a beach might lead you or your interviewee to forget your main reason for meeting.

the interviewee's role

Because most of the responsibility for planning an interview rests with the interviewer, the subject has an easier time during the planning phase. There are, however, some things a respondent can do in advance to make the interview a good one.

Clarify the interviewer's goals It's important to know just what the interviewer is seeking from you. Sometimes the interviewer's goals are obvious. The insurance sales representative who wants "to see if you're paying too much for your present coverage" is trying to sell you a new policy, and a friend who wants to know how you've repaired an object or fixed a recipe is probably looking for your expertise.

In other cases, the interviewer's goal isn't quite so clear. Sometimes you know the general goal of the interview but need to understand the specific content areas more clearly. For example, suppose you are preparing for an employment interview. You know that the company is looking for the best applicant to fill the job. But just what kinds of qualities are they seeking? Are education and training most important? Experience? Initiative? Knowing these criteria in advance will boost your chances of doing well in the interview.

There will be times when an interviewer has hidden goals, which you should do your best to discover. For instance, your boss's questions about your daily job routine might really be part of the managerial process of deciding whether to promote (or fire) you. An acquaintance's ostensible questions about factual information might really be aimed at building a friendship. This last example shows that not all hidden goals are malicious, but in any case you'll feel more comfortable and behave more effectively when you know what the interviewer wants from you.

Clarify your own goals Sometimes the subject's only role in an interview is to help the questioner. But there are other times when you, as an

---

table 7–3 checklist for interview planning

interviewer	interviewee
Goals ☐ General purpose defined ☐ Specific content areas listed	**Goals** ☐ Interviewer's goals clearly understood ☐ Interviewee's goals clearly defined
Tentative questions ☐ Cover all content areas in specific depth ☐ Each question properly phrased as factual or opinion ☐ Each question properly worded as open or closed ☐ Each question properly worded directly or indirectly	**Preparation** ☐ Necessary information, materials collected ☐ Thought given to interviewer's probable questions
Setting ☐ Best time chosen for both interviewer and subject ☐ Private, comfortable, distraction-free setting chosen	

interviewee, will have your own agenda. Although a sales representative might be trying to sell you an insurance policy, you could be interested in getting an education on the subject. When your boss conducts an interview assessing your performance, you might want to learn by observation how to do the same thing later in your career when you're a manager. Keep your own goals in mind when thinking about the upcoming session.

Do your homework   There are many cases in which a subject can make an interview run quickly and well by preparing materials or answers in advance. If you know that the interviewer will be seeking certain information, get it together before your meeting. Sometimes you'll need to bring facts and figures, as when you need to justify your claims during an income tax audit. At other times an interviewee should collect materials. For instance, an interviewer describing what college is like to a graduating high school senior might bring along class schedules, catalogs, textbooks, and exams.

Preparation is an important step in interviewing. But once the interviewer and subject get together, there's more to do than simply ask and answer the prepared questions.

stages of an interview

An interview, like the speeches you'll read about in later chapters, has three distinct parts.

Opening   This beginning stage serves two important functions. Most important, it establishes the tone of the relationship between interviewer and subject: formal or informal, relaxed or tense, serious or humorous. Just as the first stages of a date or party will generally shape what comes later, the success or failure of an interview is often determined before the first question is asked. Besides setting the tone, a good introduction will also give the interviewee a preview (or reminder) of the interviewer's goals and what subjects will be covered.

The usual format for an opening begins with some sort of greeting, which includes any introductions that are necessary. A period of informal conversation sometimes follows, in which the interviewer and subject talk about subjects of mutual interest not necessarily related to the interview topic. This period gives both people a chance to get settled and acquainted before getting down to business. This greeting stage may sound artificial—which it often is. But there's no need to discuss obviously trivial subjects or act phony here: the idea is to establish some common ground sincerely between interviewer and subject.

In the final stage of the opening, the interviewer should preview topics of discussion and brief the subject on plans for proceeding: "I appre-

conducting the interview

ciate your giving me the time. I expect my questions will take about forty-five minutes. I'd like to start by learning how you got started, then go on to talk about what you've learned during your career, and finish by asking for any suggestions you have that might help me in my career."

Body This middle stage of the interview is the longest. It's here that the interviewer asks the questions that were planned before the meeting.

Although the list of questions is important, it's sometimes a mistake to follow them precisely. Some areas will need more exploration, whereas others won't seem worth pursuing. The trick in the body of the interview is to focus on all the important content areas in a way that seems most comfortable to both interviewer and subject. (We'll have more to say about the roles of each party shortly.)

Closing In many ways, the closing is similar to the opening. Instead of previewing, however, the conclusion is a time for reviewing what's occurred during the interview. This helps ensure that the interviewer has correctly understood any points that might be unclear and has gotten the general tone of the subject matter correctly.

The closing is also a time to establish the future of the relationship between interviewer and subject: to decide if any future meetings are necessary, possibly to set a date for them. Finally, it's usually good to conclude the interview with an exchange of sincere pleasantries. Table 7–4 summarizes the points to remember when planning, conducting, and evaluating an interview.

table 7–4   checklist for evaluating interviews

Opening
☐ Sincere, appropriate pleasantries exchanged to help both parties feel comfortable
☐ Proper tone established (formal vs. informal, serious vs. casual)
☐ Interviewer previews subject and approach

Body
☐ Interviewer's nonverbal behavior reflects interest and lack of threat to subject
☐ Interviewer asks enough questions to cover all content areas established in advance
☐ Interviewer uses probes to explore client's responses (repetition, amplification, paraphrasing, silence)
☐ Interviewee gives clear, detailed answers
☐ Interviewee keeps on subject
☐ Interviewee corrects any misunderstandings of interviewer
☐ Interviewee achieves own goals

Closing
☐ Interviewer reviews results of interview
☐ Future relationship between interviewer and interviewee established
☐ Sincere pleasantries exchanged

the interviewer's role

During the session the interviewer is responsible for several areas:

Controlling and focusing the conversation The interviewer's job is to ensure that each stage of the conversation—opening, body, and closing—takes the right amount of time and that all important content areas are covered. It's easy to get off on a tangent and discover too late that the available time is up.

Help the subject feel comfortable In simplest terms this includes making sure that the setting is physically comfortable. But it's just as important that the interviewer use the listening, relational, and nonverbal skills we discussed earlier in this book to help the subject feel at ease. For example, suppose the interviewee seems reluctant to share personal information in an important content area. The interviewer might then remember that self-disclosure is reciprocal and volunteer some information such as the reasons for asking all the questions.

Probe for important information Sometimes your first question in a certain area won't give you all the information you need. At times like this it's important to probe for the facts or beliefs you're seeking by asking secondary or follow-up questions. There are several types of probes you can use as an interviewer:

1. Repeat. Either because of evasiveness or fuzzy thinking, subjects sometimes need to hear a question several times before giving a full answer.

Adult (*breaking up fight between two children*) "Hey, what's this all about?"
Child A "He's a punk!"
Adult "But what were you fighting about?"
Child B "It's not my fault! She started it!"
Adult "But what were you fighting about?"
Child A "I did *not* start it. *You* started it!"
Adult "I don't care who started it. I just want to find out what you're fighting about."

2. Amplify. When an answer is incomplete, you need to get more information.

Customer "I want to buy some running shoes."
Salesperson "What kind of running do you do?"
Customer "Oh, mostly just for fun."
Salesperson "I mean how far do you run and on what kind of surfaces?"
Customer "I mostly run on the track at the high school . . . a few miles."
Salesperson "When you say a few miles, do you mean three or four each time you run, or more?"

3. Paraphrase. Active listening, as discussed in Chapter 4, serves two purposes. First, it helps to clarify a vague answer. In addition it encourages the speaker to give more information about the topic.

A "I'm so fed up with that class that I'm ready to drop it. I just wanted to talk it over with you before I did."
B "So you're pretty sure that the right thing to do would be to quit because the class is giving you so much trouble."
A "Well, I'm just not sure. The semester is almost over and if I did drop it now, I'd just have to repeat the class later."
B "So you're really not sure what to do, is that it?"
A "Oh, I guess I ought to stick it out. It's just that I'm really tired. I'll sure be glad when the semester is over."

4. Silence and prods. A bit of experimenting will show you how useful a pause and such brief but encouraging phrases such as "Really?" "Uh-huh," "I see," and "Tell me more about it" can be. Often a subject will be anxious to talk about a subject if simply given a sympathetic and interested ear.

the interviewee's role

There are several things you can do as a subject to make the interview a success.

Give clear, detailed answers Put yourself in the interviewer's shoes, and be as specific and helpful as you hope others would be for you. Although the interviewer ought to draw you out skillfully, make that job easier by being helpful yourself.

Keep on the subject It is sometimes tempting to go overboard with your answers, sidetracking the discussion into areas that won't help the interviewer. It's often a good idea to ask the questioner whether your answers are being helpful and then to adjust them accordingly.

Correct any misunderstandings Sometimes an interviewer will misinterpret your ideas. When this happens, be sure to correct the mistaken impression. Of course, one way to be certain that the message was received correctly is to invite the interviewer to paraphrase what he or she thinks you said. When an important issue in in question, any conscientious interviewer will be willing to do so.

Cover your own agenda As we pointed out earlier in this chapter, interviewees often have their own goals, which are sometimes different from those of the interviewer. It's important to keep these in mind during the session so that you can satisfy your own needs in a way that is compatible with the questioner's purpose.

For many people the short time spent facing a potential employer is the most important interview of a lifetime. After all, a great deal is at stake. Most of us spend the greatest part of our adult lives on the job: roughly 2,000 hours per year for a full-time employee. In addition the financial difference between an unrewarding position and a well-paying one can be staggering. Even without considering the effects of inflation, a gap of only $200 per month can amount to almost $100,000 over the course of a career. Finally, the emotional stakes of having the right position are high. A frustrating job not only can block the chances for advancement and lead to unhappiness at work; these dissatisfactions have a way of leaking into nonworking hours as well.

How important is an interview in getting the right job? The Bureau of National Affairs, a private research firm that serves both the government and industry, conducted a survey to answer this question.[3] They polled 196 personnel executives to find out what factors are most important in hiring applicants. The results of their survey showed that the employment interview is the single most important factor in landing a job.

employment strategies

Most people naively believe that the best candidate gets the job. Although this principle might be fair and logical, the employment process usually doesn't work this way. In reality, *the person who knows the most about getting hired* usually gets the desired position. Though job-getting skills are no substitute for qualifications once the actual work begins, they are necessary if you are going to be hired in the first place.

What is the best strategy for getting the job offer you want? The advice job seekers often get is certainly important: Scan sources of job announcements for positions, and prepare a thorough, professional résumé. But beyond these steps are other strategies that can often give you a critical boost over other applicants.[4]

Background research Your first step should be to explore the types of work and specific organizations for which you'd like to work. This phase involves looking into all those areas that have interested you in the past. Through library research, reading magazine and newspaper articles, taking classes, and simply fantasizing, find out as much as possible about jobs that might be interesting to you. The result of your research should be a list of organizations and of people who can tell you more about your chosen field and help you make contacts.

Background interviews At this point arrange to meet the people on the list you have just developed. These meetings are *not* employment interviews in which you're specifically asking for job. Rather, they serve three purposes:

1. To help you learn more about the fields and companies that interest you.

As you sit across the table from the man or woman you'd most like to work for, it is crucial that you relate your skills to what's going on in their head, not merely to what's going on in yours. If I'm dying for lack of a creative artist in my organization, and you walk in and show me you have a genuine skill in that area, you are interpreting your skills in terms of my problems. But if I have long since decided I don't need any more help with art work, and you try to sell me on the idea that I need one (namely, you), you are falling into the pitfall of interpreting your skills in terms of *your* problems, not mine.

Richard Bolles
What Color Is Your Parachute?

2. To help you make contacts that might later lead to a job offer from your interview subject.
3. To develop leads about other people you might contact for help in your job search.

These background interviews are information-gathering in nature, so it's wise to read the section of this chapter that deals with this subject before beginning this step.

tips for the interviewee

Once you are in the interview itself, there are several important points to keep in mind.

Follow the interviewer's lead Let the interviewer set the emotional tone of the session: amount of humor, level of formality, and so forth. A great deal depends on the personal chemistry between interviewer and candidate, so try to match the interviewer's style without becoming phony.

table 7–5 common job interview questions

questions from the employer

What makes you think you're qualified to work for this company? (How can you help us?)

What have you been doing since your last job?

Why are you interested in this company? This job?

What do you want in your career?

What would you do if . . . (hypothetical situation)

Where do you see yourself in five years?

Tell me about your experience.

What did you like (not like) about your last job?

What's your greatest strength (limitation) for this job?

questions for the employer

Will you describe the duties of the job for me, please?

Will you tell me where this job fits within the organization?

What characteristics do you most hope to find in people for this kind of assignment?

Can you tell me about the prospects for advancement beyond this level?

What is the biggest problem facing your staff now? How have past and current employees had trouble solving this problem?

What have been the best results produced by people in this job?

What are the primary results you would like to see me produce?

Can you describe the ideal candidate for this job? Then we can see how closely I fit your requirements.

table 7–6   common interviewer complaints about job applicants

1. Is caught lying.
2. Shows lack of interest in the interview, merely shopping around.
3. Has a belligerent attitude, is rude or impolite.
4. Lacks sincerity.
5. Is evasive concerning information about himself or herself.
6. Is concerned only about salary.
7. Is unable to concentrate.
8. Displays a lack of initiative.
9. Is indecisive.
10. Has an arrogant attitude.
11. Has a persecuted attitude.
12. Tries to use pull to get a job.
13. Has dirty hands or face.
14. Is cynical.
15. Is intolerant and has strong prejudices.
16. Is late for the interview.
17. Has a limp-fish handshake.
18. Is unable to express himself clearly.
19. Shows lack of planning for career.
20. Has not done research into history and products of the company.
21. Wants to start in an executive position.
22. Lacks maturity.
23. Has low moral standards.
24. Presents extreme appearance.
25. Oversells case.

Based on Charles S. Goetzinger, Jr., "An Analysis of Irritating Factors in Initial Employment Interviews of Male College Graduates," unpublished doctoral dissertation, Purdue University, 1954. Cited in Charles J. Stewart and William B. Cash, Jr., *Interviewing: Principles and Practices*, 2d ed. (Dubuque, Iowa: W. C. Brown, 1978).

Respond to the employer's needs   Though you may need a job to repay your student loan or finance your new Porsche, these concerns won't impress a potential employer. Companies hire an employee to satisfy *their* needs. Your approach in an interview, then, should be to show your potential employer how your skills match up with the company's concerns. Here's where your background research will pay off: If you've spent time learning about your potential employer, you'll be in a good position to talk about that company's concerns and how you can satisfy them.

Recognize and respond to hidden questions   As you read earlier in this chapter, some questions are indirect. For example, the question "Where do you see yourself five years from now?" most likely means "How ambitious are you? How well do your plans fit with this company's goals? How realistic are you?" In the same way, when an interviewer asks, "Why did you leave your last job?" the real questions are probably "Are you competent? Can you get along with others?"

Be honest   Whatever else an employer may be seeking, honesty is a key job requirement. If an interviewer finds that you've misrepresented yourself by lying or exaggerating about even one answer, everything else you say will be suspect. Emphasize your strengths, and downplay your weak areas, of course, but always be honest.

Keep your answers brief   It's easy to rattle on in an interview, either out of enthusiasm, a desire to show off your knowledge, or nervousness; but in most cases long answers are not a good idea. The interviewer probably has lots of ground to cover, and long-winded answers won't help this task. A good rule of thumb is to keep your responses under two minutes.

Look good and behave well   You should obviously present a good image. Dress neatly and appropriately, be on time, and bring along any necessary materials.

Have your own questions answered   Any good employer will recognize that you have your own concerns about the job. After you've answered the interviewer's questions, you should be prepared to ask a few of your own. See Table 7–5 for some suggestions.

the information-gathering interview

Although you might not label them as such, you almost certainly take part in a great many information-gathering interviews. Whenever you investigate an offer of goods or services, seek advice about the future, explore another person's opinions or background, or seek specific facts, you are conducting an interview. The following suggestions will help you do a good job.

collecting background information

Sometimes a period of research can pay dividends when the actual interview begins. Suppose, for instance, that you have decided to treat yourself to a foreign vacation. You have heard about a travel agent who arranges unusual trips—river rafting, mountain climbing, tramp steamer voyages, and so on. You've made an appointment to talk with the agent and hear some suggestions. Of course, it's the agent's job to interview *you* to find out what kind of trip suits your interests; but at the same time your advance research can help you both in answering the agent's questions and in asking some of your own. What parts of the world interest you? Read about those areas to discover any interesting features you'd like to see. What about types of transportation? Climates? Lifestyles? Having thought about areas like these will boost the chances that you'll arrange the best vacation.

choosing the right interviewee

Sometimes the most obvious subject for an interview isn't the best person to answer your questions. Asking an instructor about how a course is taught might not be as productive as talking to students who have taken it in the past. Seeking financial advice from a wealthy person might not be helpful if that subject made the money in times that were different from these or if the subject's interests or skills are different from yours. Sometimes knowing *whom* to ask is just as important as knowing *what* to ask.

informational interviewing tips

In addition to the general suggestions on pages 164–174, follow these pointers when conducting informational interviews.

Be curious Whereas matters like wording questions correctly and choosing the right environment are important, another essential ingredient for success in interviewing is honest curiosity, as shown by a willingness to follow a line of questioning until you're satisfied and to ask about points that interest you. Your sincere curiosity will often warm up an interviewee, who will be flattered by your interest. And an inquiring attitude will help you think of new and important questions during your interview, transforming it from what might be a sterile recitation of the questions you prepared in advance.

Check your understanding After reading Chapter 4 you know that much listening is inaccurate. Keeping this fact in mind, you will find it a good idea to check your understanding of important ideas with the interviewee. Sometimes the consequences of misunderstanding are fairly small: a botched recipe (was it a tablespoon or a cup of vinegar?) or getting lost (were you supposed to turn right or left?). In other cases, however, misunderstandings can be more serious. The fact that you thought you understood an instructor's explanation won't change your low grade on a final exam, and the Internal Revenue Service won't forgive your tax penalties because you thought the local agent said something that turned out to be something else. Whenever there's a chance of misinterpretation, it's a good idea to use the active listening skills you learned earlier in this book.

Use the best interviewing strategy In many cases, your best approach is to ask questions in the simplest, most straightforward manner. There are times, however, when a more strategic approach will produce better results.

You have already read about the value of asking indirect questions when direct ones will be embarrassing or difficult to answer. Instead of asking a merchant, "Will your advice about products or service be any good?" you could ask about some product that you already know about.

Hal Higdon once started an interview with, "Why don't you tell me a little bit about what you've done?" "If you don't know," retorted the subject, "what are you doing here?"

John Brady
The Craft of Interviewing

He who asks is a fool for five minutes. He who does not ask is a fool forever.

Chinese proverb

There are also times when the personality of your interviewing subject calls for a strategic way of presenting yourself. For instance, if you are talking to someone whose self-image is one of being an authority or a wise person, you might take a *naive* approach: "Gee, I'm new at this, and you know so much." A little flattery never hurts. At other times you might want to act more like an *interrogator,* particularly when you think a subject is trying to treat you like a fool. For instance, you could show your knowledge and seriousness to a car mechanic by saying, "Why did you suggest a valve job without running a compression check?" (Here's one case where gathering background information on automotive repair could improve your interviewing and save you a healthy chunk of money.) In still other cases a *sympathetic* or *chummy* approach can be helpful. Investing the time and money to chat over coffee or beers can shake loose information a subject might be unwilling to share in a more formal setting.

other interview types

the persuasive interview

The most recognizable type of persuasive interview involves the selling of some commercial product, either merchandise or service. But there are also noncommercial situations in which the interview aims at changing the attitudes or behavior of a subject. Candidates meet with prospective voters, either in person or via broadcast media; religious people try to influence the beliefs of others; and representatives of charitable organizations are constantly seeking more funds for their causes, often in interview settings.

There are several steps to follow for a successful persuasive interview:

Define your goal In Chapter 11 we'll talk in detail about defining a public speaking goal. Some of the same principles apply here. You ought to have a clear idea of just what kind of change you're seeking in your subject. Your goal should be specifically worded, and it should be a realistically attainable one.

Understand the interviewee A persuasive approach that will convince one person will be ineffective with others. Your best chance of success will come from understanding your subjects—their interests, concerns, level of knowledge, and background.

Use persuasive strategies Chapter 15 contains a list of persuasive strategies that are useful in both public speaking and interview settings. In addition to the items there, you should consider these guidelines:[5]

1. Welcome the subject's questions and reactions. They tell you how the interviewee is responding to your approach, giving you a chance to adapt and keep on target. It is important, however, for you to choose the time when the other person voices his or her concerns. You should keep control of the interview to avoid complicating the discussion.

2. Show that you understand the interviewee's position. The fact that you understand will leave the other person feeling more positive about you, diminishing the "hard-sell" image.

3. Keep your approach clear and simply stated. Only bring up one subject at a time, and organize your presentation logically. See Chapters 12 and 13 for more suggestions in this area.

the appraisal interview

Appraisal interviews are most common in school and job settings, where a student or employee's performance is judged. At its best, the appraisal process is a tool for recognizing accomplishments and finding ways to improve performance in problem areas. But in practice things sometimes work out differently. It's not hard to see why: Appraisal is a form of evaluation, and as such has a high potential for arousing defensiveness. Here are a few suggestions for making appraisal interviews truly productive.

As an interviewee:

1. Remember that criticism of your work in one area doesn't mean you're no good as a person or even in other areas in which you interact with the interviewer.

2. Approach the interview with a sincere desire to do better. View the interview as a chance to start improving your performance. This attitude will impress the interviewer and will help you grow.

3. When faced with vague descriptions of your behavior ("You're doing well" or "You're not keeping up"), ask the interviewer for specific examples. Your goal here isn't to be argumentative but to understand exactly what the interviewer is talking about.

4. Do your best to avoid behaving defensively by counterattacking or withdrawing. Though reactions like these are understandable, they probably won't make you feel any better and are likely to lower your stature in the interviewer's eyes.

As an interviewer:

1. Acknowledge good work as well as pointing out problem areas.

2. Be improvement-oriented. Try to focus on making things better rather than simply criticizing. Set specific behavioral goals (see Chapter 3) for the upcoming evaluation period.

3. Be descriptive, not evaluative. Describe how the interviewee's behavior affects you and the organization.

4. Be a good listener. Try really to understand the respondent's point of view. Remember the value of active listening when someone else is upset.

interviewing

181

the counseling interview

Few people are professional counselors or therapists, but at one time or another we're all faced with the chance to help solve another person's problem: love, career, family, money . . . the list of troublesome areas is a long one.

There are two approaches to counseling others with problems—directive and nondirective. The directive approach includes a good deal of question asking, analysis, and advice. There are definitely situations in which this approach is the best one, most often when the counselor has greater knowledge than the interviewee. For example, a friend might approach you for advice on how to get help from some consumer-protection agency. If you know the right procedure, you surely would share this information and suggest how your friend ought to proceed.

There are many other cases when a directive approach isn't the best one. Suppose your problem-ridden friend asks for advice about whether or not to get married. Even the best advice can be ignored or rejected at times like this. There is another risk in giving advice: If your friend follows your suggestions and things don't work out, you are the one who's likely to be held responsible.

The most important decision in counseling interviews, then, is whether to use a directive or nondirective approach. Be sure to base your decision on knowledge of the person seeking help and on the nature of the problem. In any case, it's essential to know just how much

help and guidance one can give as a friend and when it's dangerous to begin playing counselor without the necessary training. It's better to say, "I don't know what to tell you" than to give bad advice to a person in need.

the survey interview

Surveys are a type of information gathering in which the responses of a sample of a population are collected to disclose information about a larger group. Surveys are used in government, businesses, and educational concerns. Interviews are a valuable way of surveying, for they provide greater respondent cooperation, depth of response, and flexibility than other means of gathering data, such as questionnaires.

In order to be effective, survey interviews must collect data from a representative sample of the population in question. A classic example of poor sampling occurred in the 1936 presidential election, when a popular magazine, *Literary Digest,* interpreted the results of over two million surveys to mean that Alfred Landon would beat Franklin D. Roosevelt by a landslide. Hindsight showed that the incorrect prediction arose from the fact that the respondents were chosen from telephone directories and automobile registration lists. During the Great Depression only upper- and middle-class people fell into these categories. Thus, the survey failed to give adequate representation to the millions of less affluent Democrats who were to choose Roosevelt.

Most survey interviews are highly structured, with respondents all being asked identical questions in identical order. This sort of structure ensures that all respondents are, in fact, being approached in the same way. Survey interviewers are trained to standardize their approach, even to the extent of repeating the same nonverbal behaviors from one situation to the next. For example, a smile in one interview might encourage responses that would differ from those elicited by a more restrained approach.

Interviewing is a special kind of conversation, being more purposeful, structured, controlled, and one-sided than other types of two-party interaction. There are many types of interviews—information gathering, selection, problem and evaluation, and persuasive. Each of these types contains several subcategories, which are listed in Table 7–1.

A successful interview begins with a planning phase before the parties meet. During that time, the interviewer should define the goal of the session, develop tentative questions, and arrange the setting. The questions should be closely related to the purpose of the interview. Thought should also be given as to whether questions will be factual or opinion seeking, open or closed, and direct or indirect. When necessary, primary questions should be followed up by secondary inquiries. In the preparation stage, the interviewee should clarify the interviewer's goals

summary

as much as possible and do whatever planning will help the session run smoothly.

Interviews consist of three stages—opening, body, and closing. During the session the interviewer should control and focus the conversation, help the subject feel comfortable, and probe for important information. The interviewer's role includes giving clear, detailed answers, keeping on the subject, and correcting any misunderstandings. In addition interviewers should also be sure to accomplish their own goals.

Though the steps outlined early in the chapter are useful in all contexts, specific types of interviews have their own requirements. Selection and information-gathering interviews were discussed in some detail; and persuasive, appraisal, counseling, and survey interviews were briefly described.

activities

1. Almost everybody takes part in interviews. This exercise will help you identify the subjects and types of interviews that play a role in your life.

   a. Use Table 7–2 to identify interviewing situations that you have experienced. In addition to noting situations in which you have been involved in the past, you can also list the kinds of interviews in which you will be involved in the future. (For example, you may know you'll take part in an employment interview and realize that you should also seek advice about potential employers before doing so.)

   b. For each subject indicate the type of interview in which you'll be involved, using Table 7–1 as a guide.

   c. For each situation indicate whether you will play the role of interviewer or interviewee.

   d. Finally, for each item you've checked, write the name of the person or persons with whom you'll be speaking. If you don't know any names, describe them as best you can (for example, potential boss, irate customer).

2. Choose one situation in which you'll be an interviewer. Using that situation:

   a. List your objectives for the interview.

   b. Translate these goals into content areas.

   c. Write a list of tentative questions sufficient to explore each content area. Be sure your questions follow the suggestions in this chapter.

3. How well do you understand the nature of interview questions? Find out by identifying each of the following questions as either open or closed, factual or opinion-seeking, primary or secondary. For each primary question you identify, write two secondary questions. For each closed question, write an open question that would generate additional useful information.

a. "Have you been hospitalized in the last five years?"
b. "I don't blame you for wanting good roommates. What kinds of things do you think make a roommate good?"
c. "You've been awfully quiet lately. Are you upset?"
d. "Now that you've told me which parkas you have in stock, do you think the more expensive one is worth the extra money?"
e. "Can you give me some examples of the type of questions we'll need to answer in each area?"

4. This exercise will help you build your skill at probing for more information when interviewing subjects. For each statement that follows write an appropriate probing response. Be sure to use each of the following types of response at least once:
a. "I'd never hire her!"
b. "Career advice? I'd check with the placement office on campus." (You asked about advice from people already in business.)
c. "I'm not sure how to answer that."
d. "I'm probably wasting your time."
e. "I guess what I'm looking for are some useful courses."
f. "The book by Jones and Smith might help you."

notes

1. Robert S. Goyer, W. Charles Redding, and John T. Rickey, *Interviewing Principles and Techniques: A Project Text* (Dubuque, Iowa: Kendall-Hunt, 1968), pp. 6–7.
2. Charles J. Stewart and William B. Cash, Jr., *Interviewing: Principles and Practices*, 3d ed. (Dubuque, Iowa: W. C. Brown, 1982), p. 10.
3. Cited in Richard N. Bolles, *What Color Is Your Parachute?: A Practical Manual for Job-Hunters and Career Changers,* rev. ed. (Berkeley, Calif.: Ten Speed Press, 1980), p. 140.
4. These steps are based on the suggestions of Bolles, op. cit.
5. Cal Downs, Wil Linkugel, and David M. Berg, *The Organizational Communicator* (New York: Harper & Row, 1977), pp. 120–121.

part 3 communication in groups

eight

the nature of groups

After reading this chapter, you should understand:

1. The characteristics that distinguish groups from other collections of people.
2. The types of goals that operate in groups.
3. The various types of groups.
4. The characteristics of groups described in this chapter.
5. The advantages and disadvantages of the decision-making methods introduced in this chapter.

You should be able to:

1. Identify the groups you presently belong to and those you are likely to join in the future.
2. List the personal and group goals in groups you observe or belong to.
3. Identify the norms, roles, and interaction patterns in groups you observe or belong to.
4. Choose the most effective decision-making method for a group task.

How important are groups?

You can answer this question for yourself by trying a simple experiment. Start by thinking of all the groups you belong to now and have belonged to in the past: the family you grew up with, the classes you have attended, the teams you have played on, the many social groups you have been a member of. . . . The list is a long one. Now, one by one, imagine that you had never belonged to each of these groups. Start with the less important ones, and the results aren't too dramatic; but very soon you will begin to see that a great deal of the information you have learned, the benefits you have gained . . . even your very identity have all come from group membership.

This doesn't mean that every group experience is a good one. Some are vaguely unrewarding, rather like eating food that has no taste and gives no nourishment. And others are downright miserable. Sometimes it is easy to see why a group succeeds or fails, but in other cases matters aren't so clear.

This chapter will help you understand better the nature of group communication. It will start by explaining just what a group is—for not every collection of people qualifies. It will go on to examine the reasons people form groups and then look at several different types of groups. Finally, it will conclude by looking at some common characteristics all groups share.

what is a group?

Imagine that you are taking a test on group communication. Which of the following would you identify as groups?

a crowd of onlookers gawking at a burning building

several passengers at an airline ticket counter discussing their hopes to find space on a crowded flight

an army battalion

As all these situations seem to involve groups, your experience as a canny test taker probably tells you that a commonsense answer will get you in trouble here—and you're right. When social scientists talk about groups, they use the word in a special way that excludes each of the preceding examples.

What are we talking about when we use the term *group?* For our purposes a group consists of *a small collection of people who interact with each other, usually face to face, over time in order to reach goals.* A closer examination of this definition will show why none of the collections of people described in the preceding quiz qualify as groups.

interaction

Without interaction a collection of people isn't a group. Consider, for example, the onlookers at a fire. Though they all occupy the same area at a given time, they have virtually nothing to do with each other. Of

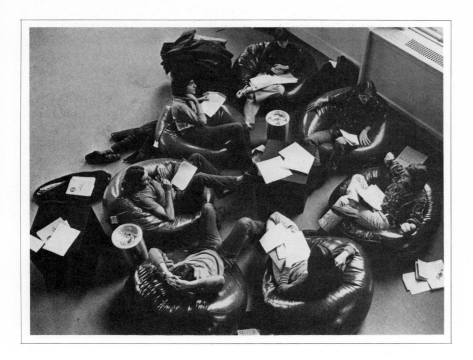

course, if they should begin interacting—working together to give first aid or to rescue victims, for example—the situation would change. This requirement of interaction highlights the difference between true groups and collections of individuals who merely *coact*—simultaneously engaging in a similar activity without communicating with one another. For example, students who passively listen to a lecture don't technically constitute a group until they begin to exchange messages with each other and their instructor. (This explains why some students feel isolated even though they spend so much time on a crowded campus. Despite being surrounded by others, they really don't belong to any groups.)

As you read in Chapters 3 and 5, there are two types of interaction that go on in any communication setting. The most obvious type is verbal, in which group members exchange words either orally or in writing. But people needn't talk to each other in order to communicate as a group: Nonverbal channels can do the job, too. We can see how by thinking again about a hypothetical classroom. Imagine that the course is in its tenth week and the instructor has been lecturing nonstop for the entire time. During the first few meetings there was very little interaction of any kind: Students were too busy scribbling notes and wondering how they would survive the course with grade-point averages and sanity intact. But as they became more used to the class, the students began to share their feelings with each other. Now there's a great amount of eye rolling and groaning as the assignments are poured on, and the students exchange resigned sighs as they hear the same tired jokes for the second and third time. Thus, even though there's no verbal exchange of sentiments, the class has become a group—interestingly, in this sense a group that doesn't include the professor.

time

A collection of people who interact for a short while don't qualify as a group. As you'll soon read, groups that work together for any length of time begin to take on characteristics that aren't present in temporary aggregations. For example, certain standards of acceptable behavior begin to evolve, and the way individuals feel about each other begins to affect their behavior toward the group's task and toward each other. According to this criterion, onlookers at a fire might have trouble qualifying as a group even if they briefly cooperated with one another to help out in the emergency. The element of time clearly excludes temporary gatherings such as the passengers gathered around the airline ticket counter. Situations like this simply don't follow many of the principles you'll be reading about in the next two chapters.

size

Our definition of groups included the word *small*. Most experts in the field set the lower limit of group size at three members. This decision isn't arbitrary, for there are some significant differences between two-

Is this a group?

and three-person communication. For example, the only way two people can resolve a conflict is either to change one another's mind, give in, or compromise; in a larger group, however, there's a possibility of members forming alliances either to put increased pressure on dissenting members or to outvote them.[1]

There is less agreement about when a group stops being small. Though no expert would call a 500-member army battalion a group in our sense of the word (it would be labeled an organization), most experts are reluctant to set an arbitrary upper limit. Probably the best description of smallness is the ability for each member to be able to know and react to every other member. It's sufficient to say that our focus in these pages will be on collections of people ranging in size from three to between seven and twenty.

goals

Group membership isn't always voluntary, as most draftees and prison inmates will testify. But whenever people choose to join groups, they do so because membership will help them achieve one or more goals. At first the goal-related nature of group membership seems simple and obvious. In truth, however, there are several types of goals, which we will now examine.

We can talk about two types of goals when we examine groups. The first category deals with the motives of individual members whereas the second involves the goals of the group itself.

individual goals

Task-related goals   The most obvious reason individuals join groups is to accomplish some task—to get a job done. Some people join study groups, for example, in order to improve their knowledge. Others belong to religious groups as a way of improving the quality of their lives and those of others. (There may be additional reasons for going to school and church, as we will soon see.)

Sometimes a member's task-related goals will have little to do with a group's stated purpose. Many merchants, for example, join service clubs such as Kiwanis, Rotary, or Lions primarily because doing so is good for business. The fact that these groups help achieve worthy goals such as helping the blind or disabled is fine, of course, but for many people it is not the prime motive for belonging.

Social goals   What about groups with no specifically defined purpose? Consider, for instance, a gathering of regulars at the beach on sunny weekends or a group of friends who eat lunch together several times a week. Collections such as these meet the other criteria for being groups:

goals of groups and their members

They interact, meet over time, and have the right number of members. But what are the members' reasons for belonging? In our examples here, the goals can't be sunbathing or eating because these activities could be carried out alone. The answer to our question introduces the second type of group goals, which are social. In many cases, people join together in order to get the inclusion, control, and affection we mentioned in Chapter 1.

We join many, if not most, groups in order to accomplish both task and social goals. School becomes a place both to learn important information and to meet desirable friends. Our work becomes a means of putting food on the table and getting recognition for being competent. The value of making a distinction between task and social goals comes from recognizing that the latter are usually important but often not stated or even recognized by group members. Thus, asking yourself whether social goals are being met can be one way of identifying and overcoming blocks to group effectiveness.

group goals

So far we have discussed the forces that motivate individual group members. In addition to these individual motives, there also exist group goals. For example, athletic teams exist to compete with each other, and academic classes strive to transmit knowledge.

Sometimes there is a close relationship between group and individual goals. In athletic teams the group goal is to win whereas individual members' goals include helping the group succeed. If you think about it for a moment, however, you'll see that the individual members have other goals as well: improving their physical ability, having a good time, overcoming the personal challenges of competition, and often gaining the social benefits that come from being an athlete. The difference between individual and group goals is even more pronounced when the two are incompatible. Consider, for instance, the case of an athletic team that has one player more interested in being a "star" (satisfying personal needs for recognition) than in helping the team win. Or recall classes you have known in which a lack of student enthusiasm made the personal goal of many students getting by with the smallest possible amount of work—hardly consistent with the stated group goal of conveying information. Sometimes the gap between individual and group goals is public whereas in other cases an individual's goal becomes a *hidden agenda*. In either case, this discrepancy can be dangerous for the well-being of the group and needs to be dealt with. We'll have more to say about this subject in Chapter 9.

types of groups

So far we have seen that there are a variety of goals that groups fulfill. Another way of examining groups is to look at some of the functions they serve.

learning groups

When the term "learning" comes up, most people think first about school. Although academic settings certainly qualify as learning groups, they aren't the only ones. Members of a scuba diving class, friends who form a Bible study group, and members of a League of Women Voters chapter all belong to learning groups. Whatever the setting or subject, the purpose of learning groups is to increase the knowledge or skill of each member.

Learning groups take a variety of formats. Most familiar is the lecture, in which one or more speakers dispense information to several listeners. Learning also takes place in two-way exchanges of information, when each member is both a contributor and receiver of knowledge. Sometimes the learning becomes more active, as when skiers or aspiring musicians develop their skill by practicing it.

growth groups

Unlike learning groups, in which the subject matter is external to the members, growth groups focus on teaching the members more about themselves. Consciousness-raising groups, Marriage Encounter workshops, counseling, and group therapy are all types of growth groups. These are unlike most other types of groups in that there is no real collective goal: The entire purpose of the group is to help the members identify and deal with their personal concerns.

problem-solving groups

Problem-solving groups work together to resolve a mutual concern. Sometimes the concern involves the group itself, as when a family decides how to handle household chores or when co-workers meet to coordinate vacation schedules. In other instances, the problem is external to the group. For instance, neighbors who organize themselves to prevent burglaries or club members who plan a fund-raising drive are focusing on external problems.

Problem-solving groups can take part in many activities: One type is gathering information, as when several students compile a report for a class assignment. At other times a group makes policy—a club deciding whether or not to admit the public to its meetings being an example. Some groups make individual decisions; an interview committee deciding which candidate to hire is fulfilling this function.

social groups

We have already mentioned that some groups serve strictly to satisfy the social needs of their participants. Some social groups are organized whereas others are informal. In either case the inclusion, control, and affection that such groups provide are reason enough for belonging.

characteristics of groups

Whatever their function, all groups have certain characteristics in common. Understanding these characteristics is a first step to behaving more effectively in your own groups.

norms

Norms are agreements about how people should behave toward one another.[2] Some norms—called "laws" or "rules" by sociologists—are *explicit,* spelling out what behaviors are appropriate and prohibited. In a classroom, explicit norms include matters such as the number of permissible absences, whether papers must be typed or may be handwritten, and so on. Although *implicit* norms are just as powerful and important as explicit ones, they are not stated overtly. For instance, you probably won't find a description of what jokes are and aren't acceptable in the bylaws of any groups you belong to, yet you can almost certainly describe the unstated code if you think about it. Is sexual humor acceptable? How much, and what types? What about religious jokes? How much kidding of other members is proper? Matters such as these vary from one group to another, according to the norms of each one.

There are three categories of group norms: social, procedural, and task.[3] *Social* norms govern the relationship of members to each other. How honest and direct will members be with one another? What emotions will and won't be expressed, and in what ways? Matters such as these are handled by the establishment of social norms, usually implicit ones. *Procedural* norms outline how the group should operate. Will the group make decisions by accepting the vote of the majority, or will the members keep talking until consensus is reached? Will one person run

A fighter pilot soon found he wanted to associate only with other fighter pilots. Who else could understand the nature of the little proposition (right stuff/death) they were all dealing with? And what other subject could compare with it? It was riveting! To talk about it in so many words was forbidden, of course. The very words *death, danger, bravery, fear* were not be uttered except in the occasional specific instance or for ironic effect. Nevertheless, the subject could be adumbrated in *code* or *by example* . . . They diced that righteous stuff up into little bits, bowed ironically to it, stumbled blindfolded around it, groped, lurched, belched, staggered, bawled, sang, roared, and feinted at it with self-deprecating humor. Nevertheless!—they never mentioned it by name.

Tom Wolfe
The Right Stuff

---

meetings, or will discussion be leaderless? *Task* norms focus on how the job itself should be handled. Will the group keep working on a problem until everyone agrees that its product is the best one possible, or will members settle for an adequate, if imperfect solution? The answer to this question results in a task-related norm. All groups have social norms whereas problem-solving, learning, and growth groups also have procedural and task norms.

Table 8–1 lists some of the norms most people bring to a task-oriented group's first meeting. It is important to realize that cultural

table 8–1 expected norms for a discussion group's first meeting

social	procedural	task
Do	Do	Do
—serve refreshments	—introduce people	—criticize ideas, not people
—dress casually	—plan to participate	—support the best idea
—use first names	—establish goals	—commit yourself to group
—discuss uncontroversial	—build agenda	solutions
subjects	—hold routine meetings one	—share in the workload
—tell humorous jokes	hour in length	—say so if you disagree
—tell political jokes (they will	—have someone in charge	—ask questions about group
be tolerated)	—sit face-to-face	ideas
—tell trend or one-line jokes		
—tell cultural truisms	Don't	Don't
	—leave meetings without	—push your idea on the
Don't	cause	group
—smoke (perhaps)	—monopolize conversation	—support ideas just because
—swear	—stand up and speak in	of people who presented
—arrive late	small-group meetings	them
—be absent without apology	(generally)	—be verbally violent if you
—tell sexist, racist, ethnic,	—demand to lead	disagree with ideas
agist, or religious jokes	—refuse to speak when	—consider your ideas as the
	addressed	only ones of merit

"What are we? Humans? Or animals? Or savages? What's grownups going to think? Going off—hunting pigs—letting fires out—and now!"

A shadow fronted him tempestuously.

"You shut up, you fat slug!"

There was a moment's struggle and the glimmering conch jigged up and down. Ralph leapt to his feet.

"Jack! Jack! You haven't got the conch! Let him speak."

Jack's face swam near him.

"And you shut up! Who are you, anyway? Sitting there telling people what to do. You can't hunt, you can't sing—"

"I'm chief. I was chosen."

"Why should choosing make any difference? Just giving orders that don't make any sense—"

"Piggy's got the conch."

"That's right—favor Piggy as you always do—"

"Jack!"

Jack's voice sounded in bitter mimicry.

"Jack! Jack!"

"The rules!" shouted Ralph. "You're breaking the rules!"

"Who cares?"

Ralph summoned his wits.

"Because the rules are the only thing we've got!"

William Golding
Lord of the Flies

norms such as these are *idealized* and that a group's actual norms emerge as its members spend time together. Consider the matter of punctuality, for example. A cultural norm in our society is that meetings should begin at the scheduled time, yet some groups soon generate the usually unstated agreement that the real business won't commence until ten or so minutes later. On a more serious level, one cultural norm is that other people should be treated politely and with respect, but in some groups failure to listen, sarcasm, and even outright hostility make the principle of civility a sham.

roles

Where norms define acceptable group standards, roles refer to the patterns of behavior expected of individual members.[4] Just like norms, some roles are formally recognized. These explicit roles usually come with a label, such as "professor," "chairperson," or "student." Other roles are informal; they are very real although group members may not acknowledge—or even consciously realize—their existence. For instance, you can probably think of many informal groups in which some members are clearly leaders and others followers, although these positions have never been discussed.

Social scientists have found that there are certain functions (see Table 8–2) that must be carried out if a group is to operate effectively. Each function corresponds to a role that one or more members must fulfill. Although some theorists have argued with details of this list, it remains a valuable tool for two reasons. First, it is easily understandable: The role names provide a clear description of each function. The second advantage of the list is the distinction it makes between two types of functions, task and maintenance. *Maintenance* functions help keep the personal relationships of group members running smoothly, whereas *task* functions help learning, growth, and problem-solving groups accomplish their goals.

Role emergence We said earlier that most group members aren't aware of the existence of functional roles. You will rarely find members saying things like "You ask most of the questions, I'll give opinions, and she can be the summarizer." Yet it's fairly obvious that over time certain members do begin to fulfill specific functions. How does this process occur?

There are two answers to this question. One factor in role differentiation is certainly the personal characteristics of each member. Some people, for example, seem to be more critical than others and thus feel comfortable as diagnosers and evaluators. Others are particularly aware of personality dynamics and find it easy to get along with other members, which makes them good harmonizers and interpersonal problem solvers.

In addition to the personal skills and traits of individual members, the idiosyncrasies of each particular group shape the roles that each member takes. In other words, each of us plays a different role in different

table 8–2 functional roles of group members

task functions	maintenance functions
1. Information giver	12. Participation encourager
2. Opinion giver	13. Harmonizer
3. Information seeker	14. Tension reliever
4. Opinion seeker	15. Evaluator of emotional climate
5. Starter	16. Process observer
6. Direction giver	17. Praise giver
7. Summarizer	18. Empathetic listener
8. Diagnoser	19. Interpersonal problem solver
9. Energizer	
10. Reality tester	
11. Evaluator	

Adapted from Kenneth D. Benne and Paul Sheats, "Functional Roles of Group Members," *Journal of Social Issues* 4 (1948): 41–49.

groups. For example, a normally nonassertive person might act as a starter or direction giver in a group where no one else was performing that necessary task. In some cases, this assumption of uncharacteristic roles isn't voluntary: Members informally assign functions to members who wouldn't otherwise have taken them. This kind of role assignment shows up in movies, where the hapless passenger or the untrained but courageous flight attendant saves the plane after an accident wipes out the pilot. In more humdrum but common situations you've probably heard people assigning roles by saying things like "You know something about that, what do you think?"—a clear invitation to become an information or opinion giver.

Role-related problems Groups can suffer from at least two role-related problems. The first occurs when one or more important functional roles go unfilled. The most common example of this happens in groups where there is no information giver to provide some vital knowledge. A more subtle (but equally dangerous) role vacuum occurs when maintenance functions aren't filled. If nobody relieves interpersonal tensions, gives praise, or solves interpersonal problems at critical times, a group will have a hard time accomplishing its task. There are other cases when the problem isn't an *absence* of candidates to fill certain roles, but an *overabundance* of them. This situation can lead to unstated competition between members, which gets in the way of group effectiveness. You have probably seen groups in which two people both want to be the tension-relieving comedian. In such cases, the problem arises when the members in question become more concerned with getting laughs than with getting the group's job done.

patterns of interaction

In Chapter 1 we said that communication involves the flow of information between and among people. It almost goes without saying that this exchange needs to be complete and efficient for the communicators to reach their goals. In interpersonal and group settings, information exchange is relatively uncomplicated, taking basically two routes: either between the two individuals in an interpersonal dyad or between speaker and audience in a public speaking situation.* In groups, however, things aren't so simple. The mathematical formula that identifies the number of possible interactions between individuals is

$$\frac{N(N-1)}{2}$$

---

* Actually this is a slight oversimplification. In public-speaking situations members of an audience also exchange messages with one another with their laughter, restless movements, and so on. It's still fair to say, however, that the exchange of information is basically two-way.

where N equals the number of members in a group. Thus, in even a relatively small five-member group, there are ten possible combinations of two-person conversations and a vastly greater number of potential multiperson interactions. Besides the sheer quantity of information exchange, the more complex structure of groups affects the flow of information in other ways, too.

Physical arrangement It's obviously easier to interact with someone you can see well. Lack of visibility isn't a serious problem in dyadic settings, but it can be troublesome in groups. For example, group members seated in a circle are more likely to talk with persons across from them than those on either side.[5] Different things happen when members are seated in rectangular arrangements. Research with twelve-person juries showed that those sitting at either end of such tables participated more in discussions and were viewed by other members as having more influence on the decision-making process.[6] Rectangular seating patterns have other consequences as well. Research conducted on six-person groups seated at rectangular tables showed that as distance between two persons increased, other members perceived them as being less friendly, less talkative, and less acquainted with each other.[7]

Bill Bernbach, when he was building the most exciting advertising agency of his time, had a round conference table in his office. He tried the customary rectangular one, but, as he said, ''The junior men always sat at the foot and I sat at the head, and I learned that the light of conviction is often in the eyes of junior men. With a round table, I was closer to them and less likely to miss it.''

Robert Townsend
Up the Organization

figure 8–1
Small group communication networks

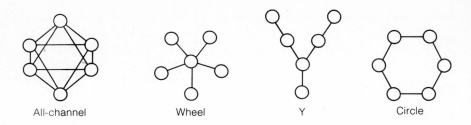

All-channel   Wheel   Y   Circle

Communication networks When group members meet face-to-face, information flows freely among them. But this open structure doesn't always exist. For instance, think about working groups in which members occupy separate offices or even social groups where members talk with each other one at a time over the telephone. The patterns that individual channels of communication form between group members are called networks. Figure 8–1 pictures several communication networks for five-person groups. The circles represent group members, and lines represent communication among them.

Does the structure of a communication network have any effect on group interaction? Much experimentation indicates that it does. Perhaps the most significant effect involves leadership emergence. In groups with no formal leader, the person who occupies a central position in any network has the greatest chance of emerging as a leader.[8] This principle contains a practical tip for aspiring leaders: Do whatever you can to become the clearinghouse for your group's information. Offer to keep members informed of any news, collect information from them, be present whenever there's a subgroup meeting, and chat casually with other members whenever you get the chance.

Communication networks also affect group problem solving. As Figure 8–1 shows, there are two basic types of networks, centralized and each-to-all. In the centralized pattern, one person serves as the clearinghouse for all information and solves the problem, using the information provided from others. In each-to-all groups, on the other hand, every member has equal access to information and potentially has an equal chance to contribute to solving the group's problems. Extensive research has shown that centralized networks work better in some situations whereas each-to-all arrangements are more productive in others. When the group faces an ambiguous task, an each-to-all approach works most effectively—probably because the greater amount of input boosts the chances of finding a good solution.* A centralized approach works best with simple, routine tasks, because there is less time occupied by communication that interferes with getting the job done.[9]

* Centralized group structures such as chains and stars (see Fig. 8–1) can still manage tasks in an each-to-all manner by using memos, verbal message passing, and other methods. Although such feats are possible, they are difficult. When decentralized communication is appropriate, it's far better to structure the group accordingly.

communication in groups

202

decision-making methods

Another way to classify groups is according to the approach they use to make decisions. There are several methods a group can use to decide matters. We'll look at each of them now, examining their advantages and disadvantages.[10]

Authority rule without discussion   This is the method most often used by autocratic leaders (see Chapter 9). Though it sounds dictatorial, there are times when such an approach has its advantages. First, the method is quick: There are some cases when there simply isn't time for a group to decide what to do. The method is also perfectly acceptable with routine matters that don't require discussion in order to gain approval. When overused, however, this approach causes problems. As Chapter 9 will show, much of the time group decisions are of higher quality and gain more support from members than those made by an individual. Thus, failure to consult with members can lead to a decrease of effectiveness, even when the leader's decision is a reasonable one.

Expert opinion   Sometimes one group member will be defined as an expert and, as such, will be given the power to make decisions. This method can work well when that person's judgment is truly superior. For example, if a group of friends are backpacking in the wilderness and one becomes injured, it would probably be foolish to argue with the advice of a doctor in the group. In most cases, however, matters aren't so simple. Who is the expert? There is often disagreement on this question. Sometimes a member might think he or she is the best qualified to make a decision, but others will disagree. In a case like this, the group probably won't support that person's advice, even if it is sound.

Authority rule after discussion   The method of authority rule after discussion is less autocratic than the preceding two, for it at least takes into consideration the opinions of more than one person. Thus, the unilateral decisions of an open-minded authority gain some of the increases in quality and commitment that come from group interaction while also enjoying the quickness that comes from avoiding extensive discussion. This approach has its disadvantages, however. Often other group members will be tempted to tell the leader what they think he or she wants to hear, and in other cases they will compete to impress the decision-maker.

Majority control   A naive belief of many people (perhaps coming from overzealous high school civics teachers) is that the democratic method of majority rule is always superior. This method does have its advantages in cases where the support of all members isn't necessary; but in more important matters it is risky. Remember, if a 51 percent majority of the members favor a plan, then 49 percent oppose it—hardly sweeping

During a [second grade] science project . . . one of the 7 year olds wondered out loud whether the baby squirrel they had in class was a boy or a girl. After pondering the issue for a few minutes, one budding scientist offered the suggestion that they have a class discussion about it and then take a vote.

Cal Downs, Wil Linkugel, and David M. Berg
The Organizational Communicator

support for any decision that needs the support of all members in order to work.

Minority control Sometimes a few members of a group will decide matters. This approach works well with noncritical questions that would waste the whole group's time. In the form of a committee, a minority of members also can study an issue in greater detail than can the entire group. When an issue is so important that it needs the support of everyone, it's best at least to have the committee report its findings for the approval of all members.

Consensus Consensus occurs when all members of a group support a decision. The advantages of consensus are obvious: Full participation can increase the quality of the decision as well as the commitment of members to support it. Consensus is especially important in decisions on critical or complex matters; in such cases, methods using less input can diminish the quality of or enthusiasm for a decision. Despite its advantages, consensus also has its drawbacks. It takes a great deal of time, which makes it unsuitable for emergencies. In addition, it is often very frustrating: Emotions can run high on important matters, and patience in the face of such pressures is difficult. Because of the need to deal with these emotional pressures, consensus calls for more communication skill than do other decision-making approaches. As with many things in life, consensus has high rewards, which come at a proportionately high cost.

Which of these methods is best? There's no single answer. The most effective method in a given situation depends on the circumstances: the amount of time available, the importance of the decision, the abilities of the group's leader, and the members' attitudes toward that person. The best approach might be to use the preceding descriptions of each method as guidelines in deciding which method to use in a particular situation.

summary

Groups play an important role in many areas of our lives—families, education, on the job, and in friendships, to name a few. Groups possess several characteristics that distinguish them from other communication contexts. They involve interaction over time among a small number of participants with the purpose of achieving one or more goals. Groups have their own goals, as do individual members. Member goals fall into two categories: task-related and social. Sometimes individual and group goals are compatible, and sometimes they conflict.

Groups can be put into several classifications—learning, growth, problem-solving, and social. All these types of groups share certain characteristics: the existence of group norms, individual roles for members, patterns of interaction that are shaped by the group's structure, and the choice of one or more ways of reaching decisions.

activities

1. Think about two groups to which you belong.
   a. What are your task-related goals in each?
   b. What are your social goals?
   c. Are your personal goals compatible or incompatible with those of other members?
   d. Are they compatible or incompatible with the group goals?
   e. What effect does the compatibility or incompatibility of goals have on the effectiveness of the group?

2. You can understand the nature of norms by thinking of one specific group to which you belong as you answer the following questions.
   a. What explicit norms govern your group's behavior? How were they announced?
   b. What implicit norms are in operation? What is the evidence of their existence?
   c. Use the examples from the preceding steps plus others to identify two social norms, two procedural norms, and two task norms.

3. Think of a group to which you belong.
   a. What functional roles do you fill in that group?
   b. Are those roles similar or different in other groups to which you belong?
   c. Are there any roles that are going unfilled in your group? How does this absence affect the group's functioning?

4. Draw a visual representation of the shape of the communication network in one group to which you belong. How does this type of network affect the decisions the group makes? Would a different type of network be better?

5. What is the physical setting in which your group meets? What effect does that setting have on the communication? Consider factors such as seating arrangement, level of light, ventilation, background noise, and degree of privacy. Are there any changes in the physical environment that could improve the group's effectiveness? How could you help make those changes?

6. Describe the methods of decision making used in family, classroom, and on-the-job groups to which you have belonged. Then answer the following questions for each group:
   a. Does the group use the same decision-making method in all circumstances, or does it use different methods at different times?
   b. After reading the advantages and disadvantages of each method, do you think the methods used by each group are appropriate? If not, what methods would be better? Why?

notes

1. C. David Mortensen, *Communication: The Study of Human Interaction* (New York: McGraw-Hill, 1972), pp. 267–268.
2. Earl R. Babbie, *Society by Agreement: An Introduction to Sociology* (Belmont, Calif.: Wadsworth, 1977).
3. John F. Cragan and David W. Wright, *Communication in Small Group Discussions: A Case Study Approach* (St. Paul, Minn.: West Publishing, 1980), p. 56.
4. Albert C. Kowitz and Thomas J. Knutson, *Decision Making in Small Groups: The Search for Alternatives* (Boston: Allyn & Bacon, 1980), p. 98.
5. B. Steinzor, "The Spatial Factor in Face-to-Face Discussion Groups," *Journal of Abnormal and Social Psychology* 45 (1950): 552–555.
6. F. L. Strodtbeck and L. H. Hook, "The Social Dimensions of a Twelve Man Jury Table," *Sociometry* 24 (1961): 397–415.
7. N. F. Russo, "Connotations of Seating Arrangements," *Cornell Journal of Social Relations* 2 (1967): 37–44.
8. Marvin E. Shaw, *Group Dynamics: The Psychology of Small Group Behavior,* 3d ed. (New York: McGraw-Hill, 1981), p. 153.
9. Ibid., p. 156.
10. Adapted from David W. Johnson and Frank P. Johnson, *Joining Together: Group Theory and Group Skills* (Englewood Cliffs, N.J.: Prentice-Hall, 1975), pp. 80–81.

nine

solving problems in groups

After reading this chapter, you should understand:

1. The advantages of solving problems in groups.
2. The four basic problem-solving steps.
3. The importance of effective listening and conflict resolution methods in group problem solving.
4. The factors that contribute to group cohesiveness.
5. The factors that contribute to balanced participation in groups.
6. The differences between "leader" and "leadership."
7. The various types of power in groups.
8. The various approaches to studying leadership.
9. The dangers in group discussion outlined in this chapter.

You should be able to:

1. Use the problem-solving steps outlined in this chapter in a group task.
2. Suggest ways to build the cohesiveness and participation in a group.
3. Analyze the sources of leadership and power in a group.
4. Suggest the most effective leadership approach for a specific group task.
5. Identify the obstacles to effective functioning of a specific group and suggest more effective ways of communicating.

209

Chapter 8 described various types of groups—learning, growth, social, and problem-solving. Of all these, problem-solving groups have been studied most intensively by social scientists. Once we understand the nature of problem solving, the reason becomes clear. "Problems," as we define them here, don't only refer to situations where something is wrong. Perhaps "meeting challenges" and "performing tasks" are better terms. Once you recognize this, you can see that problem solving not only occupies a major part of our working life, but plays an important role in other areas as well. At one time or another, all groups need to solve problems.

There are two sets of communication skills that any group must possess in order to come up with successful solutions. The first has to do with the group task itself: how to analyze the problem, choose the best solution, and make it work. A second area involves building and maintaining good relationships: making sure, first, that members feel good about each other to get the job done and, second, that they enjoy the experience of working together.

This chapter will focus on both the task and relational aspects of problem-solving groups. In addition, it will explore the nature of leadership, defining that important term and suggesting how groups can be led most effectively. Finally, it will list several common problems task-oriented groups can encounter and describe how to overcome them.

why use groups for problem solving?

To many people, groups are to communication what Muzak is to music or Twinkies are to food—a joke. The snide remark, "A camel is a horse designed by a committee," reflects this attitude as does this ditty:

Search all your parks in all your cities . . .
You'll find no statues to committees![1]

This unflattering reputation is at least partly justified. Most of us would wind up with a handsome sum if we had a dollar for every hour wasted in groups. On the other hand, it's unfair to view all groups as bad, especially when this accusation implies that other types of communication are by nature superior. After all, we also have wasted time listening to boring lectures, reading worthless books, and making trivial conversation.

So what's the truth: Is group problem solving a waste of effort, or is it the best way to manage a task? As with most matters, the truth falls somewhere between these two extremes. Groups do have their shortcomings, which we will discuss in a few pages. But extensive research has shown that when these shortcomings can be avoided, groups are clearly the most effective way to handle many tasks.

Over fifty years of research that has compared problem solving by groups and by individuals shows that in most cases groups can produce more solutions to a problem than individuals working alone . . . and that the solutions will be of higher quality.[2]

once upon a september day—

Another meeting! One after another without coming up with a proposal that would fly.

This one took place in early September and (not surprisingly) only a few people showed up—12, to be precise. And so they talked for some days and finally came up with a plan for still another meeting, eight months hence. It was hoped this would offer sufficient time to generate interest in the matter.

They also moved the location. It was not that the September site had been unpleasant—on the contrary, the facilities were quite good—but variety in meeting places might induce more individuals to attend.

Of the 74 invitees, 55 showed up. But they didn't all come at once. They were supposed to convene on Monday, May 14, but it wasn't until Friday, May 25, that enough were present to conduct business. They decided to work diligently from that day on until they finished their proposal. They even agreed to put a lid on their deliberations.

They were a relatively young group; the average age was 42. The youngest was 30 and the oldest 82 and prone to nod during long meetings. Although some were lackluster in ability, most were able and would later move to high executive positions.

They were together for 116 days, taking off only Sundays and 12 other days. And you might have guessed it: During a very hot summer they were without air conditioning. In addition to the formal sessions of the entire group, much of their work was done in committee and after hours.

The formal sessions sometimes got out of hand. One faction had come with a proposal that was almost the reverse of an outline offered by another group. The advocates of each seemed unwilling to bend, and by the end of June tempers were flaring so much that the oldest participant suggested beginning each session with an invocation.

By early June, they got wind of a way out of their impasse: Adopt a portion of each plan. By compromising, they might be better able to sell their product to a broad market. Yet even this task of drawing the line between two extremes was not easy, and so some decided to go home or back to their offices. It simply was not worth the effort.

Even among those who remained there was still criticism of the final proposal. It was much too short, some argued—only 4,000 words. Four months of work and only 4,000 words! It was scarcely enough to fill a few sheets of paper. But 39 of them felt it was the best they could come up with. It was good enough to sign, which they did on the 17th day of September, 1787.

And they called their proposal the Constitution of the United States.

Thomas V. DiBacco

Groups have proved superior at a wide range of tasks—everything from assembling jigsaw puzzles to solving complex reasoning problems. There are several reasons why groups are effective.[3]

resources

For many tasks, groups possess a greater collection of resources than do most individuals. Sometimes the resources are physical. For example, three or four people can put up a tent or dig a ditch better than a lone person. But on other problems the pooled resources lead to *qualitatively* better solutions. Think, for instance, about times when you have studied with other students for a test, and you will remember how much better the group was at imagining all the possible questions that might be asked and at developing answers to them. (This, of course, assumes that the study group members cared enough about the exam to have studied for it before the group meeting.) Groups not only have more resources than individuals; through interaction among the members they also are better able to mobilize them. Talking about an upcoming test with others can jog your memory about items you might not have thought of if you had been working alone.

accuracy

Another benefit of group work is the increased likelihood of catching errors. At one time or another, we all make stupid mistakes, like the man who built a boat in his basement and then wasn't able to get it out through the door. Working in a group increases the chance that foolish errors like this won't slip by. Sometimes, of course, errors aren't so obvious, which makes groups even more valuable as an error-checking mechanism. Another side to the error-detecting story is the risk that group members will support each other in a bad idea. We'll discuss this problem when we focus on comformity later in this chapter.

commitment

Besides coming up with superior solutions, groups also generate higher commitment to carrying them out. Members are most likely to accept solutions they have helped create, and they will work harder to carry out those actions. This fact has led to the principle of *participative decision making,* in which the people who will live with a plan help make it.[4] This is an especially important principle for those in authority such as supervisors, teachers, and parents. As professors, we have seen the difference between the sullen compliance of students who have been forced to accept a policy with which they disagree and the much more willing cooperation of classes who have helped develop it. Though the benefits of participative decision making are great, we need to insert a qualification here: There are times when an autocratic approach of imposing a decision without discussion is most effective. We will discuss this question of when to be democratic and when to be authoritarian in the section on leadership later in this chapter.

steps in problem solving

By now you can see that groups have the potential to be effective problem solvers. This doesn't mean that all groups are successful. What makes some succeed and others fail? To a great degree the answer lies in whether or not they have followed several necessary steps. Just as a poor blueprint or a shaky foundation can weaken a house, groups can fail by skipping one or more of the principles that follow. These principles were developed by John Dewey in 1910[5] and have been recommended with only slight variations by most experts on group process ever since.

identify the problem

Sometimes a group's problem is easy to identify. The crew of a sinking ship, for example, doesn't need to conduct a discussion to understand that its goal is to avoid drowning or being eaten by some large fish.

There are many times, however, when the problems facing a group aren't so clear. As an example, think of an athletic team stuck deep in last place well into the season. At first the problem seems obvious: an inability to win any games. But a closer look at the situation might show that there are other unmet goals—and thus other problems. For instance, individual members may have goals that aren't tied directly to winning: making friends, receiving acknowledgment as good athletes . . . not to mention the simple goal of having fun—of playing, in the recreational sense of the word. You can probably see that if the coach or team members took a simplistic view of the situation, looking only at the team's win-lose record, analyzing player errors, training methods, and so on, some important problems would probably go overlooked. In this situation, the team's performance could probably be best improved by working on the basic problems—the frustration of the players about having their personal needs met. What's the moral here? That *the way to start understanding a group's problem is to identify the concerns of each member.*[6]

What about groups that don't have problems? Several friends planning a surprise birthday party or a family deciding where to go for its vacation don't seem to be in the dire straits of a losing athletic team: They simply want to have fun. In cases like these, it may be helpful to substitute the word *challenge* for the more gloomy term *problem*. However we express it, the same principle applies to all task-oriented groups: The best place to start work is to identify what each member seeks as a result of belonging to the group.

B.C. by permission of Johnny Hart and Field Enterprises. Inc.

analyze the problem

Once you have identified the general nature of the challenge facing the group, you are ready to look at the problem in more detail. There are several steps you can follow to accomplish this important job.

Word the problem as a probative question[7] If you have ever seen a formal debate, you know that the issue under discussion is worded as a proposition: "The United States should reduce its foreign aid expenditures," for example. Many problem-solving groups define their task in much the same way. "We ought to spend our vacation in the mountains," suggests one family member. The problem with phrasing problems as propositions is that such wording invites people to take sides. Though this approach is fine for formal debates (which are contests rather like football or card games), premature side-taking creates unnecessary conflict in most problem-solving groups.

A far better approach is to state the problem as a question. Note that this question should be *probative*—one that encourages exploratory thinking. Asking, "Should we vacation in the mountains or at the beach?" still forces members to choose sides. A far better approach involves asking a question to help define the general goals that came out during the problem-identification stage: "What do we want our vacation to accomplish?" (that is, "relaxation," "adventure," "low cost," and so on).

Notice that this question is truly exploratory. It encourages the family members to work cooperatively, not forcing them to make a choice and then defend it. This absence of an either-or situation boosts the odds that members will listen openly to one another rather than listening selectively in defense of their own positions. There is even a chance that the cooperative, exploratory climate that comes from wording the question probatively will help the family arrive at consensus about where to vacation, eliminating the need to discuss the matter any further.

Gather relevant information Groups often need to know important facts before they can make decisions or even understand the problem. We remember one group of students who determined to do well on a class presentation. One of their goals, then, was "to get an *A* grade." They knew that to do so they would have to present a topic that interested both the instructor and the students in the audience. Their first job, then, was to do a bit of background research to find out what subjects would be well received. They interviewed the instructor, asking what topics had been successes and failures in previous semesters. They tested some possible subjects on a few classmates and noted their reactions. From this research they were able to modify their original probative question—"How can we choose and develop a topic that will earn us an *A* grade?"—into a more specific one—"How can we choose and develop a topic that contains humor, action, and lots of information (to demonstrate our research skills to the instructor) and that contains practical information that will either improve the audience's social life, academic standing, or financial condition?"

Identify impelling and restraining forces Once members understand what they are seeking, the next step is to see what forces stand between the group and its goals. One useful tool for this kind of analysis is the *force field analysis.*[8] The easiest way to understand the force field concept is to look at Figure 9–1. By returning to our earlier example of the troubled team, we can see how the force field operates. Suppose the group defined its problem-question as "How can we (a) have more fun and (b) grow closer as friends?"

One restraining force in area (a) was clearly the team's losing record. But more interestingly, discussion revealed that another damper on enjoyment came from the coach's obsession with winning and his infectiously gloomy behavior when the team failed. The main blocking force in area (b) proved to be the lack of socializing between team members in nongame situations. The driving forces in the first area included the sense of humor possessed by several members and the confession by most players that winning wasn't nearly as important to them as everyone had suspected. The impelling force in the area of friendship was the desire of all team members to become better friends. In addition, the fact that members shared many interests was an important plus.

It's important to realize that most problems have many impelling and constraining forces, all of which need to be identified during this stage. This may call for another round of research.

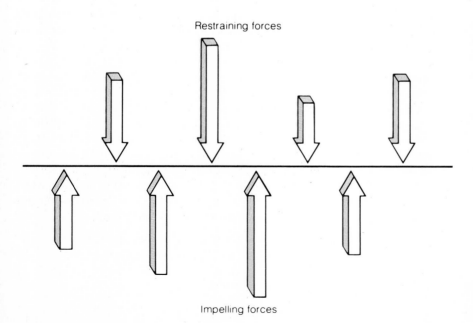

Restraining forces

Impelling forces

figure 9–1
Force field. The arrows pointing downward represent forces that keep a group from reaching its goal whereas the upward arrows reflect the forces that support change. Notice that the arrows are of different lengths, representing the fact that some forces are stronger than others.

solving problems in groups

215

creativity killers in group discussion

Nothing squelches creativity like criticism. While evaluating ideas is an important part of problem solving, judging suggestions too early can discourage members from sharing potentially valuable ideas. Here is a list of creativity-stopping statements that people should avoid making in the development phase of group work.

"That's ridiculous."
"It'll never work."
"You're wrong."
"What a crazy idea!"
"We tried it before and it didn't work."
"It's too expensive."
"There's no point in talking about it."
"It's never been done like that."
"We could look like fools."
"It's too big a job."
"We could never do that."
"It's too risky."
"You don't know what you're talking about."

Once the force field is laid out, the group is ready to move on to the next step—namely, deciding how to strengthen the impelling forces and weaken the constraining ones.

develop and evaluate alternative solutions

Once the group has set up a list of criteria for success, its next job is to consider a number of ways to reach its goal. There are actually two parts to this process: development of possible solutions and their evaluation.

During the development phase, creativity is essential. The goal is to generate a number of approaches, not to choose just one. The biggest danger here is the tendency of members to defend their own idea and criticize others'. This kind of behavior leads to two problems. First, evaluative criticism almost guarantees a defensive reaction from members whose ideas have been attacked. A second consequence is the stifling of creativity. People who have just heard an idea rebuked—however politely—will find it hard even to think of more alternatives, let alone share them openly and risk possible criticism.

Probably the best-known method for encouraging creativity and avoiding the dangers just described is the process of *brainstorming*.[9] There are four important rules connected with this approach:

1. **Criticism is forbidden.** As we have already said, nothing will stop the flow of ideas more quickly than negative evaluation.
2. **"Freewheeling" is encouraged.** Sometimes even the most outlandish ideas prove workable, and even an impractical suggestion might trigger a workable idea.

3. **Quantity is sought.** The more ideas generated, the better the chance of coming up with a good one.
4. **Combination and improvement are desirable.** Members are encouraged to "piggyback," by modifying ideas already suggested, and to combine previous suggestions.

Once it has listed possible solutions, the group can evaluate the usefulness of each. One good way of identifying the most workable solutions is to ask three questions:[10]

1. **Will this proposal produce the desired changes?** One way to find out is to see whether it successfully overcomes the restraining forces in your force field analysis.
2. **Can the proposal be implemented by the group?** Can the members strengthen impelling forces and weaken constraining ones? Can they influence others to do so? If not, the plan isn't a good one.
3. **Does the proposal contain any serious disadvantages?** Sometimes the cost of achieving a goal is too great. For example, one way to raise money for a group is to rob a bank. Although this plan might be workable, it raises more problems than it solves.

implement the plan

Everyone who makes New Year's resolutions knows the difference between making a decision and carrying it out. There are several important steps in developing and implementing a plan of action.[11]

Identify specific tasks to be accomplished What needs to be done? Even a relatively simple job usually involves several steps. Now is the

---

table 9–1   steps in group problem solving

1. Identify the problem.
   a. What are group's goals?
   b. What are individual members' goals?

2. Analyze the problem.
   a. Word problem as probative question.
   b. Gather relevant information.
   c. Identify impelling and restraining forces.

3. Develop and evaluate alternative solutions.
   a. Brainstorm possible solutions.
   b. Choose most effective solution (see the three criteria above).

4. Implement the plan.
   a. Identify specific tasks.
   b. Determine necessary resources.
   c. Define individual responsibilities.
   d. Provide for emergencies.

time to anticipate all the tasks facing the group. Remember everything now, and you will avoid a last-minute rush later.

Determine necessary resources Identify the equipment, material, and other resources the group will need in order to get the job done.

Define individual responsibilities Who will do what? Do all members know their jobs? The safest plan here is to put everyone's duties in writing, including due date. This might sound compulsive, but experience shows that it increases the chance of having jobs done on time.

Provide for emergencies Murphy's Law states, "Whatever can go wrong, will." Anyone experienced in group work knows the truth of this statement. People forget or welsh on their obligations, get sick, or quit. Machinery breaks down. (One corollary of Murphy's Law is "the copying machine will be out of order whenever it's most needed.") Whenever possible, you ought to develop contingency plans to cover foreseeable problems. Probably the single best suggestion we can give here is to plan on having all work done well ahead of the deadline, knowing that even with unforeseen problems, you will probably finish on time.

The second part of the implementation phase occurs when the group's decision is being carried out. Despite the best planning, it's possible that the group will need to make midcourse corrections, rather like the navigator of a ship or the coach of a team.

maintaining positive relationships

The task-related advice in the preceding pages will be little help if the members of a group don't get along. We, therefore, need to look at some ways to maintain good relationships among members. Many of the principles described in Chapters 4 and 6 apply here. Because these principles are so important, we will review them here.

basic skills

Probably the most important ingredient in good personal relationships is mutual respect, and the best way to demonstrate respect for the other person is to *listen* carefully. A more natural tendency, of course, is to assume you understand the other members' positions and to interrupt or ignore them. Even if you are right, however, these reactions can create a residue of ill feelings. On the other hand, careful listening can at least improve the communication climate ... and it may even teach you something.

Groups are bound to disagree sooner or later. When they do, the win-win, problem-solving methods outlined in Chapter 6 boost the odds of solving the immediate issue in the most constructive way. As you read in Chapter 8, taking votes and letting the majority rule can often leave a sizable minority whose unhappiness can haunt the group's future work.

Consensus is harder to reach in the short term, but far more beneficial in the long run.

building cohesiveness

Cohesiveness can be defined as the totality of forces that cause members to feel themselves a part of a group and make them want to remain in that group. You might think of cohesiveness as the glue that bonds individuals together, giving them a collective sense of identity. Groups become cohesive when certain conditions exist. If you understand these conditions, you can apply them to any group. You will then have a way of both measuring the group's cohesiveness and understanding how to increase it. There are eight factors that lead to increased cohesiveness.[12]

Shared or compatible goals People draw closer when they share a similar aim or when their goals can be mutually satisfied. For example, members of a conservation group might have little in common until a part of the countryside they all value is threatened by development. Some members might value the land because of its beauty; others, because it provides a place to hunt or fish; and still others, because the nearby scenery increases the value of their property; but as long as their goals are compatible, this collection of individuals will find that a bond exists that draws them together.

Progress toward these goals While a group is making progress, members feel highly cohesive; when progress stops, cohesiveness decreases. All other things being equal, members of an athletic team feel closest when the team is winning. During extended losing streaks, it is likely that players will feel less positive about the team and less willing to identify themselves as members of the group.

Shared norms and values Although successful groups will tolerate and even thrive on some differences in members' attitudes and behavior, wide variation in the group's definition of what actions or beliefs are proper will reduce cohesiveness. If enough members hold different ideas of what behavior is acceptable, the group is likely to break up. Disagreements over values or norms can fall into many areas, such as humor, finance, degree of candor, and proportion of time allotted to work and play.

Lack of perceived threat between members Cohesive group members see no threat to their status, dignity, and material or emotional well-being. When such interpersonal threats do occur, they can be very destructive. Often competition arises within groups, and as a result members feel threatened. Sometimes there is a struggle over who will be nominal leader. At other times members view others as wanting to take over a functional role (problem solver, information giver, and so on), either through competition or criticism. Sometimes the threat is real, and sometimes it's only imagined, but in either case the group must neutralize it or face the consequences of reduced cohesiveness.

Interdependence of members Groups become cohesive when their needs can be satisfied only with the help of other members. When a job can be done just as well by one person alone, the need for membership decreases. This factor explains the reason for food cooperatives, neighborhood yard sales, and community political campaigns. All these activities enable the participants to reach their goal more successfully than if they acted alone.

Threat from outside the group When members perceive a threat to the group's existence or image (groups have self-concepts, just as individuals do), they grow closer together. Almost everyone knows of a family whose members seem to fight constantly among themselves—until an outsider criticizes one of them. At this point the internal bickering stops, and for the moment the group unites against its common enemy. The same principle works on a larger scale when nations often bind up their internal differences in the face of external aggression.

Mutual perceived attractiveness and friendship This factor is somewhat circular, because friendship and mutual attraction often are a result of the points just listed; yet groups often do become close simply because members like each other.

Shared group experiences When members have been through some unusual or trying experience, they draw together. This explains why soldiers who have been in combat together often feel close and stay in touch for years after; it also accounts for the ordeal of fraternity pledging and other initiations. Many societies have rituals that all members share, thus increasing the group's cohesiveness.

It's important to realize that the eight factors just described interact with one another, often in contradictory ways. For instance, members of many groups are good friends who have been through thick and thin together (cohesiveness builders), but find themselves less dependent on each other than before and now struggle over playing certain roles. In cases like this, cohesiveness can be figured as the net sum of all attracting and dividing forces.

encouraging participation

In most groups there is an unequal amount of participation from member to member. Though it probably isn't desirable to have every person speak equally on every subject, neither is it good to have one or more members keep almost totally quiet. There are two reasons why: First, the group could probably benefit from hearing the additional information; second, having wallflowers in a group can become nerve-racking, both for the quiet ones themselves and for the contributors. How, then, can participation be encouraged?

solving problems in groups

221

Keep the group small Common sense suggests that as a group grows larger, there is less time for each member to speak. But, just as important, the imbalance between talkers and nontalkers grows with membership.[13] In small groups of three or four members, participation is roughly equal, but once the size increases to between five and eight, there's a dramatic gap between the contributions of members. Therefore, one simple way to increase participation is to keep the group small whenever the task permits.

Solicit contributions from quiet members Sometimes contributions from quiet members can be obtained by simply asking for a member's input, ideally using open questions to guarantee a complete response: "What can you suggest to improve that idea, Gus?" In other cases, the nominal leader can assign quiet members certain tasks that will ensure their participation, such as reporting to the group on research.

Reinforce contributions When a quiet member does make a contribution, it is especially important for others in the group to acknowledge it. Acknowledgment can be direct: "Thanks for suggesting that, Lisa." Another way to reinforce a comment is to refer to it later in the discussion: "That ties in with what Will said a while ago about . . ."

Of course, there's a danger of becoming a phony, being overly complimentary. Gushing undeserved praise at shy people will probably discourage them from contributing again, so be sure to keep your reinforcements sincere and not effusive.

When we first read over these suggestions for encouraging participation, they sounded so obvious that we almost tossed them in the trash basket. But before doing so, we took a look at groups we belong to and realized that following these three simple steps really does draw out quiet speakers. So we encourage you not to discount these obvious but effective suggestions.

leadership in groups

For most of us, leadership ranks not far below motherhood in the heirarchy of values. "What are you, a leader or a follower?" we're asked, and we know which position is the good one. On the job, for instance, leadership means promotion. Even in the earliest grades of school, we knew who the leaders were, and we admired them. What is leadership all about?

leadership and leaders: an important distinction

Most people use the terms *leader* and *leadership* interchangeably, when in fact there is a big difference between these two concepts. Some leaders don't exert leadership, and much leadership doesn't come from leaders . . . or at least people we identify by that term. Let us explain.

We can begin by defining leadership as *the ability to influence the behavior of others in a group.* And how are people influenced? By some sort of power. Power comes in several forms.[14]

Legitimate power   The ability to influence others through legitimate power comes from the position one holds—supervisor, parent, professor, and so on. In many situations, this sort of power comes from the title alone: We follow the directions of police officers in traffic because we figure they know what they're doing. At other times, however, a person's title isn't the prime motivation.

Coercive power   Sometimes we do what the boss tells us, not out of any respect for the wisdom of the decision, but because the consequences of not obeying would be unpleasant. Economic hardship, social disapproval, unpleasant work, even physical punishment . . . all are coercive forces that can shape behavior.

Reward power   The ability to reward is the reverse side of coercive power. Like punishments, rewards can be social, material, or physical.

Expert power   Sometimes we are influenced by people because of what they know or can do. For example, when a medical emergency occurs, most group members would gladly let a doctor, nurse, or paramedic call the shots (no pun intended) because of that person's obvious knowledge.

Referent power   We might regard referent power as social power because we are talking about the influence that comes from the members' respect, attraction, or liking for someone in the group.

Logic suggests that if leadership is the power to influence others, then the leader is someone who exerts that influence. But a look at the list you have just read shows that matters aren't this simple. For instance, there are some times when the *nominal leader*—the person whose title suggests a great deal of power—really has very little influence on a group. We remember those happy days of junior high school when a certain substitute teacher took control (and we use that term loosely) of one civics class. She may have reigned, but she certainly didn't rule. Instead, a band of rowdy students, headed by two ringleaders with great referent power, ran the show: telling jokes, falling out of chairs, and finally escaping from the room through open windows. In the end the dean's coercive power was the only way to put down the rebellion.

The lesson in this story of teenage mayhem is that some nominal leaders don't really lead and that some superficially powerless members are, in fact, the real movers and shakers of the group. One way to analyze the influence of a nominal leader is to identify that person's true power in the group by applying the five dimensions we just listed. If the nominal leader scores high in most of these categories, we can say

A leader is best
When people barely know
    that he exists,
Not so good when people
    obey and acclaim him,
Worse when they despise
    him.
"Fail to honor people,
They fail to honor you";
But of a good leader who
    talks little,
When his work is done, his
    aim fulfilled,
They will say, "We did it
    ourselves."

Lao-tzu

solving problems in groups
223

that he or she is a "strong leader." If the power is spread throughout the group, however, that leader's influence isn't as great.

Don't conclude from this that highly visible, powerful, centralized leadership is the best way to get a job done. There are many cases in which shared leadership is very effective. One mark of many effective leaders is their ability to enlist subtly the powerful support—reward, coercive, expert, and referent—of other members to support a policy. Even leaders who want to take a highly influential and visible role can't do everything. Recall our discussion of functional roles in Chapter 8 and you'll realize that no single person can possibly perform every task necessary to have the group achieve its goal. We will have more to say about the pros and cons of directive, centralized leadership in a few pages, when we discuss autocratic and democratic styles of designated leaders.

what makes leaders effective?

Because the position of nominal leader is such an important one in our society, the next few pages will describe the factors that contribute to leader effectiveness.

Trait analysis   Over 2,000 years ago Aristotle proclaimed, "From the hour of their birth some are marked out for subjugation, and others for command."[15] This is a radical example of the "great man" (or "great woman") view of leadership. Social scientists began their studies of leader effectiveness by conducting literally hundreds of studies that compared leaders with nonleaders. The results of all this research were mixed. Yet a number of distinguishing characteristics did emerge in several categories:[16]

Physical appearance   As a rule, leaders tend to be slightly taller, heavier, and physically more attractive than others. They also seem to possess greater athletic ability and stamina.

Sociability   The category of sociability involves behaviors related to maintaining personal relationships within the group. For example, leaders talk more often and more fluently and are regarded as more popular, cooperative, and socially skillful.

Goal facilitation   Leaders have skills that help groups perform their tasks. They are somewhat more intelligent, possess more task-relevant information, and are more dependable than other members.

Desire for leadership   Leaders *want* that role and act in ways that will help them get it. They exercise initiative, are persistent, and express their beliefs assertively.

Despite these general findings, the research on leader traits is of only limited practical value: Later research has shown that many other factors are important in determining leader success, and not everyone who possesses these traits becomes a leader. We'll now examine this body of knowledge.

Leadership style Some leaders are *authoritarian,* using legitimate, coercive, and reward power to dictate what will happen in a group. Others are more *democratic,* inviting other members to share in decision making. In a third style, called *laissez-faire,* the leader gives up the power to dictate, transforming the group into a leaderless collection of equals. Early research suggested that the democratic style produced the highest-quality results,[17] but later experiments showed that matters weren't so simple. For instance, groups with autocratic leaders proved more productive under stressful conditions, but democratically led groups did better when the situation was nonstressful.[18]

Contemporary approaches After more than half a century of research, it seemed that certain types of leadership worked well in one set of circumstances but poorly in another. In an effort to pin down what approach works best in a given type of situation, psychologist Fred Fiedler attempted to find out when a task-oriented approach was most effective and when a more relationship-oriented style produced the best results.[19] From his research, Fiedler developed a *situational* theory of leadership. Although the complete theory is too complex to describe here, its general conclusion is that a leader's style should change with the circumstances. A task-oriented approach works best when conditions are either highly favorable (good leader-member relations, strong leader power, and clear task structure) or highly unfavorable (poor leader-member relations, weak leader power, and an ambiguous task) whereas a more relationship-oriented style is appropriate in moderately favorable or moderately unfavorable conditions.

Two researchers in the field of organizational communication, Robert R. Blake and Jane S. Mouton, have also examined the interaction of task and relationship factors in leadership, but with somewhat different conclusions.[20] They developed a managerial Grid® consisting of a two-dimensional model (see Figure 9–2). The horizontal axis measures the leader's concern for production. This involves a focus on accomplishing the organizational task, with efficiency being the main concern. The vertical axis measures the leader's concern for people's feelings and ideas. Blake and Mouton suggest that the most effective leader is one who adopts a 9,9 style—showing high concern for both task and relationships.

To summarize, situational theorists suggest that a good leader doesn't adopt either a 1,9 (high-relationship) or 9,1 (high-task) approach and stick with it; rather, effectiveness comes from adjusting to whatever approach the situation demands. Grid proponents urge leaders to exhibit

figure 9-2
The managerial Grid. From Robert R. Blake and Jane S. Mouton, *The New Managerial Grid,* Houston: Gulf Publishing Co., Copyright © 1978, p. 11. Reproduced by permission.

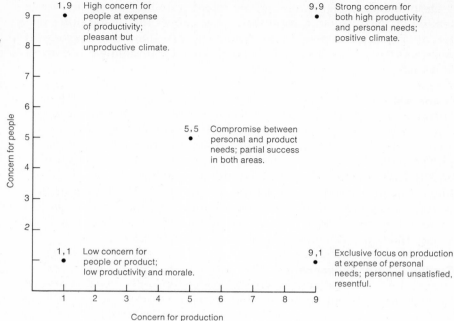

1,9 High concern for people at expense of productivity; pleasant but unproductive climate.

9,9 Strong concern for both high productivity and personal needs; positive climate.

5,5 Compromise between personal and product needs; partial success in both areas.

1,1 Low concern for people or product; low productivity and morale.

9,1 Exclusive focus on production at expense of personal needs; personnel unsatisfied, resentful.

Concern for people

Concern for production

high concern for both task and relationships at all times.[21] This book isn't the place to settle the dispute between situational and "one best style" adherents. Despite the unresolved controversy, one important and useful point emerges: Leaders need to consider the relationship needs of their subordinates as well as the demands of the task at hand.

dangers in group discussion

Even groups with the best of intentions often find themselves unable to reach satisfying decisions. At other times, they make decisions that later prove to be wrong. Though there's no foolproof method of guaranteeing high-quality group work, there are several dangers to avoid.

absence of critical information

Many groups are so anxious to make decisions that they do so without having important information. We know of one group that scheduled a fund-raising party without enough forethought and later found that their event had to compete with a championship football game. A bit of checking could have prevented much disappointment and earned the group more sorely needed funds.

domination by a minority

We have already said that participation in most groups is unequal. Besides leaving quieter members feeling hurt and unenthusiastic, domination by the vocal few can reduce a group's ability to solve a problem effectively. Research shows that the proposal receiving the largest number of favorable comments is usually the one chosen, even if it isn't the best one.[22] Furthermore, ideas of high-status members (who aren't always talkers) are given more consideration than those of lower-status people.[23] The moral to this story? Don't assume that quantity of speech or the status of the speaker automatically defines the quality of an idea: Instead, seek out and seriously consider the ideas of quieter members.

pressure to conform

There's a strong tendency for group members to go along with the crowd, which often results in bad decisions. A classic study by Solomon Asch illustrated this point.[24] College students were shown three lines of different lengths and asked to identify which of them matched with a fourth line. Although the correct answer was obvious, the experiment was a setup: Asch had instructed all but one member of the experimental groups to vote for the wrong line. As a result, fully one-third of the uninformed subjects ignored their own good judgment and voted with the majority. If simple tasks like this one generate such conformity, it is easy to see that following the (sometimes mistaken) crowd is even more likely in the much more complex and ambiguous tasks that most groups face. It's interesting to note that pressures toward conformity are strongest when group members have low confidence in their ability to solve a problem and are highly attracted to the group and when the conforming majority is relatively large.[25]

Drawing by Levin; © 1983. The New Yorker Magazine, Inc.

solving problems in groups

227

When we look a little closer, we see an inconsistency in the way our society seems to feel about conformity (team playing) and nonconformity (deviance). For example, one of the great best sellers of the 1950s was a book by John F. Kennedy called *Profiles in Courage,* wherein the author praised several politicians for their courage in resisting great pressure and refusing to conform. To put it another way, Kennedy was praising people who refused to be good team players, people who refused to vote or act as their parties or constituents expected them to. Although their actions earned Kennedy's praise long after the deeds were done, the immediate reactions of their colleagues were generally far from positive. The nonconformist may be praised by historians or idolized in films or literature long after the fact of his nonconformity, but he's usually not held in high esteem, at the time, by those people to whose demands he refuses to conform.

Elliot Aronson
The Social Animal

premature decision making

Probably because uncertainty is not a happy state, many groups become emotionally attached to an alternative early in the decision-making process.[26] Such attachment leads members to ignore other ideas that might prove to be better. This tendency explains why the brainstorming process described on pages 216–217 stipulates that all ideas should be considered without criticism during early stages of discussion.

confusing disagreement with dislike

Many group members see criticism of their ideas as a personal attack. This often leads them to either withdraw from the discussion or to lash back at the personality or proposal of the original critic. Hard as it sometimes is, it's important to distinguish disagreement from dislike.[27]

summary

Despite the bad reputation of groups in some quarters, research shows that they are often the most effective setting for problem solving. They command greater resources, both quantitatively and qualitatively, than either single individuals or a collection of persons working in isolation; their work can result in greater accuracy; and the participative nature of the solutions they produce generates greater commitment from members.

Groups stand the best chance of developing effective solutions to problems if they begin their work by identifying the problem, avoiding the mistake of failing to recognize hidden needs of individual members. Their next step is to analyze the problem, including identification of forces both favoring and blocking progress. Only at this point should the group begin to develop possible solutions, taking care not to stifle creativity by evaluating any of them prematurely. During the implementation phase of the solution the group should monitor the situation carefully and make any necessary changes in its plan.

Groups that only pay attention to the task dimension of their interaction risk strains in the relationships among members. Many of these interpersonal problems can be avoided by using the skills described in Chapter 6 as well as by following the guidelines in this chapter for building group cohesiveness and encouraging participation.

Many naive observers of groups confuse the concepts of leader and leadership. We defined leadership as the ability to influence the behavior of other members through the use of one or more types of power—legitimate, coercive, reward, expert, or referent. We saw that many nominal leaders share their power with other members. Leadership has been examined from many perspectives—trait analysis, leadership style, and situational variables.

The chapter concluded with a list of several common dangers that can hamper the effectiveness of problem-solving groups: lack of critical information, domination by vocal members, pressures to conform, premature decision making, and the confusion of disagreement and dislike among members.

1. Apply the principles summarized in Table 9–1 to a problem-solving group you belong to. (Class projects or informal study groups are good subjects to study here.) Do your best to follow each step carefully, and note any differences between the results of this approach and others you've tried in the past.

2. Observe a problem-solving group in action and use Table 9–1 to see whether the group follows each of the steps thoroughly. What are the consequences of omitting one or more of the steps? Ib the group hired you as a consultant, how could you advise them to increase their problem-solving effectiveness?

3. Recall two groups to which you have belonged: one with a low level of cohesiveness and one highly cohesive one. Use the factors listed on pages 219–221 to analyze what contributed to the level of commitment of each group. How could matters be improved in the low-cohesiveness group?

4. Think of one low-level participator in a group you have observed. Using the guidelines on pages 221–222, suggest how the quiet member's contributions could be increased.

5. Think of two effective leaders you have known. How would you describe the style of each one: autocratic, democratic, or laissez-faire;

activities

task- or relationship-oriented? Imagine that the two leaders were transferred, so that each one was directing the other's group. Would the same approach work equally well in each situation? Why or why not?

notes

1. Cal Downs, David M. Berg, and Wil A. Linkugel, *The Organizational Communicator* (New York: Harper & Row, 1977), p. 127.
2. Marvin E. Shaw, *Group Dynamics: The Psychology of Small Group Behavior,* 3d ed. (New York: McGraw-Hill, 1981), pp. 61–64.
3. Ibid., p. 391.
4. Charles W. Redding, *Communication Within the Organization* (New York: Industrial Communication Council, 1972).
5. John Dewey, *How We Think* (New York: Heath, 1910).
6. Bobby R. Patton and Kim Giffin, *Problem-Solving Group Interaction* (New York: Harper & Row, 1973), p. 131.
7. Adapted from David Potter and Martin P. Andersen, *Discussion in Small Groups: A Guide to Effective Practice* (Belmont, Calif.: Wadsworth, 1976), pp. 20–22.
8. Kurt Lewin, *Field Theory in Social Science* (New York: Harper & Row, 1951), pp. 30–59.
9. Alex Osborn, *Applied Imagination* (New York: Scribner's, 1959).
10. Patton, op. cit., pp. 167–168.
11. Ibid., adapted from pp. 182–185.
12. Adapted from Ernest G. Bormann, *Discussion and Group Methods: Theory and Practice,* 2d ed. (New York: Harpar & Row, 1975), pp. 141–171.
13. R. F. Bales, F. L. Strodtbeck, T. M. Mills, and M. E. Roseborough, "Channels of Communication in Small Groups," *American Sociological Review* 16 (1951): 461–468.
14. John R. French and Bertram Raven, "The Basis of Social Power," in Dorwin Cartwright and Alvin Zandler (eds.), *Group Dynamics* (New York: Harper & Row, 1968), p. 565.
15. Aristotle, *Politics* (New York: Oxford University Press, 1958), Book 7.
16. John F. Cragan and David W. Wright, *Communication in Small Group Discussions: A Case Study Approach* (St. Paul, Minn.: West Publishing, 1980), p. 74.
17. Kurt Lewin, R. Lippitt, and R. K. White, "Patterns of Aggressive Behavior in Experimentally Created Social Climates," *Journal of Social Psychology* 10 (1939): 271–299.
18. L. L. Rosenbaum and W. B. Rosenbaum, "Morale and Productivity Consequences of Group Leadership Style, Stress, and Type of Task," *Journal of Applied Psychology* 55 (1971): 343–358.
19. Fred E. Fiedler, *A Theory of Leadership Effectiveness* (New York: McGraw-Hill, 1967).
20. Robert R. Blake and Jane S. Mouton, *The Managerial Grid* (Houston: Gulf Publishing, 1964).
21. Robert R. Blake and Jane S. Mouton, *Toward Resolution of the Situationalism vs. "One Best Style . . ." Controversy in Leadership Theory, Research, and Practice* (Austin, Tex.: Scientific Methods, 1981).

22. L. Richard Hoffman and Norman R. F. Maier, "Valence in the Adoption of Solutions by Problem-Solving Groups: Concept, Method, and Results," *Journal of Abnormal and Social Psychology* 69 (1964): 264–271.

23. E. P. Torrence, "Some Consequences of Power Differences on Decision Making in Permanent and Temporary Three-Man Groups," *Research Studies,* Washington State College, 22 (1954): 130–140.

24. Solomon E. Asch, "Effects of Group Pressure upon the Modification and Distortion of Judgments," in H. Guetzkow (ed.), *Groups, Leadership and Men* (Pittsburgh: Carnegie Press, 1951), pp. 177–190.

25. Shaw, op. cit., p. 398.

26. Hoffman and Maier, op. cit.

27. Patton and Giffin, op. cit., p. 158.

ten

communicating in organizations

After reading this chapter, you should understand:

1. The frequency and importance of communication in organizations.
2. The characteristics that define an organization and the role communication plays in each characteristic.
3. The characteristics of upward, downward, and horizontal communication in formal organizational networks.
4. The characteristics of informal communication networks.

You should be able to:

1. Identify the organizations you presently deal with and those you are likely to deal with in the future.
2. Identify the purpose, order, specialization, replaceability, uniformity, authority, and identifying signs and symbols in an organization you deal with.
3. Describe the types of upward, downward, and horizontal communication in an organization and suggest ways each could be improved.
4. Describe the informal communication networks in an organization and suggest ways you can use these networks to your advantage.
5. Define a personal goal within an organization, choose the best audience to deal with, and select the best channel to deliver your message.

"Because we can talk, we all assume we can communicate. That assumption is proved incorrect daily. In business, it costs millions daily in lost time, productivity, profit. Programs are desperately needed to increase awareness of effective communication techniques. I think no other skills can so dramatically aid one's climb up the corporate ladder."

Phil Matteis, President
Integrated Management Systems, Inc.

Organizations occupy a major part of almost everyone's life. Their most obvious role is in one's career, for most workers belong to organizations. Some of these organizations are commercial (Giovanni's Pizza Parlor, General Motors); some are governmental (the city planning department, U.S. Army); still others are not-for-profit organizations of one type or another (educational, religious, medical, or charitable).

Even people who don't work *in* organizations work *with* them. Colleges and universities are organizations. So are the gas, electric, and phone companies; the Internal Revenue Service; libraries; hospitals; traffic courts; and commercial stores. Like it or not, dealing with organizations like these is a daily fact of life.

Because organizations are so pervasive and important, we will spend this chapter looking at them in detail. We will explain how their basic structure makes organizational communication different from what takes place in other settings. We will describe the patterns of communication—both formal and informal—that occur in organizations. Finally, we will offer some specific suggestions that will help you communicate more effectively within and with organizations.

the importance of organizational communication

Organizational communication is worth studying for two reasons. First, it is frequent—perhaps more frequent than any other activity. Second, the quality of communication in an organization often determines whether it will succeed or fail.

communication is frequent

Whatever the job, people communicate. In fact, research shows that in most jobs people spend more time sending and receiving messages than in any other activity—between 50 and 90 percent, according to most studies.[1] The amount of time spent communicating increases along with responsibility: First-line managers may spend 60 percent of their working hours communicating.[2] For higher level executives, the figure is even greater—70 to 80 percent or even more.[3]

Communication isn't only common in people-oriented jobs like sales or personnel; it is also necessary in fields that seem to deal more with things. An engineer, for example, has to communicate with designers and production staff to get a job done. Researchers work with associates in the lab. Artisans have to deal with customers and suppliers. Accountants have to work with clients, staff, and government personnel. As Table 10-1 shows, communication on the job is the rule, not the exception.

Dealing with organizations as an outsider is, of course, almost totally a matter of communication. You must communicate effectively to show the credit card company that your bill is wrong, to convince the emergency room clerk that your medical problem can't wait, or to persuade

table 10–1   types of organizational communication

interviews
Information-gathering (survey, research, investigation)
Information-giving (orientations, instructions)
Selection (screening, hiring, placement)
Problem-solving/goal-setting (performance appraisal, complaint/grievance, task-related)

personal and group activities
Exchanging information
Analyzing problems
Promoting a point of view
Evaluating ideas
Building rapport

presentations
Briefings
Reports
Explanations
Training
Proposals
Motivational speeches
Goodwill speeches

the service manager that your car problem is indeed covered by the warranty.

communication is important

Communication is not only frequent; it is also vitally important in the success of an organization and its employees. College alumni recognize this fact. Graduates in every field who were surveyed one, seven, and ten years after leaving school all identified communication as critical for job success. In fact, the majority of graduates ranked communication as more important than the major subject they studied.[4]

Employers also recognize the importance of communication skills. When 170 well-known firms were asked to list the most common reasons they did not hire applicants, the most frequent replies were "poor communication skills" and "inability to communicate."[5]

Once on the job, communication is just as important. In one survey, business executives in over fifty of America's largest corporations unanimously agreed that communication skills had played a part in their advancement. Two-thirds believed that the ability to communicate well played a major role in their success.[6] In another survey, subscribers to the *Harvard Business Review*—primarily successful managers—rated the ability to communicate as more important in gaining promotions than ambition, education, and the capacity for hard work.[7]

Without communications, the only thing I can command is my desk.

General Curtis LeMay
Former Commander, Strategic Air Command

communicating in organizations
235

characteristics of organizational communication

You might agree that organizational communication is important, but still wonder why it requires a chapter of its own in this book. After all, other sections introduce skills commonly used in organizations: interviewing, working in groups, communicating interpersonally, and speaking to an audience. Although the information in these chapters is helpful, organizations possess certain characteristics that make communication in them different from what takes place in other settings. We will examine those characteristics now.[8]

purpose

Organizations always exist to serve a purpose—to get a job done efficiently. This emphasis on efficiency makes organizational communication different from that of many other groups, which focus more on social relationships and less on efficiency. In many nonorganizational groups, the only "job" is to have members enjoy one another's company and gain a sense of belonging. Other groups may have a task dimension, but efficiency still is not a critical concern. Neighbors organizing a blockwide yard sale or a softball team planning the end-of-season party aren't likely to worry much about getting the job done with as few people as possible in the shortest time. In a formal organization, however, the goal—at least in principle—is to finish the task quickly and then get on with business. Even the inevitable small talk that occurs is expected to serve the goal of building goodwill.

This doesn't mean that members of organizations are machinelike human robots who care only about the job. In fact, organizational experts increasingly recognize that the personal needs of their employees are important. As John Nasbitt says in his best-seller *Megatrends,* "high tech" organizations must also be "high touch"—recognizing and filling the needs of their staff members to be consulted and appreciated.[9] Social goals do exist, then, but the organization cares about them only to the degree that they affect the job at hand. This doesn't necessarily make organizational managers cruel, just realistic.

order

It is almost inconceivable that an organization could exist without any structure. Imagine the chaos that would occur in even a small office if the employees showed up every morning and had to ask, "Who'll do what today?" or "How should we do it?"

Every organization (the term itself implies order) creates structures to perform its job by defining policies and procedures for handling common tasks. A department store chain outlines the steps to follow when a customer returns an item, the fire department decides in advance which station will handle emergencies in each part of town, and a university publishes the steps students must take to withdraw from a class or to seek a grade change.

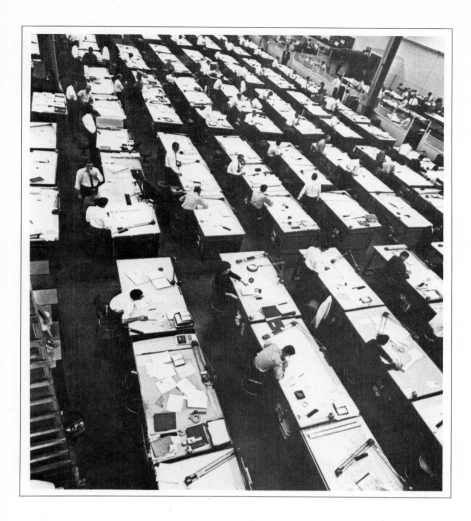

Organizations create order in other ways that are so common we hardly notice them. They conduct business at a regular location, and they publicize and follow regular hours of operation. You can count on this hospital's always being open, on school to follow a predictable schedule, and on your favorite restaurant to be open on Saturday night.

Having a well-constructed organizational plan isn't enough by itself: The people who are involved—both inside and outside the organization—must understand that plan. Communicating information about these sorts of order is one characteristic of organizations. Your bank, for instance, almost certainly has several large books that outline its policies and procedures. Your college or university has an official catalog. In addition to these Biblelike publications, most organizations are characterized by a constant series of written and oral messages outlining new information about how things will operate.

communicating in
organizations

237

specialization

Members of organizations have roles that are strictly defined. Their responsibilities are made clear from the start, usually in the form of a job description. This fact is reflected in the fact that virtually everyone in an organization has a title that describes his or her duties: new accounts manager, customer service representative, or assistant dishwasher.

This specialization is certainly useful, for it boosts the odds that every job has someone to do it. On the other hand, specialization also affects communication in some troublesome ways. One problem that flows from specialization is lack of understanding. Workers whose duties are limited often don't understand why other parts of the organization operate as they do. For example, an advertising copy writer or an automobile parts clerk may resent the paperwork that is essential to the accounting department because they don't understand why it is important.

Specialization of roles also inhibits the exchange of ideas. Workers with narrow jobs are often unlikely to talk to people from other areas or to care much about those areas even if they do talk. This lack of concern and understanding inhibits the kind of creativity that helps the organization do a better job.

Because a great deal of specialization is necessary in most organizations, the challenge is to get members sith differing specialties to communicate with and understand one another. Enlightened managers use a number of methods to accomplish this goal. They cross-train workers, who gain at least a basic understanding of other parts of the operation. They often create project teams that join together from various departments to work on a specific task. They also circulate companywide newsletters and other media that keep workers posted on what is going on in other areas of the organization.

replaceability

A family can't "fire" its members without breaking up the unit. Friends can't throw one or more people out of their group without changing its nature. Organizations, however, strive to create structures in which individual members can be replaced. As the president of one growing corporation put it, "If I were to drop dead tomorrow, we'd be in trouble. Nobody else could do my job. We have to work out long-range plans, job descriptions, and cross-training so nobody is indispensable."

This sort of indispensability is difficult to achieve at the highest levels of management, where individual managers set the tone and goals of organizations. The directors of the Chrysler Corporation recognized this fact when, in late 1983, they offered Lee Iacocca over $4 million in stock to stay in office for three additional years. "His importance to the company cannot be overstated," declared one board member.[10] At lower levels, employees can be replaced with little disruption. If airline pilots, bus drivers, or phone workers strike, business can go on as long as man-

agement can replace the absent employees with competent workers. The replaceability of almost everyone in an organization has a strong effect on communication. A person will behave carefully if his or her position will be jeopardized by stepping too far out of line. This kind of pressure leads to another characteristic of organizations, namely, uniformity.

uniformity

The range of acceptable behaviors is narrower in organizations than in other types of groups. Formal and informal rules cover everything from the hours overtime workers are expected to put in to the kind of language they use with the public. Clothing styles in organizations illustrate this principle of uniformity. The military and police have official uniforms. Bankers and stockbrokers usually dress conservatively. Even college and university faculty are governed by a range of acceptable clothing styles. If you doubt this fact, imagine your reaction if your professor came to class on a warm day dressed in a skimpy swimming suit.

authority

One obvious element of organizational structure is authority. Certain people are responsible for supervising the work of others, so that it is clear who is ultimately responsible for getting the job done.

Once an organization grows beyond just a few members, the authority structure usually becomes hierarchical, with a chain of command. This hierarchical structure is usually pictured in an organizational chart, such as the one in Figure 10–1.

communicating in
organizations

239

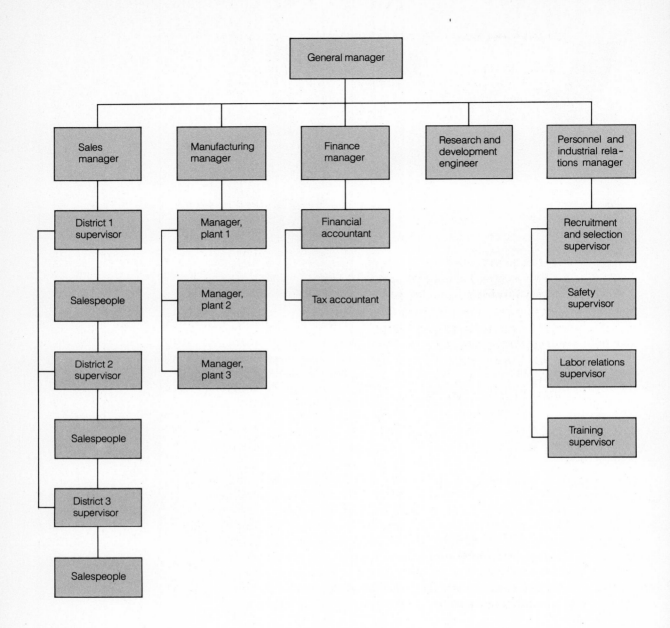

figure 10-1
Simplified organizational chart

Every organization has some sort of authority structure, though not all are the same. The military, for example, is extremely hierarchical, with the chain of command stretching clearly from the newast recruit to the commander in chief. Other organizations are less centralized, though an authority structure still exists. In some companies, operating groups have freedom to handle their work as they see fit. If, however, the group fails to carry its weight, top management will assert its authority to make changes.

signs and symbols

All organizations have identifying symbols or signs that identify them. The most obvious of these is the organization's name itself. There is only one United Airlines, McDonald's, or Los Angeles Raiders. These names are so important that they are registered and protected legally. Organizations also invest a great deal in publicizing identifying trademarks (for example, McDonald's golden arches and Disney's Mickey Mouse) and slogans (for example, "You're in good hands" or "Leave the driving to us").

Although this book deals primarily with verbal, face-to-face interaction, other means of communication are also frequent: written correspondence (letters, memos, and reports), telephone conversations, and electronic telecommunications (teleconferencing and electronic mail) also play a role. Whatever the medium, organizational communication falls into several categories.

types of organizational communication

formal communication

Formal communication networks are management's idea of who ought to work with whom to accomplish the organization's mission. Organizational charts like the one in Figure 10–1 describe some, but not all, kinds of formal communication networks. An organizational chart doesn't include interaction among people from different departments or among members of the organization and the public. To outline all the formal communication involved in getting a job done, one must construct a *flowchart.* The flowchart in Figure 10–2 illustrates the communication that occurs when a college or university introduces a new course into its curriculum.

Notice that the information described in Figure 10–2 doesn't flow only from superiors to subordinates. In fact, information within an organization can pass in three directions: upward, downward, and horizontally.

Downward communication Downward communication occurs when a superior sends a message to one or more subordinates. The most obvious type of downward communication is *job instructions,* but there are other types of downward messages that are equally important.[11]

A second type of downward communication involves *job rationale:* explanations of why a task needs to be performed. An office manager might offer job rationale by explaining the reason behind an apparently useless order: "I know it seems foolish both to type up a repair order and to phone it in, but we've found that a phone call gets the custodians out here much faster. It's definitely worth the few extra minutes."

Downward communication can also deal with *procedures and practices.* Information about rules and regulations falls into this category.

communicating in organizations

241

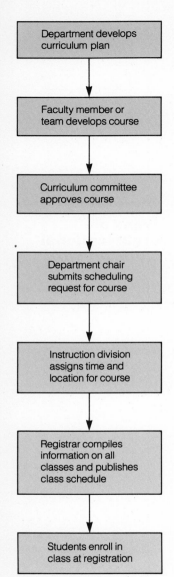

Department develops
curriculum plan

↓

Faculty member or
team develops course

↓

Curriculum committee
approves course

↓

Department chair
submits scheduling
request for course

↓

Instruction division
assigns time and
location for course

↓

Registrar compiles
information on all
classes and publishes
class schedule

↓

Students enroll in
class at registration

figure 10–2
Flowchart

For example, the boss might send out a memo stating the company's policy on a personal use of the copying machine, and a sales manager might announce that his or her approval is required for all deals over a certain amount.

A fourth type of downward communication conveys *feedback* from the top down. This feedback can be praise ("You really handled that job well") or constructive criticism ("We could have made the deadline if you'd sent the contracts by Express Mail"). Sometimes, of course, criticism isn't constructive at all: "That was a stupid thing to do. One more stunt like that and you're finished!"

Finally, some downward messages *indoctrinate* employees, motivating them to perform better. Sales meetings are often aimed at motivating employees, as are some performance appraisal interviews and "state of the company" speeches by top management.

Upward communication As its name suggests, upward communication occurs when subordinates send messages to their superiors. Upward communication can convey four types of information.[12]

First, it can tell superiors *what subordinates are doing*. How much longer will the job take? Where can you be reached when you leave the office? When will you be back? Questions like these may be obvious, but they need to be answered if management is to know what is going on.

Upward communication can also deal with *unsolved work problems*. Some of these problems are mundane, though important. A boss might not know why last week's sales figures are so hard to get (too many people using one computer terminal) unless somebody tells him. Some bosses discourage this sort of communication, either actively by lashing out at the bearers of bad news or passively by failing to invite reports on problems that need solving.

Employees can also approach their superiors with *suggestions for improvement*. How could we get more repeat business? How can the turnaround time on a job be shortened? Employees who are willing to initiate this type of upward communication show that they have potential to move higher in the organization.

Finally, upward communication can describe *how subordinates feel about themselves and the job*. If you want more responsibility or are interested in learning a different part of the business, it is probably wise to let your superiors know. Matters become a bit more delicate when you have complaints about the job. Unmitigated complaining usually isn't well received, so it's important to phrase your message positively. Instead of saying, "I'm bored" or "I can't stand Charlie," you might say, "I'd like to tackle a bigger challenge" or "I'd like to get experience working with other people."

Horizontal communication Horizontal communication goes on among members with equal power. Some horizontal exchanges occur among

"Season's greetings from Slug Wassleman, on forklift twenty-seven, Container Division, Fulton, New York, plant."

Drawing by H. Martin; © 1981. The New Yorker Magazine, Inc.

people who work closely together in the same group. Other horizontal messages flow from one part of the organization to another—between departments, for example. In either case, horizontal messages can serve several functions.[13]

First, they can improve *task coordination*. "When can we meet to talk about those new electronic typewriters?" you might ask a purchasing agent. "Let's work out a vacation schedule that keeps both our departments covered," a fellow worker might suggest to you.

Other horizontal messages involve *problem solving*. Quality control personnel might meet with assembly line supervisors before work to figure out how mistakes can be cut on a new procedure. Likewise, an office manager might ask the maintenance staff how the fresh air circulation can be improved in the work area.

communicating in organizations

243

A third type of horizontal communication involves *sharing information*. The change-of-shift briefings common in nursing and police operations are primarily information-sharing sessions, as are meetings in which a sales staff explains customer needs to designers.

Horizontal communication also can focus on *conflict resolution*. Some conflicts are personal. One employee might be offended by another's ethnic jokes, for example. Other disputes focus on job-related issues, such as who was responsible for losing a major account or whether women are being excluded from top management positions.

A final type of horizontal communication can *build rapport*. You might have lunch or play tennis with someone in another department, knowing that a good relationship between your divisions will help work run more smoothly.

informal communication

Not all communication in organizations follows formal channels. Consider these examples:

- You overhear the personnel talking about a new job opening. You mention the opening to a fellow worker, who asks for and gets reassigned to the new position before the opening is formally announced.
- Your running partner is secretary to the boss. She tells you that the boss was grumbling about the way salary expenses have gotten out of hand. You decide to postpone your request for a raise.

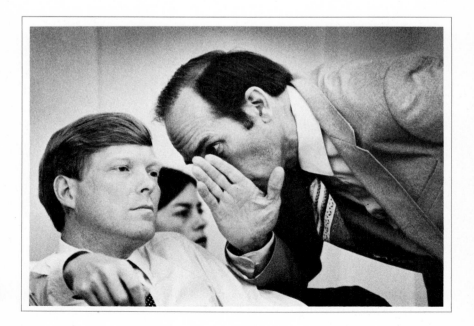

- At the annual Christmas party, you mention to the data-processing manager that you've been having trouble understanding the weekly progress report printouts. As a result of your conversation, the format of the reports is reorganized in a clearer format.

Informal communication networks connect people in ways that have little or nothing to do with organizational tables or flowcharts. Informal networks arise for a number of reasons, including proximity, similar interests, and personal friendships.

Whatever their basis, informal networks can be a useful way to send and receive information. One advantage of informal networks is their speed. Because they are based on personal relationships, informal messages usually travel much more quickly than more formal ones that must follow official channels. In one organization, for example, 46 percent of the management staff heard about one member's newborn child within thirteen hours after the birth.[14]

The off-the-record nature of informal messages allows them to convey information that simply can't be sent officially. A friend who might tell you over a cup of coffee that Jones is a two-faced liar certainly wouldn't put the message into a memo. Likewise, your supervisor might relay management's announcement that use of the copying machine is absolutely forbidden and yet make it clear from his or her tone of voice that he or she thinks the rule is too strict.

Informal networks often are described as "grapevine" communication, a term that has connotations of an inaccurate rumor mill. How reliable is grapevine information? Surprisingly, research shows that its accuracy is surprisingly high—between 80 and 90 percent, according to many studies.[15] Not all grapevine information is equally reliable: Noncontroversial information is more likely to be transmitted accurately than is more sensational news. Also, accuracy decreases as the number of people passing along a message grows. (This is also true for formal messages that travel through a long chain of senders and receivers.)

So far this chapter has given an overview of how communication operates in organizations. In the following pages, we will take a more personal focus, describing how you can become more effective in your communication, both as a member of organizations and as an outsider who has to deal with them.

The communication challenges that involve organizations are frequent and varied. Consider a few examples:

- After negotiating a new car price that is really more than you can afford, you arrive at the dealer's to take delivery and find that a few "additional charges" add $500 to the price. You're angry and vow "not to stand for this."
- Two months ago your boss assured you that your work would be rewarded. Yesterday you found that the assistant manager's position

improving your organizational communication

you were hoping for went to an outsider. You are angry and disappointed.

- You have an idea of how some computer programming methods you learned in school might improve the efficiency of the company you've just joined. You know, however, that the president of the company is an old-fashioned operator who mistrusts new "gadgets," as he calls them. Despite this attitude, you still decide to promote the idea.

Your success in situations like these depends partly on the skills introduced elsewhere in this book: the ability to handle yourself well in an interview, to work in a group, to participate in meetings, and to express your ideas in a presentation. In addition to these contextual skills, however, there are some general principles that apply to every type of organizational communication.

define your goal

People communicate to get results, but they don't always know exactly what results they are seeking. Consider the earlier example of the added-on charges on the new car. Would you try to have the extra charges dropped, or would you rather have the dealer—and the public—know how unreputable you think he is? Now think about the case of the promotion you didn't receive: Would your goal be to persuade the manager to reconsider and give you the position you believe you are entitled to? Would you hope to get the next opening? To receive a raise, regardless of a promotion? To hear where you stand with the boss?

As these examples show, most opportunities for organizational communication can have several goals. Before you speak or write, you ought to define yours by answering two questions:

1. **Exactly what do you want to happen?** Be sure to state your goal in terms of the results you are seeking. Don't say, "I want to complain about how badly I've been treated." After all, you don't even need an audience to do this! Instead, say, "I want the sales manager to agree that I've been treated badly and to make an adjustment.

Be sure your goal is specific. Take another look at the statement in the last paragraph, and you will see it isn't especially clear. What kind of "adjustment" will you ask for, and what is the least that will satisfy you? Without knowing this, you are not ready to deliver a message.

2. **Is your goal realistic?** It is probably unrealistic to expect that your boss will give you a job that has already been promised to someone else. It is also unlikely that a skeptical customer will be converted to your product in one presentation. Your goal, then, ought to be one that has a chance of success. You might, for instance, aim to get your boss to agree that you are, indeed, entitled to a promotion and that you deserve a raise in the meantime. Likewise, you might try to analyze your customer's needs in a first session and then use that information to demonstrate in later sections how your product can satisfy those needs.

choose the best audience

Suppose you were a parent who was unhappy with the health and safety conditions at your child's school. You could aim your message at several audiences: the teacher, the school principal, the superintendent of the system, the elected school board, the news media, and governmental agencies. Which audience is best? The answer will depend on many factors: the personalities of each receiver, the way each might regard the sender, and the political climate, to mention a few.

Almost every message has several potential audiences. Communicating with each one requires a different approach and is likely to get different results. Within an organization, protocol usually requires you to clear any ideas or problems with your immediate superior, and most of the time this is a good idea. There are instances, however, when your boss will be too hostile, busy, uninterested, or stupid to appreciate your ideas. There are still ways to deliver a message to the outside world without going over your boss's head. You can mention it in a meeting where others are present: "I've had some ideas on cost cutting that might work for other departments, and I can share them if you're interested . . ." You can put the idea in a memo to your boss and send copies to others. You can discuss the idea with people not in your chain of command as long as the subject is related to their work: "You guys in purchasing are always telling us to keep costs down. I heard about a new software program that might be able to save us some money . . ."

use the best channel

How you deliver a message can be as important as what you say. You have several communication channels available when sending organizational messages: face-to-face conversation, telephone, and writing. As Table 10-2 shows, there are separate varieties within each of these channels.

Ready. Fire. Aim.

Executive at Cadbury's, quoted by Thomas J. Peters and Robert H. Waterman, Jr.

communicating in organizations

247

table 10—2   communication channels in organizations

Face-to-face
   Two-person
   Group
   Speaker-to-audience

Telephone
   Personal contact
   Through intermediary (secretary, co-worker, and so on)
   Recording device

Written
   Personal letter or memo (handwritten or typed)
   Duplicated letter (copies to several recipients)
   Printed publication (newsletter, mass mailing, and so on)
   Mailgram, telegram
   Electronic mail

Choosing one channel over another shouldn't be a casual decision. Each method of delivery has advantages and disadvantages, which we will now consider.[16]

Oral communication   The biggest advantage of oral communication—both face-to-face and by telephone—is its *speed*. Once you have made contact with your receiver, the message is conveyed instantly. This speed is especially valuable when time is of the essence. Should a customer's check be approved? Are the parts you desperately need available? An oral response can answer questions like these in a timely manner.

A second advantage of oral communication is the *instant feedback* it provides. Do your listeners have any questions? Did you forget to say anything? A conversation can let you know. Nonverbal reactions are just as revealing as the words your receiver speaks. Does the other person look bored? Do your remarks get enthusiastic nods and smiles or frowns and head shaking? You can even get valuable feedback in telephone conversations from the speaker's tone of voice.

Finally, oral communication gives you *control* of the situation—far more than you have with written messages. Your receivers might briefly scan the letter you worked so hard on and toss it aside. Even worse, they might not read it at all. In a conversation, however, the audience has at least to pretend to pay attention; and if you use the speaking skills outlined in Chapters 12 to 15, your message ought to be clear and effective enough to be well received.

Written communication   Written communication also has advantages. First, it is *permanent*. Most members of organizations file all correspondence, which means a record of your message exists. Listeners might forget three of the five reasons outlined in your oral presentation, but with a written document they have a record of your ideas.

Written records also *prevent distortion* of your ideas. As you read in Chapter 4, listeners routinely filter comments through their own experiences and prejudices. A letter or memo can guarantee that what you say is what they will receive. Then, if someone makes an unfair accusation, a record of your message is available: "Sure I told you about the problem. Here's a copy of my March 15 memo to you."

Written messages also have the advantage of being most easily *planned in advance*. You can take all the time you want to shape their content and tone. You can test out several versions on sample audiences to predict the response of your real audience, and you can make modifications until you get the desired result. In contrast, oral messages are more difficult to plan. You can rehearse a presentation, but one unforseen question from a listener can throw your whole plan off track. A personal conversation is even harder to plan because you can only guess at what the other person will say.

Which method is best? There is no single answer to this question. As Table 10–3 shows, some messages are most effective when delivered orally whereas others ought to be committed to paper. Oral communication is usually advisable when your message needs to be personal. It also works best with ideas that have a strong need for visual support: demonstrations, charts, slides, and so on. Oral communication also is usually best when you need immediate feedback—either an answer from the other party or assurance that your message has been understood.

Written communication is the best choice when you want your message to be more formal. It is also better than oral channels when you

table 10–3 oral vs. written communication

oral communication	written communication
More personal	More formal
Effective for relatively simple ideas	Effective for relatively complex ideas
Provides immediate feedback	Feedback delayed or nonexistent
Off-the-record	Formal record exists
Effective for messages with visual or hands-on elements	Less effective for visual or hands-on messages
Effective when seeking immediate, emotional response (motivation, sales, and so on)	Effective when seeking delayed, thoughtful response

must choose your words carefully. Written messages are also better when you are communicating complicated ideas. Finally, written messages are best for any message when you want a record to exist.

Sometimes it is wise to send a message in both oral and written forms. You might write a note of thanks to a potential employer (adding an impressive document to your application file) and then phone to express your appreciation personally. You could express a complaint in person to a merchant and follow it up with a letter (with a copy to the Better Business Bureau).

summary

Communicating within and with organizations is a fact of life for almost everyone. Within organizations, most employees spend more time communicating than in any other activity, and the amount of communication increases with the responsibility of a job. College alumni and employers agree that the ability to communicate well is an essential ingredient for a successful career. Even people who do not work in organizations must communicate with them.

Organizations possess several defining characteristics, each of which involves communication. They must define and explain their purpose. They have ordered structure that enables them to carry out their task. Their personnel have specialized roles and, for the most part, are replaceable. Organizations demand a degree of uniformity from employees and have an authority structure. Finally, organizations create unique signs and symbols to identify themselves.

Within an organization, formal communication networks are management's idea of who ought to communicate with whom. Information flows within these networks upward, downward, and horizontally. Informal networks also carry information. They are based on proximity, shared interests, and personal friendships. Informal networks are an important and useful means of receiving and sending information.

Individuals can improve the effectiveness of their communication, both within organizations and as outsiders. Defining a realistic and specific goal can contribute to success. Choosing the best audience can also produce desired results. Finally, choosing the best channel to deliver a message can often make the difference between success and failure.

activities

1. Identify the organizations you belong to and those you communicate with as an outsider. Use the criteria on pages 236–241 to identify the organizations on your list.

2. Using an organization from your own experience, describe the types of communication you initiate and receive:
   a. Downward (job instructions, job rationale, policies and procedures, feedback, and indoctrination).
   b. Upward (what subordinates are doing, unsolved work problems,

suggestions for improvement, how subordinates feel about themselves and the job).

   c. Horizontal (task coordination, problem solving, sharing information, resolving conflict, building rapport).

How could each type of communication be improved?

3. What informal networks do you belong to in organizations? Who are the other members? What types of information does each network carry? How reliable is it? How can you use these networks to your advantage?

4. Choose a personal goal you have as a member of an organization.

   a. Define the results you seek in realistic, specific terms.

   b. Identify the best audience or audiences to approach.

   c. Describe the best channel or channels to convey your message.

   d. Construct the message you could send.

notes

1. D. Stine and D. Skarzinski, "Priorities for the Business Communication Classroom: A Survey of Business and Academe," *Journal of Business Communication* 16 (1979): 25.

2. Raymond Lesiker, *Business Communication: Theory and Application,* 4th ed. (Homewood, Ill.: R. D. Irwin, 1980), p. 5.

3. C. S. Goetzinger and M. A. Valentine, "Problems in Executive Interpersonal Communication," *Personnel Administration* 27 (1964): 24–29.

4. A. S. Bisconti and L. C. Solmon, *College Education on the Job—The Recent Graduates' Viewpoint* (Bethlehem, Pa.: The College Placement Council Foundation, 1976), p. 43.

5. F. S. Endicott, "The Endicott Report: Trends in the Employment of College and University Graduates in Business and Industry 1980" (Evanston, Ill.: Placement Center, Northwestern University, 1979).

6. J. C. Bennett, "The Communication Needs of Business Executives," *Journal of Business Communication* 9 (1971): 5–12.

7. G. W. Bowman, "What Helps or Harms Promotability?" *Harvard Business Review* (January–February 1964): 14.

8. Adapted from A. Tannenbaum, *Social Psychology of the Work Organization* (Belmont, Calif.: Brooks/Cole, 1966), pp. 2–6.

9. John Nasbitt, *Megatrends: Ten New Directions Transforming Our Lives* (New York: Warner Books, 1982), Chapter 2.

10. Donald Woutat, "Chrysler Gets 3 More Years from Iacocca," *Los Angeles Times,* December 9, 1983, Part IV, p. 1.

11. D. Katz and R. Kahn, *The Social Psychology of Organizations,* 2d ed. (New York: Wiley, 1978).

12. Adapted from Katz and Kahn, op. cit., p. 245.

13. Adapted from G. Goldhaber, *Organizational Communication,* 3d ed. (Dubuque, Iowa: Wm. C. Brown, 1983), p. 162.

14. Keith Davis, "Management Communication and the Grapevine," *Harvard Business Review* (September–October 1953): 43–49.

15. Keith Davis, *Human Behavior at Work* (New York: McGraw-Hill, 1972).

16. Adapted from Betsy Yarrison and Ronald B. Adler, *The Business of Communication* (New York: Random House, 1986).

communicating in organizations

part 4 **public communication**

eleven

choosing and developing a topic

After reading this chapter, you should understand:

1. The importance of defining a clear speech purpose.
2. The difference between a general and a specific speech purpose.
3. The necessity of analyzing a speaking situation.
4. The importance of audience analysis.

You should be able to:

1. Choose an effective topic.
2. Formulate a purpose statement that will help you develop that topic.
3. Analyze the three components of a speaking situation.
4. Perform an audience analysis.
5. Gather information on the topic from a variety of sources.

unaccustomed as i am . . .

. . . I am, God help me, about to do it for the fifth time. My hands I know will be wet and my mouth dry. There will even be an actual bumping inside my chest as I scrape back my chair and walk unsteadily to the podium. ''Thank you very much'' (gulp . . . weak smile), ''and good evening, ladies and gentlemen.''

My horror of stages, speeches, spotlights and footlights is old stuff. I am a born spectator. My natural habitat is the audience. I know my place and it is not in the spotlight. It is back up there in the snug anonymous dark. . . .

I first emerged from the wings in a walnut shell towed by two mice. It was a fourth-grade production of *Thumbelina,* and my mortifying costume was a leaf. Merciful obscurity closed in after that until the time came to make a speech at my eighth-grade graduation. By then I was burdened with 20 pounds of overweight, a mouthful of braces and a broken leg. The event was so traumatic that for the next 20 years I stayed resolutely off the stage, refusing to take part in school plays, team athletics, dance contests or campus politics. I even got my college diploma by mail. Though my wedding took place in the relative privacy of my parents' living room, I would have preferred the even greater anonymity of city hall.

For years I refused all invitations to participate in panel discussions, disk-jockey interviews, political rallies, awards ceremonies or tree plantings. I never asked questions from the floor at lectures or volunteered to help the magician in the nightclub. At raffles, half of me hoped I didn't have the lucky number.

The carrot that finally coaxed me out of the wings was of all things a journalism award. No acceptance speech, they said, no award. O vanity, vanity! I said I'd be there.

But there was something more to it than that. I really started speaking for the same reason that I stopped smoking. I was ashamed of myself. It was time to grow up. But the older one gets, it seems, the harder that is to do.

As my D-day approached, I retreated. Friends had rallied round with all sorts of advice, mostly contradictory. Don't be afraid to write it out. Read it. Memorize it. Put it on cards. Speak it off the cuff. Start funny. Start dull—an early joke lets them off the hook of curiosity. Turn from side to side so they can all see you. Find one nice face in the audience and tell it all to him. Get a new dress. Get a little drunk.

By the afternoon of the speech, trying to follow all this advice at once, I sat stupefied with terror in my room in the hotel where the banquet was to be held. My new gown hung on the back of the door, flowers and telegrams began to arrive. Were they condolences? Had I already died? . . . I barely remember going downstairs to the hotel ballroom, or the dais, or the dinner, or anything at all until I felt my wet palms gripping the smooth sides of the lectern, and heard my own weird, oddly magnified voice rumble out over the crowd.

I was most unprepared for my own total unpreparedness: I didn't know where to look, where to put my hands, where to pitch my voice, when to pause, when to smile. To be *that* unknowing rarely happens to an adult; it gave me a giddy feeling; nothing to do but push on.

After a few moments I heard faint laughter. I was not quite conscious of it at first, but then it came again a bit stronger, until I was sure I heard it, and then as I was reading I began to wait for it, and to make spaces in sentences for it, to enjoy it, and finally to play with the words and with the audience, to swoop and glide and describe arabesques with all the nutty abandon of Donald Duck on ice skates.

Success. Triumph. Waves of applause. The night came to a kind of crescendo Andy Hardy finish that I have never been able to recapture. In the next three speeches I was nearly as scared as the first time, but not nearly as good. But I am going to try it again. I am getting to know the ropes.

Shana Alexander

256

Most people view the prospect of standing before an audience with the same enthusiasm that accompanies a trip to the dentist or the tax auditor. In fact, giving a speech seems to be one of the most anxiety-producing things we can do: *The Book of Lists* claims that Americans fear public speaking more than they do insects, heights, accidents, and even death.[1]

Despite the discomfort that speech giving causes, sooner or later most of us will need to talk to an audience of some kind: while giving a class report, as part of our jobs, or as part of a community-action group. And even in less "speechlike" situations, we often need the same skills good speakers possess: the ability to talk with confidence, to organize ideas in a clear way, and to make those ideas interesting and persuasive.

Getting to "know the ropes" in public speaking is, as Shana Alexander suggests in the reading on page 256, at least partially a matter of practice. But practice doesn't always make perfect; without a careful analysis of *what* you are practicing, practice has a tendency to make old public speaking habits permanent rather than perfect. The final section of this book will provide you with some tools to analyze your performance as a public speaker.

all communication is purposeful

No one gives a speech—or expresses *any* kind of message—without having a reason to do so. This is easy to see in those messages that ask for something: "Pass the salt" or "How about a movie this Friday?" or "Excuse me, that's my foot you're standing on." But even in more subtle messages the speaker always has a purpose—to evoke a response from the listener.

Sometimes purposes are misunderstood or confused by the speaker. This causes wasted time both in the preparation and the presentation of the speech. It is essential, therefore, that the speaker keep in mind a clear purpose.

The first step in understanding your purpose is to formulate a clear and precise purpose statement. This requires an understanding of both *general purpose* and *specific purpose*.

general purpose

Most students, when asked *why* they are giving a speech in a college class, will quickly cite course requirements. But you have to analyze your motives more deeply than that to develop a complete speech purpose. Even if you are only giving your speech for the grade, you still have to affect your audience in some way to earn that grade.

> The secret of success is constancy of purpose.
>
> Disraeli

If your motive for speaking is to learn effective speech techniques (as we hope it is), you still have to influence your audience to accomplish your goal because that is what effective speaking is all about.

Now, when we say you have to influence your audience, we mean you have to *change* them in some way. If you think about all the possible ways you could change an audience, you'll realize that they all boil down to three options, which happen to be the three basic general purposes for speaking:

1. **To entertain:** To relax your audience by providing them with a pleasant listening experience.
2. **To inform:** To enlighten your audience by teaching them something.
3. **To persuade:** To move your audience toward a new attitude or behavior.

A brief scrutiny of these purposes will reveal that no speech could ever have *only* one purpose. These purposes are interrelated because a speech designed for one purpose will almost always accomplish a little of the other purposes; even a speech designed purely to entertain might change audience attitudes or teach that audience something new. In fact, these purposes are *cumulative* in the sense that to inform an audience you have to provide them with "a pleasant listening experience" at least long enough to get their attention and to persuade them you have to inform them about arguments and evidence.

Deciding your general purpose is like choosing the "right" answer on one of those multiple-choice tests in which *all* the answers are right to a certain degree, but *one* answer is more right than the others. Thus, we say that any speech is *primarily* designed for one of these purposes. A clear understanding of your general purpose gets you on the right track for choosing and developing a topic. Understanding your *specific* purpose will keep you on that track.

specific purpose

Whereas your general purpose is only a one-word label, your specific goal is expressed in the form of a *purpose statement,* which is a complete sentence that tells exactly what you want your speech to accomplish. The purpose statement usually isn't used word for word in the actual speech; its purpose is to keep you focused as a speaker.

There are three criteria for a good purpose statement.[2]

1. **A purpose statement must be audience-oriented.** As we mentioned earlier, all communication seeks some response from a receiver. This receiver orientation should be reflected in your purpose statement. For example, if you were giving an informative talk on gourmet cooking, this would be an inadequate purpose statement:

   "My purpose is to tell my audience about gourmet cooking."

   As that statement is worded, your purpose is "to tell" an audience something, which means that the speech could be successful even if no one listens. Your purpose statement should refer to the response you want from your audience: It should tell what the audience members will know or do or be able to do after listening to your speech. Thus, the purpose statement above could be improved this way:

"After listening to my speech, my audience will know more about gourmet cooking."

That's an improvement because you now have stated what you expect from your audience. But this purpose statement could still be improved through the judicious application of a second criterion:

2. **A purpose statement must be precise.** To be effective, a purpose statement should be worded specifically, with enough details so that you would be able to measure or test your audience, after your speech, to see if you had achieved your purpose. In the example given earlier, simply "knowing about gourmet cooking" is too vague; you need something more specific, such as:

"After listening to my speech, my audience will be able to cook *coq au vin* at home."

At least now you've limited your purpose to a single dish rather than the entire world of gourmet cooking. This is an improvement, but it can still be made better by applying a third criterion:

3. **A purpose statement must be attainable.** You must be able to accomplish your purpose as stated. Some speakers insist on formulating purpose statements such as "My purpose is to convince my audience to make governmental budget deficits illegal." Unfortunately, unless your audience happens to be a joint session of Congress, it won't have the power to change United States fiscal policy. But any audience can write their congressional representative or sign a petition. Similarly, an audience will not "learn how to play championship tennis" or "understand the dangers of business regulation" in one sitting. You must aim for an audience response that is possible to accomplish. In your gourmet cooking speech, it would be impossible for you to be sure that each of your audience members will actually be able to cook a meal. You might have no idea, for example, if they all have access to a kitchen. So a better purpose statement for this speech might sound something like this:

"After listening to my speech my audience will be able to list the five steps for preparing *coq au vin* at home."

A good speech purpose should be attainable, but it's impossible to know just *what* you can expect to attain and the best way to go about attaining it without analyzing the speaking situation.

There are three components to analyze in any speaking situation: the speaker, the audience, and the occasion. To be successful, every choice you make in putting together your speech—your choice of purpose,

analyzing the speaking situation

topic, and all the material you use to develop your speech—must be appropriate to all three of these components.

you, the speaker: self-analysis

"Above all else," Polonius urged Hamlet, "to thine own self be true." This is good advice to follow in speech preparation. Don't become so involved in finding a "correct" topic or material that you lose yourself. Stay in touch with your own purpose, feelings, and unique knowledge and interests.

Purpose We already discussed one step in self-analysis when we considered your purpose as a speaker. The first question to ask yourself when planning a speech (or any other act of communication) is "What do I want to accomplish?" Having answered this question, you should check every decision that follows to be sure it contributes to your goal.

Your feelings After your purpose has been clarified, a second kind of self-analysis involves your feelings about yourself in the specific speaking situation. As we discussed in Chapter 2, the perceptions of both the speaker and the listener can greatly alter the outcome of any act of communication. Your perception of yourself as a speaker will influence you along every step of the speech-preparation process. If you have a negative self-concept or if you feel negative about the topic, those feelings will show through in the final product. You will be just a little "off" in terms of the topic you've selected, the information you've gathered, the way you present that information, and in every other aspect of your speech. Therefore it's important to look at yourself objectively and to choose a purpose, topic, and material about which you can feel confident and enthusiastic. If you really don't care about gourmet cooking, then that's not an appropriate topic for you as a speaker—no matter how potentially interesting that topic is to your audience.

Your unique knowledge and interests A third step in your self-analysis involves recognizing and building upon your uniqueness as a person. Though you are obviously similar in many ways to your audience, there are also many respects in which you are different. You can capitalize on this uniqueness by offering the audience something new—your knowledge, your experiences, or perhaps your opinions. Analyze yourself from the point of view of how you are different from your audience. This will give you insight into what you have to offer them. For example, if you spend a lot of time rock climbing or if you know a lot about the sport and you have reason to believe the rest of your audience doesn't, then you have an area of uniqueness to talk about.

At the same time, this third step in your self-analysis will help you keep your message close to the listeners' interests and backgrounds; if you know where you're different from them, you'll know where you have to explain things in depth and add human-interest touches to keep from losing their attention. This brings us to our second step in analyzing the situation: your analysis of the audience.

the listeners: audience analysis

When you choose a gift, it's important to consider the person who will receive it; what would be an ideal present for one person could be a disaster for another. In the same way you need to think about your audience—especially in terms of their interests—when planning a speech. There are several factors to consider in audience analysis.

Audience type   There are at least three types of audience you are likely to encounter—"passersby," "captives," and "volunteers." Each type suggests different audience interests.[3]

"Passersby," as the name implies, are people who aren't much interested—at least not in advance—in what you have to say. A crowd milling around the student union or a shopping mall would fit into this category. With this type of audience, your first concern is to make them aware of you as a speaker, either by interesting them in the topic or in you as a speaker. You might have to pick a really sensational topic or begin developing your topic by using some kind of device or gimmick to get their attention, such as the loud costumes or wild theatrics street speakers often rely upon.

Think before thou speakest.

Cervantes
Don Quixote

"Captives" are audience members who have gathered for some reason besides the joy of hearing you speak. Students in a required class often begin as a type of "captive" audience. So do military formations, mandatory work meetings, and other "required" gatherings. With captives you don't have to worry about devices and gimmicks to make them aware of you as a speaker; you do, however, have to use material that will get them interested and keep them interested in what you have to say.

"Volunteers" are audience members who have gathered together because of a common interest. Students in elective courses, especially those with long waiting lists, would fit into this category. So would gatherings of most clubs, social organizations, and "action" groups. Even with an audience of volunteers, you still have to maintain the listeners' interest; you never lose that responsibility. But when the audience is informed and involved, as volunteers tend to be, you can treat your topic in greater depth without worrying about *losing* their interest.

Most college speech classes are a mixture of captives and volunteers, which means that you don't have to sensationalize your topic or use gimmicks, but you do have to maintain interest and provide depth.

Audience purpose Just as you have a purpose for speaking, the audience members have a purpose for gathering. Sometimes virtually all members of your audience will have the same, obvious goal. Expectant parents at a natural childbirth class are all seeking a healthy, relatively painless delivery, and people attending an investment seminar are looking for ways to increase their net worth.

There are other times, however, when audience purpose can't be so easily defined. In some instances, different listeners will have different goals, some of which might not be apparent to the speaker. Consider a church congregation, for example. Whereas some members might listen to a sermon with the hope of applying religious principles to their lives, others might be interested in being entertained or in appearing pious. In the same way, the listeners in your speech class probably have a variety of motives for attending; becoming aware of as many of these motives as possible will help you predict what will interest them.

Demographics Demographics are characteristics of your audience that can be labeled, such as number of people, age, sex, group membership, and so on. In any speech most of these characteristics should affect your planning in some way.[4] For example:

1. Number of people. Topic appropriateness varies with the size of an audience. With a small group you can be less formal and more intimate—you can, for example, talk more about your own inner feelings and personal experiences. If you gave a speech before five people as impersonally as if they were a standing-room-only crowd in a lecture hall, they would probably find you stuffy. On the other hand, if you talked to 300 people about your unhappy childhood, you'd probably make them uncomfortable. Also, the larger your audience, the broader the range of interests and knowledge; with a small audience, you can choose a more specific topic.

2. **Sex.** Traditionally, men and women have tended to be interested in different topics. These differences are becoming less pronounced as time goes on because men and women are becoming conscious of sexual stereotypes and are rebelling against them. Still, the differences in interest that prevail are of concern to a speaker in choosing and developing a topic. There are still more men than women interested in automotive engineering and more women than men interested in cooking. The guideline here might be: *Do not exclude or offend any portion of your audience on the basis of sex.* Every speech teacher has a horror story about a student getting up in front of a class composed primarily, but not entirely, of men and speaking on a subject such as "Picking up Chicks." The women, once they realize that the speech is not about methods of handling poultry, are invariably offended. And most of the men will feel the same way.

As with any of these demographic characteristics, the point is to *adapt* your idea (rather than throwing it away) according to who is in your audience. The speaker who wants to speak on how boy meets girl, or vice versa, may still do so; the topic of the speech, however, should be "meeting people." That way it can be treated in a manner that would be appropriate for both men and women. This is true of topics like "weight lifting" (which could be changed to "body conditioning") and "home economics" (which could be changed to "survival for singles").

3. **Age.** In many areas younger people and older people have different interests. Topics such as social security, child rearing, and school success are all influenced by the age of the audience. These differences run relatively deep; Aristotle observed long ago that young people "have strong passions," that "their lives are spent not in memory but in expectation," and that they have high ideals because "they have not been humbled by life or learnt its necessary limitations." Older people, on the other hand, tend to have more practical interests.

4. **Group membership.** Organizations to which the audience members belong provide more clues to audience interests. By examining the groups to which they belong, you can surmise an audience's political leanings (Young Republicans or Young Democrats), religious beliefs (CYO or Hillel), or occupation (Bartenders Union or Speech Communication Association). Group membership is often an important consideration in college classes. Consider the difference between "typical" college day classes and "typical" college night classes. At many colleges the evening students are generally older and tend to belong to civic groups, church clubs, and the local chamber of commerce. Daytime students tend to belong to sororities and fraternities, sports clubs, and social-action groups.

choosing and developing a topic

263

These four demographic characteristics are important examples, but the list goes on and on. Other demographic characteristics include ethnic background, religion, educational level, economic status, and occupation; demographics that might be important in a college class include home town, year in school, and major subject. In short, any demographic characteristic of the audience that you can identify should be used as part of your audience analysis.

A final factor to consider in audience analysis concerns their attitudes, beliefs, and values.

Attitudes, beliefs, and values Structured in human consciousness like layers of an onion are people's attitudes, beliefs, and values. They are all closely interrelated, but attitudes lie closest to the surface whereas beliefs and values underlie them. An *attitude* is a predisposition to respond to something in a favorable or unfavorable way. A *belief* is an underlying conviction about the truth of something, which is sometimes based on cultural or religious training. A *value* is a deeply rooted belief about a concept's inherent worth or worthiness. An audience might hold the value that "freedom is a good thing," for example, which will be expressed in a belief such as "people should be free to choose their political leaders," which in turn will lead to the attitude that "voting is an important right and responsibility for all citi-

zens." This, in short, leads to a predisposition to vote—in other words, a positive attitude toward voting.

You can often make an inference about audience attitudes by recognizing beliefs and values they are likely to hold. For example, a group of religious fundamentalists might hold the value of "obeying God's word." This might lead to the belief—based on their interpretation of the Bible—that women are not meant to perform the same functions in society as men. This in turn might lead to the attitude that the Equal Rights Amendment should not be supported.

You can also make a judgment about one attitude your audience members hold based on your knowledge of other attitudes they hold. If your audience is made up of undergraduates who have a positive attitude toward sexual-liberation movements, it is a good bet they also have a positive attitude toward civil rights and ecology. If they have a negative attitude toward collegiate sports, they probably also have a negative attitude toward fraternities and sororities. This should not only suggest some appropriate topics for each audience, it should also suggest ways that those topics could be developed.

the occasion

The third phase in analyzing a speaking situation focuses on the occasion. The "occasion" of a speech is determined by the circumstances surrounding it. Three of these circumstances are time, place, and audience expectations.

Time Your speech occupies a space in time that is surrounded by other events. For example, other speeches might be presented before or after yours, or comments might be made that set a certain tone or mood. There are also external events (such as elections, the start of a new semester, or disasters) that color the occasion in one way or the other. The date on which you give your speech might have some historical significance. If that historical significance relates in some way to your topic, you can use it to help build audience interest.

The time *available* for your speech is also an essential consideration. You should choose a topic that is broad enough to say something worthwhile but brief enough to fit your time limits. "Wealth," for example, might be an inherently interesting topic to some college students, but it would be difficult to cover such a broad topic in a ten-minute speech and still say anything significant. But a topic like "How to Make Extra Money in Your Spare Time" could conceivably be covered in ten minutes in enough depth to make it worthwhile. All speeches have time limitations, whether they are explicitly stated or not. If you are invited to say a few words and you present a few volumes, you won't be invited back.

Place Your speech also occupies a physical space. The beauty or squalor of your surroundings or the noise or stuffiness of the room

length versus depth

The speaker steps up on the podium
To give his speech of praise or odium,
And as he lays his papers out
And ranges them with care about
And thinks, "My speech is for the ages,"
His hearers try to count the pages.

Richard Armour

sample analysis of a speaking situation

Audience: Sons of Italy Club

Situation: Acceptance speech for scholarship award

Purposes:
1. The audience will know that I'm grateful for receiving the scholarship.
2. The audience will realize that I'm not the stereotyped bookworm that scholarship recipients are usually viewed as.
3. The audience will think that they've given the scholarship to the right person.

When I began planning the speech, I couldn't decide if I wanted to do it in Italian or English. I was considering Italian because of the nature of the club and because I thought it would impress the audience if I used that language: They might think "She's a good Italian" and "She's bright." In the end I decided to speak in English. Even though most of the audience would understand my Italian, there were a few important people who don't speak it.

My audience consisted of mostly middle-aged and older people. There were about 150–200 of them. Among the special guests were the mayor and some club representatives from out of town. I knew that I had to sound sincere, and yet be organized enough to show that I had a "good head on my shoulders." On the other hand, I didn't want to give the audience the impression that I was superstudious and did nothing but study. For this reason I began the speech by acknowledging the audience's feelings of boredom after sitting through forty minutes of other speeches. I thought this would show that I was one of them. I acknowledged this feeling because from past experiences with this particular audience I know that they are more interested in the festivities and dancing following dinner than with any ceremonies.

Also to get away from the bookworm stereotype I dressed in a very sophisticated (yet not too sexy—I'm a "nice Italian girl"!) manner, in a black midcalf dress.

My entire speech supported the idea that I was honored to receive the scholarship by describing my sincere feelings of enthusiasm. I also threw in a few Italian phrases for authenticity and concluded the speech by encouraging everyone to have a great time that evening.

The speech was a big success. I was very sincere and emotional while giving it, so the audience knew it was coming from my heart. My happiness showed in my smile. I felt comfortable looking at the audience a lot because I had practiced the speech well, and because I knew they were behind me. Because of my nervousness and excitement my voice was quivery, but I think even this helped my purpose, although I didn't plan it that way.

The reception I received from the audience was tremendous, which made me feel good because it made me realize that I had accomplished my purposes.

---

should all be taken into consideration. These physical surroundings can be referred to in your speech if appropriate. If you were talking about world poverty, for example, you could compare your surroundings to those that might be found in a poorer country.

Audience expectation Finally, your speech is surrounded by audience expectations. A speech presented in a college class, for example, is usually expected to reflect a high level of thought and intelligence. This doesn't necessarily mean that it has to be boring or humorless; wit and humor are, after all, indicative of intelligence. But it does mean that you have to put a little more effort into your presentation than if you were discussing the same subject with friends over coffee.

When considering the occasion of your speech, as well as when considering your audience and yourself as a speaker, it pays to remember that every occasion is unique. Although there are obvious differences between the occasion of a college class, a church sermon, and a bachelor party "roast," there are also many subtle differences that will apply only to the circumstances of each unique event.

This discussion about planning a speech purpose and analyzing the speech situation should make it apparent that it takes time, interest, and knowledge to develop a topic well. This leads us to our final three guidelines for choosing a topic:

guidelines on choosing a topic

look for a topic early

Ideas seem to come automatically to speakers who have a topic in mind; things they read or observe or talk about that might have otherwise been meaningless suddenly relate to their topic, providing material or inspiration for sources of material.[5] The earlier you decide on a topic, the more of these happy coincidences you can take advantage of; the

choosing and developing a topic

267

best student speakers usually choose a topic as soon as possible after a speech is assigned by their instructor, and then they stick with it.

choose a topic that interests you

If you are not interested in your topic, it will be difficult for you to interest anyone else. Your interest in a topic will improve your ability to investigate it. It will also increase your confidence when it comes time to present it.

Needless to say, your topic should also have the potential of being interesting to your audience. But no matter how "good" the topic, if it isn't interesting to you, you'll have a hard time involving your audience.

Sometimes it's difficult to remember *what* your interests are—especially when you're being pressed to come up with a speech topic. If that happens to you, we suggest the following steps:

1. Review a few recent issues of your favorite newspapers and magazines—which articles did you find interesting?
2. Browse through your bookshelf at home, or mentally review the books you've read—any consistent themes or topics?
3. Inspect your possessions—any equipment for sports, hobbies, or interests that would suggest a topic?
4. Think about the way you spend your free time—anything there that would suggest a major interest?

These steps are just examples, of course. Television programs, films, bookstores, walks in the neighborhood, talks with friends, and dozens of other activities can all spur your memory about the things that interest you.

choose a topic you know something about

The main problem for most people is not generally "knowing something," but realizing how *much* they know. It is a mistake to think that you have nothing new to say; your experiences, your thoughts, and your investigation of a topic will be, by definition, unique.

gathering information

Much of the information you present in your speech will be based on your own thoughts and experience. Setting aside a block of time to reflect on your own ideas is essential. However, you will also need to gather information from outside sources.

There are three types of information you need for a speech. We've already discussed the first category, which is information dealing with the speaking situation (you, the audience, and the occasion). In addition, you also need information about the *ideas* you use and *facts* to substantiate and help develop your ideas. By this time, of course, you are familiar with library research as a form of gathering information. Some-

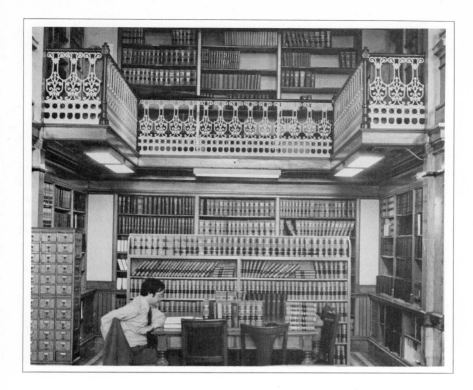

times, however, speakers overlook some of the less obvious resources of the library; more often they also overlook interviewing, personal observation, and survey research as equally effective methods of gathering information. We will review all of these methods here and perhaps provide a new perspective on one or more of them.

library research

Libraries, like people, tend to be unique. It's important to get to know your own library, to see what kind of special collections and services it offers, and just to find out where everything is. There are, however, a few resources that are common to most libraries, including the card catalog, reference works, periodicals, and nonprint materials.

The card catalog The card catalog is an ancient and noble information-storing device. It is your key to all the books in the library, filed according to subject, author, and title, so you can look under general topics as well as for specific books and authors.

Reference works Reference works will also be listed in the card catalog, but it would be a better idea to spend some time wandering

Knowledge is of two kinds:
We know a subject
ourselves, or we know where
we can find information upon
it.

Samuel Johnson

through the reference room yourself. There are wonders there that could turn you into a trivia expert for life. There are encyclopedias galore, even specialized ones such as *The Encyclopedia of Social Sciences* and *The Encyclopedia of American History;* there are statistical compilations such as *The World Almanac, Facts on File,* and *The Guinness Book of World Records;* you can find out *Who's Who in America* or even *Who Was Who.* You can collect a lot of facts in a short time in the reference room.

Periodicals Magazines, journals, and newspapers are good resources for finding recently published material on interesting topics. Indexes such as *The Readers' Guide to Periodical Literature* will enable you to find popular magazine articles on just about any subject. Specialized indexes such as *The Education Index* and *Psychological Abstracts* can be used to find articles in specific fields, and newspaper indexes such as *The New York Times Index* can be used to find microfilmed newspaper articles.

Nonprint materials Most libraries are also treasuries of nonprint and audiovisual materials. Films, records, tapes, and videotapes can be used not only as research tools but as aids during your presentation. Your library probably has an orientation program that will acquaint you with what it has to offer in the way of nonprint materials.

Library "gnomes" If you have done everything mentioned earlier and you still can't find exactly what you need, seek out the gnome in your library. In folklore, gnomes (the term comes from the Greek word "to know") were ageless dwarfs who guarded precious ores and treasures. The modern library variety are real, though rarely dwarflike—and they themselves are the treasures. These people seem to know where to find almost any bit of information. They are usually located behind the reference desk, but they might be anywhere. Find the gnome in your library, and you have half the battle won.

On-line databases A growing number of libraries have access to on-line databases. These are computerized collections of information that can be searched via telephone link. One popular collection of databases is Dialog Information Retrieval Service. Dialog contains over 80,000,000 records from news services, magazines, scholarly journals, conference papers, books, and other sources. With the right search strategy, you can locate scores of citations on your topic in just a few minutes rather than spending hours or weeks looking manually. Once you have located the items you want, it is possible to read abstracts or even entire articles on the screen of the library's computer terminal—or even have printouts mailed to you. For more information on databases, contact your local library gnome.

interviewing

As we discussed in Chapter 7, the information-gathering interview is an especially valuable form of research on a college campus because so many experts of every stripe run loose there. The interview allows you to view your topic from an expert's perspective, to take advantage of that expert's years of experience, research, and thought. You can use an interview to collect facts and to stimulate your own thinking. Often the interview will save you hours of library research and allow you to present ideas that you could not have uncovered any other way. And because the interview is a face-to-face interaction with an expert, many ideas that otherwise would be unclear can become more understandable.

personal observation

Personal *experience* is one of the basic ingredients of any speech, but unsupported personal *opinions* can be detrimental. As a method of gathering information, personal observation gives some extra weight to your personal opinion. For example, if you were suggesting to an audience that the TV sets in your student union should be removed, you might say this:

> I think people would interact more here if the televisions were removed from the student union.

But all you have there is personal opinion, which could be based on anything, including a purely emotional hatred of television or of college students. The use of personal observation, however, might allow you to say this:

> Last Wednesday I spent 7:00 to 10:00 P.M. in the lounge of the student union. Only three times during the evening did anyone attempt to start a conversation. Two of those attempts were met with a request for silence in deference to the television.

If you wanted to prove your point further, you could go one step further and observe the same situation under different circumstances:

> This Wednesday I received permission to remove the television from the student union. During those same hours, 7:00 to 10:00 P.M., I observed the following behavior in that lounge, this time without television:
>
> 1. Thirty conversations were begun.
> 2. Twenty-four of these conversations continued, in depth, for more than ten minutes.
> 3. Seven groups of students decided on alternative entertainment for the evening, including table games, singing, dancing, and going to the library.
> 4. Four new male-female acquaintances were made, one of which resulted in a TV date for the following Wednesday night.

Personal observation is used to collect information about human beings. Because your job as a public speaker is communicating with human beings, and because human beings love information about themselves, observing their behavior firsthand can be an extremely valuable form of investigation. Survey research is also valuable in this respect.

survey research

One advantage of handing out a survey to your audience (a week or so before your speech) is that it gives you up-to-date answers concerning "the way things are" in a fast-moving, constantly changing world. Consider the following ideas, either of which might be presented in a speech on giving children a right to divorce their parents:

> A survey conducted in 1980 suggests that five out of ten college students are in favor of greater civil rights for children. (library-type data)

> According to a survey I conducted last week, nine out of ten students in this class are in favor of greater civil rights for children. And yet the same proportion—nine out of ten—are undecided about granting children the right to divorce their parents. (survey-type data)

That second statement would probably be of more immediate interest to an audience of students. That is one advantage of conducting your own survey. Another advantage is that it is one of the best ways to find out about your audience: It is in fact *the* best way to collect the demographic data mentioned earlier. The one disadvantage of conducting your own survey is that, if it is used as evidence, it might not have as much credibility as published evidence found in the library. But all in all the advantages seem to outweigh the disadvantages of survey research in public speaking.

No matter how you gather your information, remember that it is the *quality* rather than the quantity of the research that is important. The key is to determine carefully what type of research will answer the questions you need to have answered. Sometimes only one type of research will be necessary; at other times every type mentioned here will have to be used.

summary

This chapter dealt with your first tasks in preparing a public speech: choosing and developing a topic.

One of your tasks is to understand your purpose so that you can stick to it as you prepare your speech. General purposes include entertaining, informing, and persuading. Specific purposes are expressed in the form of purpose statements, which must be audience-oriented, precise, and attainable.

Another first task is to analyze the three components of the speaking situation—yourself, the audience, and the occasion. When analyzing yourself, you should consider your feelings about your topic, your unique knowledge and interests, as well as your purpose. When analyzing your audience, you should consider the audience type (passersby, captives, volunteers), purpose, demographics, attitudes, beliefs, and values. When analyzing the occasion, you should consider the time (and date) your speech will take place, the time available, the location, and audience expectations.

Some final guidelines for choosing a topic evolve out of these preliminary concepts: Look for a topic early and stick with it, choose a topic you find interesting, and choose a topic you know something about to begin with.

Although much of your speech will be based on personal reflection about your own ideas and experiences, it is usually necessary to gather some information from outside sources. Techniques for doing so include interpersonal research (such as interviewing), personal observation, and surveys, as well as library research.

Throughout all these preliminary tasks you will be organizing information. This process will be discussed in the next chapter.

activities

1. Analyze your strengths and weaknesses as a speaker. Think back to the most recent ''speech'' you gave—a class presentation, for example. Answer the following questions about that speech:
   a. How interested was your audience in what you had to say?
   b. How well did they understand you?
   c. Did your speech accomplish what you wanted it to accomplish?
   d. How did *you* feel about your presentation?

2. For practice in formulating purpose statements that adhere to the criteria mentioned in this chapter, try writing one for each of the following speeches:
   a. An after-dinner speech at an awards banquet in which you will honor a team that has a winning, but not championship, record. (You pick the team.)
   b. A classroom speech in which you explain how to do something. (Once again, you choose the topic: rebuilding an engine, cooking a favorite dish, playing a guitar, or whatever.)
   c. A campaign speech in which you support the candidate of your choice.

   Answer the following questions about each of your purpose statements: Is the purpose audience-oriented? Is it precise? Is it attainable?

3. For practice in choosing topics through self-analysis, list the following:
   a. Three topics you feel are *inappropriate* for you as a speaker.
   b. Three topics you feel are *appropriate* for you.

choosing and developing a topic

273

Briefly explain *why* each of these topics is appropriate or inappropriate.

4. For practice in analyzing speech situations, carry out the following exercise with your classmates:
   a. Prepare, in advance, three index cards: one with a possible topic for a speech, one with a possible audience, and one with a possible occasion.
   b. Form groups of three members each, and place your cards face down, with one member's "audience" matched with a second member's "topic" and a third member's "occasion," and so on.
   c. Turn the cards over. For each set, decide which characteristics of the audience, topic, and occasion would most likely affect the way the speech was developed.
   d. Compare notes with the other groups to see who had the most unlikely matchup, as well as the best analysis.

   A sample set of cards might look like this:

   Topic: Morals on campus.
   Audience: The women's auxiliary for the local ambulance squad. All women, all between the ages of thirty-five and fifty, and all married to members of the volunteer ambulance squad.
   Occasion: Annual awards banquet, at which you're about to receive an award for special achievement in your topic area.

5. This exercise will give you practice in gathering information.
   a. Choose a current expression with a derivation that you are interested in but unsure about. For example, you might choose a term in general usage such as *nerd, gut course,* or *cramming;* or you might choose one that enjoys only local currency, such as *megabooking* now has on at least one large Eastern campus.
   b. Once you have decided on an expression, try to find out as much as you can about its derivation. Use the library, conduct an interview or two, do a survey, and observe the context in which your chosen expression is used around your campus and among your friends and acquaintances.

notes

1. David Wallechinsky, Irving Wallace, and Amy Wallace, *The Book of Lists* (New York: William Morrow, 1977), p. 469.
2. Leon Fletcher, *How to Design and Deliver a Speech* (New York: Chandler, 1973).
3. Different theorists mention different audience "types." See, for example, H. L. Hollingsworth, *The Psychology of the Audience* (New York: American Book, 1935), pp. 19–32.
4. An example of how demographics such as race, age, and union membership affect an audience's perception of messages can be found in Carl H. Botan

and Lawrence R. Frey, "Do Workers Trust Labor Unions and Their Messages?" *Communication Monographs* 50 (September 1983): 233–244.

5. For a recent article that offers advice on choosing and developing a topic for *written* communication, see B. F. Skinner, "How to Discover What You Have to Say: A Talk to Students," *Behavior Analyst* 4 (September 1981): 1–7.

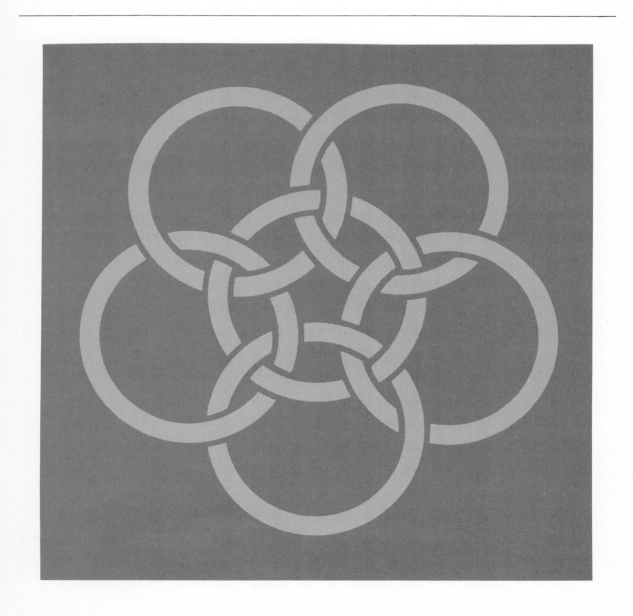

twelve

organization and support

After reading this chapter, you should understand:

1. The importance of clear speech organization.
2. The basic structure of a speech.
3. The steps involved in organizing the body of a speech.
4. The importance of effective introductions, conclusions, and transitions.
5. The functions and types of supporting material.

You should be able to:

1. Formulate a clear, accurate thesis statement.
2. Construct an effective formal speech outline, using the organizing principles described in this chapter.
3. Develop an effective introduction, conclusion, and transitions.
4. Choose supporting material for a speech to make your points clear, interesting, memorable, and convincing.

Knowing what you want to say and *communicating* that knowledge aren't the same thing. It's frustrating to know you aren't expressing your thoughts clearly, and it's equally unpleasant to know another speaker has something worth saying, yet be unable to figure out just what it is.

In the following pages, you will learn methods of organizing your thoughts in a way that others can follow. Clarity isn't the only benefit of good organization: Structuring a message effectively will help you refine and clarify your own ideas and then present them in a way that is not only comprehensible, but persuasive.

structuring the speech

A good speech is like a good building: Both grow from a careful plan. In Chapter 11 you began this planning by analyzing your audience, formulating a purpose, and conducting research. Now you will learn how to apply the information you developed there.

the thesis statement

A *thesis statement* is a one-sentence statement of the central idea in your speech. Your thesis should answer the audience's inevitable question, "What's the speaker trying to say?"

A thesis statement differs from the purpose statement described in Chapter 11. The purpose statement is personal: a note to yourself expressing what you want your speech to accomplish. Your thesis statement, on the other hand, is public, telling your audience what you want them to believe.

Although it is almost always advisable to state your thesis, you might decide not to share your purpose. For example:

Purpose: After hearing me speak, I want several students to open accounts in the bank I represent on campus.
Thesis: My bank offers the widest range of services for the lowest price.

Purpose: As a result of my talk, I want the audience to sign a petition to the state legislature opposing an increase in tuition fees.
Thesis: An increase in fees is unfair and excessively burdensome to many students.

The thesis statement is the cornerstone of a speech. Once you have developed your thesis, you are ready to build an outline that helps lead your audience both to understand and to agree with it.

outlining the speech

An outline is the framework upon which your speech is built. It contains your main ideas and shows how they relate to one another and your thesis. Virtually every speech outline ought to follow the same basic structure:

I. Introduction
  A. Attention-getter
  B. Preview
II. Body
  A.
  B.
  •   —2–5 main points
  •
  •
III. Conclusion
  A. Review
  B. Final remarks

This structure demonstrates the old aphorism for speakers: "Tell what you're going to say, say it, and then tell what you said." Although this structure sounds redundant, the research on listening cited in Chapter 4 demonstrated that receivers forget most of what they hear. The clear, repetitive nature of the basic speech structure reduces the potential for memory loss, because audiences have a tendency to listen more carefully during the beginning and ending of a speech.[1]

Outlines come in all shapes and sizes, but they can generally be classified in one of three categories.

1. Formal outlines The basic pattern given earlier is a formal outline. It uses a consistent format and set of symbols to identify the structure of ideas. Roman numerals are usually used to separate the main divisions of the speech: introduction, body, and conclusion. Each of those sections is then divided and subdivided with capital letters, Arabic numerals, and lowercase letters. Formal outlines can be writ-

ten in full-sentence or key-word form. Examples of each type appear in this chapter.

A formal outline can be used as a visual aid (on posterboard, for example, or distributed as a handout) or as a record of a speech that was delivered (many organizations send outlines to members who miss meetings at which presentations were given; in speech classes outlines are often used by the instructor to analyze student speeches).

A formal outline contains only the structural units of a speech—main points and subpoints (the division of main points, including sub-subpoints and sub-sub-subpoints). In formal outlines, main points and subpoints almost always represent a division of a whole. As it is impossible to divide something into less than two parts, you will usually have at least two main points for every topic. Then, if your main points are divided, you will always have at least two subpoints, and so on. Thus, the rule for formal outlines is, never a "I" without a "II," never an "A" without a "B," and so on.*

2. **Working outlines.** Working, or "scratch," outlines are construction tools used in building your speech. Unlike a formal outline, a working outline is a constantly changing, personal device. You begin organizing your speech material from a rough working outline; then, as your ideas solidify, your outline changes accordingly.

A working outline is for your eyes only. No one else need understand it, so you can use whatever symbols and personal shorthand you find functional. In fact, your working outline will probably become pretty messy by the time you complete your speech.

3. **Speaking notes.** Like your working outline, your speaking notes are a personal device, so the format is up to you. Many teachers suggest that speaking notes should be in the form of a brief key-word outline, with just enough information listed to jog your memory but not enough to get lost in.

* Supporting points (discussed later in this chapter) are not divisions of a whole and may be listed singly in an outline.

There are three principles that relate to all outlines, working or formal. A good outline will follow all three—division, coordination, and order.

Division The first principle of outlining is to divide your topic into main points that completely cover your thesis. Correct division is said to be *essential, exhaustive,* and *focused.* "Essential" in this sense means that those points are the most important parts of your central idea. If you are speaking on jury selection and are explaining that lawyers are able to recognize certain biases in prospective jurors, you might divide the idea of bias like this:

A. Racial bias
B. Sexual bias

If those are the two most important parts of the idea of bias, then it can be said that the divisions of that idea are "essential." If, however, you divided the idea into "racial bias, sexual bias, and lawyers' biases," that third point might *not* be essential to the idea of biases in prospective jurors.

"Exhaustive" means that all the necessary information can be included under one of the divisions of that idea. For example, if you also want to discuss the fact that some jurors are biased in terms of the defendant's age, you might have to divide the idea of bias like this:

A. Racial bias
B. Sexual bias
C. Age bias

If everything you want to say could be included under one of these three subpoints, then the idea is properly divided. If not, the division of the idea would not be exhaustive.

"Focused" means that each division should contain one, and only one, idea. If you were discussing hangover cures, your topic might be divided incorrectly if your main points looked like this:

I. "Preventive cures" help you before drinking.
II. "Participation cures" help you during and after drinking.

You might actually have three ideas there and thus three main points:

I. Preventive cures (before drinking)
II. Participation cures (during drinking)
III. Postparticipation cures (after drinking)

It is important for all messages to be divided in an essential, exhaustive, and focused manner. But speeches have one further requirement: They should have no more than five main points (three or four are considered ideal), and each point should be broken up into no more than five subpoints (and so on for sub-subpoints). Research shows that this will allow for maximum comprehension within the limits of human information processing.[2]

First, you must know the truth about the subject you speak or write about; that is to say, you must be able to isolate it in definition, and having so defined it you must understand how to divide it into kinds, until you reach the limit of division.

Plato

Coordination Coordination is the state of being equal in rank, quality, or significance. The principle of coordination requires that all your main points be of *similar importance* and that they be *related* to one another. The principle of coordination is reflected in the wording of your main points. Points that are equal in significance and related to one another can easily be worded in a similar manner. Because of this, the principle of coordination is sometimes referred to as the principle of "parallel wording." For example, if you are developing a speech against capital punishment, your main points might look like this:

A. Crime did not decrease during the 1950s, when capital punishment was enforced.
B. The Eighth Amendment to the U.S. Constitution protects against cruel and unusual punishment.
C. Most civilized countries have abandoned the notion of capital punishment.

The relationship of those points might seem obvious to you as a speaker, but chances are they would leave the audience confused. Parallel wording, which requires that each of these main points be written in a similar way, helps to guard against this confusion.

A. Capital punishment is not effective: It is not a deterrent to crime.
B. Capital punishment is not constitutional: It does not comply with the Eighth Amendment.
C. Capital punishment is not civilized: It does not allow for a reverence for life.

Order An outline should reflect a logical order for your points. You might arrange them from newest to oldest, largest to smallest (or vice versa), best to worst (or worst to best), or in a number of other ways we will soon discuss. The organizing pattern you choose ought to be the one that best develops your thesis.

developing the body

The body makes up the bulk—usually 80 percent or more—of the speech. Because the body contains the main ideas you will express, it makes sense to begin preparing the actual speech by starting here rather than with the introduction or conclusion.

The body of any speech should contain two types of information: the points you want to make and supporting material to back up those points. The last half of this chapter will focus on supporting material. In the next pages we will examine the various ways in which you can organize the main points themselves.

Time patterns Arrangement according to periods of time, or chronology, is one of the most common patterns of organization. The period of time could be anything from centuries to seconds. The "hangover cures" example given earlier is an example of a time pattern. In a speech on the history of the ASPCA, a time pattern might look like this:

A. Early attempts by the city to control animals, 1900–1920.
B. The ASPCA takes over: 1920–present.
C. The outlook for the future.

Arranging points according to the steps that make up a process is another form of time patterning. The topic "Getting That Big Date" might use this type of patterning:

A. The first step: Choosing an appropriate person.
B. The second step: Breaking the ice.
C. The third step: Asking for the date.

Space patterns Space patterns are organized according to area. The area could be stated in terms of continents or centimeters or anything in between. If you were discussing the ASPCA in New York City, for example, you could arrange your points according to borough:

A. Manhattan
B. Queens
C. Brooklyn
D. Bronx
E. Staten Island

Topic patterns A topical arrangement is based on types or categories. These categories could be either well known or original; both have their advantages. For example, a division of college students according to well-known categories might look like this:

A. Freshmen
B. Sophomores
C. Juniors
D. Seniors

Well-known categories are advantageous because audiences are generally more receptive to ideas that they can associate with their present knowledge. But familiarity also has its drawbacks. One disadvantage is the "Oh, this again" syndrome. If members of an audience feel they have nothing new to learn about the components of your topic, they might not listen to you. To avoid this, you could invent original categories that freshen up some topics by suggesting an original analysis. For example, original categories for "college students" might look like this:

A. Grinds—the students who go to every class and read every assignment before it is due, who are usually seen in dormitories telling everyone to turn their stereos down.
B. Renaissance students—the students who find a satisfying blend of scholarly and social pursuits. They go to most of their classes and do

most of their assignments, but they don't let school get in the way of their social life.

C. Burnouts—the students who have a difficult time finding the classroom, let alone doing the work.

Problem-solution patterns The problem-solution pattern, as you might guess from its no-nonsense title, describes what's wrong and proposes a way to make things better. It is usually (but not always) divisible into these two distinct parts. One variation of the problem-solution arrangement contains five steps and has come to be known as the motivated sequence.[3]

1. **The attention step** draws attention to your subject. (For example, "Have you ever gotten all dressed up to go out for a meal in a nice restaurant and then been choked by smoke from the table next to you?")
2. **The need step** establishes the problem. ("Ambient smoke—that is, smoke from someone else's cigarette, cigar, or pipe—is a threat to your health as well as a general nuisance.")
3. **The satisfaction step** proposes a solution. ("The State Clean Air Act will provide for separate smoking and nonsmoking areas in restaurants.")
4. **The visualization step** describes the results of the solution. ("Imagine—clean air in every public place, without denying smokers their rights in any way.")
5. **The action step** is a direct appeal for the audience to do something. ("Sign this petition, and you will have done your part.")

Cause-effect patterns Cause-effect patterns are similar to problem-solution patterns in that they are basically two-part patterns: First you discuss something that happened; then you discuss its effects. For example, many speakers feel that the topic of inflation is amenable to this pattern because the reason people tend to misunderstand inflation is that they confuse causes with effects. These speakers would organize a speech on inflation as follows:

A. Causes:
   1. Government budget deficits
   2. Increase in money supply
B. Effects:
   1. Rising prices
   2. Rising wages

A variation of this pattern is reversing the order and presenting the effects first and then the causes. Effect-to-cause patterns would work well with a topic such as "rising gasoline prices"; the audience would presumably already be interested in and knowledgeable about the effects, and discussing them first might increase interest in your analysis of the causes.

Climax patterns   Patterns that build to a climax are used to create suspense. For example, if you wanted to create suspense in a speech about military intervention, you could chronologically trace the steps that eventually led us into World War II or Korea or Vietnam in such a way that you build up your audience's curiosity. If you told of these steps through the eyes of a soldier who was drafted into one of those wars, you would be building suspense as your audience wonders what will become of him.

This pattern can also be reversed. When it is, it is called *anticlimactic* organization. If you started your military-intervention speech by telling the audience that you were going to explain why so-and-so was killed in such-and-such a war, and then you went on to explain the things that caused him to become involved in that war, you would be using anticlimactic organization. This pattern is helpful when you have an essentially uninterested audience and you need to build interest early in your speech to get them to listen to the rest of it.

Once you have organized the body of your speech, you can turn to your introduction and conclusion.

beginning and ending the speech

The introduction and conclusion of a speech are vitally important, although they usually will occupy less than 20 percent of your speaking time. Listeners form their impressions of a speaker early, and they remember what they hear last; it is, therefore, vital to make those few moments at the beginning and end of a speech work to your advantage.

> The beginning is the most important part of the work.
>
> Plato

The introduction   As you have already read, the first part of your introduction should capture the attention of your listeners. There are several ways to get an audience's attention. The following list shows how some of these ways might be used in a speech entitled "Communication Between Plants and Humans."

1. **Refer to the audience.** This technique is especially effective if it is complimentary, such as "It's great to have the opportunity to address a group of America's brightest young scholars . . ." Of course, to be effective the compliment has to be sincere.

2. **Refer to the occasion.** A reference to the occasion could be a reference to the event of your speech, such as "We are gathered here today, as we are on every Tuesday and Thursday at this time, to examine the phenomenon of human communication . . ." This might also be a reference to the date, such as "On this date, just five years ago, a little-known botanist made a breakthrough that set the scientific world on its ear . . ." This type of reference naturally must relate to the topic.

3. **Refer to the relationship between the audience and the subject.** "My topic, 'Communicating with Plants,' ties right in with our study of human communication. We can gain several insights into our

communication with one another by examining our interactions with our little green friends."

4. **Refer to something familiar to the audience.** This technique is especially effective if you are discussing a topic that might seem new or strange to the audience. Audience attention will be attracted to the familiar among the new, in much the same way that we are able to pick out a friend's face in a crowd of strangers. For example, "See that lilac bush outside the window? At this very moment it might be reacting to the joys and anxieties that you are experiencing in this classroom."

5. **Cite a startling fact or opinion.** A statement that surprises an audience is bound to make them sit up and listen. This is true even for a topic that the audience considers old hat; if the audience members think they've heard it all before about plant-human communication, you might mention, "There is now actual scientific evidence that plants appreciate human company, kind words, and classical music."

6. **Ask a question.** A rhetorical question is one that causes your audience to think rather than to answer out loud. "Have you ever wondered why some people seem to be able to grow beautiful, healthy plants effortlessly whereas others couldn't make a weed grow in the best soil you could get?" This question is designed to make the audience respond mentally, "Yeah, why is that?"

7. **Tell an anecdote.** A personal story perks up audience interest because it shows the human side of what might otherwise be dry, boring information. "The other night, while taking a walk in the country, I happened upon a small garden that was rich with lush vegetation. But it wasn't the lushness of the vegetation that caught my eye at first. There, in the middle of the garden, was a man who was talking quite animatedly to a giant sunflower."

8. **Use a quotation.** Quotable quotes sometimes have a precise, memorable wording that would be difficult for you to say as well. Also, they allow you to borrow from the credibility of the quoted source. For example, "Thorne Bacon, the naturalist, recently said about the possibility of plants and humans communicating, 'Personally, I cannot imagine a world so dull, so satiated, that it should reject out of hand arresting new ideas which may be as old as the first amino acid in the chain of life on earth.'"

9. **Tell a joke.** If you happen to know, or can find, a joke that is appropriate to your subject and occasion, it can help you build audience interest: "We once worried about people who talked to plants, but that's no longer the case. Now we only worry if the plants talk back." Be sure, though, that the joke is appropriate to the audience, as well as to the occasion and you as a speaker.

After you capture the attention of the audience, an effective introduction will almost always state the speaker's thesis and give them an idea of the upcoming main points. Katherine Graham, the chairperson of the board of the Washington Post Company, addressed a group of businessmen and their wives this way:

Copyright, 1980, Universal Press Syndicate. All rights reserved. Reprinted by permission of Jerry Marcus.

I am delighted to be here. It is a privilege to address you. And I am especially glad the rules have been bent for tonight, allowing so many of you to bring along your husbands. I think it's nice for them to get out once in a while and see how the other half lives. Gentlemen, we welcome you.

Actually, I have other reasons for appreciating this chance to talk with you tonight. It gives me an opportunity to address some current questions about the press and its responsibilities—whom we are responsible to, what we are responsible for, and generally how responsible our performance has been.[4]

Thus, Mrs. Graham previewed her main points:

I. To explain whom the press is responsible to.
II. To explain what the press is responsible for.
III. To explain how responsible the press has been.

Sometimes your preview of main points will be even more straight-forward:

"I have three points to discuss: They are _____, _____, and _____.

Sometimes you will not want to refer directly to your main points in your introduction. Your reasons might be based on a plan calling for suspense, humorous effect, or stalling for time to win over a hostile audience. In that case, you might preview only your thesis:

"I am going to say a few words about _____."
"Did you ever wonder about _____?"
"_____ is one of the most important issues facing us today."

The attention-getter and preview of every speech should accomplish two functions in addition to their stated purposes:

1. **Setting the mood and tone of your speech.** Notice, in the example just given, how Katherine Graham began her speech by joking with her audience. She was speaking before an all-male organization; the only women in the audience were the members' wives. That is why Mrs. Graham felt it necessary to put her audience members at ease by joking with them about women's traditional role in society. By beginning in this manner, she assured the men that she would not berate them for the sexist bylaws of their organization. She also showed them that she was going to approach her topic with wit and intelligence. Thus, she set the mood and tone for her entire speech. Imagine how different that mood and tone would have been if she had begun this way:

   > Before I start today, I would just like to say that I would never have accepted your invitation to speak here had I known that your organization does not accept women as members. Just where do you Cro-Magnons get off, excluding more than half the human race from your little club?

2. **Demonstrating the importance of your topic to your audience.** Your audience will listen to you more carefully if your speech relates to them as individuals. Based on your audience analysis, you should state directly *why* your topic is of importance to your audience. This importance should be related as closely as possible to their specific needs at that specific time. For example, if you were speaking to your class about why they should help support the Red Cross, you might begin like this:

   > Lives have been lost in the time it takes an ambulance or doctor to reach the victim of accidents. Too many people have died from accidentally severed veins or arteries, drowning, choking on food, or swallowing iodine, plant-spray, arsenic, or other poisons.
   >
   > If someone on the scene had known what emergency measures to take, tragedy could have been averted.
   >
   > The Red Cross, with vast experience in the latest, most successful lifesaving techniques, has put together a handy, easy-to-follow manual, *Standard First Aid and Personal Safety*. The information it contains could save your life—or that of someone dear to you. This book is available only through the Red Cross, and we'd like to send it to you *free*.[5]

This introduction establishes an immediate importance: The audience members don't have to wait until they need blood or until an emergency or a disaster strikes. Acquiring the free booklet is something that is important to them right now as healthy, reasonably secure members of a college class.

The conclusion   The conclusion, like the introduction, is an especially important part of your speech. Your audience will have a tendency to listen carefully as your speech draws to a close; they will also have a tendency to consider what you say at the end of your speech as important. Because of this, the conclusion has two important functions: to review the thesis and to leave the audience remembering your speech by using effective final remarks. You can review your thesis either through direct repetition or by paraphrasing it in different words. Either way your conclusion should include a short summary statement:

> And so, after listening to what I had to say this afternoon, I hope you agree with me that the city cannot afford to lose the services of the ASPCA.

You might also want to review your main points. This can be done directly thus: "I made three main points about the ASPCA today. They are . . ."

The review of your main points can also be done artistically. For example, first look back at that example of an introduction by Katherine Graham; then read her conclusion to that speech:

> . . . So instead of seeking flat and absolute answers to the kinds of problems I have discussed tonight, what we should be trying to foster is respect for one another's conception of where duty lies, and understanding of the real worlds in which we try to do our best. And we should be hoping for the energy and sense to keep on arguing and questioning, because there is no better sign that our society is still healthy and strong.[6]

Let's take a closer look at how and why this conclusion was effective. Mrs. Graham posed three questions in her introduction. She dealt with those questions in her speech and reminded her audience, in her conclusion, that she had answered the questions.

preview	review
1. Whom is the press responsible to?	**1.** To its own conception of where its duty lies.
2. What is the press responsible for?	**2.** For doing its best in the "real world."
3. How responsible has the press been?	**3.** It has done its best.

Your final remarks are important because they are the last words your audience will hear from you in the speech. You can make them most effective by avoiding the following mistakes:

1. Do not end abruptly. Make sure that your conclusion accomplishes everything it is supposed to accomplish. Develop it fully. You might want to use a "pointer phrase" such as "and now, in conclusion . . ." or "to sum up what we've been talking about here . . ." to let your audience know that you have reached the conclusion of the speech.

2. But don't ramble, either. Prepare a definite conclusion and never, *never* end by mumbling something like "Well, I guess that's about all I wanted to say . . ."

3. Don't introduce new points. The worst kind of rambling is "Oh, yes, and something I forgot to mention is . . ."

A speech is like a love affair. Any fool can start it, but to end it requires considerable skill.

Lord Mancroft

organization and support
289

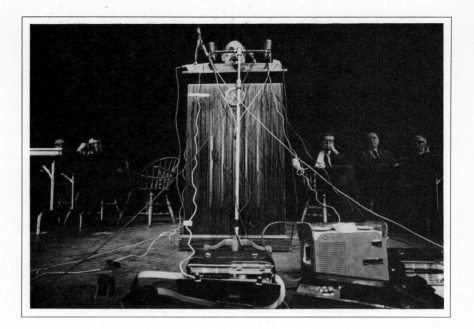

4. Don't apologize. Don't say, "I'm sorry I couldn't tell you more about this" or "I'm sorry I didn't have more time to research this subject" or any of those sad songs. They will only highlight the possible weaknesses of your speech, and there's a good chance those weaknesses were far more apparent to you than to your audience.

Instead, it is best to end strong. You can use any of the attention-getters suggested for the introduction to make the conclusion memorable. In fact, one kind of effective closing is to refer to the attention-getter you used in your introduction and remind your audience how it applies to the points you made in your speech.

You can use elements of surprise or suspense to make a point memorable; you can also use mnemonic devices, which are often formulated as collections of meaningful letters:

> Think of recycling in the same terms as you think of gas mileage: MPG. Only in recycling MPG stands for *metals, paper,* and *glass,* the three materials you stand to conserve.

Whatever device you use, end with a flourish, as John F. Kennedy did when he said, "Ask not what your country can do for you; ask what you can do for your country," in the conclusion of his inaugural address, or as General MacArthur did when he said, "Old soldiers never die; they just fade away."

transitions

You should tie all your ideas together through the use of transitions, which join ideas together by showing how one is related to another.

table 12–1 steps in speech organization

I. Formulate thesis statement

II. Organize body of speech
   A. Divide points
   B. Coordinate points
   C. Order points

III. Organize introduction
   A. Gain audience attention
   B. Preview thesis and/or main points
   C. Set mood and tone of speech
   D. Demonstrate importance of idea to audience

IV. Organize conclusion
   A. Review thesis and/or main points
   B. Plan memorable ending

V. Check transitions from point to point

They keep your message moving forward, they tell how the introduction relates to the body of the speech, they tell how one main point relates to the next main point, they tell how your subpoints relate to the points they are part of, and they tell how your supporting points relate to the points they support. Transitions, to be effective, should refer to the previous point and to the upcoming point and relate both of them to the thesis. They usually sound something like this:

"... Like (*previous point*), another important consideration in (*topic*) is (*upcoming point*).

"... But _____ isn't the only thing we have to worry about. _____ is even more potentially dangerous."

"... Yes, the problem is obvious. But what are the solutions? Well, one possible solution is ..."

Sometimes a transition includes an internal review, a preview of upcoming points, or both:

"... So far we've discussed _____, _____, and _____. Our next points are _____, _____, and _____."

As you can see, the actual process of organizing a speech usually takes place in the order outline in Table 12–1.

It should be obvious from the preceding discussion that it is important to organize ideas clearly and logically. But clarity and logic by themselves won't guarantee that you'll interest or persuade others; these functions call for the use of supporting materials. These materials—the facts and information that back up and prove your ideas and opinions—are the flesh that fills out the skeleton of your speech.

There are four purposes for supporting material:

1. To clarify. As we explained in Chapter 3, people of different backgrounds tend to attach different meanings to words. For example, if

supporting material

291

you were talking about recycling, every member of your audience could have a different idea about what you meant. To some, recycling refers just to aluminum beer cans; to others, the term means reusing everything that is normally thrown away as refuse. You could us a supporting material to clarify this idea:

> The type of recycling I'm talking about here involves separating from the rest of your trash all glass, metals, newspapers, and magazines. The papers and magazines must be bundled, the containers must be uncapped and washed, and labels must be removed from the cans. The material is then placed in a separate container for removal once a week to a municipal recycling center.

2. To make interesting. A second use of support is to make an idea interesting or to catch your audience's attention. The audience might know what you mean by "recycling" now, but still not care. Supporting material could be used to bolster their interest in your topic:

> Outside New York City, where garbage has been dumped into the ocean for years, a large mass of thick, life-choking sludge is slowing inching its way toward the shore. It might be too late for New York, but *we* might be able to avoid the same problem here, if we take action now.

3. To make memorable. A third purpose of supporting material, related to the one above, is to make a point memorable. We have already mentioned the importance of "memorable" statements in a speech conclusion; use of supporting material in the body of the speech provides another way to help your audience retain important information.

The most common way to make a point memorable is to use supporting material that is impressive because it stresses the importance of the point. For example:

> The State Environmental Protection Agency recently measured the air in this area, and what they found suggests that each and every one of us, at this moment, are breathing poisons into our systems. These are cumulative, carcinogenic, chemical toxins, and they are caused by our township incinerator burning garbage that could just as easily be sold and reused.

4. To prove. Finally, supporting material can be used as evidence, to prove the truth of what you are saying. For example, if you said, "The way our local landfill area is filling up, it might have to be closed in a year or so," your audience would find it easy to disagree with you. But supporting material makes it less easy to disagree:

> According to Tom Murray, our village chief sanitation engineer and the man in charge of landfill areas, all our landfills will be filled to capacity and closed within one year. This means, in no uncertain terms, that we are not going to have anywhere to put our garbage.

As you may have noted, each function of support could be fulfilled by several different types of material. An examination of these different types of supporting material follows.

definitions

It's a good idea to give your audience definitions of your key terms, especially if those terms are unfamiliar to them or are being used in an unusual way. A good definition is simple and concise and is stated in such a way that no other terms within the definition need to be defined.

Dictionary definitions are a handy way of determining the most acceptable meaning for a word, but you should be careful about using them to define terms in your speech. Your own carefully chosen words are usually more interesting and clearer than a dictionary definition. Dictionaries are written for very general audiences. If you were speaking on the abortion issue and relying on a dictionary definition, you might be stuck with:

> By abortion I mean the expulsion of a nonviable fetus . . .

This might be an accurate definition, but it is probably too clinical for a college audience. It might be clearer to say:

> By abortion I mean the termination of pregnancy before the twelfth week of gestation . . .

if that's what you mean.

Another problem with dictionaries is that they sometimes give you a definition that includes the term itself and that will sometimes make it seem as if you are clarifying an idea when you actually aren't:

> By abortion, I mean the abortion of a fetus . . .

One last problem with dictionary definitions is that they have a tendency to change more slowly than the reality they represent. You might use the term *female chauvinist sexist* in a speech about women employers who discriminate against men. However, if you looked up those terms in *The Random House College Dictionary,* 1972 edition, you would find that *female* means "woman" (as you might expect), but *chauvinist* means "patriot," and *sexist* means "someone who discriminates against women." According to this dictionary, therefore, a female chauvinist sexist is a woman patriot who discriminates against women!

There are two different types of definitions: traditional and operational. A traditional definition places something in a class and tells how it is different from other things in that class. The classic example of this is proposed by Aristotle: "Man [or "woman," we might add] is a featherless biped." Man is therefore defined as belonging to a class (bipeds) but different from that class in that he does not have feathers.

Operational definitions tell what you would have to do to experience the thing being described. We could use an operational definition to define recycling: First you separate glass, metals, newspapers, and magazines from the rest of your trash, and so on. Operational definitions for the term *man* might sound something like this:

> You want to know what a man is? Go down to the graduation ceremonies for marine boot camp. Now *those* are men.

or,

> You want to know what a man is? Go to the state school for the retarded, and watch the men who work with those kids every day with compassion and unfailing patience. Those are men.

detailed description

A description is a "word picture," a direct rendering of the details that summarize an idea from your perspective. Martin Luther King, Jr., used description in his famous "I Have a Dream" speech, when he described the plight of the black American:

> There are those who are asking the devotees of civil rights, "When will you be satisfied?" We can never be satisfied as long as our bodies, heavy with the fatigue of travel, cannot gain lodging in the motels of the highways and the hotels of the cities. We cannot be satisfied as long as the Negro's basic mobility is from a smaller ghetto to a larger one. We can never be satisfied as long as our children are stripped of their selfhood and robbed of their dignity by signs stating "for whites only."[7]

Dr. King's description helps us to imagine pain and fatigue as well as the sight of a sign that says "for whites only." These things can be truly perceived only through the senses, but he manages to give us an image of them by capturing their essence in a few words. In his description, as in all good description, it is the choice of details that makes the difference.

analogies / comparison-contrast

We use analogies, or comparisons, all the time, often in the form of figures of speech such as similes and metaphors. A simile is a direct comparison that usually uses *like* or *as* whereas metaphor is an implied comparison that does not use *like* or *as*. So if you said, "Student unrest is like psoriasis: It flares up, then subsides, but never quite goes away," you would be using a simile. If you used phrases such as "simmering student unrest" or "an avalanche of student unrest," you would be using metaphors because you have implied comparisons between student unrest and slowly boiling liquids and snow slides.

Analogies are extended metaphors. We run across analogies all the time. Here, for example, is the way Ingmar Bergman describes old age:

> Old age is like climbing a mountain. You climb from ledge to ledge. The higher you get, the more tired and breathless you become, but your view becomes much more extensive.

Here's the way Carl Sagan explains the age of the universe through analogy:

The most instructive way I know to express this cosmic chronology is to imagine the fifteen-billion-year lifetime of the universe (or at least its present incarnation since the Big Bang) compressed into the span of a single year. . . . It is disconcerting to find that in such a cosmic year the Earth does not condense out of interstellar matter until early September: Dinosaurs emerge on Christmas Eve; flowers arise on December 28th; and men and women originate at 10:30 P.M. on New Year's Eve. All of recorded history occupies the last ten seconds of December 31; and the time from the waning of the Middle Ages toflthe present occupies little more than one second.[8]

Here's how a newspaper reporter pointed out how relatively inexpensive bike lanes can be:

The proposed four-mile long freeway in New York City at $1.6 billion could finance 100,000 miles of rural bikeways. Or, alternatively, ribbon bikeways could be built paralleling the whole 40,000-mile national Interstate System of highways.[9]

Analogies can be used to compare or contrast an unknown concept with a known one. For example, if you had difficulty explaining to a public speaking class composed mostly of music majors why they should practice their speeches out loud, you might use this analogy:

We all realize that great masters often can compose music in their heads; Beethoven, for example, composed his greatest masterpieces after he had gone deaf and couldn't even hear the instruments play out his ideas. However, beginners have to sit down at a piano or some other instrument and play their pieces as they create them. It is much the same way for beginning public speakers. When composing their speeches, they need to use their instruments—their voices—to hear how their ideas sound.

For an audience of music majors, this analogy might clarify the concept of practicing a speech. For a class of electrical engineers who may not know Beethoven from the Bee Gees, this analogy might confuse rather than clarify. It is important to remember to make your analogies appropriate to your audience.

anecdotes

An anecdote is a brief story with a point, often (but not always) based on personal experience. (The word *anecdote* comes from the Greek meaning "unpublished item.") Anecdotes can add a lively, personal touch to your explanation. For example, a minister used the following anecdote to demonstrate the communication problems he sometimes has with members of his congregation.

I ought not to be surprised by anything at my time of life, but one of my flock did manage to take my breath away. I was preaching about the Father's tender wisdom in caring for us all; illustrated by saying that the Father knows which of us grows best in sunlight and which of us must have shade. "You know you plant roses in the sunshine," I said, "and heliotrope and geraniums; but if you want your fuchsias to grow they must be kept in a shady nook." After the sermon, which I hoped would be a comforting one, a woman came up to me, her face glowing with pleasure that was evidently deep and true. "Oh, Dr. _____, I am so grateful for that sermon," she said, clasping my hand and shaking it warmly. My heart glowed for a moment, while I wondered what tender place in her heart and life I had touched. Only for a moment, though. "Yes," she went on fervently, "I never knew before what was the matter with my fuchsias."[10]

The minister's anecdote contains an analogy, which makes it a good example of how two types of supporting material can be combined. And that brings us to our next type of supporting material: examples.

examples

An example is a specific case that is used to demonstrate a general idea. Examples can be either factual or hypothetical, personal or borrowed. They can also be combined with another type of support. Senator Edward Kennedy, in his speech before the 1980 Democratic convention, wanted to stress economic problems. He relied on an anecdote that contained several examples:

> Among you, my golden friends across this land, I have listened and learned.
> I have listened to Kenny Dubois, a glass-blower in Charleston, W. Va., who has 10 children to support but has lost his job after 35 years, just three years short of qualifying for his pension.
> I have listened to the Trachta family, who farm in Iowa and who wonder whether they can pass the good life and the good earth on to their children.
> I have listened to the grandmother in East Oakland who no longer has a phone to call her grandchildren, because she gave it up to pay the rent on her small apartment.
> I have listened to young workers out of work, to students without the tuition for college and to families without the chance to own a home. I have seen the closed factories and the stalled assembly lines of Anderson, Indiana, and Southgate, California. And I have seen too many—far too many—idle men and women desperate to work. I have seen too many—far too many—working families desperate to protect the value of their wages from the ravages of inflation.[11]

Hypothetical examples can be even more powerful than factual examples because hypothetical examples ask the audience to imagine something—thus causing them to become active participants in the thought. If you were speaking on the subject of euthanasia (mercy killing), you might ask your audience to imagine that someone they loved was suffering and being kept alive by a machine.

Examples can be effective in clarifying information and making it interesting and memorable. Strictly speaking, however, they do not prove a point because they refer only to isolated instances that might not be representative. To prove an idea with examples, you have to collect a number of them; at that point they become statistics.

quantification and statistics

Quantification is the use of numbers to clarify a concept, to make it more specific. One example of quantification comes from a lecture given by a professor at Columbia University. He wanted to develop the idea that inflation lowers the value of paper currency, so he used quantification (developed in an anecdote) in the following way:

> Some time ago, I found a postcard which I had written to my father on November 23, 1923, while I was attending a boarding school in Germany. The card asked that my father send the bursar "immediately 1.2 trillion marks. If the tuition is not paid by the end of the month, you will have to pay four gold marks."
>
> Those two figures—1.2 trillion paper and four gold marks—illustrate the catastrophic fraud of the great German inflation which resulted in a revolutionary change in the economic and above all the social order of the country.[12]

Statistics are numbers that are arranged or organized to show how a fact or principle is true for a large number of cases. Statistics are actually collections of examples, which is why they are often more effective as proof than are isolated examples. For example, if you wanted to develop the idea that American youths are not well informed about the American economic system, the following example would be insufficient proof:

> I asked my younger brother the other day if he knew the difference between collectivism and a free-enterprise society, and he had no idea. He didn't even know that the U.S. economy is based on free enterprise.

Proof based on *lots* of people's younger siblings would be more effective:

> A 1981 study by the Joint Council on Economic Education showed that 50 percent of high school students could not distinguish between collectivism and a free-enterprise society, and 50 percent did not know the U.S. economy was based on free enterprise.

Because statistics are potentially powerful proof, you have the ethical responsibility to cite them exactly as they were published or tabulated. It's usually all right to "round off" a percentage or other figure, but it's considered bad form to manipulate your statistics so they sound better than they are. For example, the term *average* is often used to manipulate statistics. As there are actually three measures of central tendency, or "averages" (mean, median, and mode), it is important to be clear about which one you mean. Imagine that you had the following list of annual incomes for a group of five people:

1. $0
2. $0
3. $500
4. $750
5. $23,750

The mode (most frequent value) for that group would be $0, the mean (arithmetic average) would be $5,000, and the median (the point at which 50 percent of the values are greater and 50 percent are less) would be $500. Any of these could be cited as the "average" by an unscrupulous speaker.

Another responsibility calls for you to cite the complete source of your statistic along with any other information that would have a bearing on its validity. Established professional pollsters such as Gallup, Roper, and Harris, as well as the best magazines and newspapers, have reputations for accuracy. If you cite them, your audience can be relatively sure that your statistics are reliable. Sometimes the source of a statistic will cause it to be suspect, as when, years ago, a cigarette company mailed cartons of cigarettes to doctors and then sent those same doctors a questionnaire asking which brand of cigarettes they were then smoking. Shortly afterward, advertising for the company stated that seven out of ten doctors reported smoking that brand.

A third rule about the use of statistics is based on effectiveness rather than ethics. You should reduce the statistic to a concrete image, if possible. For example, $1 billion in $100 bills would be about the same height as a sixty-story building. Using concrete images such as this will make your statistics more than "just numbers" when you use them.

If you are going to refer extensively to statistical data, they could be tabulated on a chart for clarity. This brings us to the next type of support.

visual aids

Sometimes information is clearer, more interesting, more persuasive, and more memorable when it is presented visually. Figure 12–1 provides one example. Saying that a billion is a thousand millions isn't nearly as effective as demonstrating that fact graphically. (Imagine how you might use this display in a speech on the increasing national debt.)

Visual aids serve several purposes. They can show how things look (photos of your trek to Nepal or the effects of malnutrition). They can show how things work (demonstration of a new ski binding, a diagram of how sea water is made drinkable). Visual aids can also show how things relate to one another (the million-billion example in Figure 12–1; a graph showing the relationship between gender, education, and income). Finally, they can show important information clearly (steps in filing a claim in small claims court, symptoms of anemia).

Table 12–2 lists several types of visual aids. Whatever types you use, keep the following points in mind:

1. Keep your visual aids simple. Your goal is to clarify, not confuse. Cover only one idea per visual. Use only key words or phrases, not sentences. Use eight or fewer lines of text, each with 25 or fewer characters. Keep all printing horizontal. Omit all nonessential details.

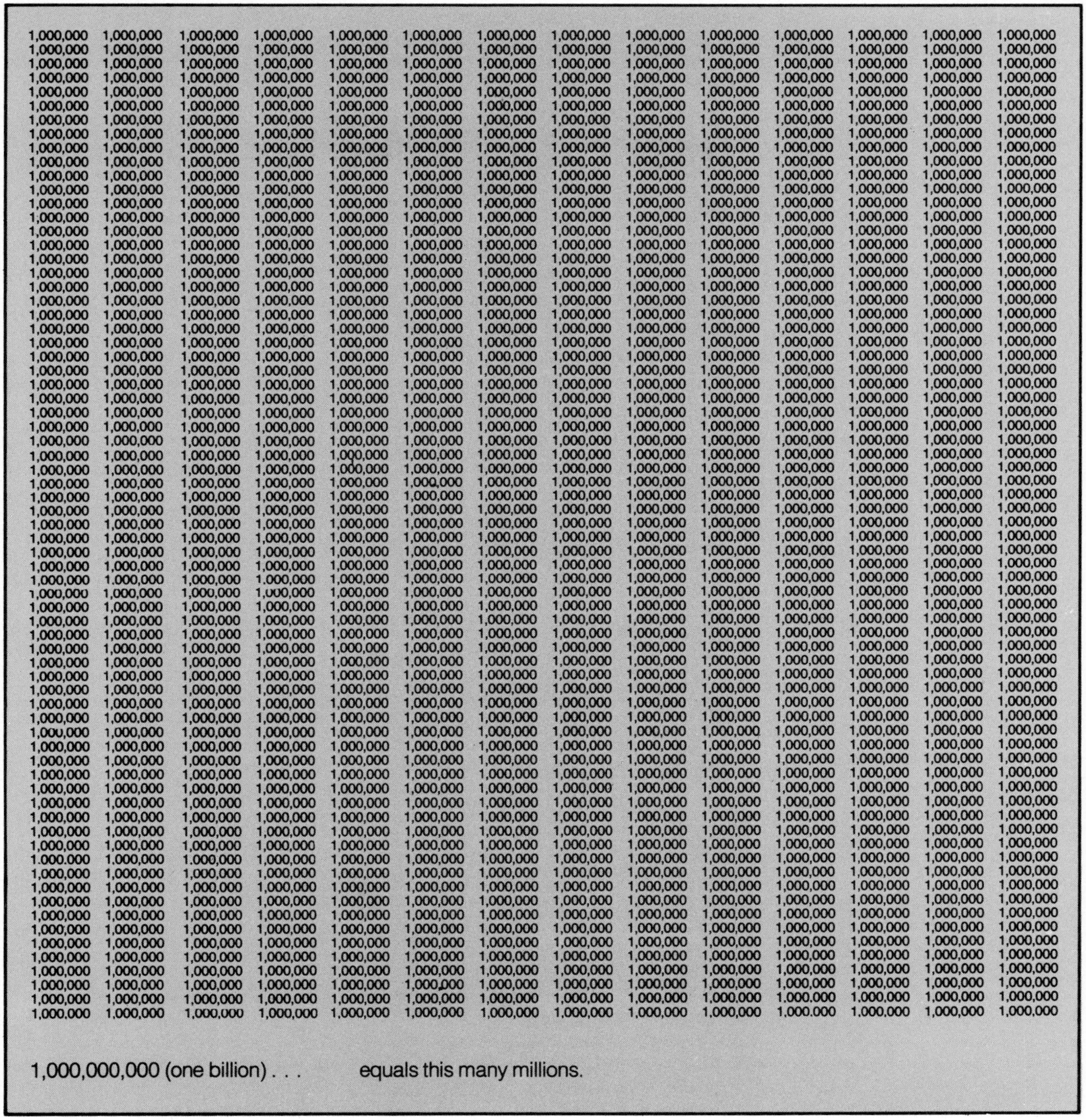

1,000,000,000 (one billion) . . .   equals this many millions.

2. Visual aids should be large enough for your entire audience to see them at one time, but portable enough so you can get them out of the way when they no longer pertain to the point you are making.
3. They should be visually interesting and as neat as possible. If you don't have the necessary skills, try to get help from a friend or at the audiovisual center on your campus.

figure 12–1
Visual aids often have more impact than words

organization and support
299

table 12–2   types of visual aids

Objects
  Real-life (for example, samples of poisonous plants)
  Models (for example, architectural plan)
Demonstrations
  Process (for example, first aid procedures)
  Product use (for example, fire extinguisher)
  Behavior (for example, job interview)
Illustrations
  Slides (for example, enlargements of microscopic samples)
  Drawings (for example, blueprints, plans)
  Artwork (for example, portraits)
  Photographs (enlargements)
Tables and charts
  Graphs (for example, sales curve)
  Lists (for example, key personnel)
Handouts
  Lists (for example, addresses and phone numbers)
  Instructions (for example, steps in C.P.R.)
  Outlines
Audiovisuals
  Audiotape (musical recordings)
  Videotape (excerpt from TV broadcast)
  Film
  Sound-on-slides

Be sure of it; give me the ocular proof.

Shakespeare
Othello

4. They must be appropriate to all the components of the speaking situation—you, the audience, and your topic—and they must emphasize the point you are trying to make. Often a speaker will grab a visual aid that has *something* to do with the topic and use it even though it is not directly related—such as showing a map of a city transit system while talking about the condition of the individual cars.

5. You must be in control of your visual aid at all times. Wild animals, chemical reactions, and gimmicks meant to shock a crowd are often too likely to backfire.

When it comes time for you to *use* the visual aid, remember one more point:

6. Talk to your audience, not to your visual aid. Some speakers become so wrapped up in their props that they turn their backs on their audience and sacrifice all their eye contact.

Aids that extend senses other than sight are also effective in some circumstances. If you were speaking about perfume, skunks, or the effects of a chemical plant on a community, actually producing the appropriate smells might help explain your point. If you were talking about baking brownies or brewing beer, a taste probably wouldn't hurt. And you could incorporate something to touch if you were speaking about the texture of a substance or how it feels.

Audio aids such as tape recordings and records can supply information that could not be presented any other way (comparing musical styles, for example, or demonstrating the differences in the sounds of gas and diesel engines), but in most cases you should use them sparingly. Remember that your presentation already relies heavily on your audience's sense of hearing; it's better to use a visual aid, if possible, than to overwork the audio. Of course there are audiovisual aids, including films, videotapes, and sound-on-slide. These should also be used sparingly, however, because they allow the audience members to receive information passively, thus relieving them of the responsibility of becoming active participants in the presentation.

quotation/testimony

Using a familiar, artistically stated saying will enable you to take advantage of someone else's memorable wording. For example, if you were giving a speech on the pros and cons of personal integrity, you might quote Mark Twain, who said, "Always do right. This will gratify some people, and astonish the rest." A quotation like that fits Alexander

Pope's definition of "true wit": "What was often thought, but ne'er so well expressed."

You can also use quotations as *testimony,* to prove a point by using the support of someone who is more authoritative or experienced on the subject than you.

One speaker recently used quotation for this purpose when he began a speech on stage fright this way:

> According to Professor Hans Larson, a highly respected psychologist and editor of *The Anxiety Quarterly,* speech anxiety is one of the most prevalent fears in contemporary society.

In this example the speaker used a well-known, authoritative source. If you quote testimony from a source that your audience will not immediately recognize, it is important to introduce that source to them.

You can usually signal to your audience that you are using a quotation simply by pausing or by changing your pace or inflection slightly. If you want to be more formal, you can preface the quotation with some variation of "And I quote . . ." and end it with some variation of "end of quote," although that technique becomes tiresome if used too often.

audience analysis and forms of support

We discussed audience analysis in Chapter 11, mostly in terms of how this form of analysis can be used to help you choose a suitable topic for a speech. But we would be remiss if we did not mention the importance of audience analysis to effective support.

Before you decide to use a particular form of support, remember to ask yourself if this material will make your point either clearer, more interesting, more memorable, or more convincing *for this particular audience.* Look at factors such as audience purpose, attitudes, beliefs, and values; and if the answer to your question is not yes, find some other form of support.

summary

This chapter dealt with speech organization and supporting material. Speech organization is a process that begins with the formulation of a thesis statement to express the central idea of a speech. The thesis is established in the introduction, developed in the body, and reviewed in the conclusion of a structured speech. The introduction will also gain the audience's attention, set the mood and tone of the speech, and demonstrate the importance of your topic to the audience.

Organizing the body of the speech will begin with a list of points you might want to make in your speech. These points are then organized according to the principles of outlining. They are divided, coordinated, and placed in a logical order. Transitions from point to point help make this order apparent to your audience.

Organization follows a pattern such as that of time, space, topic, problem-solution, cause-effect, and climax arrangements. Along with reviewing your thesis and/or main points, the conclusion also supplies the audience with a memory aid. Supporting materials are the facts and information you use to back up what you say. Supporting material has four purposes: to clarify, to make interesting, to make memorable, and to prove. Any piece of support could perform any or all of these functions, and any of the functions could be fulfilled by any of the types of support.

Types of support include *definitions,* which can be either *traditional* or *operational; detailed descriptions,* which create word pictures, that enable an audience to visualize an idea; *analogies,* which compare and/ or contrast an unknown or unfamiliar concept with a known or familiar one; *anecdotes,* which add a lively, personal touch; *examples,* which can be either real or hypothetical; *quantification,* which makes an idea more specific; *statistics,* which show that a fact or principle is true for a large number of cases; *visual aids,* which help clarify complicated points and keep an audience informed on where you are in the general scheme of things; and *quotations,* which are used for memorable wording as well as testimony from a well-known or authoritative source. Any piece of support might combine two or more of these types. The final test for effectiveness of support is audience analysis.

activities

1. For practice in formulating thesis statements, turn each of the following purpose statements into a statement that expresses a possible central idea:
   a. At the end of my speech the audience members will be willing to sign my petition requesting our congressional representative to support a balanced federal budget.
   b. After listening to my speech, the audience members will be able to list five advantages of recycling.
   c. During my speech on the trials and tribulations of sailing, the audience members will show their interest by paying attention and their amusement by occasionally laughing.

2. For practice in formulating thesis statements, try the following: Imagine that Congress has just passed a law requiring that all young people—male and female, without exception—perform two years of required national service immediately after high school (or at the age of eighteen, for those who don't finish high school). This period of national service could be spent in the military, park service, or any government agency. Pay would be at the subsistence level, below minimum wage.
   The exercise proceeds as follows:
   a. Decide whether you will support or oppose this law.
   b. Write a purpose statement for a speech in support of your position.

c. Draw up a list of points you might like to make in the speech.

d. With the help of this list, select your thesis and main point.

If you do this exercise, save your notes and materials so you can build on them in one or two of the other exercises that follow. Your instructor may ask you to do some research on the topic of mandatory national service.

3. For practice in outlining, take your list of points on ''mandatory national service,'' and turn it into a key-word outline.

4. For practice in dividing ideas, divide each of the following into subcategories that are essential, exhaustive, and focused:
   a. Transportation
   b. Careers
   c. U.S. Government
   d. The National Park System
   e. Balanced diets
   f. Television programs
   g. Houseplants

5. To practice coordinating points, write out the following ''steps in studying'' in parallel wording:
   a. Preview quickly
   b. Read slowly
   c. Take notes
   d. Review notes
   e. Test yourself

6. To test your skills in ordering points according to your purpose before a specific audience, try the following exercise. Use your list of points for the ''required national service'' exercise or one for a topic of your own choice.
   a. Identify a hypothetical audience before whom you would give a speech supporting your position on this issue. The audience should be identified according to the following characteristics: age, sex, occupations, reason for gathering, and group membership.
   b. Develop an outline for the body of the speech. Arrange your points in the order you believe will best achieve your stated purpose.
   c. Be prepared to discuss why you organized the points as you did.

7. For practice in formulating definitions, see if you can come up with both a traditional and an operational definition for each of the following terms:
   a. politician   **c.** automobile
   b. living room   **d.** college student

8. For practice in recognizing the functions of support, identify three instances of support in each of the speeches at the end of Chapters 14 and 15. Explain the function of each instance of support. (Keep in mind that any instance of support *could* perform more than one function.)

9. One of the best ways to practice description is to paint a word picture of something you're so familiar with that you don't normally take the time to observe it carefully. Consider the room you're in right now—how would you describe it in one written paragraph? What details would you include so that someone else could visualize it from your description?

10. For practice in formulating analogies, provide one for each of the following: deficit spending, inflation, shopping, studying, infatuation, true love, and a job interview.

Once again these particular terms are not essential to the exercise. Use any terms you like but try to make them original. It was a good use of analogy when Vince Lombardi said that tying a football game was like "kissing your sister," but just to dredge up an analogy like that from your memory is less useful in this exercise than making up one of your own.

11. For practice in using anecdotes, try the following: first, identify an anecdote to prove a point of your choice ("college is a rewarding experience," for example, or "power corrupts" or "love is blind"). Whatever point you choose, make sure you start with the point first and then think up the anecdote to support it. Then reverse the exercise: Think of one of your favorite stories or personal experiences, and then identify a point that story could be used to support.

12. For practice in using examples to support points, team up with someone else and take turns supplying examples for points each of you identify. These points could be well-established truisms ("cheaters never prosper," "better safe than sorry") or more specific ideas ("Robert DeNiro is a great actor," "the Bermuda Triangle is a dangerous place"). Take note of those examples that combine with other forms of support.

13. For practice in quantifying vague statements, try supporting statements such as the following with specific numbers:
"Servicing your own car saves money."
"It takes a lot of time to write a good speech."
"Local housing is very expensive."

14. To practice using statistics, dig up a copy of this year's *Information Please Almanac, Statistical Abstract of the United States, World Almanac and Book of Facts,* or any other statistical yearbook or almanac. Then support these statements statistically:

a. There are a lot of people out of work today.

b. The United States imports a lot of oil.

c. A lot of people die of heart attacks.

d. Crime is on the rise.

e. More and more people are getting divorced these days.

f. There are a lot of people on welfare these days.

15. This exercise will give you practice with the different forms of support. It can be done individually or in a group.

a. Choose one of the following situations:

(1) You have just received a lower grade on a term paper than you think you deserve because the instructor thinks your topic was inappropriate. You would like to convince your instructor to change your grade.

(2) You finally summon the courage to ask out a person to whom you have been strongly attracted for months. The person thinks about it and says, ''Convince me.''

(3) Someone you really don't care for has just asked you out. You need to explain to that person why it isn't a good idea.

(4) You've just found a classified ad for the ideal job. Answer it, explaining why they should hire you.

(5) Your best friend, a varsity athlete, has broken a leg the night before the opening game. You go to the hospital to cheer up your friend.

b. Fill in the missing details of the situation you chose, such as the topic in (1), the people in (2) and (3), the job in (4), and the type of sport in (5).

c. Come up with one example of each type of support for the chosen situation.

16. For practice in designing visual aids, describe three different visual aids that could be used to clarify the following ideas:

a. Unemployment.

b. Inflation.

c. The difference between cheaply made and good-quality clothing.

d. The operation of an internal combustion engine (or some other piece of machinery).

e. How to juggle.

notes

1. Research into this effect is summarized in G. Cronkhite, *Persuasion: Speech and Behavioral Change* (Indianapolis: Bobbs-Merrill, 1969), pp. 195–196.
2. See, for example, George A. Miller, "The Magical Number Seven, Plus or Minus Two: Some Limits on Our Capacity for Processing Information," in Richard C. Anderson and David P. Ausubel (eds.), *Readings in the Psychology of Cognition* (New York: Holt, Rinehart and Winston, 1965), pp. 242–267.
3. Alan H. Monroe, *Principles and Types of Speech* (Glenview, Ill.: Scott, Foresman, 1935).
4. Katherine Graham, "The Press and Its Responsibilities," *Vital Speeches of the Day* 42 (April 15, 1976).
5. From Red Cross fund-raising material.
6. Katherine Graham, op. cit.
7. Martin Luther King, Jr., "I Have a Dream," speech at civil rights rally, Washington, D.C., August 28, 1963. See James C. McCroskey, *An Introduction to Rhetorical Communication* (Englewood Cliffs, N.J.: Prentice-Hall, 1968), pp. 248–249, for transcript.
8. Carl Sagan, *The Dragons of Eden: Speculations on the Evolution of Human Intelligence* (New York: Ballantine, 1978), pp. 13–17.
9. Bob Burgess, "Hiking/Biking," *Santa Barbara News Press* (February 25, 1978).
10. Edmund Fuller, *2500 Anecdotes for All Occasions* (New York: Avenel Books, 1970), p. 275. Copyright © 1970 by Crown Publishers, Inc. Reprinted by permission.
11. Edward M. Kennedy, speech before Democratic National Convention, New York City, August 12, 1980. See *The New York Times* (August 13, 1980), p. B2, for transcript.
12. G. C. Wiegand, "Inflation," *Vital Speeches of the Day* 43 (June 15, 1978).

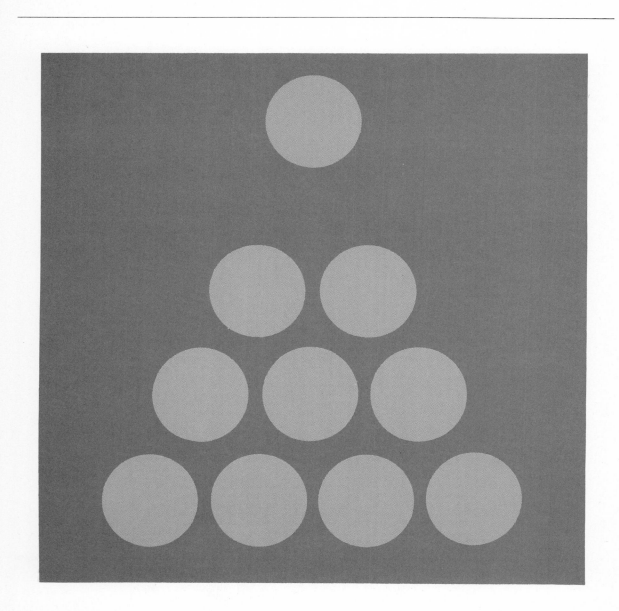

thirteen

presenting your message

After reading this chapter, you should understand:

1. The difference between facilitative and debilitative stage fright.
2. The sources of debilitative stage fright.
3. The differences among the various types of delivery.
4. The visual and auditory aspects of delivery that help you choose the best type of delivery for a particular speech.

You should be able to:

1. Overcome debilitative stage fright.
2. Choose the most effective type of delivery for a particular speech.
3. Follow the guidelines for effective extemporaneous, impromptu, manuscript, and memorized speeches.

"So far, so good," you may be thinking to yourself. You've developed a purpose; you've chosen and researched a topic that suits your own interests, your audience, and the occasion. You feel confident about your ability to organize your ideas in a logical, effective way, and you've built up a healthy reserve of supporting material.

But then comes a problem: When you think about the actual act of standing before a group, your self-confidence begins to erode. How will you act? Should you be formal or casual? Should you memorize your remarks, read from a script, or use notes? How loudly should you speak, and how quickly? And what about your nerves? The prospect of talking to an audience probably seems much more threatening than expressing yourself in a blue book or even mixing chemicals in a laboratory.

Because the act of speaking before a group of listeners may be a new one for you, we'll look at the process now. The purpose of this chapter is to make you feel more confident about yourself as a speaker and to give you a clearer idea of how to behave before an audience.[1]

speaking with confidence

The terror that strikes into the hearts of so many beginning speakers is called communication apprehension or speech anxiety by communication scholars, but it is more commonly known to those who experience it as stage fright.

facilitative and debilitative apprehension

Although stage fright is a very real problem for many speakers, it is a problem that can be overcome. Interestingly enough, the first step in feeling less apprehensive about speaking is to realize that a certain amount of nervousness is not only natural but facilitative. That is, it's a factor that can help improve your performance. Just as totally relaxed athletes or musicians aren't likely to perform at the top of their potential, speakers think more rapidly and express themselves more energetically when their level of tension is moderate.

It is only when the level of anxiety is intense that it becomes debilitative, inhibiting effective self-expression. Intense fear causes trouble in two ways. First, the strong emotion keeps you from thinking clearly. Second, intense fear leads to an urge to do something, anything, to make the problem go away. This urge to escape often causes a speaker to speed up delivery, which results in a rapid, almost machine-gun style. As you can imagine, this boost in speaking rate leads to even more mistakes, which only adds to the speaker's anxiety. Thus, a relatively small amount of nervousness can begin to feed on itself until it grows into a serious problem.

sources of debilitative apprehension

Before we describe how to manage debilitative stage fright, it might be helpful to look at some reasons people are afflicted with the problem.[2]

I have a slight inferiority complex still. I go into a room and have to talk myself into going up to people . . . If I'm the epitome of a woman who is always confident and in control, don't ever believe it of anyone.

Barbara Walters

Previous experience One reason people feel apprehensive about speech giving is because of unpleasant past experiences. A traumatic failure at an earlier speech or low self-esteem from critical parents during childhood are common examples. You might object to the idea that past experiences cause stage fright. After all, not everyone who has bungled a speech or had critical parents is debilitated in the future. To understand why some people are affected more strongly than others by past experiences, we need to consider another cause of speech anxiety.

Irrational thinking Cognitive psychologists argue that it is not *events* that cause people to feel nervous, but rather the beliefs they have about those events.[3] Certain irrational beliefs leave people feeling unnecessarily apprehensive. Psychologist Albert Ellis lists several such beliefs, which we will call "fallacies" because of their illogical nature.[4]

1. **The fallacy of catastrophic failure.** People who adopt this belief operate on the assumption that if something bad can happen, it probably will. Their thoughts before and during a speech resemble these:

   "As soon as I stand up to speak, I'll forget everything I wanted to say."
   "Everyone will think my ideas are stupid."
   "Somebody will probably laugh at me."

   Although it is naive to imagine that all your speeches will be totally successful, it is equally wrong to assume they will all fail misera-

A man is hurt not so much by what happens as by his opinion of what happens.

Montaigne

I never was what you would call a fancy skater—and while I seldom actually fell, it might have been more impressive if I had. A good resounding fall is no disgrace. It is the fantastic writhing to avoid a fall which destroys any illusion of being a gentleman. How like life that is, after all!

Robert Benchley

I believe that courage is all too often mistakenly seen as the absence of fear. If you descend by rope from a cliff and are not fearful to some degree, you are either crazy or unaware. Courage is seeing your fear in a realistic perspective, defining it, considering the alternatives and choosing to function in spite of the risk.

Leonard Zunin
Contact: The First Four Minutes

bly. One way to escape from the fallacy of catastrophic failure is to take a more realistic look at the situation. Would your audience really hoot you off the stage? Will they really think your ideas are stupid? Even if you did forget your remarks for a moment, would the results be a genuine disaster?[5]

2. **The fallacy of perfection.** Speakers who accept this belief expect themselves to behave flawlessly. Whereas such a standard of perfection might serve as a target and a source of inspiration (rather like making a hole-in-one for a golfer), it is totally unrealistic to expect that you will write and deliver a perfect speech—especially as a beginner.

3. **The fallacy of approval.** This mistaken belief is based on the idea that it is vital—not just desirable—to gain the approval of everyone in their audience. It is rare that even the best speakers please everyone, especially on topics that are at all controversial. To paraphrase Abraham Lincoln, you can't please all the people all the time . . . and it is irrational to expect you will.

4. **The fallacy of overgeneralization.** This might also be labeled the fallacy of exaggeration, for it occurs when a person blows one poor experience out of proportion. Consider these examples:

"I'm so stupid! I mispronounced that word."
"I completely blew it—I forgot one of my supporting points."
"My hands were shaking. The audience must have thought I was a complete idiot."

A second type of exaggeration occurs when a speaker treats occasional lapses as if they were the rule rather than the exception. This sort of mistake usually involves extreme labels such as "always" and "never."

"I *always* forget what I want to say."
"I can *never* come up with a good topic."
"I can't do *anything* right."

overcoming stage fright

There are four fairly simple ways to overcome debilitative stage fright. The first, as suggested earlier, is to be rational about the beliefs that cause your stage fright. The other three are to be receiver-oriented, positive, and prepared.

1. **Be rational.** Listen to your thought processes, your internal voice, and try to figure out if the basis for your stage fright is rational. Then dispute any irrational beliefs. Use the list given earlier to discover which of your internal statements are based on mistaken thinking.

2. **Be receiver-oriented.** Concentrate on your audience rather than on yourself. Worry about whether they are interested, about whether they understand and about whether or not you are maintaining human contact with them.

In speaking to the Winnipeg Rotary Club, I arrived a little early for the meeting and was greeted by an attractive lady who asked, "What are you doing here?"

She looked a little familiar. I thought perhaps I had met her at a convention two years earlier. "I'm here to give a speech to the Rotary Club," I replied.

"Do you do this often?" she asked.

"Quite often," I said.

"Are you nervous before you talk?" she demanded.

"I don't think so," I replied.

She retorted, "Then what are you doing in the ladies' washroom?"

Ross Smyth

3. **Be positive.** It is important to build and maintain a positive attitude toward your audience, your speech, and yourself as a speaker. Some communication consultants suggest that public speakers should concentrate on three statements immediately before speaking. The three statements are:

"I'm glad I'm here."
"I know my topic."
"I care about you" ("you" of course being the audience).

Keeping these ideas in mind can help you maintain a positive attitude.

4. **Be prepared.** If you are fully prepared, your speech will represent less of a threat. Devote enough time to each step of message preparation so you can feel secure. Be especially sure to leave enough time to *practice* your presentation. And when it comes time to give your presentation, keep in mind that nervousness is normal. Expect it, and remember that its symptoms—even shaky knees and trembling hands—are more obvious to you than they are to the audience. Beginning public speakers, when congratulated for their poise during a speech, are apt to make such remarks as "Are you kidding? I was *dying* up there."

These four guidelines will enable most speakers to control their stage fright to the point where it will be facilitative rather than debilitative. Speakers who find these methods inadequate have two other options: They might enlist the help of a professional counselor (these services are often provided free by colleges), or they could research a more extensive procedure for themselves, such as systematic desensitization. Ron Adler's book *Confidence in Communication: A Guide to Assertive and Social Skills*[6] outlines several procedures for managing communication anxiety.

Improving the way you feel as a speaker plays an important role in your effectiveness. Now we will turn to another vital part of your delivery: How you look and sound as a speaker. The first thing to consider in this area is the style of delivery you choose.

types of delivery

There are four basic types of delivery—extemporaneous, impromptu, manuscript, and memorized. Each type creates a different impression and is appropriate under different conditions. Any speech may incorporate more than one of these types of delivery. For purposes of discussion, however, it is best to consider them separately.

extemporaneous speeches

An extemporaneous speech is planned in advance but presented in a direct, spontaneous manner. This style of speaking is generally accepted to be the most effective, especially for a college class. In a classroom you generally speak before a small audience (five to fifty people) made up of people with diverse backgrounds. Spontaneity is essential with this type of audience, but so is careful message planning. Extemporaneous speaking allows you to benefit from both careful planning and spontaneous delivery. A speech presented extemporaneously will be focused, organized, and planned out in advance, but the exact wording of the entire speech will not be memorized or otherwise predetermined.

Because you speak from only brief, unobtrusive notes, you are able to move and maintain eye contact with your audience.

Extemporaneous speaking is not only the most effective type of delivery for a classroom speech, but it is also the most common type of delivery in the "outside" world. Most of those involved in communication-oriented careers find that the majority of their public speaking is done before audiences that, in terms of size and diversity of interests represented, resemble those found in a college classroom. Professional public speakers recognize the advisability of both careful planning and spontaneity with such an audience.

The extemporaneous speech does have some disadvantages. It is difficult to keep exact time limits, to be exact in wording, or to be grammatically perfect with an extemporaneous speech. Therefore, if you are speaking as part of a radio or television broadcast or if your speech will be reproduced "for the record," you might want to use a manuscript or to memorize your speech. Also, an extemporaneous speech requires time to prepare. If you don't have that time, an impromptu speech might be more appropriate.

impromptu speeches

An impromptu speech is given off the top of one's head, without preparation. An impromptu speech is often given in an emergency, such as when a scheduled speaker becomes ill and you are suddenly called upon:

> Grunt Johnson couldn't make it this evening, folks, but I notice in our audience another Sioux U student leader who I am sure would be glad to say a few words . . .

Impromptu speeches are sometimes given when speakers forget they are scheduled for extemporaneous speeches. In fact, a certain amount of confusion exists between the terms *extemporaneous* and *impromptu.*

The problem with an impromptu speech is that it is given on the spur of the moment and, as Monroe and Ehninger have pointed out, "Too often the 'moment' arrives without the necessary informed and inspired 'spur.'"[7] There are, however, advantages to impromptu speaking. For one thing, an impromptu speech is by definition spontaneous. It is the delivery style necessary for informal talks, group discussions, and comments on others' speeches. It also can be an effective training aid; it can teach you to think on your feet and organize your thoughts quickly. To take full advantage of an impromptu speaking opportunity, remember the following points:

1. Take advantage of the time between being called on to speak and actually speaking. Review your personal experiences and use them. Don't be afraid to be original; you don't have to remember what every other expert says about your topic—what do *you* say about it? If nothing else, consider the questions "Who? What? When? Where?

It usually takes me more than three weeks to prepare a good impromptu speech.

Mark Twain

How?" and formulate a plan to answer one or more of them. Even if you have only a minute, you can still scribble a few brief notes to protect against mental blocks.

2. Observe what is going on around you and respond to it. If there were other speakers, you might agree or disagree with what they said. You can comment on the audience and the occasion, too, as well as on your topic.

3. Keep a positive attitude. Remember that audience expectations are low. They know you haven't prepared in advance, and they don't expect you to be Patrick Henry.

4. Finally, and perhaps most important, keep your comments brief. Especially, do not prolong your conclusion. If you have said everything you want to say or everything you can remember, wrap it up as neatly as possible and sit down. If you forgot something, it probably wasn't important anyway. If it was, the audience will ask you about it afterward.

manuscript speeches

Manuscript speeches are necessary when you are speaking "for the record," as at legal proceedings or when presenting scientific findings. The greatest disadvantage of a manuscript speech is the lack of spontaneity that may result. Manuscript readers have even been known to read their directions by mistake: "And so, let me say in conclusion, look at the audience with great sincerity . . . oops!" Needless to say, this can lead to extreme embarrassment.

Manuscript speeches are difficult and cumbersome, but they are sometimes necessary. If you find occasion to use one, here are some guidelines:

1. When writing the speech, recognize the differences between written essays and speeches. Speeches are usually less formal, more repetitive, and more personal than written messages.[8]

2. Use short paragraphs. They are easier to return to after establishing eye contact with your audience.

3. Type the manuscript triple-spaced, in all caps, with a dark ribbon. Underline the words you want to emphasize. (See Figure 13-1.)

4. Use stiff paper, so it won't fold up or fly away during the speech. Type on only one side, and number the pages as visibly as possible.

5. Rehearse until you can "read" whole lines without looking at the manuscript.

6. Take your time, vary your speed, and try to concentrate on ideas rather than words.

memorized speeches

Memorized speeches are the most difficult and often the least effective. They usually seem excessively formal. They tend to make you think of

TO SUMMARIZE, WE ARE IN THE EARLY STAGE OF DEVELOPMENTS IN THE SCIENCE AND TECHNOLOGY OF INFORMATION PROCESSING THAT WILL TRULY REVOLUTIONIZE OUR SOCIETY. ADVANCES ARE OCCURRING AT SUCH A FAST PACE THAT RECENT EXPERIENCE IS NOT ALWAYS A GOOD GUIDE TO THE FUTURE. IN THE PAST 30 YEARS, COMPUTER COMPUTATIONS HAVE GONE FROM A FEW INSTRUCTIONS PER SECOND AT A COST OF SEVERAL DOLLARS TO MILLIONS OF INSTRUCTIONS PER SECOND AT A COST OF LESS THAN 1 CENT. BUT SUCH DRAMATIC INDICATORS OF PROGRESS DO NOT MEASURE THE FULL IMPACT OF WHAT IS TAKING PLACE OR WHAT IS LIKELY TO OCCUR IN THE NEXT 30 YEARS. THERE CAN BE LITTLE DOUBT THAT THESE CHANGES WILL ALTER THE WAY PEOPLE LIVE AND EARN A LIVING, AND THE WAY THEY PERCEIVE THEMSELVES AND RELATE TO ONE ANOTHER.

words rather than ideas. However, like manuscript speeches, they are sometimes necessary. They are used in oratory contests and on very formal occasions such as eulogies or church rituals. They are used as training devices for memory. They are also used in some political situations. For example, in the 1980 presidential debates, Jimmy Carter and Ronald Reagan were allowed to make prepared speeches, but they were not allowed to use notes. Thus they had to memorize precise, "for-the-record" wording.

There is only one guideline for a memorized speech: practice. The speech won't be effective until you have practiced it so you can present it with what actors and term-paper recyclers call "the illusion of the first time."

figure 13–1
Sample page from manuscript speech

You will want to choose the appropriate delivery style for the type of speech you are giving. The best way to assure that you are on your way to an effective delivery is to practice in front of a small sample audience—perhaps one or two friends—and have them comment on it.

guidelines for delivery

The best way to consider guidelines for delivery is through an examination of the nonverbal aspects of presenting a speech. As we pointed out in Chapter 5, nonverbal messages can change the meaning assigned to the spoken word and in some cases can contradict that meaning entirely. In fact, if the audience wants to interpret how you *feel* about something, they are likely to trust your nonverbal communication more than the words you speak. If you tell an audience, "It's good to be here today," but you stand before them slouched over with your hands in your pockets and an expression on your face as if you were about to be shot, they are likely to discount what you say. This might cause your audience to react negatively to your speech, and their negative reaction might make you even more nervous. This cycle of speaker and audience reinforcing each other's feelings can work *for* you, though, if you approach a subject with genuine enthusiasm. One way that enthusiasm will be manifested is through the visual aspects of your delivery.

visual aspects of delivery

Visual aspects of delivery include such things as appearance, movement, posture, facial expressions, and eye contact.

Appearance Appearance is not a presentation variable as much as a preparation variable. Some communication consultants suggest new clothes, new glasses, and new hairstyles for their clients. In case you consider any of these, be forewarned that you should be attractive to your audience, but not flashy. Research suggests that audiences like speakers who are similar to them, but they prefer the similarity to be shown conservatively. For example, studies run in 1972, when long hair on males was becoming popular, showed that even long-haired listeners considered long-haired speakers less credible than shorter-haired speakers.[9]

Movement Movement is an important visual aspect of delivery. The way you walk to the front of your audience, for example, will express your confidence and enthusiasm. And once you begin speaking, nervous energy can cause your body to shake and twitch, and that can be distressing both to you and to your audience. One way to control involuntary movement is to move voluntarily when you feel the need to move. Don't feel that you have to stand in one spot or that all your gestures need to be carefully planned. Simply get involved in your message, and let your involvement create the motivation for your movement. That way, when you move, you will emphasize what you are saying in the same way you would emphasize it if you were talking to a group of friends. If you move voluntarily, you will use up the same energy that would otherwise cause you to move involuntarily.

Movement can help you maintain contact with *all* members of your audience. Those closest to you will feel the greatest contact with you whereas the people who are less interested will have a tendency to sit farther away to begin with. This creates what is known as the "action

Gesture, but do not *make* gestures. Let your gestures spring from the impulse common to all expression through action.

James A. Winans

zone" of audience members sitting in the front and center of the room. Movement enables you to extend this action zone, to include in it people who would otherwise remain uninvolved. Without overdoing it, you should feel free to move toward, away, or from side to side in front of your audience.

Remember: Move with the understanding that it will add to the meaning of the words you use. It is difficult to bang your fist on a podium or to take a step without conveying emphasis. Make the emphasis natural by allowing your message to create your motivation to move.

Posture Generally speaking, good posture means standing with your spine relatively straight, your shoulders relatively squared off, and your feet angled out to keep your body from falling over sideways. In other words, rather than standing at military attention, you should be comfortably erect.

Of course, you shouldn't get *too* comfortable. There are speakers who are effective in spite of the fact that they sprawl on tabletops and slouch against blackboards, but their effectiveness is usually in spite of their posture rather than because of it. Sometimes speakers are so awesome in stature or reputation that they need an informal posture to encourage their audience to relax. In that case, sloppy posture is more or less justified. But because awesomeness is not usually a problem for beginning speakers, good posture should be the rule.

Good posture can help you control nervousness by allowing your breathing apparatus to work properly; when your brain receives enough oxygen, it's easier for you to think clearly and dispel irrational fears. Good posture will also help you get a positive audience reaction because standing up straight makes you more visible. It also increases your audience contact, because the audience members will feel that you are interested enough in them to stand formally, yet relaxed enough to be at ease with them.

Facial expressions The expression on your face can be more meaningful to an audience than the words you say. Try it yourself with a mirror. Say, "College is neat," with a smirk, with a warm smile, deadpan, and then with a scowl. It just doesn't mean the same thing. When speaking, keep in mind that your face might be saying something in front of your back. Remember also that it is just about impossible to control facial expressions from the outside. Like your movement, your facial expressions will reflect your involvement with your message. Don't try to fake it. Just get involved in your message, and your face will take care of itself.

Eye contact This is perhaps the most important nonverbal facet of delivery. Eye contact not only increases your direct contact with your audience, it also should increase their interest in you by making you more attractive. Eyes are beautiful things; much more beautiful than eyelids, foreheads, or scalps. Furthermore, and contrary to popular opinion, eye contact can be used to help you control your nervousness. Direct eye contact is a form of reality testing. The most frightening aspect of speaking is the unknown. How will the audience react? What will they think? Direct eye contact allows you to test your perception of your audience as you speak. Usually, especially in a college class, you will find that your audience is more "with" you than you think. We found that out ourselves through personal experience; when we first began teaching, we were terrified of the students who would slither down in their chairs, doodle, and generally seem bored. These students upset us so thoroughly that we usually would try *not* to look at them. And that made matters worse. Eventually, by deliberately establishing eye contact with the apparently bored students, we found that they often *were* interested; they just weren't showing that interest because they didn't think anyone was looking. Once these bored-looking students realized that someone was actually looking at them, noticing their existence, they made their attention more obvious by sitting up and looking back at us. The more eye contact they received, the more interested they became.

To maintain eye contact you might try to meet the eyes of each member of your audience, squarely, at least once during any given presentation. Once you have made definite contact, move on to another audience member. You can learn to do this quickly, so you can visually latch onto every member of a good-sized class in a relatively short time.

The characteristics of appearance, movement, posture, facial expression, and eye contact are visual, nonverbal facets of delivery. Now consider the auditory, nonverbal messages that you might send during a presentation.

auditory aspects of delivery

As you read in Chapter 5, the way you use your voice—your paralanguage—says a great deal about you: most notably about your sincerity and enthusiasm. In addition, using your voice well can help you control your nervousness. It's another cycle: Controlling your vocal characteristics will decrease your nervousness, which will enable you to control your voice even more. But this cycle can also work in the opposite direction. If your voice is out of control, your nerves will probably be in the same state. Controlling your voice is mostly a matter of recognizing and using appropriate *volume, rate, pitch,* and *articulation.*

Volume Volume—the loudness of your voice—is determined by the amount of air you push past the vocal folds in your throat. The key to controlling volume, then, is controlling the amount of air you use. The key to determining the *right* volume is audience contact. Your delivery should be loud enough so that your audience can hear everything you say but not so loud that they feel you are talking to someone in the next

I walked to the lectern. I hemmed. Then I hawed. I cleared my throat. Then I said:

"I shall give an illustrated lecture on the interior of the human mouth—the teeth, the tongue, the upper palate, the lower palate and other points of interest."

Then, to illustrate my lecture, I stuck my finger in my mouth, as if to point out the various things I was talking about, and for five solid minutes I spoke totally unintelligible gibberish, never removing the finger from my mouth and sometimes inserting my entire fist.

Alan Sherman
A Gift of Laughter

---

room. Too much volume is seldom the problem for beginning speakers. Usually they either are not loud enough or have a tendency to fade off at the end of a thought. Sometimes, when they lose faith in an idea in midsentence, they compromise by mumbling the end of the sentence so it isn't quite coherent. That's an unfortunate compromise, rather like changing your mind in the middle of a broad jump.

One contemporary speaker who has been criticized for inappropriate volume is Senator Edward M. Kennedy. L. Patrick Devlin recently pointed out that "... Kennedy tended to shout when an audience was small or uninterested or when he sensed he was losing them. Thus, his volume was often inappropriate to the time and place."[10] *Newsweek's* John Walcott observed, "When he had an unresponsive audience—300 Iowa farmers who were not jumping up on their chairs—he tended to shout more and it became more and more incongruous."[11]

Rate Rate is your speed in speaking. Normal speaking speed is around 150 words per minute. If you talk at a slower rate than that, you may tend to lull your audience to sleep. Faster speaking rates are stereotypically associated with speaker competence,[12] but if you talk too rapidly, you will tend to be unintelligible. Once again, your involvement in your message is the key to achieving an effective rate.

Pitch Pitch—the highness or lowness of your voice—is controlled by the frequency at which your vocal folds vibrate as you push air through them. Because taut vocal folds vibrate at a greater frequency, pitch is influenced by muscular tension. This explains why nervous speakers have a tendency occasionally to "squeak" whereas relaxed speakers seem to be more in control. Pitch will tend to follow rate and volume. As you speed up or become louder, your pitch will have a tendency to rise. If your range in pitch is too narrow, your voice will have a singsong quality. If it is too wide, you may sound overly dramatic. You should control your pitch so your listeners believe you are talking *with* them rather than performing in front of them. Once again, your involvement in your message should take care of this naturally for you.

When considering volume, rate, and pitch, keep *emphasis* in mind. You have to use a variety of vocal characteristics to maintain audience interest, but remember that a change in volume, pitch, or rate will result in emphasis. If you pause or speed up, your rate will suggest emphasis. Words you whisper or scream will be emphasized by their volume. One of our students once provided an example of how volume can be used to emphasize an idea. He was speaking on how possessions like cars communicate things about their owners. "For example," he said, with normal volume, "a Lincoln Continental says, 'I've got money!' But a Rolls Royce says, *'I'VE GOT MONEY!'* " He blared out those last three words with such force the podium shook.

Articulation The final auditory nonverbal behavior, articulation, is perhaps the most important. For our purposes here, articulation means saying all the parts of all the necessary words and nothing else.

It is not our purpose to condemn regional or ethnic dialects within this discussion. Native New Yorkers can continue to have their "hot dawgs" with their "cawfee," and Southerners can drawl as much as they-all please. You *should* know, however, that a considerable amount of research suggests that regional dialects can cause negative impressions.[13] But it is also true that an honest regional accent can work in your favor. For example, when Paul Volcker was president of the Federal Reserve Bank of New York, he used his accent to his benefit when he began a speech this way:

> Fellow New Yorkers: I am emboldened to use that simple salutation tonight for more than one reason. At the most personal level, I was reminded the other day where my own roots lay. I heard a tape recording of some remarks I had made. After spending three quarters of the past 16 years in Washington, I confess to being startled by what I heard—the full, rounded tones of a home-grown New York accent.[14]

The purpose of this discussion is to suggest *careful,* not standardized, articulation. Incorrect articulation is nothing more than careless articulation. It usually results in (1) leaving off parts of words (deletion), (2) replacing part of a word (substitution), (3) adding parts to words (addition), or (4) overlapping two or more words (slurring).

Deletion The most common mistake in articulation is deletion, or leaving off part of a word. As you are thinking the complete word, it is often difficult to recognize that you are only saying part of it. The most common deletions occur at the end of words, especially "-ing" words. "Going," "doing," and "stopping" become "goin'," "doin'," and "stoppin'." Parts of words can be left off in the middle, too, as in "natully" for "naturally" and "reg'lar" for "regular."

Substitution Substitution takes place when you replace part of a word with an incorrect sound. The ending "-th" is often replaced at the end

he talks bawlamerese, duddney?

BAWLAMER, Sept. 20—Following is a brief glossary of "Bawlamerese" compiled as a traveler's guide to the local patois by the Citizens Planning and Housing Association of this city, which outsiders often mispronounce "BALT-i-more" and local residents pronounce "BAWL-uh-mer." The excerpts from the association's list are reproduced with its permission from its handbook, "Bawlamer":

AIG   The thing with a yoke.
ARSH   People from Arlin.
AWL   Goes into the crankcase.
ARN   What you do on an arnin board.
BLOW   Opposite of above.
COLE RACE BEEF   A favorite sandwich.
CALF LICK   Protestant, Jewish and . . .
DRAFF   Animal with the longest neck.
DRUCKSTEWER   Drugstore.
DUDDNEY   Doesn't he.
ELFIN   Animal with a trunk.
ERF   Planet on which we live.
FARN GIN   Used for fighting fars.
FARST FARS   Smokey Bear fights them.
GRANITE   What you don't want to be taken for.
HOSKULL   Where you went before cahwidge.
IGGGLE   Our national symbol.
JEET?   Did you eat? Usually answered by "no, jew?"
LOBBLE   Responsible for.
MERLIN   The Free State.
MACELY   Mostly.
MORALITY   The race for mayor.

MEER   What you look at in the morning.
MURIEL   A large painting on a large wall.
NAPLIS   The state capital.
OLTNO   I don't know.
OLL   What you walk down when you get married.
OLLIN   A piece of land surrounded by water.
PO-LEECE   A single police officer.
PLEECE   Two or more po-leece.
PARAMOUR   What your neighbor uses at 8 A.M. Sundays.
PHANE   What you answer when it rings.
QUARR   Sings in Church.
ROSTRUM   Where the ladies go after dinner.
SORE   Drainage area under streets.
TORST   Tourist.
WARSHNIN   Our nation's capital.
WRENCH   Rinse, as in "wrench your hands in the zinc."
WOODER   What you wrench your hand with.
YERP   Europe.
ZOLLAFANE   Xylophone.

of a word with a single "t," as when "with" becomes "wit." (This tendency is especially prevalent in many parts of the northeastern United States.) The "th-" sound is also a problem at the beginning of words, as "this," "that," and "those" have a tendency to become "dis," "dat," and "dose."

Addition   This articulation problem is caused by adding extra parts to words that are already perfectly adequate, such as "incentative" for "incentive," "athalete" instead of "athlete," and "orientated" instead of "oriented." Sometimes this type of addition is caused by incorrect word choice, such as when "irregardless" (which is not a word) is used for "regardless."

Another type of addition is the use of "tag questions," such as "you know?" or "you see?" or "right?" To have every other sentence punctuated with one of these barely audible superfluous phrases can be maddening.

Probably the worst type of addition, or at least the most common, is the use of "uh" and "anda" between words. "Anda" is often stuck between two words when "and" isn't even needed. If you find yourself doing that, you might want just to pause or swallow instead.

Slurring Slurring is caused, in effect, by trying to say two or more words at once—or at least overlapping the end of one word with the beginning of the next. Word pairs ending with "of" are the worst offenders in this category. "Sort of" becomes "sorta," "kind of" becomes "kinda," and "because of" becomes "becausa." Word combinations ending with "to" are often slurred, as when "want to" becomes "wanna." Sometimes even more than two words are blended together, as when "that is the way" becomes "thatsaway." Careful articulation means using your lips, teeth, tongue, and jaw to bite off your words, cleanly and separately, one at a time.

The general rule for articulation in extemporaneous speaking is to be both natural and clear. Be yourself, but be an understandable, intelligent-sounding version of yourself. The best way to achieve this goal is to accept your instructor's evaluation of whether you add, substitute, drop, or slur word sounds. Then you can, as Shakespeare had King Lear suggest, "Mend your speech a little, lest you may mar your fortune."

This chapter dealt with the problems inherent in the actual delivery of your speech. The most serious of these problems is debilitative (as opposed to facilitative) stage fright. Sources of debilitative stage fright include irrational thinking, which might include a belief in one or more of the following fallacies: the fallacy of perfection (a good speaker never does anything wrong), the fallacy of absolute approval (*everyone* has to like you), the fallacy of overgeneralization (you *always* mess up speeches), the fallacy of helplessness (there's nothing you can do about it), and the fallacy of catastrophic failure (all is lost if this speech bombs).

There are several methods of overcoming speech anxiety. The first is to refute the irrational fallacies just listed. The others include being receiver-oriented, positive, and prepared.

There are four types of delivery: extemporaneous, impromptu, manuscript, and memorized. In each type, the speaker must be concerned with both visual and auditory aspects of the presentation. Visual aspects

summary

include appearance, movement, posture, facial expressions, and eye contact. Auditory aspects include volume, rate, pitch, and articulation. The four most common articulation problems are deletion, substitution, addition, and slurring of word sounds.

activities

1. For practice in recognizing the symptoms of stage fright, identify a speech you either gave or witnessed someone else give. This speech might be something as ordinary as a classroom response or as eventful as a presidential debate. In your opinion, what was the effect of stage fright in this speech? Was it facilitative or debilitative?

2. To become better at understanding how your thoughts shape your feelings about speechmaking, think about the following situations, and list two opposite ways you could interpret each situation. Take note of the feelings that would follow from each interpretation.
   a. While researching your topic you find it difficult to find material.
   b. While organizing your ideas, you come to one that all the experts agree upon but that you're not too sure about.
   c. When you get up to give your speech, someone giggles.
   d. In the middle of an important point you're making, one audience member yawns emphatically.
   e. Toward the end of your presentation, you notice an attractive person staring at you and smiling.

3. To analyze your own reaction to stage fright, think back to your last public speech, and rate yourself on how ''rational, receiver-oriented, positive, and prepared'' you were. How did these attributes affect your anxiety level?

4. You can analyze speech delivery problems either by examining yourself or other speakers. Try one of the following:
   a. Make a list of your own problems in speech delivery. See if you can either (1) add to that list or (2) list some possible solutions to your problems from what you read in this chapter.
   b. Name two good and two bad speakers you have heard. Identify the good and bad features of each style, and suggest an alternative style, if appropriate.

5. For practice in analyzing visual aspects of delivery, pick a favorite celebrity (comedian, actor, newscaster, or talk-show host) whose delivery you find effective. What are the visual aspects of his or her delivery that help make it effective?

6. When examining your own articulation, it is sometimes helpful to use a tape recorder. Because we hear our own voices partially through our cranial bone structure, we are sometimes surprised at what we sound

like to others. Try the following classic articulation exercises with your own recorder:

a. Nonsense syllables: Run through all the consonants of the alphabet, pronouncing them with the five vowels: *Ba, be, bi, bo, bu* (pronounced bay, be, buy, beau, boo); *ca, ce, ci, co, cu; da, de, di, do, du,* and so on. As you do so, try to overarticulate; that is, move the tongue, jaw, and lips in an exaggerated manner. (There will be some duplication of consonant sounds with *c/s, x/z,* or *k/q.* However, all others—such as *f/v*—should be distinctly different.)

b. Tongue twisters: Repeat the following several times as quickly as possible:

''She sells seashells on the seashore.''
''Rubber baby buggy bumpers.''
''Saw some sleek, slim, slender saplings.''

You probably know more of these, or you can make them up. Feel free to do so.

c. Poetry: Recite the following clearly and dramatically:

To sit in solemn silence in a dull, dark dock
In a pestilential prison, with a lifelong lock,
Awaiting the sensation of a short, sharp shock,
From a cheap and chippy chopper on a big black block!
(Gilbert and Sullivan)

d. Prose selection: Read the following in the grand style its author obviously intended:

Shakespeare was an intellectual ocean whose waves touched all the shores of thought; within which were all the tides and waves of destiny and will; over which swept all the storms of fate, ambition, and revenge; upon which fell the gloom and darkness of despair and death, and all the sunlight of content and love, and within which was the inverted sky lit with the eternal stars—an intellectual ocean—toward which all rivers ran, and from which now the isles and continents of thought receive their dew and rain.
(Robert G. Ingersoll, Lecture on Shakespeare, 1894)

e. Get an idea of how you sound in normal conversation by leaving a tape recorder running in everyday situations: at the dinner table, while you're using the telephone, when studying with friends, and so on. The results can be surprising!

notes

1. We will not, at this point, get into the age-old argument of the relative importance of substance (what you say) and style (how you say it). Suffice it to say that this question is as old as the study of public speaking. See, for example, Barbara Warnick, "The Quarrel Between the Ancients and the Moderns," *Communication Monographs* 49 (December 1982): 263–276. One recent study pointed out that media commentators viewed substance as *less* important than delivery, appearance, and manner in the 1980 presidential debates. See Goodwin F. Berquist and James L. Goldin, "Media Rhetoric, Criticism, and the Public Perception of the 1980 Presidential Debates," *Quarterly Journal of Speech* 67 (May 1981), pp. 125–137.

2. A substantial body of research literature on communication apprehension and anxiety has accumulated. See James C. McCroskey, "Oral Communication Apprehension: A Summary of Recent Theory and Research," *Human Communication Research* 4 (1977): 78–96.

3. See John O. Greene and Glenn G. Sparks, "Explication and Test of a Cognitive Model of Communication Apprehension: A New Look at an Old Construct," *Human Communication Research* 9 (Summer 1983): 349–366. See also Ralph R. Behnke and Michael J. Beatty, "A Cognitive–Physiological Model of Speech Anxiety," *Communication Monographs* 48 (June 1981): pp. 158–163.

4. Adapted from Albert Ellis, *A New Guide to Rational Living* (North Hollywood, Calif.: Wilshire Books, 1977).

5. Expectations are a significant predictor of communication apprehension. See, for example, John O. Greene and Glenn G. Sparks, "The Role of Outcome Expectations in the Experience of a State of Communication Apprehension," *Communication Quarterly* 31 (Summer 1983): 212–219.

6. Ronald B. Adler, *Confidence in Communication: A Guide to Assertive and Social Skills* (New York: Holt, Rinehart and Winston, 1977).

7. Alan H. Monroe and Douglas Ehninger, *Principles and Types of Speech Communication,* 7th ed. (Glenview, Ill.: Scott, Foresman, 1974), p. 142.

8. For a recent synthesis of findings on these differences, see F. Niyi Akinnaso, "On the Differences Between Spoken and Written Language," *Language and Speech* 25 (March–June 1982): 97–125.

9. These studies are reviewed in Lawrence R. Rosenfeld and Jean M. Civikly, *With Words Unspoken* (New York: Holt, Rinehart and Winston, 1976), p. 62.

10. L. Patrick Devlin, "An Analysis of Kennedy's Communication in the 1980 Campaign," *Quarterly Journal of Speech* 68 (November 1982): 397–417.

11. Ibid.

12. A recent study demonstrating this is Richard L. Street, Jr., and Robert M. Brady, "Speech Rate Acceptance Ranges as a Function of Evaluative Domain, Listener Speech Rate, and Communication Context," *Speech Monographs* 49 (December 1982): 290–308.

13. See, for example, Anthony Mulac and Mary Jo Rudd, "Effects of Selected American Regional Dialects upon Regional Audience Members," *Communication Monographs* 44 (1977): 184–195. Some research, however, suggests that nonstandard dialects do not have the detrimental effects on listeners that were once believed. See, for example, Fern L. Johnson and Richard Buttny, "White Listener's Responses to 'Sounding Black'

and 'Sounding White': The Effects of Message Content on Judgments about Language," *Communication Monographs* 49 (March 1982): 33–49.

14. Paul A. Volcker, "The Dilemmas of Monetary Policy," *Vital Speeches of the Day* 42 (January 15, 1976).

fourteen

informative speaking

After reading this chapter, you should understand:

1. The importance of having a specific informative purpose.
2. The importance of creating information hunger.
3. The importance of using clear language.
4. The importance of generating audience involvement.

You should be able to:

1. Formulate an effective informative purpose statement.
2. Create "information hunger" by stressing the relevance of your material to your listeners' needs.
3. Emphasize important points in your speech.
4. Generate audience involvement.

Informative speaking is especially important in the dawning "age of information" in which transmitting knowledge will account for most of the work we do and, in a large part, for the quality of our lives. Although much of the information of the future will be transmitted by machines—computers and electronic media—the spoken word will continue to be the best way to reach small audiences with messages tailored specifically for them. And at least some of these messages will be designed to help people make sense of the glut of information that surrounds them.

Informative speaking seeks to increase the knowledge and understanding of an audience. This type of speaking goes on all around you: in your professors' lectures, in news reports on radio and TV, in a mechanic's explanation of how to keep your car from breaking down. All demonstrations and explanations are forms of informative speaking, and you probably engage in this type of speaking often, whether you realize it or not. Sometimes it's formal, as when you're giving a report in class. At other times it's more informal, as showing a friend how to prepare your favorite dish. It is often this everyday, informal type of informative speaking that we find most frustrating. One of the objectives of this chapter is to bolster some skills that can help relieve that frustration.

techniques of informative speaking

define a specific informative purpose

We explained in Chapter 11 (pp. 257–259) that any speech must be based on a purpose statement that is audience-oriented, precise, and attainable. When you are preparing an informative speech, it is especially important to define, in advance, for yourself, a clear informative purpose. The purpose statement for an informative speech will generally be worded in such a way that audience knowledge and/or ability will be stressed:

"After listening to my speech the audience will be able to name three types of _____."

"After listening to my speech the audience will be able to list the three main reasons that _____."

"After listening to my speech the audience will be able to recall the four major components of _____."

Notice that in each of these purpose statements a specific verb such as "to name," "to list," or "to recall" is used to point out the kind of thing the audience will be able to do after hearing the speech. Other key verbs for informative purpose statements include:

analyze	contrast	explain	recognize
apply	describe	identify	summarize
compare	discuss	integrate	support

Setting a clear informative purpose will help keep you focused as you prepare and present your speech. But no matter what your purpose, you have to keep your audience interested so that they will listen to what you have to say. That brings us to our second technique for effective informative speaking.

create "information hunger"

In informative speaking, you must create a reason for your audience to want to listen to and learn from your speech. The most effective way to do that is to respond in some way to their needs—either those general needs that all human beings feel or more specific needs that are unique to your audience.

Maslow's (general) needs To relate your speech to general human needs, Maslow's analysis, as discussed in Chapter 1, can be used as a guide. You could tap into *physiological needs* by relating your topic to your audience's survival or to the improvement of their living conditions. If you gave a speech on food (eating it, cooking it, or shopping for it), you would automatically be dealing with a basic audience need. If you gave a speech on water pollution, you could relate to physiological needs by listing the possible pollutants in one of your local lakes or streams and explaining what each one could do to a human body. In the same way, you could tap into *safety needs* by relating your topic to your audience's security; you could tap into *esteem needs* by showing your audience how to be respected—or simply by showing them that *you* respect them.

You can appeal to *self-actualization needs,* those based on the need to accomplish as much as possible with our lives, by showing your audience some way to improve themselves. Self-actualization needs are particularly important in a college classroom because of the audience's need to grow intellectually. This helps explain the importance of supporting material in a college speech, especially supporting material that includes a historical or literary reference. For example, consider the following introduction to a speech given by a professor of philosophy at the University of Michigan:

> Of all that was done in the past
> You eat the fruit
> Either rotten or ripe
> (T. S. Eliot)
>
> We are a daring civilization. An adventurous civilization. But in the last analysis, we are a stupid civilization. We are a civilization afflicted with a death wish. We are destroying (not just using, but destroying) natural resources, ecological habitats, the tissue of which society is made. We are destroying, by the increasing number and magnitude of various stresses, individual human beings. We are destroying life at large. The civilization which intentionally or unintentionally does all these things cannot be called either judicious or wise. We are a stupid civilization.[1]

Along with demonstrating the use of a literary reference, this example also shows how you can create information hunger by appealing to sev-

Because information can change society, and because the amount of information doubles every fifteen years, our culture, if it is to become enriched and improved by its information, needs speakers to digest and assimilate this information and present it with clarity.

Otis Walter
Speaking to Inform and Persuade

eral audience needs at once. The professor focused on his audience's esteem needs by enhancing that esteem ("We are a daring civilization") and also by threatening it ("We are a stupid civilization"). He also tapped into his audience's safety and physiological needs ("We are a civilization afflicted with a death wish") and social needs ("We are destroying individual human beings").

Specific needs Maslow's analysis of needs should be kept in mind for all audiences, for these needs are shared by all human beings. And yet the closer you can come to the specific needs of your audience, the more "information hunger" you will generate. If a large percentage of your audience is graduating soon, they will be eager to hear about job opportunities; if many of them commute to school, they will be eager to hear about the prospects for the availability of gasoline. If most of them live in dormitories, they will be eager to hear how they can keep from going crazy while trying to study.

emphasize important points

Along with defining a specific informative purpose and creating information hunger, you should stress the important points in your speech through *repetition* and *"signposts."*

Repetition Chapter 12 discusses ways that you can emphasize material through clear organization: limiting your speech to two to five main points; dividing, coordinating, and ordering those main points; using a strong introduction that previews your ideas; using a conclusion that reviews them and makes them memorable; and using lots of transitions, internal summaries, and internal previews. Strong organization, in effect, provides your listeners with a repetition of important points, and that repetition will help them understand and remember those points. You can also be repetitive stylistically by saying the same thing in more than one way: "It is a known fact that jogging is good for your heart; medical research is unequivocal in supporting the fact that jogging builds up heart muscle by increasing the flow of blood that nourishes the muscular tissue of the heart itself."

Redundancy is no crime when you are using it to emphasize important points; it is only a crime when (1) you're redundant with obvious, trivial, or boring points, or (2) you run an important point into the ground. Unfortunately there is no sure rule for making sure you haven't overemphasized a point. You just have to use your own best judgment to make sure that you've stated the point enough that your audience "gets" it without repeating it so often that they want to give it back.

Signposts Another way to emphasize important material is by using "signposts" to warn your audience that what you're about to say is important. You can say, simply enough, "What I'm about to say is important." Or you can use some variation of that statement: "But listen to this . . ." or "The most important thing to remember is . . ." or "The three keys to this situation are . . ." and so on.

use supporting materials effectively

Our fourth technique for effective informative speaking has to do with the supporting material we discussed in Chapter 12. Three of the purposes of support (to clarify, to make interesting, and to make memorable) are essential to informative speaking. Therefore, you should be careful to do the following:

- Define your key terms if there is any chance that the audience might be confused by them.
- Provide detailed descriptions to increase audience involvement in the information you are presenting.
- Use analogies to enable your audience to view your information from a different perspective.
- Use quantification and statistics to make your information more authoritative and accurate.
- Use anecdotes and examples to make your information more interesting and memorable.
- Use visual aids to take advantage of the huge amount of information that audience members can take in through their sense of sight.

use clear language

Another technique for effective informative speaking is to use clear language—which means the use of clear, simple vocabulary and definitions of any obscure but necessary terms.

Use precise vocabulary   Clarity, simply stated, is the process of saying what you mean. Saying what you mean requires precise word choice. When planning an informative speech, you have to be a wordsmith, an artisan just like a silversmith or a watchsmith, only with words as your raw materials and dictionaries (or even a thesaurus, which is really just a dictionary of synonyms) as your tools. You should use these tools to find the most precise word to say what you want to say. If you have any doubt about the clarity of something you are saying, then you should devise several different ways of saying it and choose the best way. Most of the memorable phrases that are so familiar to us now started off in some different form and were then refined by the speaker. Consider the following expressions and see if they ring a bell:

"Eighty-seven years ago . . ."
"Don't fire until they get right up next to you."
"Old soldiers don't die; they just leave."
"Why, I'd sooner die than not have liberty."
"You should ask what services you can perform for your country rather than asking what it can do for you."

The whole art of informing is only the art of awakening the natural curiosity of a mind for the purpose of satisfying it afterwards.

Anatole France

Use simple vocabulary Finding the right word, the most precise word, seldom means finding the most obscure or complicated word. In fact, just the opposite is true. Important ideas don't have to sound complicated. Consider the following passage:

> Objective considerations of contemporary phenomena compel the conclusion that success or failure in competitive activities exhibits no tendency to be commensurate with innate capacity, but that a considerable element of the unpredictable must invariably be taken into account.[2]

That is George Orwell's satirical idea of how a biblical passage would be written in twentieth-century jargon. The original verse, from the King James translation of Ecclesiastes, reads:

> . . . the race is not to the swift, nor the battle to the strong, neither yet bread to the wise, nor yet riches to men of understanding, nor yet favor to men of skill; but time and chance happeneth to them all.

Define obscure but necessary terms It is a good idea to define key terms that you use; it is also a good idea to define any words that might be obscure or misunderstood in the context in which they are used. This is especially necessary if the word you're using qualifies as jargon, which is a word of a specialized nature that is used, and therefore understood, only by specific groups of people. Educators, for example, talk of "empirically validated learning" and "multimode curricula" and rather than saying that a child can do better, they say that "academic achievement is not commensurate with abilities." Doctors and military strategists are famous for their use of jargon also. A heart attack is a "coronary thrombosis" or a "cardiovascular accident" for doctors whereas air raids are "routine limited duration protective reactions" for military folks. Business people, religious groups, sports enthusiasts, lawyers, and many other groups have semiprivate vocabularies that are clearly understood only by those who use them regularly. When speaking to an outsider, jargon should probably be avoided; if it turns out to be absolutely necessary, it should be defined.

generate audience involvement

Our fifth and final technique for effective informative speaking is to get your audience involved in your speech. Educational psychologists have long known that the best way to *teach* someone something is to have them *do* it; social psychologists have added to this rule by proving, in many studies, that involvement in a message increases audience comprehension of, and agreement with, that message.

There are many ways to encourage audience involvement in your speech. One way is by following the rules for good delivery by maintaining enthusiasm, energy, eye contact, and so on. Other techniques include audience participation, the use of volunteers, and a question-and-answer period.

Audience participation   One way to increase audience involvement is to have the audience members actually *do* something during your speech. For example, if you were giving a demonstration on isometric exercises (which don't require too much room for movement), you could have the entire audience stand up and do one or two sample exercises. (That not only involves them psychologically, it also keeps them more alert physically by increasing the flow of blood and adrenalin in their systems.) If you were explaining how to fill out a federal income tax long form, you could give each class member a sample form and have him or her fill out each section as you explain it. Outlines and checklists could be used in a similar manner for just about *any* speech.

Use volunteers   If the action you are demonstrating is too expansive or intricate to allow all the class members to take part in it, you can select one or two volunteers from the audience to help you out. This will increase the psychological involvement of all the members because they will tend to identify with the volunteers.

Question-and-answer period   One way to increase audience involvement that is nearly *always* appropriate if time allows is to answer

The chief merit of language is clearness, and we know that nothing detracts so much from this as do unfamiliar terms.

Galen (A.D. 129–199)

questions at the end of your speech. You should encourage your audience to ask questions. Solicit questions and be patient waiting for the first one. Often no one wants to ask the first question. When the questions do start coming, the following suggestions might increase your effectiveness in answering them:

1. **Listen to the substance of the question.** Don't zero in on irrelevant details; listen for the big picture—the basic, overall question that is being asked. If you're not really sure *what* the substance of a question is, ask the questioner to paraphrase it. Don't be afraid to let the questioners do their share of the work.
2. **Paraphrase confusing questions.** Use the active listening skills described in Chapter 4. You can paraphrase the question in just a few words: "If I understand your question, you are asking _____. Is that right?"
3. **Avoid defensive reactions to questions.** Even if the questioner seems to be calling you a liar or stupid or biased, try to listen to the substance of the question and not to the possible personality attack.
4. **Answer the question as briefly as possible.** Then check the questioner's comprehension of your answer. Sometimes you can simply check their nonverbal response—if they seem at all confused, you can ask, "Does that answer your question?"

Audience involvement, along with the other techniques mentioned earlier, are exemplified in the sample speech that follows.

a sample speech

The following speech was given by Professor Jerry Tarver of the University of Richmond. Professor Tarver, discussing the use of language in speech writing, spoke before a group of professional speech writers in Hartford, Connecticut.

can't nobody here use this language?
function and quality in choosing words

I learned last May you have to be careful in speaking to a group of professional communicators. After I conducted a writer's workshop at the Toronto Conference of the International Association of Business Communicators, Janine Lichacz wrote asking me to speak here tonight and used the communication techniques I had recommended. She even included a footnote citing my lecture. I am susceptible to good communication—and to flattery—so I am pleased to be with you to discuss your topic for the evening, the use of language in the art of speech writing.

I suppose we must begin by shaking our heads woefully over the sad state of language today, whether in formal speeches, casual conversation, or in writing. Most of us in this room no doubt agree with the generally negative tone of *Time Magazine's* year-end assessment of 1978 which claims "our language has been besieged by vulgarities." But to perserve our sanity as professionals in communication, most of us would probably join *Time* in optimistically expecting English somehow to survive and even to prosper.

On the negative side, if I may use a vulgarity to criticize vulgarity, I am often moved in my own profession to paraphrase Casey Stengel and ask, "Can't nobody here use this language?"

To generalize about the language ability of students, I would say far too many of them can't express themselves well, and they don't seem to care. The most significant hollow verbalization among students today is not "y'know." It is "needless to say."

I have a respectful appreciation of the rules of the classical rhetoricians, and on occasion I have discussed in class the stylistic device of antithesis. One of my students, quite unconsciously I am sure, gave the technique a try in a speech on physical fitness and said, "A well-rounded body makes for a well-rounded mind." We've come a long way down from *mens sana in corpore sano.*

Faculty members are often worse. Some time back I attended a conference on setting standards for language competence in Virginia's schools. In one presentation a professor from a distinguished university repeatedly used the expression "scribal language." I finally turned to someone to ask what the devil that meant and was told the term was a fancy synonym for "writing." I wrote a letter to the professor suggesting a requirement for a report on competence in language should be competence in language. He did not take it well.

One of my colleagues wrote a lengthy document on the proper use of classrooms and stated forthrightly, "It is necessary to employ characteristics of uniqueness where uniqueness is held to be important. The idea of flexibility should be placed in a balanced way with other particular instructional and design needs to achieve a maximized learning atmosphere. In some instances, degrees of flexibility may have to give way to other equally creative and significant dimensions of a classroom environment."

some comments
Introduction: Reference to audience and conference coordinator increases audience interest.

He begins to develop his first main point: the current state of language. (See outline further on.)

quotation as supporting material
another reference to audience

He increases "information hunger" by stressing the magnitude of today's language problems.

example used as supporting material

example

example

example

informative speaking

339

I happen to know what that means, and I will be happy to provide a translation at twenty cents a word. If you want the answer, send your dollar to me at the University of Richmond.

example

A certain church group which supports many colleges throughout the South regularly sends me a publication which purports to be educational. Leaders of this group use up a goodly portion of the alphabet with the impressive degrees they attach to their names and employ this publication to increase the size of the audience for their various pronouncements. The quality of the writing is so gloriously and innocently bad that the entire magazine could easily pass as a satire written by a clever member of a high school debating team. One of the speeches from a couple of months ago contained the striking statement, "Drifting causes a loss of direction." That was one of the major points in the speech which incidently was delivered at the inauguration of a college president.

quotation

On the positive side, *Time* finds our language "enriched by vigorous phrases and terms" from such sources as CB radio and situation comedies. The major bright spots I see are the writing in advertising and on the bathroom wall. Let me quickly add that the *worst* writing also appears in these two places. Some of the most crude and senseless tripe I have encountered has appeared in ads or graffiti. But when they are good, they are very, very good. Both the ad writer and the graffiti artist must work within a small compass. They must be concise. To the point. And each is moved, urgently moved, to communicate. Unfortunately for the motivation of the advertiser, I am one of those people who can enjoy the sizzle and forgo the steak. I don't smoke cigars, and I don't even remember the brand

examples

involved, but who can forget the classic commercial in which Edie Adams used to urge, "Why don't you pick one up and smoke it sometime?" I admit I don't have a Texaco credit card, but little I read of modern academic poetry moves me as much as the soothing jingle, "You can trust your car to the man who wears the star."

My favorite graffiti are the plaintive sort. A poor soul eloquently crying out to be understood. In the men's room just down from my office, someone in apparent anguish wrote with painstaking care in the grout between the tiles, "What in the hell am I doing here?" Weeks passed before someone undertook a reply. Whether done in a spirit of helpfulness or malice, I cannot say, but finally in different hand-

example/anecdote

writing, there appeared, "If this is an existential question, contact Dr. Hall in the Philosophy Department. If this is a theological question, contact Dr. Alley in the Religion Department. If this is a biological question, take a look."

Years ago I saw a quotation printed on a little gummed paper strip which had been attached to the wall of a men's room off the New Jersey Turnpike. It offered a simple Biblical text and had apparently come to the attention of a tired truck driver. The quotation asked the question, "If God be for us, who can be against

example/anecdote

us?" No doubt in despair, the truck driver had replied underneath, "The dispatcher."

stresses importance of point to audience

How can we capture the vitality of the best of graffiti and advertising in our own writing and speaking? Perhaps some of you would agree with a sociologist friend of mine, Dr. James Sartain. Whenever Jim is offered a chance to improve his teaching, he says, "I already know how to teach better than I do." I suspect this is

public communication

340

true for most of us. So, we may not be discovering tonight as much as reminding.

But there could be some ground for controversy. Let me first of all attempt to play down the current emphasis on correctness. Grammar—much like spelling—is one of the manual skills of expression. Almost any fool can learn to make a subject agree with a verb according to the standard rules of English.

I think the pseudo-objectivity of correctness attracts many followers. But grammatical systems are, after all, themselves arbitrary. We could change the rules if we wanted to. Our failure to alter our grammar to include a sexless pronoun can hardly be blamed on the sanctity of the rules. If you wish to attack the sentence, "He done done it," you can't attack it by claiming it does not follow a rigid set of rules. It just doesn't follow the system most widely taught.

I'm not suggesting you break rules at random. Just don't be too proud of yourself for not using "very unique" or "hopefully, it will rain." And remember George Orwell's advice that you should break any rule rather than "say anything outright barbarous."

I suggest to write and speak our best we need, first, a grasp of the function of language and, second, a sensitivity to the quality of our words.

My desk dictionary includes among its definitions of the word *function,* "The action for which a . . . thing is specially fitted or used or for which a thing exists." The concept of function reminds us that words act upon people.

Let me give you an example of a piece of communication which illustrates function. You may recall in *Catch 22,* Lt. Milo Minderbinder at one point instituted an elaborate procedure for going through the chow line. It involved signing a loyalty oath, reciting the pledge of allegiance and singing "The Star-Spangled Banner." But the entire system was destroyed one day when Major de Coverly returned from a trip and cut through the red tape with two words: "Gimme eat."

That simple, and quite ungrammatical, phrase shows language in action. Words at work. Expression that eliminates the unnecessary and gets down to cases.

A grasp of function causes a writer to think of results. Impact. Effect. Audience becomes important. Who will read or listen? Why? Function calls for the communicator to examine the reason for the existence of a given communication and to choose words that will be a means of expression and not an end.

Next, as I said, we must be sensitive to quality. I know of no objective way to determine quality. But I agree with Robert Persig who insists in *Zen and the Art of Motorcycle Maintenance* that most people intuitively know quality in language when they encounter it.

Most of us have written material we knew was merely adequate. No errors. All the intended ideas in place. No complaints from the boss or the editor. But deep down inside we knew we had done a pedestrian job.

I use a chill bump test for quality. For poor writing or speaking I get one type of chill bumps. For good language, a better brand of chill bumps. For most of the mediocre stuff in between, no chill bumps at all.

Quality does not mean fancy. When General McAuliffe reportedly answered a Nazi surrender ultimatum with the word "nuts," his language had no less quality than the declaration of the Indian Chief Joseph, "From where the sun now stands, I will fight no more forever." Either of my examples would probably not fare well in a classroom exercise in English composition. But anyone who objected to the use of such language in that situation would be guilty of ignoring the concept of function.

analogy—comparing grammar with manual skill—used as supporting material

example

examples/quotation

definition of key term

example

operational definition of key term

example

example/quotation

example/quotation

informative speaking
341

Transition: internal preview of following points.

He stresses the importance of these points by listing them as numbered "guidelines."

Only after we agree that we must be concerned about function and quality can we properly turn our attention to rules. I offer the following ten guidelines for the speech writer. Some of the guidelines apply primarily to the language of speeches; some apply to almost any kind of writing. I do not consider my list exhaustive, and I should point out that the items on it are not mutually exclusive.

Guideline Number One. Be simple. Tend toward conversational language. Earlier this month I conducted speaker training for a corporation which distributed a speech manuscript containing such expressions as "difficult to ascertain" and "management audits attest." There's nothing wrong with these phrases in print, but I wouldn't say ascertain or attest out loud in front of the Rotary Club. "Find out" and "show" would sound more natural.

Guideline Number Two. Be expansive. Speeches use more words per square thought than well-written essays or reports. The next time you get a speech writing assignment, see if you can't talk your boss into throwing out two-thirds of the content and expanding the remainder into a fully developed expression of a limited topic. I realize gobbledygook is wordy, but I assume none of us will be writing gobbledygook. And I don't know of anyone who has suggested that Martin Luther King's "I Have a Dream" speech suffered from excessive repetition.

example

Guideline Number Three. Be concrete. Specific terms limit a listener's chances to misunderstand. Back in November, Combined Communications Corporation President Karl Eller gave a speech out in Phoenix in which he used a glass of milk to describe our free enterprise system. He said, "Some farmer bred and raised the cow. Some farmer owned and tended the land it grazed on. He bought special feed from someone. Some farmer milked the cow or cows and sold the milk to someone else who processed it, pasteurized it, and packaged it. He sold it to a wholesaler who sold it to a retailer. And all along the line the product was either made better or its distribution was simplified and narrowed, and a lot of people had jobs. Wealth was created." I've quoted less than a fifth of Eller's description. I'm convinced nobody left his speech confused.

example

Guideline Number Four. Be vivid. Appeal to the senses. President Carter's speech writers attempted to paint a word picture in the state of the union address when they wrote of the power of nuclear weapons "towering over all this volatile changing world, like a thundercloud in a summery sky." I am reminded of Mark Twain's distinction between the lightning and the lightning bug. The Carter image fails to stir the imagination. But vivid language can be effective.

example/quotation

In demonstrating the point that his company's nuclear plants are safe, Ontario Hydro Board Chairman Robert Taylor told members of the Kiwanis Club of Ottawa, "You could sit naked, if you had a mind to, at the boundary fence around the Pickering nuclear station for a year, drink the water and eat the fish from nearby Lake Ontario, and you would pick up a total of five units of radiation. That's less than you would get from natural sources such as rocks, good air and cosmic rays. A single chest X-ray would give you eight times that exposure."

example/analogy

Guideline Number Five. Be personal. Use the personal pronoun. Don't be afraid of making a speaker sound egotistical. Ego springs from attitude, not language. A modest speaker can say "I know" and "I did" and "I was" with no problem. But I know a fellow who is so egotistical he can say "Good morning" and seem to take credit for it. Still, it's hard to imagine Caesar saying, "One comes, one sees, one conquers."

Guideline Number Six. Be smooth. Speech demands uncluttered rhythm. Avoid clauses which interrupt your idea. It's a bit awkward for a speaker to say, "William Safire, former Nixon speech writer," but "former Nixon speech writer William Safire" flows a bit better. If you must add a clause, make a big deal out of it. For example, you might say, "Jogging—which can have a fantastically positive effect on your sex life—may clear up minor sinus problems."

Feel free to use contractions if they help the flow of the speech. In conversation the absence of contractions often becomes a device for emphasis. If you don't use contractions in speaking, you risk overemphasis.

In writing jokes into a speech, be sure to put the "they saids" *before* the quoted material, especially in punch lines. Observe the effect of reading: "Why does a chicken cross the road?" she asked. "To get to the other side," he answered.

Guideline Number Seven. Be aggressive. Don't use the loaded language of your enemies. Let me get my prejudice clearly before you. As a consumer, I deeply resent the careless use of the term "consumer advocate." As a breather of air and drinker of water and observer of sunsets, I resent the haphazard application of the term "environmentalist" to anyone who can gather six friends in a living room to organize a Snailshell Defiance. My sympathy goes out to the engineer who finds it all but impossible to explain how fish like warm water without describing the fish as victims of thermal pollution.

I do not assume that American business and industry always have in mind the best interests of consumers, the environment, and fish, but we need to avoid one-sided language if we are to have an honest discussion of the issues. I would prefer to keep away from loaded words or to qualify them with "so-called" or "self-styled."

Guideline Number Eight. Be purposeful. Meaning is assigned to words by listeners; your intent is less important than your listener's perception. The controversy over sexism and racism in language can be settled if we remember words are symbols which listeners interpret. I will not use the phrase "girls in the office" because a significant number of people who hear me will react negatively. For the same reason, avoid "a black day" on the market, in favor of a bleak day or a bad day. We need not resort to awkward constructions. You might not want to say "unmanned boat," but this does not mean you must blunder along with "unpeopled boat." What about "a boat with no one aboard?"

Guideline Number Nine. Be eloquent. Use an occasional rhetorical device to enhance your expression of an idea. Indulge at times in a little light alliteration. Balance a pair of phrases: "Ask not what the country can do for General Motors, ask what General Motors can do for the country."

Guideline Number Ten. Be adaptable. Write to suit your speaker. A speech writer for Phillips Petroleum once described his role as being that of a clone. A writer must know the speaker's feelings and the speaker's style. And remember your speaker may need a tersely worded speech one week and a flowery one the next.

example/anecdote/example

examples

One of the few points not supported with an example. Clear as is.

examples

example

examples

example

description

a short, concise
conclusion

My guidelines are far easier to express than to execute. Writing a good speech requires talent, brains, and effort. If you write for others, add to the requirements a self-effacing attitude and a thick skin.

Our language will not be saved by the exhortations of evangelists in the Church of the Fundamental Grammar. It can be saved by writers and speakers with a grasp of function and a sense of quality. We should be proud of your organization's contribution; it enrolls and nurtures communicators who use language well.

Jerry Tarver

---

analysis of the speech

From the marginal comments you can see that Professor Tarver followed many of the techniques mentioned in this chapter. For example, he seemed to have a clear-cut, specific, informative purpose:

> After listening to my speech, my audience members will be able to recall five or six of my ten guidelines for the speech writer.

If he had wanted his audience to remember more, or to have a copy of his guidelines for future reference, he might have handed out a list of guidelines or provided an outline as a visual aid.

Professor Tarver taps into general audience social and esteem needs by reminding his audience that "our language is being besieged by vulgarities." He taps into self-actualization needs by showing his audience how to improve themselves. And he taps into their specific needs by telling them that good English preserves their "sanity as professionals."

He emphasizes his important points by using numbered "guidelines" as signposts. His use of language throughout is precise and simple; he defines his meaning of a key term, *function*. He uses supporting material—especially examples and quotations—to back up his ideas. Finally, he generates audience involvement by using several references to his audience during his speech and by soliciting questions afterward.

We should also note the organization of this speech. It follows this outline:

I. Introduction
II. Body
   A. The present state of language
      1. The negative side
         a. Students: "Needless to say"
         b. Faculty: "Scribal language"
      2. The positive side
         a. Graffiti
         b. Advertising
   B. First concerns
      1. Function: Words act upon people.
      2. Quality: We know it intuitively.

C. The ten guidelines
   1. Be simple.
   2. Be expansive.
   3. Be concrete.
   4. Be vivid.
   5. Be personal.
   6. Be smooth.
   7. Be aggressive.
   8. Be purposeful.
   9. Be eloquent.
   10. Be adaptable.
III. Conclusion

summary

This chapter dealt with informative speaking and suggested a number of techniques for effectiveness in this type of speaking. These suggestions include the use of a specific informative purpose, the creation of "information hunger" by tapping into both general and specific audience needs, the emphasis of important points through repetition and "signposts," and the use of clear language (defined here as language that incorporates precise vocabulary, simple vocabulary, and definitions of key or obscure-but-necessary terms).

activities

1. For practice in defining informative speech purposes, reword the following statements so they specifically point out what the audience will be able to do after hearing the speech.
   a. My purpose is to tell my audience about Hitler's rise to power.
   b. I'm going to talk about internal combustion engines.
   c. My speech is about the causes and cures of premature baldness.

2. For practice in analyzing audience needs, take a minute and consider your classmates as an audience. How does Maslow's analysis of needs relate to these people? What other, more specific needs do they have? How could the following speech topics be related to these needs?
   a. The Changing Climate of the United States
   b. Civil Rights
   c. Gun Control
   d. U.S. Foreign Policy

3. For practice in using clear language, select an article from any issue of a professional journal in your major. Using the suggestions mentioned in this chapter, rewrite a paragraph from the article so that it will be clear and interesting to the layperson.

4. To analyze an informative speech, you go through it and point out where the speaker used effective techniques; if necessary, you point out places where effective techniques are still needed, making specific

suggestions for improvement. To hone your skills in recognizing effective informative speaking, try one of the following analyses:

a. Go over our analysis of the sample speech on pages 339–344. See which of our points you agree and / or disagree with, and tell why. What would you add to our analysis?

b. Select an informative speech from *Vital Speeches of the Day*, *Representative American Speeches*, a newspaper, or any other source. Analyze this speech in terms of its effectiveness as an informative message. Use our analysis of the sample speech as a model.

c. Perform your analysis on your own informative speech, as delivered or to be delivered in class.

notes

1. Henryk Skolimowski, "The Last Lecture," *Vital Speeches of the Day* 43 (January 1, 1977).

2. George Orwell, "Politics and the English Language," in *Shooting an Elephant and Other Essays* (New York: Harcourt, Brace, 1945).

fifteen

persuasive speaking

After reading this chapter, you should understand:

1. That persuasion can be worthwhile and ethical.
2. The difference between direct and indirect approaches.
3. The basic idea of a persuasive strategy.
4. The functions of the three types of persuasive appeals.
5. The importance of analyzing and adapting to your audience.

You should be able to:

1. Formulate an effective persuasive strategy.
2. Choose the appropriate appeal for a particular persuasive point.
3. Use the techniques for effective persuasive speaking that are discussed in this chapter.

Persuasion is the act of convincing someone, through communication, to change a particular belief, attitude, or behavior. You can appreciate the importance of this skill by imagining how your life would be without the ability to persuade others. Your choice would be limited either to accepting people as they were or to coercing them to acquiesce.

This last point is worth further comment, for persuasion is not the same thing as coercion. If you held a gun to someone's head and said, "Do this or I'll shoot," you would be acting coercively. Besides being illegal, this approach would probably be ineffective. Once you took the gun away, the person would probably stop following your demands.

The failure of coercion to achieve lasting results is apparent in less dramatic circumstances. Children whose parents are coercive often rebel as soon as they can, students who perform from fear of an instructor's threats rarely appreciate the subject matter, and employees who work for abusive and demanding employers are often unproductive and eager to switch jobs as soon as possible. Persuasion, on the other hand, makes a listener *want* to think or act differently.

Even when they understand the difference between persuasion and coercion, some students are still uncomfortable with the idea of persuasive speaking. They see it as the work of high-pressure hucksters: salespeople with their feet stuck in the door, unscrupulous politicians taking advantage of beleaguered taxpayers, and so on. Indeed, many of the principles we are about to discuss have been used by unethical speakers for unethical purposes, but that isn't what all—or even most—persuasion is all about. Ethical persuasion plays a necessary and worthwhile role in everyone's life.

persuasion can be worthwhile

It is through persuasion that we influence others' lives in worthwhile ways. The person who says, "I don't want to influence other people," is really saying, "I don't want to get involved with other people," and that is an abnegation of one's responsibilities as a human being. Look at the good you can accomplish through persuasion: You can convince a loved one to give up smoking or to give up some other destructive habit; you can get members of your community to conserve energy or to join together in some other beneficial action; you can persuade an employer to hire you for a job where your own talents, interests, and abilities will be put to their best use.

persuasion can be ethical

Persuasion is considered *ethical* if it conforms to accepted standards. But what are the accepted standards today? Whose opinion should you accept for what is good or bad? If your plan is a selfish one and perhaps not in the best interest of your audience—but you're honest about your motives—is that ethical? If your plan *is* in the best interest of your audience, yet you lie to them to get them to accept the plan, is *that* ethical?[1]

These are thorny questions. Eventually the answer will depend on a set of moral values you decide to live by. For our purposes here, however, a simple general definition is sufficient: Ethical persuasion is communication that does not depend on false or misleading information to induce attitude change in an audience.

Not all persuasion is ethical, even by this simple standard. Some messages are unethical because they border on deception, such as "Enter the Burpo sweepstakes and win a million dollars a week for the rest of your life" or "You may have already won a small country in the Burpo sweepstakes." Those appeals make it sound as though just entering the sweepstakes makes you an automatic winner when your chances are actually pretty slim.

Other messages are unethical because they are absolutely false. They purposely seek to mislead the audience. An example of this type of message might be: "Congratulations! You have won a free one-year supply of Burpo, and all you need to pay is the cost of postage and han-

the merits of persuasion

He that complies against his will
Is of his own opinion still.

Samuel Butler

dling!" This strategy is used in door-to-door magazine con games. After people sign for the "free magazines," they wind up paying more for the "postage and handling" than they would for a regular subscription.

types of persuasion

There are several ways to categorize types of persuasion. For our purposes here, categorization according to *outcomes* and *approach* is most convenient.

desired outcomes

We divide persuasion according to two major outcomes: *convincing* and *actuating*.

Convincing When you set about to convince an audience, you want to change the way they think. There are two ways that you can do that; the first is to change their beliefs about the *truth* of a fact. If you wanted to convince the Sons of Columbus that the Vikings were the first Europeans to discover America, you would be using this type of persuasion.

The second way to change the way your audience thinks is to change their *evaluation* of something. If you try to convince your audience that a certain type of diet is good or that a certain government action is bad, you would be using this type of persuasion.

When we say that convincing an audience changes the way they think, we don't mean that you have to swing them from one belief or attitude to a completely different one. Sometimes an audience will already think the way you want them to, but they won't be firmly enough committed to that way of thinking. When that is the case, you simply need to *reinforce*, or strengthen, their opinions. For example, if your audience already believed that the federal budget should be balanced but didn't consider the idea very important, your job would be to reinforce their current beliefs. Reinforcing is still a type of change, however, because you are causing an audience to think more strongly about a belief or attitude.

Actuating When you set about to actuate an audience, you want to move them to immediate action. Whereas a speech to convince might move an audience to action at some future, indefinite time, a speech to actuate asks for action right then, on the spot.

There are two types of action you can ask for—*adoption* or *discontinuance*. The former asks an audience to engage in a new behavior; the latter asks them to stop behaving in an established way. Thus, if you gave a speech for a political candidate and then asked for contributions to that candidate's campaign, you would be asking your audience to adopt a new behavior. If you gave a speech against smoking and then asked your audience to sign a pledge to quit or to throw away the cigarettes they were carrying, you would be asking them to discontinue an established behavior.

direct and indirect approaches

We can also categorize persuasion according to the directness of the approach employed by the speaker.

Direct persuasion Direct persuasion will not try to disguise the desired audience response in any way. "Use seat belts—save lives" is a direct persuasive approach. Direct persuasion is the best strategy to use with a friendly audience, especially when you are asking for a response that the audience is reasonably likely to give you:

"I'm here today to let you know what you can do to take part in the Red Cross blood drive."

"Have you ever wished that students had more rights and power? They can, if they organize effectively. I'm here today to show you how to do just that."

"I'm going to try to convince you today that Candy Tate is the best choice for city council and that she needs your vote."

In a speech that uses a direct persuasive strategy, you announce the desired audience response right away in the introduction of the speech. Then that response can act as the focus of the speech.

Indirect persuasion Indirect persuasion disguises or deemphasizes the desired audience response in some way. The question "Is a season ticket to the symphony worth the money?" (when you intend to prove that it is) is based on indirect persuasion, as is any strategy that doesn't express the speaker's purpose at the outset. Indirect persuasion is not necessarily unethical. Sometimes, in fact, it is necessary to gain acceptance of a completely legitimate message. When the audience is hostile to either you or your topic, you might want to ease into your speech slowly.[2] You might want to take some time to make your audience feel good about you or the social action you are advocating. So if you are speaking in favor of Candy Tate for city council, but Candy is in favor of a tax increase and your audience is not, you might want to talk for a while about the benefits they might derive from that increase. You might even want to change your desired audience response. Rather than trying to get them to rush out and vote for Candy, you might want them simply to read a recent newspaper article about her or attend a speech she will be giving. But one thing you can't do in this instance is to begin by saying, "I'm not here to speak in support of Candy Tate"— that would be a false statement. It is more than indirect; it is unethical.

With the concepts of ethics, outcomes, and approaches in mind, we can move on to the idea of a basic persuasive strategy.[3]

The credit goes to the person who convinces the world, not to the one to whom the idea first occurs.

Sir Francis Darwin

persuasive strategy

Earlier we mentioned that the basic message strategies are cumulative. When you seek to persuade, you are still interested in maintaining audience interest by relating to needs. Psychologist James V. McConnell sums it up this way:

"The best 'persuader' appears to be whatever best satisfies the deep-felt needs of the audience."[4]

You are still concerned with explanation, too. In fact a persuasive speech is actually like three different "informative" speeches. You have to explain the problem, the solution, and the part your audience can play in that solution. Each one of these explanatory tasks requires the same kind of planning that a full "speech to inform" would require.

the problem

In order to convince someone that something needs to be changed, you have to convince that person that something is wrong; you have to establish the problem. One way to establish a problem is to answer three basic questions. First, *Is there a problem from the audience's point of view?* After all, what seems like a problem to you might not seem like a problem to other people. For example, your topic might be "Legalizing Prostitution." You might, therefore, want to show that laws against prostitution are a problem. What would make those laws a problem for your audience? Does the absence of legal prostitution lead to profits for organized crime? Does it lead to disease, or sex crimes? What arguments could you use to establish these things as problems for your audience?

The second question you need to answer is: *How does this problem relate to the audience?* Here you get back to the idea of audience needs. Do the profits of organized crime represent a threat to your audience's safety and security? Could they become infected with a dread social disease? Are their children safe from perverts? In other words, you must prove the relationship of your problem to your audience.

The final question is: *Does this problem actually require a change?* For example, if your main argument is that organized criminals benefit from illegal prostitution, your audience might mentally refute that argument by reminding themselves that there are laws against organized crime; therefore, the real problem would be a lack of law enforcement. Also, some problems will go away if you ignore them long enough. How can you prove that your problem doesn't fit into this category?

Basically, then, this first task requires you to figure out why your audience might think that your problem was not a problem for them. You have to impress them with the importance and personal relevance of your problem. For example, let's say that you are proposing a program in which students will do volunteer counseling and tutoring at a nearby prison. Your first step in planning your message would be to analyze why the students would *not* want to take advantage of such a project. If you thought about it, you might come up with reasons like these:

1. They are too busy with activities that are more important to them.
2. They believe that their participation in such a program would not make a difference.
3. They do not feel that the prisoners are their concern anyway.

You now have a guide for establishing the problem. You now proceed to answer those arguments:

1. Show that the program *will* be a valuable experience for them. You could explain what they are likely to learn or the feeling of fulfillment they are likely to achieve or how good "Tutor, State U Prison Project" will look on their résumés when it is time to look for a job.
2. Show that their participation *will* make a difference. You can cite prison programs at other universities to prove this point.
3. Show that the prisoners *should* be their concern. You might explain that the more prisoners who return to their community without being rehabilitated, the more dangerous those communities will be.

Thus, there are at least two requirements for the problem you establish:

1. It must relate directly to your audience. If you live in New Jersey, the repeal of the Nebraska state income tax would be an inappropriate problem.
2. It must be a problem that your audience can play some part in correcting. The existence of cancer would be an inappropriate problem, but the lack of funds for cancer research would be appropriate because your audience could contribute money or sign a petition supporting government funding.

You should take both of these requirements into consideration when establishing the problem. Then you will be ready to consider the solution.

the solution

Your next step in getting your audience to change something is to convince them that a change is possible. You do this by establishing a solution, which is a plan proposed to correct a problem.

Once again you might want to answer three questions to establish your plan as the answer to the problem. First: *Will the plan work?* If your plan is to legalize prostitution so that prostitutes can be regulated and therefore protected against crime and disease, can you give evidence to suggest that our frequently inept bureaucracy is actually capable of such regulation?

A second question is: *Will the plan be practical?* Perhaps the bureaucracy is capable of regulating legalized prostitution. But what would be the cost of such regulation? If the cost is too great, then the plan would not be practical. How can you prove that your plan will not cost more than it is worth?

The final question might be: *What advantages or disadvantages will result from your plan?* This question takes into account that there are costs and rewards besides economic ones. In changing laws against prostitution there could be costs to our religious beliefs, our national self-concept, and our ability to teach morality to our young. How could you prove that your plan would not create more problems than it would solve?

the desired audience response

Once the audience realizes that a change is possible, they next have to realize that they can take some part in that change. A speaker convinces them of that by establishing the desired audience response. This step, like the first two, should answer three questions. First: *What part can the audience play in putting the plan into action?* It doesn't help much if your audience simply agrees with you but does not do anything to help bring about change. The most brilliant speech is not good enough if your audience leaves thinking, "That kid sure was right. There's a real problem there. Yup, there sure is. I wonder what's for dinner tonight."

The second question that you might ask is: *How do the audience members go about playing their part?* The behavior you ask your audience to adopt should be made as simple as possible for them. If you want them to vote in a referendum, tell them when to vote, where to go to vote, and how to go about registering, if necessary. Be very specific in your request. Don't ask them to write their congressional representative. *You* write the letter (to the congressional representative who is in charge of the subcommittee that is investigating the problem, perhaps) and ask your audience members to sign it. Don't ask them to start a petition. *You* draw up the petition and have them sign it. Don't ask them to picket. Give them the placards and tell them what time to meet you at the picket site.

Finally you might want to answer the question: *What are the direct rewards of this response?* Your solution might be of importance to society, but this is just one of the possible rewards that you can offer to your audience for responding the way you want them to. If you think about it, there are probably some direct personal rewards involved also. Is there a chance that the congressional representative will answer them personally? Will the picket session be fun as well as meaningful? Will there be coffee and doughnuts and interesting people at the polling place?

The study of persuasion is as complex as the study of human communication. In fact, some people believe the terms *persuasion* and *communication* are synonymous. To reduce persuasion to three steps is a tricky business, and even then it is complex. Even then it requires you to do everything listed in Table 15–1.

table 15–1 checklist for persuasion

  I. Establish the problem
    A. Analyze the arguments that the audience might have against the importance of the problem
    B. Answer those arguments
  II. Establish the solution
    A. Analyze the arguments the audience might have against the solution
    B. Answer those arguments
  III. Establish the desired audience behavior
    A. Analyze the arguments against this behavior
    B. Answer those arguments

A persuasive strategy is put into effect through the use of persuasive appeals. Persuasive appeals supply your audience with reasons to say yes to a plan. In other words, they make an audience *want* to adopt your plan.

The early Greeks first outlined a set of devices through which reasons could be given convincingly. Aristotle labeled these *ethos, logos,* and *pathos*.[5] These correspond roughly to appeals based on credibility, logic, and emotion.

types of persuasive appeals

credibility-based appeals

An audience's evaluation of a speaker is based on their perception of many of the speaker's characteristics,[6] but the two most important facets of credibility, at least for our purposes here, are *authoritativeness* and *trustworthiness*.

Authoritativeness, the most important determinant of credibility, refers to the speaker's competence to discuss the topic. Trustworthiness refers to the speaker's believability. The speaker's perceived honesty, integrity, and impartiality are all part of the audience's perception of that speaker's trustworthiness.

Credibility can be based on either the speaker's own reputation or on the testimony of an expert the speaker cites. If the speaker is an atomic physicist who has studied the safety of nuclear power plants for many years, an audience would probably consider that speaker a credible source on the topic of safety in nuclear power plants. Chances are that if the audience members were in favor of nuclear power and this speaker told them that nuclear power was unsafe, they would have something to think about. If, on the other hand, the speaker was a student who had never even visited an atomic power plant, it would be easy for the audience members to discount the student's arguments. But

if the student quoted the expert or the results of a study the expert ran, that student would borrow some of that expert's credibility. It is important to acquire expert testimony from highly credible sources and then carefully attribute that testimony to the proper source. The student with no background in nuclear power might still be able to decide on the basis of careful research that nuclear power plants are unsafe. That student might then say:

"Nuclear power plants are unsafe."

and expect the audience to believe it. But why should they take the student's word for it? To bolster his credibility, the student might say:

"According to several books I have read, nuclear power plants are unsafe."

But what books are these? They might be works of fiction or polemics by a writer no more authoritative than the speaker. Worse yet, these books might have been distributed by special-interest groups for propaganda purposes. The best move would be for the speaker to take an extra breath and give a concise, carefully worded statement of the credibility of the outside expert:

"According to Professor A. Thom Kerschmacher, winner of the Nobel prize and highly respected for his work in nuclear safety, nuclear power plants are unsafe."

Establishing your own credibility requires a somewhat different procedure. If you are not already well known to your audience, you might have to answer the question, "Why should these people listen to *me*, anyway?" To answer this question you could make a statement about your experience concerning your topic or how important it is to you or the amount of research you have done on it.

No matter how you establish your credibility, it is important that you believe in it yourself. You don't have to jump up and down and scream, "I'm the greatest," but be wary of false modesty. As long as what you are saying about yourself is true and reasonable, don't be afraid to establish your qualifications solidly. For example, if you were giving a speech on a proposed tax cut in your community, you might begin this way:

"You might say I'm an expert in the municipal services of this town. As a lifelong resident, I've been shaped by its schools and recreation programs, protected by its police and firefighters, served by its hospitals, roads, and sanitation crews. So when a massive tax cut was proposed, I did some in-depth investigation into the possible effects. I looked into our municipal expenses and into the expenses of similar communities where tax cuts have been mandated by law . . ."

If your audience accepts you and your sources of information as being credible, they are likely to give your logical appeals a fair hearing.

logical appeals

In their purest form logical appeals supply an audience with a series of statements that lead to the conclusion the speaker is trying to establish. The most common forms of logical reasoning are *deduction* and *induction*.

Deduction Deduction is reasoning from a generality to a specific; in other words you present general evidence that leads to a specific conclusion. Deductive reasoning can be demonstrated in syllogisms, which are arguments made up of two premises (a major premise and a minor premise) and a conclusion. The classic syllogism is:

All men are mortal.
Socrates is a man.
Therefore, Socrates is mortal.

If all logical appeals were expressed as complete syllogisms, people could examine the major and minor premises and decide if the conclusions drawn from those premises were valid. Unfortunately this would make most arguments cumbersome, so we generally use *enthymemes* for logical appeals. An enthymeme is a compressed version of a syllogism in which the underlying premises are concealed, as in:

Because Socrates is a man, he's mortal.

Enthymemes become dangerous when they disguise faulty premises. Some of the best examples of this type of enthymeme are provided in the form of arbitrary rules. For example, take the rule enforced by some college-town landlords: "Because Joe Schmidlap is a college student, he will have to pay a damage deposit before he can rent an apartment." This rule is based on an enthymeme that is based on the following syllogism:

All college students wreck apartments.
Joe Schmidlap is a college student.
Therefore, Joe Schmidlap will wreck this apartment.

The conclusion, "Joe Schmidlap will wreck this apartment," is based on an untrue, unstated premise: "All college students wreck apartments."

College students often run up against this type of reasoning from landlords and utility companies. Even if they can supply letters of reference from former landlords and receipts for utility bills paid on time, they are still told things like, "I'm sorry, we don't rent to college students. It's a rule we have," or "I'm sorry, we require a seventy-five-dollar deposit to turn on your electricity. It's a rule," or "There's no sense arguing. We don't need to give you a *reason*. It's a rule."

The frustration you feel when you are subjected to illogical rules is the same frustration that an audience feels when it is subjected to an argument that does not supply valid reasons. That's basically why we take this close look at deductive reasoning: to make sure that the reasons we use in deduction are valid, we examine the underlying premises of our argument.

It is true that human reasoning is not adequately represented by formal logic.[7] Humans are not inherently logical or illogical; they are instead "psychological," which means that their reasoning processes are far more complex than any set of rules, no matter how elaborate, could encompass. However, formal logic does have at least one specific use besides being a standard for testing arguments. People who reason fallaciously are generally able to recognize their reasoning as fallacious when confronted with their errors through formal proofs. Therefore, formal logic can be used as a means to point out errors in reasoning where they exist.[8]

Induction Induction is reasoning from specific evidence to a general conclusion. In induction we observe that something is true for a specific sample. From this we reason that it is *generally* true.

Induction would be the appropriate type of reasoning to use with a skeptical or hostile audience when you don't want to state an unpopular claim right away. If you are seeking to prove that your local government is generally corrupt, for example, you might build your case with specific examples: The mayor has been convicted of bribery, the building inspector has resigned after being charged with extortion, the fire chief has been indicted for running the station's Dalmation at the track, and the chief of police has admitted to keeping his infant nephew on the police department payroll. If you used these specific instances to conclude that most of your local officials are corrupt, you would be using induction.

Although induction and deduction are the most common types of logical reasoning, there are other forms. Often these forms are combined with induction and deduction, but because they are also distinct, they are worthy of mention here. These forms include reasoning by sign, causal reasoning, and reasoning by analogy.

Reasoning by sign   Sign reasoning is reasoning from specific evidence to a specific conclusion without explaining how the evidence and conclusion are related. The classic example of sign reasoning is, "It is snowing outside; therefore it must be winter." Sign reasoning is used when the argument will be easily accepted by the audience. For example, an audience would probably accept the claim that an increase in bank robberies is a sign that a community is becoming more dangerous to live in. We wouldn't need to go into a long, logical explanation of our reasoning in that case, and the time we save could be used to develop more important aspects of the argument. For example, we might want to go on to claim a particular *cause* for the rash of bank robberies. That would require causal reasoning.

Causal reasoning   Causal reasoning, like sign reasoning, is reasoning from one specific to another specific. However, in causal reasoning you go on to prove that something happened or will happen *because* of something else. So if you claimed that the increase in bank robberies in your community was caused by a decrease in police manpower, you would be involved in causal reasoning. In that case, in fact, you would be using effect-to-cause reasoning, which is based on the organizational pattern of the same name that we discussed in Chapter 12. Effect-to-cause reasoning is used when you are talking about something that has already happened. If you were arguing about something that *will* happen (for example, the probability of future bank robberies because the police have cut the size of their force or the hours they patrol), you would be using cause-to-effect reasoning.

Reasoning by analogy   Reasoning by analogy is reasoning from specific evidence to a specific conclusion by claiming that something is *like* something else. Although this type of reasoning could not be used

persuasive speaking
361

for legal proof, it can help prove a point to an audience. For example, if you were arguing that the methods of law enforcement that curbed bank robbery in a nearby city would also work in your city, you would have to argue that your city is similar to that nearby city in all the respects that are important to your argument—number of banks, size of banks, size of police department, and so on. Thus, if you could argue that the two cities are alike except in one respect—for example, the size of their police forces—you could argue that this is what makes the difference in the incidence of bank robbery. If you did so, you would be arguing by analogy.

There are two types of analogy—*literal* and *figurative*. The analogy of two cities just given is a literal analogy because it compares two things that are really (literally) alike. A figurative analogy compares two things that are essentially different. If you argued that bank robberies are like a disease that must be treated to keep it from spreading, you would be using a figurative analogy.

No matter which type of reasoning you are using (deduction, induction, sign, causation, or analogy), you can check the validity of your arguments by checking them against the basic logical fallacies.

logical fallacies

Scholars have devoted lives and volumes to the description of various types of logical fallacies.[9] The three most common types seem to be (1) insufficient evidence, (2) non sequitur, and (3) evasion of argument. Most fallacies can be included under one of those categories.

Insufficient evidence The fallacy of insufficient evidence is sometimes difficult to recognize. This is especially true when it is caused by *ignored causes* or *ignored effects*.

Examples of *ignored causes* run rampant through everyday conversations. Take a typical discussion about college sports:

State U. beat State Tech.
State Tech creamed State Teachers.
Therefore, State U. will murder State Teachers.

This argument might ignore previously injured players who are now back in action, stars who are now injured, or a host of other variables. Logical fallacies based on *ignored effects* are even worse:

If other nations overcharge for oil that is needed for American consumers, an invasion of those countries is warranted.

That argument ignores undesirable effects of war, such as drafting college students who would rather be studying communication, and so on.

You might not recognize that an argument is based on insufficient evidence because the argument *sounds* so reasonable. One cause of this deception is reasoning according to slogan, which occurs when we use some folksy, familiar expression as proof. Max Black provides two excellent examples of this:

> We hear all too often that "the exception proves the rule." Probably not one person in a thousand who dishes up this ancient morsel of wisdom realizes that "prove" is here used in its older sense of "probe" or "test." What was originally intended was that the exception tests the rule—shows whether the rule is correct or not. The contemporary interpretation, that a rule is confirmed by having an exception, is absurd. This tabloid formula has the advantage of allowing a person to glory in the fact that his general principle does *not* square with the facts.
>
> "It's all right in theory, but it won't do in practice," is another popular way of revelling in logical absurdity. The philosopher Schopenhauer said all that needs to be said about this sophism: "The assertion is based upon an impossibility: what is right in theory *must* work in practice; and if it does not, there is a mistake in theory; something has been overlooked and not allowed for; and consequently, what is wrong in practice is wrong in theory too."[10]

Non sequiturs Fallacies of insufficient evidence are caused by not telling enough. *Non-sequitur fallacies* are those in which the conclusion does not relate to (literally, "does not follow from") the evidence. Unreasonable syllogisms such as those we described as being used by landlords and utility companies are non sequiturs based on faulty premises, but non sequiturs based on true premises can be just as dangerous. Take, for example, the non-sequitur fallacy known as *post hoc,* which is short for *post hoc ergo propter hoc.* Translated from the Latin, that means "after this, therefore because of this." This fallacy occurs when it is assumed that an action was caused by something that happened before it. Post hoc arguments are often applied to politics:

> Obviously, Jimmy Carter caused the gas shortage of 1979. It happened, after all, during his administration.

Spurious research is often post hoc:

> Nearly all heroin users started with marijuana. Marijuana obviously leads to the use of harder drugs.

Nearly all marijuana users started with aspirin, too, but aspirin doesn't necessarily lead to the abuse of drugs.

Another type of non sequitur is an *unwarranted extrapolation,* which is a statement that suggests that because something happened before, it will happen again or that because something is true for a part, it is true for a whole.

> State U. has massacred State Teachers every year for the past five years. They'll do it again this year.
>
> Ronald Reagan was a good actor. *Bonzo Goes to College* must be a good movie.

Then there is a circular argument, in which the evidence is dependent upon the truth of the argument:

Of course the administration is concerned with student welfare. It says so right in the college catalog.

Evasion of argument In this final type of argument the speaker dodges the question at hand by arguing over some other, unrelated point. This type consists of arguments such as *ad hominem,* which is the fallacy of attacking the person who brought up the issue rather than the issue itself:

Of course, Louie thinks marijuana should be legalized. Louie is an idiot.

The most common type of evasion of argument is the *red herring.* This fallacy, which derives its name from the practice of dragging an odoriferous fish across a trail when running away from bloodhounds, consists of evading an issue by concentrating on another, more volatile one:

Should cocaine be legalized? The real question here is, "Who would like to see us legalize cocaine? And the obvious answer to that question is, *the Communists.* The threat of the Communist conspiracy is as real today as it was . . .

No argument is perfect. If all the evidence were available and it related perfectly to the argument, there probably wouldn't *be* an argument in the first place. You should recognize the major fallacies, though, and watch for them in your own reasoning. If an audience is able to discount your arguments as illogical, persuasion will probably not occur.

emotional appeals

An emotional appeal uses a feeling like love, hate, fear, guilt, anger, loneliness, envy, or pity to entice an audience to change its attitude. An emotional appeal is not necessarily unethical, although it does allow the most room for an unethical speaker to operate. It is not necessarily illogical either. Emotional appeals are *psychological,* and because of this they can be particularly powerful.[11] Clarence Darrow once pointed out, "You don't have to give reasons to the jury. Make them *want* to acquit your client, and they'll find their own reasons."

It would be a good idea to accept half of Darrow's advice. Give your audience reasons, *and* make them want to accept your plan. Instead of just giving reasons from expert authorities why nuclear power plants are unsafe, you might also describe a nuclear holocaust or explain the details of radiation illness. On the other hand, if you were arguing in favor of nuclear power, you might describe what life is like without any energy sources—freezing to death and all that. Let's take a look at three emotions on which emotional appeals are sometimes based: *fear, anger,* and *pity.* (These are *examples,* of course, rather than a complete list of human emotions.)

Fear Appropriate fear appeals are sometimes effective persuaders. Modern advertising—especially the TV variety—commonly appeals to audience fears. In fact, television advertising has done more than its share of originating new fears. The fear of body odor, one of the classics of prime-time advertising, has recently been fragmented into more specific fears, like the fear of foot odor (one commercial featured a hapless father driving his entire family from the house by taking off his shoes), the fear of personal-hygiene odor, and the fear of soap odor ("But I used a deodorant soap!" cries the sweet young thing in the kissing booth. "That's just it," explains the reticent young stranger in front of her. "You *smell* like a deodorant soap.")

Fear appeals can be detrimental if they go too far. A classic study showed this.[12] High school students were presented several persuasive messages about toothbrushing. In the high-fear appeal the students were shown grotesque pictures of dental diseases, rotting gums, and black stumps of teeth. The moderate fear appeal merely mentioned tooth decay in passing, but the researchers found it to be more effective. This study, like many that have come after it, suggests that if you tap into audience fears, you should do so with moderation.

Anger If our audience is angry about something (or can be *made* angry about something), you should show them that you are angry about the same thing. This will do two things: (1) It will show that you are similar to them in this way, therefore increasing your persuasiveness (this is known as "establishing common ground," a technique we'll discuss later). (2) It will also allow you to offer your solution as a cure for whatever is causing the anger. For example, as this is being written, a few miles away there is a bandwagon full of political hopefuls who are telling people how angry they are about the rate of unemployment in the United States today. But fear not, the audience is told. There is a way to change this situation: Vote for Candidate X.

Appeals based on anger can be successful, but in order to be ethical, you have to *feel* the anger honestly. According to our definition of ethics, you can't say you're angry if you're not.

Pity Pity is the emotion that allows us to feel sorrow for the suffering of others. Pity can be used as an emotional appeal by reminding your audience that someone, somewhere, is suffering. Pity is an especially potent emotion if the sufferer comes from a group toward which we already feel sympathetic, such as children or animals. One very effective antiabortion message was delivered from the point of view of an unborn fetus, who explained that it was able to feel pain from the beginning of its development. Therefore, to allow abortion to remain legal was to allow this fetus to suffer. The listeners were thus told that a *child* was suffering; and worse yet, that they were partially responsible.

The key to an emotional appeal is sincerity. Most audiences will be able to recognize false emotions and reject appeals based on them.

Emotional appeals, as well as logical reasoning and credibility, are important to keep in mind when planning a persuasive strategy. Although any one type of appeal might dominate a particular argument, different appeals can also be *combined* to good effect.

techniques for effective persuasive speaking

The preceding discussion suggests a few techniques for effective persuasion. These techniques include the following:

set a clear persuasive purpose

As we explained in Chapter 11, your purpose statement should always be specific, attainable, and worded from the audience's point of view; in a persuasive speech this statement should also reflect the desired audience response. Remember that your objective is to move the audience to a specific, attainable attitude or behavior. "After listening to my speech my audience will save the whales" is not a well-thought-out purpose statement. "After listening to my speech the audience members will sign my petition to the UN" is a good purpose statement.

analyze and adapt to your audience

It is important to know as much as possible about your audience for a persuasive speech. For one thing, you should appeal to the existing values of your audience whenever possible even if those aren't *your* top values. Of course, this doesn't mean you should pretend to believe in something you don't. According to our definition of ethical persuasion, in fact, that's against the rules. What it does mean, however, is that you have to stress those values that are felt most forcefully by the members of your audience.[13]

establish "common ground"

It helps to stress as many similarities as possible between yourself and your audience. This helps prove that you understand them; after all, why should they listen to you if they don't feel you understand them as individuals? Also, if you share a lot of common ground, it shows you agree on many things; therefore, it should be easy to settle one disagreement—which is, of course, the one related to the attitude or behavior you would like them to change.

A good example of establishing common ground was demonstrated by the manager of public affairs for *Playboy* magazine when he reminded a group of Southern Baptists that they shared some important values with him:

> I am sure we are all aware of the seeming incongruity of a representative of *Playboy* magazine speaking to an assemblage of representatives of the Southern Baptist Convention. I was intrigued by the invitation when it came last fall, though I was not surprised. I am grateful for your genuine and warm hospitality, and I am flattered (although again not surprised) by the implication that I would have something to say that could have meaning to you people. Both *Playboy* and the Baptists have indeed been considering many of the same issues and ethical problems; and even if we have not arrived at the same conclusions, I am impressed and gratified by your openness and willingness to listen to our views.[14]

organize your material according to the expected response

It is much easier to get an audience to agree with you if they have already agreed with you on a previous point. Therefore, you should arrange your points in a persuasive speech so you develop a "yes" response. In effect, you get your audience into the habit of agreeing with you. For example, in the sample speech that follows, on the donation of body organs, the speaker begins by asking the audience if they would like to be able to get a kidney if they needed one. Then he asks them if they would like to have "a major role in curbing . . . tragic and needless dying . . ." The presumed answer to both questions is yes. It is only when he has built a pattern of yes responses that the speaker asks his audience to sign an organ donor card.

persuasive speaking

367

Another example of a speaker who was careful to organize material according to expected audience response was the late Robert Kennedy. Kennedy, when speaking on civil rights before a group of South Africans who believed in racial discrimination, arranged his ideas so that he spoke first on values that he and his audience shared—values like independence and freedom.[15]

If an audience is already basically in agreement with you, you can organize your material to reinforce their attitudes quickly and then spend most of your time convincing them on a specific course of action. If, on the other hand, they are hostile to your ideas, you have to spend more time getting the first "yes" out of them.

use a variety of appeals and supporting materials

You should examine each of your points and ask, "Is there another appeal I could use here?" If you are using only a logical appeal, you could consider emotional appeals or credibility appeals also. The same test applies to supporting material—ask, "Is there any other support I could offer to help prove this point?"

a sample speech

The following speech was given by one of our students. The student's purpose was to persuade his classmates to sign and carry an organ donor card. Some comments on his persuasive strategy are noted in the margin.

the gift of life

If any of you needed a kidney or other vital organ to live, would you be able to get one? Would you know where to begin searching for information which would lead to obtaining this needed organ?

These are questions many of us have never even considered. Yet, each year, in America alone, many people die with kidney disease because donated kidneys are not available. Now wouldn't it be nice—no; *fantastic*—to have a major role in curbing some of this tragic and needless dying? You can do just that. I'd like to show you how, today.

In researching and preparing for this speech, I had the opportunity to conduct an interview with the state secretary for the Kidney Foundation, Mrs. Florence Murray, at her home. She related some basic background information about kidneys, kidney disease, and kidney donation, and I would like to relay this information on to you.

Kidneys are vital to human life. They are the "twin organs" that perform the following vital life-maintaining functions:

1. They clean waste materials and excess fluids from the blood.
2. They filter the blood, retaining some compounds while excreting others.
3. They help regulate blood pressure and red blood cell count.

The human body cannot function without kidneys, and kidney disease is the fourth leading health problem in this country today. Over 8,000,000 Americans suffer from some type of kidney disease. Approximately 60,000 people die of it each year. In addition, over 4,000 children between the ages of 1 to 6 are stricken annually with "childhood nephrosis," which is simply medical jargon for kidney disease.

Perhaps your first question might be, "What is being done to combat this disease?" The National Kidney Foundation has many objectives, including the following:

1. It offers advice and assistance on important topics like kidney disease detection (warning signals), diagnosis (tests, X-rays, and so on), and drugs needed to treat this disease.
2. It provides assistance in obtaining artificial kidney machines, which are also called dialysis machines.
3. But most important, it coordinates the kidney donation and transplantation program, whereby donors may give one kidney while living or two kidneys posthumously in order to save another person's life.

Since the first kidney transplant back in 1954, over 5,000 of these operations have been performed. Thanks to improved medical techniques, better blood testing, and new tissue-typing processes, doctors are now reducing the risk of organ rejection. If rejection does occur, the patient can go back on dialysis to await a second, third, or even a fourth transplant, until one is successful.

some comments

His introduction suggests that this will be a direct persuasive strategy.

He begins with a moderate fear appeal. He previews his thesis.

His next statement suggests that both he and his information are credible.

He begins establishing the problem by explaining that the kidneys are essential organs.

He explains next that kidney disease is prevalent. This is basically a logical argument.

Having finished his explanation of the problem, he begins to set up his solution.

(Here he picks up one of the cards as an illustration.)

He offers some evidence that the solution is a good one. This is basically an emotional appeal.

To accelerate organ donations, the Kidney Foundation is also responsible for the widespread distribution of these uniform donor cards.

These cards enable you to donate a vital organ after your death. In order to illustrate how this program works, let me use as an example one of our neighbors, whose life was recently saved by a transplant.

I refer to a 16-year-old New Hampshire boy, John Warner, Jr., whose body had already rejected his father's kidney transplant. Now, a second transplant was essential to save the boy, whose parents could not afford the costly dialysis machine—$150 per treatment, three treatments per week. Luckily, on December 9th of this year, a matching tissue donor posthumously gave his kidney to Johnny and phe transplantation was performed and determined a success. The original transplant from his father came three years earlier and the boy had waited since then for a matching kidney. Now, thanks to this wonderful donation, no further wait was necessary. Instances like these really touch us when we stop to realize that the next victim could be someone close to us.

He misses a transition here, which is a little confusing.
He builds up credibility for his next point.

He answers some of the arguments that the audience might have.

I had the opportunity to speak with Dr. John Steinmuller, a well-known New Hampshire nephrologist and head of the "organ-retrieval team" whose job it is to go out and retrieve the organs that donors have pledged.

Dr. Steinmuller told me that skeptics always have excuses for not giving a vital organ, and he asked me tk say a few words about some of those excuses:

1. The first excuse is usually a lack of knowledge about the donation procedures. People do not know where to go or whom to contact. This is a problem I hope to solve for you in just a minute.
2. Apathy and lack of time. Some people are indifferent to the needs of others—they just do not care or they claim to be too busy to waste time on such endeavors. Actually, there is little or no time involved, and I know from personal experience that you are not apathetic people.
3. Inconvenience. Some people fear a delay in funeral and burial arrangements. However, since the operation has to be performed immediately after death, no delay is ever caused in funeral arrangements.
4. Usefulness. Some people assume that their gift will not be used. So far, however, the overwhelming problem has been a lack of donors—not recipients.

He provides his own arguments in favor of the action he wants them to take.

Consider now two reasons why each of us should give of ourselves in this worthwhile way:

1. The gift of life itself. The act of giving this organ will very probably save someone's life in the future. Isn't that a nice thought—to think that you had a part in saving another human's life?
2. Personal pride and satisfaction. How can anyone be more proud or satisfied with himself than when he has contributed to an effort which saves lives? No emotions can compare with those associated with a generous donation for the sake of others.

He answers a final argument.

Perhaps one last question in your mind might be: If I sign up at this time, can I change my mind later? The answer to this question is yes. Since the only way authorities will know you are a donor is by the donor card in your possession, you could simply tear up the card at any time and no one will be the wiser.

Now that all of you are more informed about this vital and worthy program, I would like to conclude my speech by setting the example—signing the first donor card myself. Then, I will circulate the other cards to each of you.

Please search your innermost being and conclude that such a gift would be an unselfish and generous sacrifice on your part, and then sign the donor card. Thank you very much.

Speech given by Philip L. Doughtie, University of New Hampshire, December 14, 1976.

He asks for a specific response, and he makes it as easy as possible.

This speech is included here because the speaker used so many of the techniques listed earlier, and he used them in ways that are relatively easy to point out. Your own speech might not be as direct, and it might not follow persuasive strategy in quite so lockstep a fashion. Your speech will, however, almost certainly be improved by a consideration of the techniques discussed in this chapter.

summary

Persuasion—the act of moving someone, through communication, toward some particular belief, attitude, or behavior—can be both worthwhile and ethical. It is different from coercion in that it makes an audience *want* to do what you want them to do.

Persuasion can be categorized according to its outcome (convincing or actuating) and its approach (direct or indirect). A typical persuasive strategy requires you to establish a problem, a solution, and a desired audience response. For each of these components you need to analyze the arguments your audience will have *against* accepting what you say, and then answer those arguments.

The persuasive strategy is put into effect through the use of persuasive appeals, which include credibility appeals (those based on the authoritativeness and trustworthiness of the source of information), logical appeals (such as those based on induction, deduction, sign, causation, or analogy), and emotional appeals (such as those based on fear, anger, or pity). Logical appeals must be checked for fallacies (such as insufficient evidence, non sequiturs, or evasions of argument).

Techniques for effective persuasive speaking include the use of a clear persuasive purpose, common ground, material organized according to an expected "yes" response, and a variety of appeals and supporting material.

activities

1. Identify an advertisement, editorial, or sales pitch with which you are familiar. Is this message, in your opinion, ethical or unethical? Does it conform to the definition of ethical persuasion given in this chapter?

2. For practice in analyzing different types of persuasive appeals, try one or both of the following:

a. What appeals (logical, emotional, credibility-based) might be used for each of the following:

Teacher to student: "Study diligently in this course."
Parent to kids: "Don't drink and drive."
Charity to potential donors: "Give us your money and time."

b. Examine an everyday appeal of your own choosing. This appeal might be one made by a child to a parent, one friend to another, by a student to a teacher, or by anyone else who is trying to change someone else's attitude and/or behavior. Decide which elements of this appeal are based on logic, which elements are based on emotion, and which are based on credibility.

3. For practice in formulating persuasive strategies, choose one of the following topics, and analyze it acckrding to the checklist in Table 15-1 (p. 357).

a. Parole should (should not) be abolished.

b. Standardized tests should (should not) be used as the main criteria for college admissions.

c. The capital of the United States should (should not) be moved to a more central location.

d. Police should (should not) be required to carry nonlethal weapons only.

e. Capital punishment should (should not) be abolished.

f. Bilingual education should (should not) be required for all schools serving bilingual students.

notes

1. An in-depth treatment of ethics is provided in Bert E. Bradley, *Fundamentals ofSpeech Communication: The Credibility of Ideas,* 3d ed. (Dubuque, Iowa: W. C. Brown, 1981).

2. Some research findings suggest that audiences may perceive a direct strategy as a threat to their "freedom" to form their own opinions. When this occurs, persuasion is hampered. See J. W. Brehm, *A Theory of Psychological Reactance* (New York: Academic Press, 1966). There also exists considerable evidence to suggest that announcing an intent to persuade in the introduction can reduce a message's effectiveness. Sample studies on this include J. Allyn and L. Festinger, "The Effectiveness of Unanticipated Persuasive Communications," *Journal of Abnormal and Social Psychology* 62 (1961): 35–40; C. A. Kiesler and S. B. Kiesler, "Role of Forewarning in Persuasive Communications," *Journal of Abnormal andSocial Psychology* 18 (1971): 210–221.

3. For an examination of how persuasive strategy related to the inaugurations of two presidents, see Bert E. Bradley, "Jefferson and Reagan: The Rhetoric of Two Inaugurals," *Southern Speech Communication Journal* 48 (Winter 1983): 119–136.

4. James V. McConnell, *Understanding Human Behavior* (New York: Holt, Rinehart and Winston, 1974), p. 820.

5. Aristotle, *Rhetoric,* trans. W. Rhys Roberts (New York: Modern Library, 1954).

6. Other possible credibility factors have been pointed out by various researchers, including composure, sociability, and extraverson. These factors tend to act as intensifiers of authoritativeness and trustworthiness.

7. An explanation of two theories of why reasoning breaks down is provided in Sally Jackson, "Two Models of Syllogistic Reasoning: An Empirical Comparison," *Communication Monographs* 49 (September 1982).

8. P. C. Wason and P. N. Johnson-Laird, *Psychology of Reasoning: Structure and Content* (Cambridge, Mass.: Harvard University Press, 1972), p. 2.

9. See, for example, Vincent E. Barry, *Practical Logic* (New York: Holt, Rinehart and Winston, 1976).

10. Max Black, "Fallacies," in Jerry M. Anderson and Paul J. Dovre (eds.), *Readings in Argumentation* (Boston: Allyn & Bacon, 1968), pp. 301–311.

11. Emotional proof is sometimes necessary because people will cling to unwarranted, untrue beliefs even if those beliefs have been disproved empirically. See, for example, Mary John Smith, "Cognitive Schema Theory and the Perseverance and Attenuation of Unwarranted Empirical Beliefs," *Communication Monographs* 49 (June 1982): 115–126.

12. Irving L. Janis and Seymour Feshbach, "Effects of Fear-Arousing Communications," *Journal of Abnormal and Social Psychology* 48 (1953): 78–92.

13. For an examination of how one politician adapted to his audience's attitudes, see David Zarefsky, "Subordinating the Civil Rights Issue: Lyndon Johnson in 1964," *Southern Speech Communication Journal* 48 (Winter 1983): 103–118.

14. Anson Mount, Speech before Southern Baptist Convention, in Wil A. Linkugel, R. R. Allen, and Richard Johannessen (eds.), *Contemporary American Speeches,* 3d ed. (Belmont, Calif.: Wadsworth, 1973).

15. Harriet J. Rudolf, "Robert F. Kennedy at Stellenbosch University," *Communication Quarterly* 31 (Summer 1983): 205–211.

index